THE ART OF
COMPUTER PROGRAMMING

VOLUME 4, FASCICLE 3

Generating All
Combinations and Partitions

DONALD E. KNUTH *Stanford University*

ADDISON–WESLEY

Upper Saddle River, NJ · Boston · Indianapolis · San Francisco
New York · Toronto · Montréal · London · Munich · Paris · Madrid
Capetown · Sydney · Tokyo · Singapore · Mexico City

The poem on page 83 is quoted from *The Golden Gate* by Vikram Seth (New York: Random House, 1986), copyright © 1986 by Vikram Seth

The author and publisher have taken care in the preparation of this book, but make no expressed or implied warranty of any kind and assume no responsibility for errors or omissions. No liability is assumed for incidental or consequential damages in connection with or arising out of the use of the information or programs contained herein.

For sales outside the U.S., please contact:

International Sales
international@pearsoned.com

Visit us on the Web: www.awprofessional.com

Library of Congress Cataloging-in-Publication Data

Knuth, Donald Ervin, 1938-
  The art of computer programming / Donald Ervin Knuth.
  vi,150 p.   24 cm.
  Includes bibliographical references and index.
  Contents: v. 4, fascicle 3. Generating all combinations and partitions.
  ISBN 1-201-85394-9 (pbk. : alk. papers : volume 4, fascicle 3)
1. Computer programming.   2. Computer algorithms.   I. Title.
  QA76.6.K64 2005
  005.1--dc22
                                                        2005041030

Internet page http://www-cs-faculty.stanford.edu/~knuth/taocp.html contains current information about this book and related books.

See also http://www-cs-faculty.stanford.edu/~knuth/sgb.html for information about *The Stanford GraphBase*, including downloadable software for dealing with the graphs used in many of the examples in Chapter 7.

And see http://www-cs-faculty.stanford.edu/~knuth/mmix.html for basic information about the MMIX computer.

ISBN 1-201-85394-9

Text printed in the United States, on recycled paper, at the Courier Corporation plant in Stoughton, Massachusetts

First printing, July 2005

PREFACE

In my preface to the first edition,
I begged the reader not to draw attention to errors.
I now wish I had not done so
and am grateful to the few readers who ignored my request.
— STUART SUTHERLAND, *The International Dictionary of Psychology* (1996)

THIS BOOKLET is Fascicle 3 of *The Art of Computer Programming*, Volume 4: *Combinatorial Algorithms*. As explained in the preface to Fascicle 1 of Volume 1, I'm circulating the material in this preliminary form because I know that the task of completing Volume 4 will take many years; I can't wait for people to begin reading what I've written so far and to provide valuable feedback.

To put the material in context, this fascicle contains Sections 7.2.1.3, 7.2.1.4, and 7.2.1.5 of a long, long chapter on combinatorial searching. Chapter 7 will eventually fill three volumes (namely Volumes 4A, 4B, and 4C), assuming that I'm able to remain healthy. It will begin with a short review of graph theory, with emphasis on some highlights of significant graphs in The Stanford GraphBase, from which I will be drawing many examples. Then comes Section 7.1, which deals with bitwise manipulation and with algorithms relating to Boolean functions. Section 7.2 is about generating all possibilities, and it begins with Section 7.2.1: Generating Basic Combinatorial Patterns. Details about various useful ways to generate n-tuples appear in Section 7.2.1.1, and the generation of permutations is discussed in Section 7.2.1.2. That sets the stage for the main contents of the present booklet, namely Section 7.2.1.3 (which extends the ideas to combinations of n things taken t at a time); Section 7.2.1.4 (about partitions of an integer); and Section 7.2.1.5 (about partitions of a set). Then will come Section 7.2.1.6 (about trees) and Section 7.2.1.7 (about the history of combinatorial generation), in Fascicle 4. Section 7.2.2 will deal with backtracking in general. And so it will go on, if all goes well; an outline of the entire Chapter 7 as currently envisaged appears on the `taocp` webpage that is cited on page ii.

I had great pleasure writing this material, akin to the thrill of excitement that I felt when writing Volume 2 many years ago. As in Volume 2, where I found to my delight that the basic principles of elementary probability theory and number theory arose naturally in the study of algorithms for random number generation and arithmetic, I learned while preparing Section 7.2.1 that the basic principles of elementary combinatorics arise naturally and in a highly motivated way when we study algorithms for combinatorial generation. Thus, I found once again that a beautiful story was "out there" waiting to be told.

For example, in the present booklet we find many of the beautiful patterns formed by combinations, with and without repetition, and how they relate to famous theorems of extremal combinatorics. Then comes my chance to tell the extraordinary story of partitions; indeed, the theory of partitions is one of the nicest chapters in all of mathematics. And in Section 7.2.1.5, a little-known triangle of numbers, discovered by C. S. Peirce, turns out to simplify and unify the study of set partitions, another vital topic. Along the way I've included expositions of two mathematical techniques of great importance in the analysis of algorithms: Poisson's summation formula, and the powerful saddle point method. There are games and puzzles too, as in the previous fascicles.

My original intention was to devote far less space to these subjects. But when I saw how fundamental the ideas were for combinatorial studies in general, I knew that I could never be happy unless I covered the basics quite thoroughly. Therefore I've done my best to build a solid foundation of theoretical and practical ideas that will support many kinds of reliable superstructures.

I thank Frank Ruskey for bravely foisting an early draft of this material on college students and for telling me about his classroom experiences. Many other readers have also helped me to check the first drafts; I wish to thank especially George Clements and Svante Janson for their penetrating comments.

I shall happily pay a finder's fee of $2.56 for each error in this fascicle when it is first reported to me, whether that error be typographical, technical, or historical. The same reward holds for items that I forgot to put in the index. And valuable suggestions for improvements to the text are worth 32¢ each. (Furthermore, if you find a better solution to an exercise, I'll actually reward you with immortal glory instead of mere money, by publishing your name in the eventual book:−)

Notations that are used here and not otherwise explained can be found in the Index to Notations at the end of Volumes 1, 2, or 3. Those indices point to the places where further information is available. Of course Volume 4 will some day contain its own Index to Notations.

Machine-language examples in all future editions of *The Art of Computer Programming* will be based on the MMIX computer, which is described in Volume 1, Fascicle 1.

Cross references to yet-unwritten material sometimes appear as '00' in the following pages; this impossible value is a placeholder for the actual numbers to be supplied later.

Happy reading!

Stanford, California   D. E. K.
June 2005

CONTENTS

Chapter 7 — Combinatorial Searching 0

7.2. Generating All Possibilities 0

    7.2.1. Generating Basic Combinatorial Patterns 0

        7.2.1.1. Generating all n-tuples 0

        7.2.1.2. Generating all permutations 0

        7.2.1.3. Generating all combinations 1

        7.2.1.4. Generating all partitions 36

        7.2.1.5. Generating all set partitions 61

Answers to Exercises 87

Index and Glossary 144

*Quhen a word fales to be divyded at the end of a lyne,
the partition must be made at the end of a syllab.*
— ALEXANDER HUME, *Orthographie . . . of the Britan Tongue* (c. 1620)

v

CHAPTER SEVEN

COMBINATORIAL SEARCHING

The opening sections of this chapter will appear in Volume 4, Fascicle 1, planned for publication in 2006.

7.2. GENERATING ALL POSSIBILITIES

7.2.1. Generating Basic Combinatorial Patterns

OUR GOAL in this section is to study methods for running through all of the possibilities in some combinatorial universe, because we often face problems in which an exhaustive examination of all cases is necessary or desirable.   . . .

7.2.1.1. Generating all n-tuples. Let's start small, by considering how to run through all 2^n strings that consist of n binary digits.   . . .

7.2.1.2. Generating all permutations. After n-tuples, the next most important item on nearly everybody's wish list for combinatorial generation is the task of visiting all *permutations* of some given set or multiset.   . . .

The complete texts of Sections 7.2.1.1 and 7.2.1.2 can be found in Volume 4, Fascicle 2, first published in February 2005.

7.2.1.3. Generating all combinations. Combinatorial mathematics is often described as "the study of permutations, combinations, etc.," so we turn our attention now to combinations. A *combination of n things, taken t at a time*, often called simply a *t-combination of n things*, is a way to select a subset of size t from a given set of size n. We know from Eq. 1.2.6–(2) that there are exactly $\binom{n}{t}$ ways to do this; and we learned in Section 3.4.2 how to choose t-combinations at random.

Selecting t of n objects is equivalent to choosing the $n - t$ elements not selected. We will emphasize this symmetry by letting

$$n = s + t \tag{1}$$

throughout our discussion, and we will often refer to a t-combination of n things as an "(s, t)-combination." Thus, an (s, t)-combination is a way to subdivide $s + t$ objects into two collections of sizes s and t.

> *If I ask how many combinations of 21 can be taken out of 25,*
> *I do in effect ask how many combinations of 4 may be taken.*
> *For there are just as many ways of taking 21 as there are of leaving 4.*
> — AUGUSTUS DE MORGAN, *An Essay on Probabilities* (1838)

There are two main ways to represent (s, t)-combinations: We can list the elements $c_t \ldots c_2 c_1$ that have been selected, or we can work with binary strings $a_{n-1} \ldots a_1 a_0$ for which

$$a_{n-1} + \cdots + a_1 + a_0 = t. \tag{2}$$

The latter representation has s 0s and t 1s, corresponding to elements that are unselected or selected. The list representation $c_t \ldots c_2 c_1$ tends to work out best if we let the elements be members of the set $\{0, 1, \ldots, n - 1\}$ and if we list them in *decreasing* order:

$$n > c_t > \cdots > c_2 > c_1 \geq 0. \tag{3}$$

Binary notation connects these two representations nicely, because the item list $c_t \ldots c_2 c_1$ corresponds to the sum

$$2^{c_t} + \cdots + 2^{c_2} + 2^{c_1} = \sum_{k=0}^{n-1} a_k 2^k = (a_{n-1} \ldots a_1 a_0)_2. \tag{4}$$

Of course we could also list the positions $b_s \dots b_2 b_1$ of the 0s in $a_{n-1} \dots a_1 a_0$, where

$$n > b_s > \cdots > b_2 > b_1 \geq 0. \tag{5}$$

Combinations are important not only because subsets are omnipresent in mathematics but also because they are equivalent to many other configurations. For example, every (s, t)-combination corresponds to a combination of $s + 1$ things taken t at a time *with repetitions permitted*, also called a *multicombination*, namely a sequence of integers $d_t \dots d_2 d_1$ with

$$s \geq d_t \geq \cdots \geq d_2 \geq d_1 \geq 0. \tag{6}$$

One reason is that $d_t \dots d_2 d_1$ solves (6) if and only if $c_t \dots c_2 c_1$ solves (3), where

$$c_t = d_t + t - 1, \quad \dots, \quad c_2 = d_2 + 1, \quad c_1 = d_1 \tag{7}$$

(see exercise 1.2.6–60). And there is another useful way to relate combinations with repetition to ordinary combinations, suggested by Solomon Golomb [*AMM* **75** (1968), 530–531], namely to define

$$e_j = \begin{cases} c_j, & \text{if } c_j \leq s; \\ e_{c_j - s}, & \text{if } c_j > s. \end{cases} \tag{8}$$

In this form the numbers $e_t \dots e_1$ don't necessarily appear in descending order, but the multiset $\{e_1, e_2, \dots, e_t\}$ is equal to $\{c_1, c_2, \dots, c_t\}$ if and only if $\{e_1, e_2, \dots, e_t\}$ is a set. (See Table 1 and exercise 1.)

An (s, t)-combination is also equivalent to a *composition* of $n + 1$ into $t + 1$ parts, namely an ordered sum

$$n + 1 = p_t + \cdots + p_1 + p_0, \quad \text{where } p_t, \dots, p_1, p_0 \geq 1. \tag{9}$$

The connection with (3) is now

$$p_t = n - c_t, \quad p_{t-1} = c_t - c_{t-1}, \quad \dots, \quad p_1 = c_2 - c_1, \quad p_0 = c_1 + 1. \tag{10}$$

Equivalently, if $q_j = p_j - 1$, we have

$$s = q_t + \cdots + q_1 + q_0, \quad \text{where } q_t, \dots, q_1, q_0 \geq 0, \tag{11}$$

a composition of s into $t + 1$ *nonnegative* parts, related to (6) by setting

$$q_t = s - d_t, \quad q_{t-1} = d_t - d_{t-1}, \quad \dots, \quad q_1 = d_2 - d_1, \quad q_0 = d_1. \tag{12}$$

Furthermore it is easy to see that an (s, t)-combination is equivalent to a path of length $s + t$ from corner to corner of an $s \times t$ grid, because such a path contains s vertical steps and t horizontal steps. Thus, combinations can be studied in at least eight different guises. Table 1 illustrates all $\binom{6}{3} = 20$ possibilities in the case $s = t = 3$.

These cousins of combinations might seem rather bewildering at first glance, but most of them can be understood directly from the binary representation $a_{n-1} \dots a_1 a_0$. Consider, for example, the "random" bit string

$$a_{23} \dots a_1 a_0 = 011001001000011111101101, \tag{13}$$

Table 1

THE $(3, 3)$-COMBINATIONS AND THEIR EQUIVALENTS

$a_5a_4a_3a_2a_1a_0$	$b_3b_2b_1$	$c_3c_2c_1$	$d_3d_2d_1$	$e_3e_2e_1$	$p_3p_2p_1p_0$	$q_3q_2q_1q_0$	path
000111	543	210	000	210	4111	3000	
001011	542	310	100	310	3211	2100	
001101	541	320	110	320	3121	2010	
001110	540	321	111	321	3112	2001	
010011	532	410	200	010	2311	1200	
010101	531	420	210	020	2221	1110	
010110	530	421	211	121	2212	1101	
011001	521	430	220	030	2131	1020	
011010	520	431	221	131	2122	1011	
011100	510	432	222	232	2113	1002	
100011	432	510	300	110	1411	0300	
100101	431	520	310	220	1321	0210	
100110	430	521	311	221	1312	0201	
101001	421	530	320	330	1231	0120	
101010	420	531	321	331	1222	0111	
101100	410	532	322	332	1213	0102	
110001	321	540	330	000	1141	0030	
110010	320	541	331	111	1132	0021	
110100	310	542	332	222	1123	0012	
111000	210	543	333	333	1114	0003	

which has $s = 11$ zeros and $t = 13$ ones, hence $n = 24$. The dual combination $b_s \ldots b_1$ lists the positions of the zeros, namely

$$23\ 20\ 19\ 17\ 16\ 14\ 13\ 12\ 11\ 4\ 1,$$

because the leftmost position is $n - 1$ and the rightmost is 0. The primal combination $c_t \ldots c_1$ lists the positions of the ones, namely

$$22\ 21\ 18\ 15\ 10\ 9\ 8\ 7\ 6\ 5\ 3\ 2\ 0.$$

The corresponding multicombination $d_t \ldots d_1$ lists the number of 0s to the right of each 1:

$$10\ 10\ 8\ 6\ 2\ 2\ 2\ 2\ 2\ 2\ 1\ 1\ 0.$$

The composition $p_t \ldots p_0$ lists the distances between consecutive 1s, if we imagine additional 1s at the left and the right:

$$2\ 1\ 3\ 3\ 5\ 1\ 1\ 1\ 1\ 1\ 2\ 1\ 2\ 1.$$

And the nonnegative composition $q_t \ldots q_0$ counts how many 0s appear between "fenceposts" represented by 1s:

$$1\ 0\ 2\ 2\ 4\ 0\ 0\ 0\ 0\ 0\ 1\ 0\ 1\ 0;$$

thus we have

$$a_{n-1} \ldots a_1 a_0 = 0^{q_t} 10^{q_{t-1}} 1 \ldots 10^{q_1} 10^{q_0}. \tag{14}$$

The paths in Table 1 also have a simple interpretation (see exercise 2).

Lexicographic generation. Table 1 shows combinations $a_{n-1}\ldots a_1 a_0$ and $c_t \ldots c_1$ in lexicographic order, which is also the lexicographic order of $d_t \ldots d_1$. Notice that the dual combinations $b_s \ldots b_1$ and the corresponding compositions $p_t \ldots p_0$, $q_t \ldots q_0$ then appear in *reverse* lexicographic order.

Lexicographic order usually suggests the most convenient way to generate combinatorial configurations. Indeed, Algorithm 7.2.1.2L already solves the problem for combinations in the form $a_{n-1} \ldots a_1 a_0$, since (s, t)-combinations in bitstring form are the same as permutations of the multiset $\{s \cdot 0, t \cdot 1\}$. That general-purpose algorithm can be streamlined in obvious ways when it is applied to this special case. (See also exercise 7.1–00, which presents a remarkable sequence of seven bitwise operations that will convert any given binary number $(a_{n-1} \ldots a_1 a_0)_2$ to the lexicographically next t-combination, assuming that n does not exceed the computer's word length.)

Let's focus, however, on generating combinations in the other principal form $c_t \ldots c_2 c_1$, which is more directly relevant to the ways in which combinations are often needed, and which is more compact than the bit strings when t is small compared to n. In the first place we should keep in mind that a simple sequence of nested loops will do the job nicely when t is very small. For example, when $t = 3$ the following instructions suffice:

$$\begin{aligned} &\text{For } c_3 = 2,\, 3,\, \ldots,\, n-1 \text{ (in this order) do the following:} \\ &\quad \text{For } c_2 = 1,\, 2,\, \ldots,\, c_3 - 1 \text{ (in this order) do the following:} \\ &\qquad \text{For } c_1 = 0,\, 1,\, \ldots,\, c_2 - 1 \text{ (in this order) do the following:} \\ &\qquad\quad \text{Visit the combination } c_3 c_2 c_1. \end{aligned} \qquad (15)$$

(See the analogous situation in 7.2.1.1–(3).)

On the other hand when t is variable or not so small, we can generate combinations lexicographically by following the general recipe discussed after Algorithm 7.2.1.2L, namely to find the rightmost element c_j that can be increased and then to set the subsequent elements $c_{j-1} \ldots c_1$ to their smallest possible values:

Algorithm L (*Lexicographic combinations*). This algorithm generates all t-combinations $c_t \ldots c_2 c_1$ of the n numbers $\{0, 1, \ldots, n-1\}$, given $n \geq t \geq 0$. Additional variables c_{t+1} and c_{t+2} are used as sentinels.

L1. [Initialize.] Set $c_j \leftarrow j - 1$ for $1 \leq j \leq t$; also set $c_{t+1} \leftarrow n$ and $c_{t+2} \leftarrow 0$.

L2. [Visit.] Visit the combination $c_t \ldots c_2 c_1$.

L3. [Find j.] Set $j \leftarrow 1$. Then, while $c_j + 1 = c_{j+1}$, set $c_j \leftarrow j - 1$ and $j \leftarrow j + 1$; repeat until $c_j + 1 \neq c_{j+1}$.

L4. [Done?] Terminate the algorithm if $j > t$.

L5. [Increase c_j.] Set $c_j \leftarrow c_j + 1$ and return to L2. ∎

The running time of this algorithm is not difficult to analyze. Step L3 sets $c_j \leftarrow j - 1$ just after visiting a combination for which $c_{j+1} = c_1 + j$, and the number of such combinations is the number of solutions to the inequalities

$$n > c_t > \cdots > c_{j+1} \geq j; \qquad (16)$$

but this formula is equivalent to a $(t - j)$-combination of the $n - j$ objects $\{n-1, \ldots, j\}$, so the assignment $c_j \leftarrow j-1$ occurs exactly $\binom{n-j}{t-j}$ times. Summing for $1 \leq j \leq t$ tells us that the loop in step L3 is performed

$$\binom{n-1}{t-1} + \binom{n-2}{t-2} + \cdots + \binom{n-t}{0} = \binom{n-1}{s} + \binom{n-2}{s} + \cdots + \binom{s}{s} = \binom{n}{s+1} \quad (17)$$

times altogether, or an average of

$$\binom{n}{s+1} \bigg/ \binom{n}{t} = \frac{n!}{(s+1)!\,(t-1)!} \bigg/ \frac{n!}{s!\,t!} = \frac{t}{s+1} \quad (18)$$

times per visit. This ratio is less than 1 when $t \leq s$, so Algorithm L is quite efficient in such cases.

But the quantity $t/(s + 1)$ can be embarrassingly large when t is near n and s is small. Indeed, Algorithm L occasionally sets $c_j \leftarrow j - 1$ needlessly, at times when c_j already equals $j - 1$. Further scrutiny reveals that we need not always search for the index j that is needed in steps L4 and L5, since the correct value of j can often be predicted from the actions just taken. For example, after we have increased c_4 and reset $c_3 c_2 c_1$ to their starting values 210, the next combination will inevitably increase c_3. These observations lead to a tuned-up version of the algorithm:

Algorithm T (*Lexicographic combinations*). This algorithm is like Algorithm L, but faster. It also assumes, for convenience, that $t < n$.

T1. [Initialize.] Set $c_j \leftarrow j - 1$ for $1 \leq j \leq t$; then set $c_{t+1} \leftarrow n$, $c_{t+2} \leftarrow 0$, and $j \leftarrow t$.

T2. [Visit.] (At this point j is the smallest index such that $c_{j+1} > j$.) Visit the combination $c_t \ldots c_2 c_1$. Then, if $j > 0$, set $x \leftarrow j$ and go to step T6.

T3. [Easy case?] If $c_1 + 1 < c_2$, set $c_1 \leftarrow c_1 + 1$ and return to T2. Otherwise set $j \leftarrow 2$.

T4. [Find j.] Set $c_{j-1} \leftarrow j - 2$ and $x \leftarrow c_j + 1$. If $x = c_{j+1}$, set $j \leftarrow j + 1$ and repeat this step until $x \neq c_{j+1}$.

T5. [Done?] Terminate the algorithm if $j > t$.

T6. [Increase c_j.] Set $c_j \leftarrow x$, $j \leftarrow j - 1$, and return to T2. ∎

Now $j = 0$ in step T2 if and only if $c_1 > 0$, so the assignments in step T4 are never redundant. Exercise 6 carries out a complete analysis of Algorithm T.

Notice that the parameter n appears only in the initialization steps L1 and T1, not in the principal parts of Algorithms L and T. Thus we can think of the process as generating the first $\binom{n}{t}$ combinations of an *infinite* list, which depends only on t. This simplification arises because the list of t-combinations for $n + 1$ things begins with the list for n things, under our conventions; we have been using lexicographic order on the decreasing sequences $c_t \ldots c_1$ for this very reason, instead of working with the increasing sequences $c_1 \ldots c_t$.

Derrick Lehmer noticed another pleasant property of Algorithms L and T [*Applied Combinatorial Mathematics*, edited by E. F. Beckenbach (1964), 27–30]:

Theorem L. *The combination $c_t \ldots c_2 c_1$ is visited after exactly*

$$\binom{c_t}{t} + \cdots + \binom{c_2}{2} + \binom{c_1}{1} \tag{19}$$

other combinations have been visited.

Proof. There are $\binom{c_k}{k}$ combinations $c'_t \ldots c'_2 c'_1$ with $c'_j = c_j$ for $t \geq j > k$ and $c'_k < c_k$, namely $c_t \ldots c_{k+1}$ followed by the k-combinations of $\{0, \ldots, c_k - 1\}$. ∎

When $t = 3$, for example, the numbers

$$\binom{2}{3} + \binom{1}{2} + \binom{0}{1}, \ \binom{3}{3} + \binom{1}{2} + \binom{0}{1}, \ \binom{3}{3} + \binom{2}{2} + \binom{0}{1}, \ \ldots, \ \binom{5}{3} + \binom{4}{2} + \binom{3}{1}$$

that correspond to the combinations $c_3 c_2 c_1$ in Table 1 simply run through the sequence 0, 1, 2, ..., 19. Theorem L gives us a nice way to understand the *combinatorial number system* of degree t, which represents every nonnegative integer N uniquely in the form

$$N = \binom{n_t}{t} + \cdots + \binom{n_2}{2} + \binom{n_1}{1}, \qquad n_t > \cdots > n_2 > n_1 \geq 0. \tag{20}$$

[See Ernesto Pascal, *Giornale di Matematiche* **25** (1887), 45–49.]

Binomial trees. The family of trees T_n defined by

$$T_0 = \bullet\,, \qquad T_n = \overset{\displaystyle 0 \quad 1 \qquad\qquad n-1}{\underset{\displaystyle T_0 \quad T_1 \quad \cdots \quad T_{n-1}}{\diagdown}} \qquad \text{for } n > 0, \tag{21}$$

arises in several important contexts and sheds further light on combination generation. For example, T_4 is

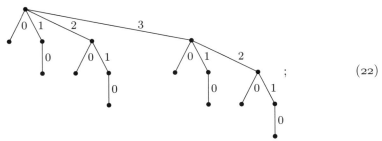

$$; \tag{22}$$

and T_5, rendered more artistically, appears as the frontispiece to Volume 1 of this series of books.

Notice that T_n is like T_{n-1}, except for an additional copy of T_{n-1}; therefore T_n has 2^n nodes altogether. Furthermore, the number of nodes on level t is the binomial coefficient $\binom{n}{t}$; this fact accounts for the name "binomial tree." Indeed, the sequence of labels encountered on the path from the root to each node on level t defines a combination $c_t \ldots c_1$, and all combinations occur in lexicographic order from left to right. Thus, Algorithms L and T can be regarded as procedures to traverse the nodes on level t of the binomial tree T_n.

The infinite binomial tree T_∞ is obtained by letting $n \to \infty$ in (21). The root of this tree has infinitely many branches, but every node except for the overall root at level 0 is the root of a finite binomial subtree. All possible t-combinations appear in lexicographic order on level t of T_∞.

Let's get more familiar with binomial trees by considering all possible ways to pack a rucksack. More precisely, suppose we have n items that take up respectively $w_{n-1}, \ldots, w_1, w_0$ units of capacity, where

$$w_{n-1} \geq \cdots \geq w_1 \geq w_0; \qquad (23)$$

we want to generate all binary vectors $a_{n-1} \ldots a_1 a_0$ such that

$$a \cdot w = a_{n-1}w_{n-1} + \cdots + a_1 w_1 + a_0 w_0 \leq N, \qquad (24)$$

where N is the total capacity of a rucksack. Equivalently, we want to find all subsets C of $\{0, 1, \ldots, n-1\}$ such that $w(C) = \sum_{c \in C} w_c \leq N$; such subsets will be called *feasible*. We will write a feasible subset as $c_1 \ldots c_t$, where $c_1 > \cdots > c_t \geq 0$, numbering the subscripts differently from the convention of (3) above because t is variable in this problem.

Every feasible subset corresponds to a node of T_n, and our goal is to visit each feasible node. Clearly the parent of every feasible node is feasible, and so is the left sibling, if any; therefore a simple tree exploration procedure works well:

Algorithm F (*Filling a rucksack*). This algorithm generates all feasible ways $c_1 \ldots c_t$ to fill a rucksack, given $w_{n-1}, \ldots, w_1, w_0$, and N. We let $\delta_j = w_j - w_{j-1}$ for $1 \leq j < n$.

F1. [Initialize.] Set $t \leftarrow 0$, $c_0 \leftarrow n$, and $r \leftarrow N$.

F2. [Visit.] Visit the combination $c_1 \ldots c_t$, which uses $N - r$ units of capacity.

F3. [Try to add w_0.] If $c_t > 0$ and $r \geq w_0$, set $t \leftarrow t + 1$, $c_t \leftarrow 0$, $r \leftarrow r - w_0$, and return to F2.

F4. [Try to increase c_t.] Terminate if $t = 0$. Otherwise, if $c_{t-1} > c_t + 1$ and $r \geq \delta_{c_t+1}$, set $c_t \leftarrow c_t + 1$, $r \leftarrow r - \delta_{c_t}$, and return to F2.

F5. [Remove c_t.] Set $r \leftarrow r + w_{c_t}$, $t \leftarrow t - 1$, and return to F4. ∎

Notice that the algorithm implicitly visits nodes of T_n in preorder, skipping over unfeasible subtrees. An element $c > 0$ is placed in the rucksack, if it fits, just after the procedure has explored all possibilities using element $c - 1$ in its place. The running time is proportional to the number of feasible combinations visited (see exercise 20).

Incidentally, the classical "knapsack problem" of operations research is different: It asks for a feasible subset C such that $v(C) = \sum_{c \in C} v(c)$ is maximum, where each item c has been assigned a value $v(c)$. Algorithm F is not a particularly good way to solve that problem, because it often considers cases that could be ruled out. For example, if C and C' are subsets of $\{1, \ldots, n-1\}$ with $w(C) \leq w(C') \leq N - w_0$ and $v(C) \geq v(C')$, Algorithm F will examine both $C \cup \{0\}$ and $C' \cup \{0\}$, but the latter subset will never improve the maximum. We will consider methods for the classical knapsack problem later; Algorithm F is intended only for situations when *all* of the feasible possibilities are potentially relevant.

Gray codes for combinations. Instead of merely generating all combinations, we often prefer to visit them in such a way that each one is obtained by making only a small change to its predecessor.

For example, we can ask for what Nijenhuis and Wilf have called a "revolving door algorithm": Imagine two rooms that contain respectively s and t people, with a revolving door between them. Whenever a person goes into the opposite room, somebody else comes out. Can we devise a sequence of moves so that each (s, t)-combination occurs exactly once?

The answer is yes, and in fact a huge number of such patterns exist. For example, it turns out that if we examine all n-bit strings $a_{n-1} \ldots a_1 a_0$ in the well-known order of Gray binary code (Section 7.2.1.1), but select only those that have exactly s 0s and t 1s, the resulting strings form a revolving-door code.

Here's the proof: Gray binary code is defined by the recurrence $\Gamma_n = 0\Gamma_{n-1}$, $1\Gamma_{n-1}^R$ of 7.2.1.1–(5), so its (s, t) subsequence satisfies the recurrence

$$\Gamma_{st} = 0\Gamma_{(s-1)t}, \; 1\Gamma_{s(t-1)}^R \qquad (25)$$

when $st > 0$. We also have $\Gamma_{s0} = 0^s$ and $\Gamma_{0t} = 1^t$. Therefore it is clear by induction that Γ_{st} begins with $0^s 1^t$ and ends with $10^s 1^{t-1}$ when $st > 0$. The transition at the comma in (25) is from the last element of $0\Gamma_{(s-1)t}$ to the last element of $1\Gamma_{s(t-1)}$, namely from $010^{s-1}1^{t-1} = 010^{s-1}11^{t-2}$ to $110^s 1^{t-2} = 110^{s-1}01^{t-2}$ when $t \geq 2$, and this satisfies the revolving-door constraint. The case $t = 1$ also checks out. For example, Γ_{33} is given by the columns of

$$
\begin{array}{llll}
000111 & 011010 & 110001 & 101010 \\
001101 & 011100 & 110010 & 101100 \\
001110 & 010101 & 110100 & 100101 \\
001011 & 010110 & 111000 & 100110 \\
011001 & 010011 & 101001 & 100011
\end{array}
\qquad (26)
$$

and Γ_{23} can be found in the first two columns of this array. One more turn of the door takes the last element into the first. [These properties of Γ_{st} were discovered by D. T. Tang and C. N. Liu, *IEEE Trans.* **C-22** (1973), 176–180; a loopless implementation was presented by J. R. Bitner, G. Ehrlich, and E. M. Reingold, *CACM* **19** (1976), 517–521.]

When we convert the bit strings $a_5 a_4 a_3 a_2 a_1 a_0$ in (26) to the corresponding index-list forms $c_3 c_2 c_1$, a striking pattern becomes evident:

$$
\begin{array}{llll}
210 & 431 & 540 & 531 \\
320 & 432 & 541 & 532 \\
321 & 420 & 542 & 520 \\
310 & 421 & 543 & 521 \\
430 & 410 & 530 & 510
\end{array}
\qquad (27)
$$

The first components c_3 occur in increasing order; but for each fixed value of c_3, the values of c_2 occur in *decreasing* order. And for fixed $c_3 c_2$, the values of c_1 are again increasing. The same is true in general: *All combinations* $c_t \ldots c_2 c_1$

appear in lexicographic order of

$$(c_t, -c_{t-1}, c_{t-2}, \ldots, (-1)^{t-1}c_1) \tag{28}$$

in the revolving-door Gray code Γ_{st}. This property follows by induction, because (25) becomes

$$\Gamma_{st} = \Gamma_{(s-1)t}, (s+t-1)\Gamma^R_{s(t-1)} \tag{29}$$

for $st > 0$ when we use index-list notation instead of bitstring notation. Consequently the sequence can be generated efficiently by the following algorithm due to W. H. Payne [see *ACM Trans. Math. Software* **5** (1979), 163–172]:

Algorithm R (*Revolving-door combinations*). This algorithm generates all t-combinations $c_t \ldots c_2 c_1$ of $\{0, 1, \ldots, n-1\}$ in lexicographic order of the alternating sequence (28), assuming that $n > t > 1$. Step R3 has two variants, depending on whether t is even or odd.

R1. [Initialize.] Set $c_j \leftarrow j - 1$ for $t \geq j \geq 1$, and $c_{t+1} \leftarrow n$.

R2. [Visit.] Visit the combination $c_t \ldots c_2 c_1$.

R3. [Easy case?] If t is odd: If $c_1 + 1 < c_2$, increase c_1 by 1 and return to R2, otherwise set $j \leftarrow 2$ and go to R4. If t is even: If $c_1 > 0$, decrease c_1 by 1 and return to R2, otherwise set $j \leftarrow 2$ and go to R5.

R4. [Try to decrease c_j.] (At this point $c_j = c_{j-1} + 1$.) If $c_j \geq j$, set $c_j \leftarrow c_{j-1}$, $c_{j-1} \leftarrow j - 2$, and return to R2. Otherwise increase j by 1.

R5. [Try to increase c_j.] (At this point $c_{j-1} = j - 2$.) If $c_j + 1 < c_{j+1}$, set $c_{j-1} \leftarrow c_j$, $c_j \leftarrow c_j + 1$, and return to R2. Otherwise increase j by 1, and go to R4 if $j \leq t$. ∎

Exercises 21–25 explore further properties of this interesting sequence. One of them is a nice companion to Theorem L: *The combination* $c_t c_{t-1} \ldots c_2 c_1$ *is visited by Algorithm R after exactly*

$$N = \binom{c_t+1}{t} - \binom{c_{t-1}+1}{t-1} + \cdots + (-1)^t \binom{c_2+1}{2} - (-1)^t \binom{c_1+1}{1} - [t \text{ odd}] \tag{30}$$

other combinations have been visited. We may call this the representation of N in the "alternating combinatorial number system" of degree t; one consequence, for example, is that every positive integer has a unique representation of the form $N = \binom{a}{3} - \binom{b}{2} + \binom{c}{1}$ with $a > b > c > 0$. Algorithm R tells us how to add 1 to N in this system.

Although the strings of (26) and (27) are not in lexicographic order, they are examples of a more general concept called *genlex order*, a name coined by Timothy Walsh. A sequence of strings $\alpha_1, \ldots, \alpha_N$ is said to be in genlex order when all strings with a common prefix occur consecutively. For example, all 3-combinations that begin with 53 appear together in (27).

Genlex order means that the strings can be arranged in a trie structure, as in Fig. 31 of Section 6.3, but with the children of each node ordered arbitrarily. When a trie is traversed in any order such that each node is visited just before or just after its descendants, all nodes with a common prefix — that is, all nodes of a subtrie — appear consecutively. This principle makes genlex order convenient, because it corresponds to recursive generation schemes. Many of the algorithms we have seen for generating n-tuples have therefore produced their results in some version of genlex order; similarly, the method of "plain changes" (Algorithm 7.2.1.2P) visits permutations in a genlex order of the corresponding inversion tables.

The revolving-door method of Algorithm R is a genlex routine that changes only one element of the combination at each step. But it isn't totally satisfactory, because it frequently must change two of the indices c_j simultaneously, in order to preserve the condition $c_t > \cdots > c_2 > c_1$. For example, Algorithm R changes 210 into 320, and (27) includes nine such "crossing" moves.

The source of this defect can be traced to our proof that (25) satisfies the revolving-door property: We observed that the string $010^{s-1}11^{t-2}$ is followed by $110^{s-1}01^{t-2}$ when $t \geq 2$. Hence the recursive construction Γ_{st} involves transitions of the form $110^a0 \leftrightarrow 010^a1$, when a substring like 11000 is changed to 01001 or vice versa; the two 1s cross each other.

A Gray path for combinations is said to be *homogeneous* if it changes only one of the indices c_j at each step. A homogeneous scheme is characterized in bitstring form by having only transitions of the forms $10^a \leftrightarrow 0^a1$ within strings, for $a \geq 1$, when we pass from one string to the next. With a homogeneous scheme we can, for example, play all t-note chords on an n-note keyboard by moving only one finger at a time.

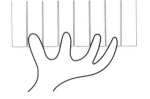

A slight modification of (25) yields a genlex scheme for (s,t)-combinations that is pleasantly homogeneous. The basic idea is to construct a sequence that begins with 0^s1^t and ends with 1^t0^s, and the following recursion suggests itself almost immediately: Let $K_{s0} = 0^s$, $K_{0t} = 1^t$, $K_{s(-1)} = \emptyset$, and

$$K_{st} = 0K_{(s-1)t}, \; 10K^R_{(s-1)(t-1)}, \; 11K_{s(t-2)} \quad \text{for } st > 0. \tag{31}$$

At the commas of this sequence we have 01^t0^{s-1} followed by $101^{t-1}0^{s-1}$, and 10^s1^{t-1} followed by 110^s1^{t-2}; both of these transitions are homogeneous, although the second one requires the 1 to jump across s 0s. The combinations K_{33} for $s = t = 3$ are

$$
\begin{array}{cccc}
000111 & 010101 & 101100 & 100011 \\
001011 & 010011 & 101001 & 110001 \\
001101 & 011001 & 101010 & 110010 \\
001110 & 011010 & 100110 & 110100 \\
010110 & 011100 & 100101 & 111000
\end{array} \tag{32}
$$

in bitstring form, and the corresponding "finger patterns" are

$$
\begin{array}{cccc}
210 & 420 & 532 & 510 \\
310 & 410 & 530 & 540 \\
320 & 430 & 531 & 541 \\
321 & 431 & 521 & 542 \\
421 & 432 & 520 & 543.
\end{array} \tag{33}
$$

When a homogeneous scheme for ordinary combinations $c_t \ldots c_1$ is converted to the corresponding scheme (6) for combinations with repetitions $d_t \ldots d_1$, it retains the property that only one of the indices d_j changes at each step. And when it is converted to the corresponding schemes (9) or (11) for compositions $p_t \ldots p_0$ or $q_t \ldots q_0$, only two (adjacent) parts change when c_j changes.

Near-perfect schemes. But we can do even better! All (s,t)-combinations can be generated by a sequence of strongly homogeneous transitions that are either $01 \leftrightarrow 10$ or $001 \leftrightarrow 100$. In other words, we can insist that each step causes a single index c_j to change by at most 2. Let's call such generation schemes *near-perfect*.

Imposing such strong conditions actually makes it fairly easy to discover near-perfect schemes, because comparatively few choices are available. Indeed, if we restrict ourselves to genlex methods that are near-perfect on n-bit strings, T. A. Jenkyns and D. McCarthy observed that all such methods can be easily characterized [*Ars Combinatoria* **40** (1995), 153–159]:

Theorem N. *If $st > 0$, there are exactly $2s$ near-perfect ways to list all (s,t)-combinations in a genlex order. In fact, when $1 \le a \le s$, there is exactly one such listing, N_{sta}, that begins with $1^t 0^s$ and ends with $0^a 1^t 0^{s-a}$; the other s possibilities are the reverse lists, N_{sta}^R.*

Proof. The result certainly holds when $s = t = 1$; otherwise we use induction on $s+t$. The listing N_{sta}, if it exists, must have the form $1X_{s(t-1)}, 0Y_{(s-1)t}$ for some near-perfect genlex listings $X_{s(t-1)}$ and $Y_{(s-1)t}$. If $t = 1$, $X_{s(t-1)}$ is the single string 0^s; hence $Y_{(s-1)t}$ must be $N_{(s-1)1(a-1)}$ if $a > 1$, and it must be $N_{(s-1)11}^R$ if $a = 1$. On the other hand if $t > 1$, the near-perfect condition implies that the last string of $X_{s(t-1)}$ cannot begin with 1; hence $X_{s(t-1)} = N_{s(t-1)b}$ for some b. If $a > 1$, $Y_{(s-1)t}$ must be $N_{(s-1)t(a-1)}$, hence b must be 1; similarly, b must be 1 if $s = 1$. Otherwise we have $a = 1 < s$, and this forces $Y_{(s-1)t} = N_{(s-1)tc}^R$ for some c. The transition from $10^b 1^{t-1} 0^{s-b}$ to $0^{c+1} 1^t 0^{s-1-c}$ is near-perfect only if $c = 1$ and $b = 2$. ∎

The proof of Theorem N yields the following recursive formulas when $st > 0$:

$$N_{sta} = \begin{cases} 1N_{s(t-1)1}, \; 0N_{(s-1)t(a-1)}, & \text{if } 1 < a \le s; \\ 1N_{s(t-1)2}, \; 0N_{(s-1)t1}^R, & \text{if } 1 = a < s; \\ 1N_{1(t-1)1}, \; 01^t, & \text{if } 1 = a = s. \end{cases} \tag{34}$$

Also, of course, $N_{s0a} = 0^s$.

Let us set $A_{st} = N_{st1}$ and $B_{st} = N_{st2}$. These near-perfect listings, discovered by Phillip J. Chase in 1976, have the net effect of shifting a leftmost block of 1s to the right by one or two positions, respectively, and they satisfy the following mutual recursions:

$$A_{st} = 1B_{s(t-1)}, \; 0A_{(s-1)t}^R; \qquad B_{st} = 1A_{s(t-1)}, \; 0A_{(s-1)t}. \tag{35}$$

"To take one step forward, take two steps forward, then one step backward; to take two steps forward, take one step forward, then another." These equations

Table 2
CHASE'S SEQUENCES FOR $(3,3)$-COMBINATIONS

$A_{33} = \widehat{C}^R_{33}$				$B_{33} = C_{33}$			
543	531	321	420	543	520	432	410
541	530	320	421	542	510	430	210
540	510	310	431	540	530	431	310
542	520	210	430	541	531	421	320
532	521	410	432	521	532	420	321

hold for all integer values of s and t, if we define A_{st} and B_{st} to be $\emptyset$ when s or t is negative, except that $A_{00} = B_{00} = \epsilon$ (the empty string). Thus A_{st} actually takes $\min(s, 1)$ forward steps, and B_{st} actually takes $\min(s, 2)$. For example, Table 2 shows the relevant listings for $s = t = 3$, using an equivalent index-list form $c_3c_2c_1$ instead of the bit strings $a_5a_4a_3a_2a_1a_0$.

Chase noticed that a computer implementation of these sequences becomes simpler if we define

$$C_{st} = \begin{cases} A_{st}, & \text{if } s + t \text{ is odd}; \\ B_{st}, & \text{if } s + t \text{ is even}; \end{cases} \qquad \widehat{C}_{st} = \begin{cases} A^R_{st}, & \text{if } s + t \text{ is even}; \\ B^R_{st}, & \text{if } s + t \text{ is odd}. \end{cases} \quad (36)$$

[See *Congressus Numerantium* **69** (1989), 215–242.] Then we have

$$C_{st} = \begin{cases} 1C_{s(t-1)}, \ 0\widehat{C}_{(s-1)t}, & \text{if } s + t \text{ is odd}; \\ 1C_{s(t-1)}, \ 0C_{(s-1)t}, & \text{if } s + t \text{ is even}; \end{cases} \quad (37)$$

$$\widehat{C}_{st} = \begin{cases} 0C_{(s-1)t}, \ 1\widehat{C}_{s(t-1)}, & \text{if } s + t \text{ is even}; \\ 0\widehat{C}_{(s-1)t}, \ 1\widehat{C}_{s(t-1)}, & \text{if } s + t \text{ is odd}. \end{cases} \quad (38)$$

When bit a_j is ready to change, we can tell where we are in the recursion by testing whether j is even or odd.

Indeed, the sequence C_{st} can be generated by a surprisingly simple algorithm, based on general ideas that apply to *any* genlex scheme. Let us say that bit a_j is *active* in a genlex algorithm if it is supposed to change before anything to its left is altered. (In other words, the node for an active bit in the corresponding trie is not the rightmost child of its parent.) Suppose we have an auxiliary table $w_n \ldots w_1w_0$, where $w_j = 1$ if and only if either a_j is active or $j < r$, where r is the least subscript such that $a_r \neq a_0$; we also let $w_n = 1$. Then the following method will find the successor of $a_{n-1} \ldots a_1a_0$:

> Set $j \leftarrow r$. If $w_j = 0$, set $w_j \leftarrow 1$, $j \leftarrow j + 1$, and repeat until $w_j = 1$. Terminate if $j = n$; otherwise set $w_j \leftarrow 0$. Change a_j to $1 - a_j$, and make any other changes to $a_{j-1} \ldots a_0$ and r that apply to the particular genlex scheme being used. $\quad (39)$

The beauty of this approach comes from the fact that the loop is guaranteed to be efficient: We can prove that the operation $j \leftarrow j + 1$ will be performed less than once per generation step, on the average (see exercise 36).

By analyzing the transitions that occur when bits change in (37) and (38), we can readily flesh out the remaining details:

Algorithm C (*Chase's sequence*). This algorithm visits all (s,t)-combinations $a_{n-1}\ldots a_1 a_0$, where $n = s + t$, in the near-perfect order of Chase's sequence C_{st}.

C1. [Initialize.] Set $a_j \leftarrow 0$ for $0 \le j < s$, $a_j \leftarrow 1$ for $s \le j < n$, and $w_j \leftarrow 1$ for $0 \le j \le n$. If $s > 0$, set $r \leftarrow s$; otherwise set $r \leftarrow t$.

C2. [Visit.] Visit the combination $a_{n-1}\ldots a_1 a_0$.

C3. [Find j and branch.] Set $j \leftarrow r$. If $w_j = 0$, set $w_j \leftarrow 1$, $j \leftarrow j + 1$, and repeat until $w_j = 1$. Terminate if $j = n$; otherwise set $w_j \leftarrow 0$ and make a four-way branch: Go to C4 if j is odd and $a_j \ne 0$, to C5 if j is even and $a_j \ne 0$, to C6 if j is even and $a_j = 0$, to C7 if j is odd and $a_j = 0$.

C4. [Move right one.] Set $a_{j-1} \leftarrow 1$, $a_j \leftarrow 0$. If $r = j > 1$, set $r \leftarrow j - 1$; otherwise if $r = j - 1$ set $r \leftarrow j$. Return to C2.

C5. [Move right two.] If $a_{j-2} \ne 0$, go to C4. Otherwise set $a_{j-2} \leftarrow 1$, $a_j \leftarrow 0$. If $r = j$, set $r \leftarrow \max(j-2, 1)$; otherwise if $r = j - 2$, set $r \leftarrow j - 1$. Return to C2.

C6. [Move left one.] Set $a_j \leftarrow 1$, $a_{j-1} \leftarrow 0$. If $r = j > 1$, set $r \leftarrow j-1$; otherwise if $r = j - 1$ set $r \leftarrow j$. Return to C2.

C7. [Move left two.] If $a_{j-1} \ne 0$, go to C6. Otherwise set $a_j \leftarrow 1$, $a_{j-2} \leftarrow 0$. If $r = j - 2$, set $r \leftarrow j$; otherwise if $r = j - 1$, set $r \leftarrow j - 2$. Return to C2. ∎

*Analysis of Chase's sequence. The magical properties of Algorithm C cry out for further exploration, and a closer look turns out to be quite instructive. Given a bit string $a_{n-1}\ldots a_1 a_0$, let us define $a_n = 1$, $u_n = n \bmod 2$, and

$$u_j = (1 - u_{j+1})a_{j+1}, \quad v_j = (u_j + j) \bmod 2, \quad w_j = (v_j + a_j) \bmod 2, \quad (40)$$

for $n > j \ge 0$. For example, we might have $n = 26$ and

$$
\begin{aligned}
a_{25}\ldots a_1 a_0 &= 11001001000011111101101010, \\
u_{25}\ldots u_1 u_0 &= 10100100100001010100100101, \\
v_{25}\ldots v_1 v_0 &= 00001110001011111110001111, \\
w_{25}\ldots w_1 w_0 &= 11000111001000000011100101.
\end{aligned}
\quad (41)
$$

With these definitions we can prove by induction that $v_j = 0$ if and only if bit a_j is being "controlled" by C rather than by $\widehat{C}$ in the recursions (37)–(38) that generate $a_{n-1}\ldots a_1 a_0$, except when a_j is part of the final run of 0s or 1s at the right end. Therefore w_j agrees with the value computed by Algorithm C at the moment when $a_{n-1}\ldots a_1 a_0$ is visited, for $r \le j < n$. These formulas can be used to determine exactly where a given combination appears in Chase's sequence (see exercise 39).

If we want to work with the index-list form $c_t \ldots c_2 c_1$ instead of the bit strings $a_{n-1}\ldots a_1 a_0$, it is convenient to change the notation slightly, writing

$C_t(n)$ for C_{st} and $\widehat{C}_t(n)$ for $\widehat{C}_{st}$ when $s + t = n$. Then $C_0(n) = \widehat{C}_0(n) = \epsilon$, and the recursions for $t \geq 0$ take the form

$$C_{t+1}(n+1) = \begin{cases} nC_t(n), \ \widehat{C}_{t+1}(n), & \text{if } n \text{ is even;} \\ nC_t(n), \ C_{t+1}(n), & \text{if } n \text{ is odd;} \end{cases} \tag{42}$$

$$\widehat{C}_{t+1}(n+1) = \begin{cases} C_{t+1}(n), \ n\widehat{C}_t(n), & \text{if } n \text{ is odd;} \\ \widehat{C}_{t+1}(n), \ n\widehat{C}_t(n), & \text{if } n \text{ is even.} \end{cases} \tag{43}$$

These new equations can be expanded to tell us, for example, that

$$\begin{aligned}
C_{t+1}(9) &= 8C_t(8), \ 6C_t(6), \ 4C_t(4), \ \dots, \ 3\widehat{C}_t(3), \ 5\widehat{C}_t(5), \ 7\widehat{C}_t(7); \\
C_{t+1}(8) &= 7C_t(7), \ 6C_t(6), \ 4C_t(4), \ \dots, \ 3\widehat{C}_t(3), \ 5\widehat{C}_t(5); \\
\widehat{C}_{t+1}(9) &= \ 6C_t(6), \ 4C_t(4), \ \dots, \ 3\widehat{C}_t(3), \ 5\widehat{C}_t(5), \ 7\widehat{C}_t(7), \ 8\widehat{C}_t(8); \\
\widehat{C}_{t+1}(8) &= \ 6C_t(6), \ 4C_t(4), \ \dots, \ 3\widehat{C}_t(3), \ 5\widehat{C}_t(5), \ 7\widehat{C}_t(7);
\end{aligned} \tag{44}$$

notice that the same pattern predominates in all four sequences. The meaning of "$\dots$" in the middle depends on the value of t: We simply omit all terms $nC_t(n)$ and $n\widehat{C}_t(n)$ where $n < t$.

Except for edge effects at the very beginning or end, all of the expansions in (44) are based on the infinite progression

$$\dots, \ 10, \ 8, \ 6, \ 4, \ 2, \ 0, \ 1, \ 3, \ 5, \ 7, \ 9, \ \dots, \tag{45}$$

which is a natural way to arrange the nonnegative integers into a doubly infinite sequence. If we omit all terms of (45) that are $< t$, given any integer $t \geq 0$, the remaining terms retain the property that adjacent elements differ by either 1 or 2. Richard Stanley has suggested the name *endo-order* for this sequence, because we can remember it by thinking "even numbers decreasing, odd $\dots$". (Notice that if we retain only the terms less than N and complement with respect to N, endo-order becomes organ-pipe order; see exercise 6.1–18.)

We could program the recursions of (42) and (43) directly, but it is interesting to unwind them using (44), thus obtaining an iterative algorithm analogous to Algorithm C. The result needs only $O(t)$ memory locations, and it is especially efficient when t is relatively small compared to n. Exercise 45 contains the details.

*Near-perfect multiset permutations. Chase's sequences lead in a natural way to an algorithm that will generate permutations of any desired multiset $\{s_0 \cdot 0, s_1 \cdot 1, \dots, s_d \cdot d\}$ in a near-perfect manner, meaning that

i) every transition is either $a_{j+1}a_j \leftrightarrow a_j a_{j+1}$ or $a_{j+1}a_j a_{j-1} \leftrightarrow a_{j-1}a_j a_{j+1}$;

ii) transitions of the second kind have $a_j = \min(a_{j-1}, a_{j+1})$.

Algorithm C tells us how to do this when $d = 1$, and we can extend it to larger values of d by the following recursive construction [*CACM* **13** (1970), 368–369, 376]: Suppose

$$\alpha_0, \ \alpha_1, \ \dots, \ \alpha_{N-1}$$

is any near-perfect listing of the permutations of $\{s_1 \cdot 1, \ldots, s_d \cdot d\}$. Then Algorithm C, with $s = s_0$ and $t = s_1 + \cdots + s_d$, tells us how to generate a listing

$$\Lambda_j = \alpha_j 0^s, \ldots, 0^a \alpha_j 0^{s-a} \qquad (46)$$

in which all transitions are $0x \leftrightarrow x0$ or $00x \leftrightarrow x00$; the final entry has $a = 1$ or 2 leading zeros, depending on s and t. Therefore all transitions of the sequence

$$\Lambda_0, \Lambda_1^R, \Lambda_2, \ldots, (\Lambda_{N-1} \text{ or } \Lambda_{N-1}^R) \qquad (47)$$

are near-perfect; and this list clearly contains all the permutations.

For example, the permutations of $\{0, 0, 0, 1, 1, 2\}$ generated in this way are

211000, 210100, 210001, 210010, 200110, 200101, 200011, 201001, 201010, 201100,
021100, 021001, 021010, 020110, 020101, 020011, 000211, 002011, 002101, 002110,
001120, 001102, 001012, 000112, 010012, 010102, 010120, 011020, 011002, 011200,
101200, 101020, 101002, 100012, 100102, 100120, 110020, 110002, 110200, 112000,
121000, 120100, 120001, 120010, 100210, 100201, 100021, 102001, 102010, 102100,
012100, 012001, 012010, 010210, 010201, 010021, 000121, 001021, 001201, 001210.

*Perfect schemes.** Why should we settle for a near-perfect generator like C_{st}, instead of insisting that all transitions have the simplest possible form $01 \leftrightarrow 10$?

One reason is that perfect schemes don't always exist. For example, we observed in 7.2.1.2–(2) that there is no way to generate all six permutations of $\{1, 1, 2, 2\}$ with adjacent interchanges; thus there is no perfect scheme for $(2, 2)$-combinations. In fact, our chances of achieving perfection are only about 1 in 4:

Theorem P. *The generation of all (s, t)-combinations $a_{s+t-1} \ldots a_1 a_0$ by adjacent interchanges $01 \leftrightarrow 10$ is possible if and only if $s \leq 1$ or $t \leq 1$ or st is odd.*

Proof. Consider all permutations of the multiset $\{s \cdot 0, t \cdot 1\}$. We learned in exercise 5.1.2–16 that the number m_k of such permutations having k inversions is the coefficient of z^k in the z-nomial coefficient

$$\binom{s+t}{t}_z = \prod_{k=s+1}^{s+t} (1 + z + \cdots + z^{k-1}) \Big/ \prod_{k=1}^{t} (1 + z + \cdots + z^{k-1}). \qquad (48)$$

Every adjacent interchange changes the number of inversions by ± 1, so a perfect generation scheme is possible only if approximately half of all the permutations have an odd number of inversions. More precisely, the value of $\binom{s+t}{t}_{-1} = m_0 - m_1 + m_2 - \cdots$ must be 0 or ± 1. But exercise 49 shows that

$$\binom{s+t}{t}_{-1} = \binom{\lfloor (s+t)/2 \rfloor}{\lfloor t/2 \rfloor} [st \text{ is even}], \qquad (49)$$

and this quantity exceeds 1 unless $s \leq 1$ or $t \leq 1$ or st is odd.

Conversely, perfect schemes are easy with $s \leq 1$ or $t \leq 1$, and they turn out to be possible also whenever st is odd. The first nontrivial case occurs for $s = t = 3$, when there are four essentially different solutions; the most symmetrical of these is

$$210 - 310 - 410 - 510 - 520 - 521 - 531 - 532 - 432 - 431 -$$
$$421 - 321 - 320 - 420 - 430 - 530 - 540 - 541 - 542 - 543 \qquad (50)$$

(see exercise 51). Several authors have constructed Hamiltonian paths in the relevant graph for arbitrary odd numbers s and t; for example, the method of Eades, Hickey, and Read [*JACM* **31** (1984), 19–29] makes an interesting exercise in programming with recursive coroutines. Unfortunately, however, none of the known constructions are sufficiently simple to describe in a short space, or to implement with reasonable efficiency. Perfect combination generators have therefore not yet proved to be of practical importance. ∎

In summary, then, we have seen that the study of (s, t)-combinations leads to many fascinating patterns, some of which are of great practical importance and some of which are merely elegant and/or beautiful. Figure 26 illustrates the principal options that are available in the case $s = t = 5$, when $\binom{10}{5} = 252$ combinations arise. Lexicographic order (Algorithm L), the revolving-door Gray code (Algorithm R), the homogeneous scheme K_{55} of (31), and Chase's near-perfect scheme (Algorithm C) are shown in parts (a), (b), (c), and (d) of the illustration. Part (e) shows the near-perfect scheme that is as close to perfection as possible while still being in genlex order of the c array (see exercise 34), while part (f) is the perfect scheme of Eades, Hickey, and Read. Finally, Figs. 26(g) and 26(h) are listings that proceed by rotating $a_j a_{j-1} \ldots a_0 \leftarrow a_{j-1} \ldots a_0 a_j$ or by swapping $a_j \leftrightarrow a_0$, akin to Algorithms 7.2.1.2C and 7.2.1.2E (see exercises 55 and 56).

*Combinations of a multiset. If multisets can have permutations, they can have combinations too. For example, consider the multiset $\{b, b, b, b, g, g, g, r, r, r,$ $w, w\}$, representing a sack that contains four blue balls and three that are green, three red, two white. There are 37 ways to choose five balls from this sack; in lexicographic order (but descending in each combination) they are

$$gbbbb, \; ggbbb, \; gggbb, \; rbbbb, \; rgbbb, \; rggbb, \; rgggb, \; rrbbb, \; rrgbb, \; rrggb,$$
$$rrggg, \; rrrbb, \; rrrgb, \; rrrgg, \; wbbbb, \; wgbbb, \; wggbb, \; wgggb, \; wrbbb, \; wrgbb,$$
$$wrggb, \; wrggg, \; wrrbb, \; wrrgb, \; wrrgg, \; wrrrb, \; wrrrg, \; wwbbb, \; wwgbb, \; wwggb,$$
$$wwggg, \; wwrbb, \; wwrgb, \; wwrgg, \; wwrrb, \; wwrrg, \; wwrrr. \qquad (51)$$

This fact might seem frivolous and/or esoteric, yet we will see in Theorem W below that the lexicographic generation of multiset combinations yields optimal solutions to significant combinatorial problems.

James Bernoulli observed in his *Ars Conjectandi* (1713), 119–123, that we can enumerate such combinations by looking at the coefficient of z^5 in the product $(1 + z + z^2)(1 + z + z^2 + z^3)^2(1 + z + z^2 + z^3 + z^4)$. Indeed, his observation is easy to understand, because we get all possible selections from the sack if we multiply out the polynomials

$$(1 + w + ww)(1 + r + rr + rrr)(1 + g + gg + ggg)(1 + b + bb + bbb + bbbb).$$

Multiset combinations are also equivalent to *bounded compositions*, namely to compositions in which the individual parts are bounded. For example, the 37 multicombinations listed in (51) correspond to 37 solutions of

$$5 = r_3 + r_2 + r_1 + r_0, \quad 0 \le r_3 \le 2, \quad 0 \le r_2, r_1 \le 3, \quad 0 \le r_0 \le 4,$$

namely $5 = 0+0+1+4 = 0+0+2+3 = 0+0+3+2 = 0+1+0+4 = \cdots = 2+3+0+0$.

Fig. 26. Examples of $(5, 5)$-combinations:

  a) lexicographic;
  b) revolving-door;
  c) homogeneous;
  d) near-perfect;
  e) nearer-perfect;
  f) perfect;
  g) suffix-rotated;
  h) right-swapped.

(a)   (b)   (c)   (d)   (e)   (f)   (g)   (h)

Bounded compositions, in turn, are special cases of *contingency tables*, which are of great importance in statistics. And all of these combinatorial configurations can be generated with Gray-like codes as well as in lexicographic order. Exercises 60–63 explore some of the basic ideas involved.

*Shadows. Sets of combinations appear frequently in mathematics. For example, a set of 2-combinations (namely a set of pairs) is essentially a graph, and a set of t-combinations for general t is called a uniform hypergraph. If the vertices of a convex polyhedron are perturbed slightly, so that no three are collinear, no four lie in a plane, and in general no $t + 1$ lie in a $(t - 1)$-dimensional hyperplane, the resulting $(t - 1)$-dimensional faces are "simplexes" whose vertices have great significance in computer applications. Researchers have learned that such sets of combinations have important properties related to lexicographic generation.

If α is any t-combination $c_t \ldots c_2 c_1$, its *shadow* $\partial \alpha$ is the set of all its $(t - 1)$-element subsets $c_{t-1} \ldots c_2 c_1$, ..., $c_t \ldots c_3 c_1$, $c_t \ldots c_3 c_2$. For example, $\partial 5310 = \{310, 510, 530, 531\}$. We can also represent a t-combination as a bit string $a_{n-1} \ldots a_1 a_0$, in which case $\partial \alpha$ is the set of all strings obtained by changing a 1 to a 0: $\partial 101011 = \{001011, 100011, 101001, 101010\}$. If A is any set of t-combinations, we define its shadow

$$\partial A = \bigcup \{ \partial \alpha \mid \alpha \in A \} \tag{52}$$

to be the set of all $(t - 1)$-combinations in the shadows of its members. For example, $\partial\partial 5310 = \{10, 30, 31, 50, 51, 53\}$.

These definitions apply also to combinations with repetitions, namely to multicombinations: $\partial 5330 = \{330, 530, 533\}$ and $\partial\partial 5330 = \{30, 33, 50, 53\}$. In general, when A is a set of t-element multisets, ∂A is a set of $(t - 1)$-element multisets. Notice, however, that ∂A never has repeated elements itself.

The *upper shadow* $\varrho \alpha$ with respect to a universe U is defined similarly, but it goes from t-combinations to $(t + 1)$-combinations:

$$\varrho \alpha = \{ \beta \subseteq U \mid \alpha \in \partial \beta \}, \qquad \text{for } \alpha \in U; \tag{53}$$
$$\varrho A = \bigcup \{ \varrho \alpha \mid \alpha \in A \}, \qquad \text{for } A \subseteq U. \tag{54}$$

If, for example, $U = \{0, 1, 2, 3, 4, 5, 6\}$, we have $\varrho 5310 = \{53210, 54310, 65310\}$; on the other hand, if $U = \{\infty \cdot 0, \infty \cdot 1, \ldots, \infty \cdot 6\}$, we have $\varrho 5310 = \{53100, 53110, 53210, 53310, 54310, 55310, 65310\}$.

The following fundamental theorems, which have many applications in various branches of mathematics and computer science, tell us how small a set's shadows can be:

Theorem K. *If A is a set of N t-combinations contained in $U = \{0, 1, \ldots, n-1\}$, then*

$$|\partial A| \geq |\partial P_{Nt}| \qquad \text{and} \qquad |\varrho A| \geq |\varrho Q_{Nnt}|, \tag{55}$$

where P_{Nt} denotes the first N combinations generated by Algorithm L, namely the N lexicographically smallest combinations $c_t \ldots c_2 c_1$ that satisfy (3), and Q_{Nnt} denotes the N lexicographically largest. ∎

Theorem M. *If A is a set of N t-multicombinations contained in the multiset $U = \{\infty \cdot 0, \infty \cdot 1, \ldots, \infty \cdot s\}$, then*

$$|\partial A| \geq |\partial \widehat{P}_{Nt}| \qquad and \qquad |\varrho A| \geq |\varrho \widehat{Q}_{Nst}|, \qquad (56)$$

where $\widehat{P}_{Nt}$ denotes the N lexicographically smallest multicombinations $d_t \ldots d_2 d_1$ that satisfy (6), and $\widehat{Q}_{Nst}$ denotes the N lexicographically largest. ∎

Both of these theorems are consequences of a stronger result that we shall prove later. Theorem K is generally called the Kruskal–Katona theorem, because it was discovered by J. B. Kruskal [*Math. Optimization Techniques*, edited by R. Bellman (1963), 251–278] and rediscovered by G. Katona [*Theory of Graphs*, Tihany 1966, edited by Erdős and Katona (Academic Press, 1968), 187–207]; M. P. Schützenberger had previously stated it in a less-well-known publication, with incomplete proof [*RLE Quarterly Progress Report* **55** (1959), 117–118]. Theorem M goes back to F. S. Macaulay, many years earlier [*Proc. London Math. Soc.* (2) **26** (1927), 531–555].

Before proving (55) and (56), let's take a closer look at what those formulas mean. We know from Theorem L that the first N of all t-combinations visited by Algorithm L are those that precede $n_t \ldots n_2 n_1$, where

$$N = \binom{n_t}{t} + \cdots + \binom{n_2}{2} + \binom{n_1}{1}, \qquad n_t > \cdots > n_2 > n_1 \geq 0$$

is the degree-t combinatorial representation of N. Sometimes this representation has fewer than t nonzero terms, because n_j can be equal to $j - 1$; let's suppress the zeros, and write

$$N = \binom{n_t}{t} + \binom{n_{t-1}}{t-1} + \cdots + \binom{n_v}{v}, \qquad n_t > n_{t-1} > \cdots > n_v \geq v \geq 1. \quad (57)$$

Now the first $\binom{n_t}{t}$ combinations $c_t \ldots c_1$ are the t-combinations of $\{0, \ldots, n_t-1\}$; the next $\binom{n_{t-1}}{t-1}$ are those in which $c_t = n_t$ and $c_{t-1} \ldots c_1$ is a $(t-1)$-combination of $\{0, \ldots, n_{t-1}-1\}$; and so on. For example, if $t = 5$ and $N = \binom{9}{5} + \binom{7}{4} + \binom{4}{3}$, the first N combinations are

$$P_{N5} = \{43210, \ldots, 87654\} \cup \{93210, \ldots, 96543\} \cup \{97210, \ldots, 97321\}. \quad (58)$$

The shadow of this set P_{N5} is, fortunately, easy to understand: It is

$$\partial P_{N5} = \{3210, \ldots, 8765\} \cup \{9210, \ldots, 9654\} \cup \{9710, \ldots, 9732\}, \quad (59)$$

namely the first $\binom{9}{4} + \binom{7}{3} + \binom{4}{2}$ combinations in lexicographic order when $t = 4$.

In other words, if we define Kruskal's function κ_t by the formula

$$\kappa_t N = \binom{n_t}{t-1} + \binom{n_{t-1}}{t-2} + \cdots + \binom{n_v}{v-1} \qquad (60)$$

when N has the unique representation (57), we have

$$\partial P_{Nt} = P_{(\kappa_t N)(t-1)}. \qquad (61)$$

Theorem K tells us, for example, that a graph with a million edges can contain at most

$$\binom{1414}{3} + \binom{1009}{2} = 470{,}700{,}300$$

triangles, that is, at most 470,700,300 sets of vertices $\{u, v, w\}$ with u — v — w — u. The reason is that $1000000 = \binom{1414}{2} + \binom{1009}{1}$ by exercise 17, and the edges $P_{(1000000)2}$ do support $\binom{1414}{3} + \binom{1009}{2}$ triangles; but if there were more, the graph would necessarily have at least $\kappa_3 470700301 = \binom{1414}{2} + \binom{1009}{1} + \binom{1}{0} = 1000001$ edges in their shadow.

Kruskal defined the companion function

$$\lambda_t N = \binom{n_t}{t+1} + \binom{n_{t-1}}{t} + \cdots + \binom{n_v}{v+1} \tag{62}$$

to deal with questions such as this. The κ and λ functions are related by an interesting law proved in exercise 72:

$$M + N = \binom{s+t}{t} \quad \text{implies} \quad \kappa_s M + \lambda_t N = \binom{s+t}{t+1}, \quad \text{if } st > 0. \tag{63}$$

Turning to Theorem M, the sizes of $\partial \widehat{P}_{Nt}$ and $\varrho \widehat{Q}_{Nst}$ turn out to be

$$|\partial \widehat{P}_{Nt}| = \mu_t N \qquad \text{and} \qquad |\varrho \widehat{Q}_{Nst}| = N + \kappa_s N \tag{64}$$

(see exercise 81), where the function μ_t satisfies

$$\mu_t N = \binom{n_t - 1}{t - 1} + \binom{n_{t-1} - 1}{t - 2} + \cdots + \binom{n_v - 1}{v - 1} \tag{65}$$

when N has the combinatorial representation (57).

Table 3 shows how these functions $\kappa_t N$, $\lambda_t N$, and $\mu_t N$ behave for small values of t and N. When t and N are large, they can be well approximated in terms of a remarkable function $\tau(x)$ introduced by Teiji Takagi in 1903; see Fig. 27 and exercises 82–85.

Theorems K and M are corollaries of a much more general theorem of discrete geometry, discovered by Da-Lun Wang and Ping Wang [*SIAM J. Applied Math.* **33** (1977), 55–59], which we shall now proceed to investigate. Consider the *discrete n-dimensional torus* $T(m_1, \ldots, m_n)$ whose elements are integer vectors $x = (x_1, \ldots, x_n)$ with $0 \le x_1 < m_1$, $\ldots$, $0 \le x_n < m_n$. We define the sum and difference of two such vectors x and y as in Eqs. 4.3.2–(2) and 4.3.2–(3):

$$x + y = \big((x_1 + y_1) \bmod m_1, \ldots, (x_n + y_n) \bmod m_n\big), \tag{66}$$

$$x - y = \big((x_1 - y_1) \bmod m_1, \ldots, (x_n - y_n) \bmod m_n\big). \tag{67}$$

We also define the so-called *cross order* on such vectors by saying that $x \preceq y$ if and only if

$$\nu x < \nu y \quad \text{or} \quad (\nu x = \nu y \text{ and } x \ge y \text{ lexicographically}); \tag{68}$$

here, as usual, $\nu(x_1, \ldots, x_n) = x_1 + \cdots + x_n$. For example, when $m_1 = m_2 = 2$ and $m_3 = 3$, the 12 vectors $x_1 x_2 x_3$ in cross order are

$$000, \ 100, \ 010, \ 001, \ 110, \ 101, \ 011, \ 002, \ 111, \ 102, \ 012, \ 112, \tag{69}$$

Table 3

EXAMPLES OF THE KRUSKAL–MACAULAY FUNCTIONS κ, λ, AND μ

$N =$	0	1	2	3	4	5	6	7	8	9	10	11	12	13	14	15	16	17	18	19	20
$\kappa_1 N =$	0	1	1	1	1	1	1	1	1	1	1	1	1	1	1	1	1	1	1	1	1
$\kappa_2 N =$	0	2	3	3	4	4	4	5	5	5	5	6	6	6	6	6	7	7	7	7	7
$\kappa_3 N =$	0	3	5	6	6	8	9	9	10	10	10	12	13	13	14	14	14	15	15	15	15
$\kappa_4 N =$	0	4	7	9	10	10	13	15	16	16	18	19	19	20	20	20	23	25	26	26	28
$\kappa_5 N =$	0	5	9	12	14	15	15	19	22	24	25	25	28	30	31	31	33	34	34	35	35
$\lambda_1 N =$	0	0	1	3	6	10	15	21	28	36	45	55	66	78	91	105	120	136	153	171	190
$\lambda_2 N =$	0	0	0	1	1	2	4	4	5	7	10	10	11	13	16	20	20	21	23	26	30
$\lambda_3 N =$	0	0	0	0	1	1	1	2	2	3	5	5	5	6	6	7	9	9	10	12	15
$\lambda_4 N =$	0	0	0	0	0	1	1	1	1	2	2	2	3	3	4	6	6	6	6	7	7
$\lambda_5 N =$	0	0	0	0	0	0	1	1	1	1	1	2	2	2	2	3	3	3	4	4	5
$\mu_1 N =$	0	1	1	1	1	1	1	1	1	1	1	1	1	1	1	1	1	1	1	1	1
$\mu_2 N =$	0	1	2	2	3	3	3	4	4	4	4	5	5	5	5	5	6	6	6	6	6
$\mu_3 N =$	0	1	2	3	3	4	5	5	6	6	6	7	8	8	9	9	9	10	10	10	10
$\mu_4 N =$	0	1	2	3	4	4	5	6	7	7	8	9	9	10	10	10	11	12	13	13	14
$\mu_5 N =$	0	1	2	3	4	5	5	6	7	8	9	9	10	11	12	12	13	14	14	15	15

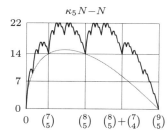
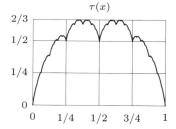

Fig. 27. Approximating a Kruskal function with the Takagi function. (The smooth curve in the left-hand graph is the lower bound $\underline{\kappa}_5 N - N$ of exercise 80.)

omitting parentheses and commas for convenience. The *complement* of a vector in $T(m_1, \ldots, m_n)$ is

$$\overline{x} = (m_1 - 1 - x_1, \ldots, m_n - 1 - x_n). \qquad (70)$$

Notice that $x \preceq y$ holds if and only if $\overline{x} \succeq \overline{y}$. Therefore we have

$$\text{rank}(x) + \text{rank}(\overline{x}) = T - 1, \qquad \text{where } T = m_1 \ldots m_n, \qquad (71)$$

if $\text{rank}(x)$ denotes the number of vectors that precede x in cross order.

We will find it convenient to call the vectors "points" and to name the points $e_0, e_1, \ldots, e_{T-1}$ in increasing cross order. Thus we have $e_7 = 002$ in (69), and $\overline{e}_r = e_{T-1-r}$ in general. Notice that

$$e_1 = 100 \ldots 00, \quad e_2 = 010 \ldots 00, \quad \ldots, \quad e_n = 000 \ldots 01; \qquad (72)$$

these are the so-called *unit vectors*. The set

$$S_N = \{e_0, e_1, \ldots, e_{N-1}\} \tag{73}$$

consisting of the smallest N points is called a *standard set*, and in the special case $N = n + 1$ we write

$$E = \{e_0, e_1, \ldots, e_n\} = \{000\ldots00, 100\ldots00, 010\ldots00, \ldots, 000\ldots01\}. \tag{74}$$

Any set of points X has a *spread* X^+, a *core* X°, and a *dual* $X^\sim$, defined by the rules

$$X^+ = \{x \in S_T \mid x \in X \text{ or } x - e_1 \in X \text{ or } \cdots \text{ or } x - e_n \in X \}; \tag{75}$$
$$X^\circ = \{x \in S_T \mid x \in X \text{ and } x + e_1 \in X \text{ and } \cdots \text{ and } x + e_n \in X \}; \tag{76}$$
$$X^\sim = \{x \in S_T \mid \overline{x} \notin X \}. \tag{77}$$

We can also define the spread of X algebraically, writing

$$X^+ = X + E, \tag{78}$$

where $X + Y$ denotes $\{x + y \mid x \in X \text{ and } y \in Y\}$. Clearly

$$X^+ \subseteq Y \quad \text{if and only if} \quad X \subseteq Y^\circ. \tag{79}$$

These notions can be illustrated in the two-dimensional case $m_1 = 4$, $m_2 = 6$, by the more-or-less random toroidal arrangement $X = \{00, 12, 13, 14, 15, 21, 22, 25\}$ for which we have, pictorially,

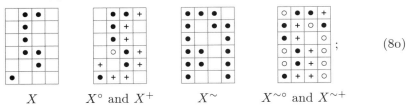

$$\qquad X \qquad\qquad X^\circ \text{ and } X^+ \qquad\qquad X^\sim \qquad\qquad X^{\sim\circ} \text{ and } X^{\sim+} \tag{80}$$

here X in the first two diagrams consists of points marked $\bullet$ or $\circ$, X° comprises just the $\circ$s, and X^+ consists of $+$s plus $\bullet$s plus $\circ$s. Notice that if we rotate the diagram for $X^{\sim\circ}$ and $X^{\sim+}$ by $180°$, we obtain the diagram for X° and X^+, but with $(\bullet, \circ, +, \ )$ respectively changed to $(+, \ , \bullet, \circ)$; and in fact the identities

$$X^\circ = X^{\sim+\sim}, \qquad X^+ = X^{\sim\circ\sim} \tag{81}$$

hold in general (see exercise 86).

Now we are ready to state the theorem of Wang and Wang:

Theorem W. *Let X be any set of N points in the discrete torus $T(m_1, \ldots, m_n)$, where $m_1 \le \cdots \le m_n$. Then $|X^+| \ge |S_N^+|$ and $|X^\circ| \le |S_N^\circ|$.*

In other words, the standard sets S_N have the smallest spread and largest core, among all N-point sets. We will prove this result by following a general approach first used by F. W. J. Whipple to prove Theorem M [*Proc. London Math. Soc.* (2) **28** (1928), 431–437]. The first step is to prove that the spread and the core of standard sets are standard:

Lemma S. *There are functions α and β such that $S_N^+ = S_{\alpha N}$ and $S_N^\circ = S_{\beta N}$.*

Proof. We may assume that $N > 0$. Let r be maximum with $e_r \in S_N^+$, and let $\alpha N = r + 1$; we must prove that $e_q \in S_N^+$ for $0 \le q < r$. Suppose $e_q = x = (x_1, \ldots, x_n)$ and $e_r = y = (y_1, \ldots, y_n)$, and let k be the largest subscript with $x_k > 0$. Since $y \in S_N^+$, there is a subscript j such that $y - e_j \in S_N$. It suffices to prove that $x - e_k \preceq y - e_j$, and exercise 88 does this.

The second part follows from (81), with $\beta N = T - \alpha(T - N)$, because $S_N^{\sim} = S_{T-N}$. ∎

Theorem W is obviously true when $n = 1$, so we assume by induction that it has been proved in $n - 1$ dimensions. The next step is to *compress* the given set X in the kth coordinate position, by partitioning it into disjoint sets

$$X_k(a) = \{\, x \in X \mid x_k = a \,\} \tag{82}$$

for $0 \le a < m_k$ and replacing each $X_k(a)$ by

$$X_k'(a) = \{\, (s_1, \ldots, s_{k-1}, a, s_k, \ldots, s_{n-1}) \mid (s_1, \ldots, s_{n-1}) \in S_{|X_k(a)|} \,\}, \tag{83}$$

a set with the same number of elements. The sets S used in (83) are standard in the $(n-1)$-dimensional torus $T(m_1, \ldots, m_{k-1}, m_{k+1}, \ldots, m_n)$. Notice that we have $(x_1, \ldots, x_{k-1}, a, x_{k+1}, \ldots, x_n) \preceq (y_1, \ldots, y_{k-1}, a, y_{k+1}, \ldots, y_n)$ if and only if $(x_1, \ldots, x_{k-1}, x_{k+1}, \ldots, x_n) \preceq (y_1, \ldots, y_{k-1}, y_{k+1}, \ldots, y_n)$; therefore $X_k'(a) = X_k(a)$ if and only if the $(n-1)$-dimensional points $(x_1, \ldots, x_{k-1}, x_{k+1}, \ldots, x_n)$ with $(x_1, \ldots, x_{k-1}, a, x_{k+1}, \ldots, x_n) \in X$ are as small as possible when projected onto the $(n-1)$-dimensional torus. We let

$$C_k X = X_k'(0) \cup X_k'(1) \cup \cdots \cup X_k'(m_k - 1) \tag{84}$$

be the compression of X in position k. Exercise 90 proves the basic fact that compression does not increase the size of the spread:

$$|X^+| \ge |(C_k X)^+|, \qquad \text{for } 1 \le k \le n. \tag{85}$$

Furthermore, if compression changes X, it replaces some of the elements by other elements of lower rank. Therefore we need to prove Theorem W only for sets X that are totally compressed, having $X = C_k X$ for all k.

Consider, for example, the case $n = 2$. A totally compressed set in two dimensions has all points moved to the left of their rows and the bottom of their columns, as in the eleven-point sets

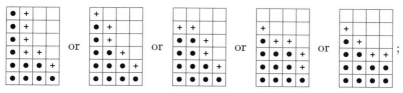

the rightmost of these is standard, and has the smallest spread. Exercise 91 completes the proof of Theorem W in two dimensions.

When $n > 2$, suppose $x = (x_1, \ldots, x_n) \in X$ and $x_j > 0$. The condition $C_k X = X$ implies that, if $0 \le i < j$ and $i \ne k \ne j$, we have $x + e_i - e_j \in X$. Applying this fact for three values of k tells us that $x + e_i - e_j \in X$ whenever $0 \le i < j$. Consequently

$$X_n(a) + E_n(0) \subseteq X_n(a-1) + e_n \quad \text{for } 0 < a < m, \qquad (86)$$

where $m = m_n$ and $E_n(0)$ is a clever abbreviation for the set $\{e_0, \ldots, e_{n-1}\}$.

Let $X_n(a)$ have N_a elements, so that $N = |X| = N_0 + N_1 + \cdots + N_{m-1}$, and let $Y = X^+$. Then

$$Y_n(a) = \big(X_n((a-1) \bmod m) + e_n\big) \cup \big(X_n(a) + E_n(0)\big)$$

is standard in $n-1$ dimensions, and (86) tells us that

$$N_{m-1} \le \beta N_{m-2} \le N_{m-2} \le \cdots \le N_1 \le \beta N_0 \le N_0 \le \alpha N_0,$$

where α and β refer to coordinates 1 through $n-1$. Therefore

$$\begin{aligned}
|Y| &= |Y_n(0)| + |Y_n(1)| + |Y_n(2)| + \cdots + |Y_n(m-1)| \\
&= \alpha N_0 + N_0 + N_1 + \cdots + N_{m-2} = \alpha N_0 + N - N_{m-1}.
\end{aligned}$$

The proof of Theorem W now has a beautiful conclusion. Let $Z = S_N$, and suppose $|Z_n(a)| = M_a$. We want to prove that $|X^+| \ge |Z^+|$, namely that

$$\alpha N_0 + N - N_{m-1} \ge \alpha M_0 + N - M_{m-1}, \qquad (87)$$

because the arguments of the previous paragraph apply to Z as well as to X. We will prove (87) by showing that $N_{m-1} \le M_{m-1}$ and $N_0 \ge M_0$.

Using the $(n-1)$-dimensional α and β functions, let us define

$$N'_{m-1} = N_{m-1},\ N'_{m-2} = \alpha N'_{m-1},\ \ldots,\ N'_1 = \alpha N'_2,\ N'_0 = \alpha N'_1; \qquad (88)$$
$$N''_0 = N_0,\ N''_1 = \beta N''_0,\ N''_2 = \beta N''_1,\ \ldots,\ N''_{m-1} = \beta N''_{m-2}. \qquad (89)$$

Then we have $N'_a \le N_a \le N''_a$ for $0 \le a < m$, and it follows that

$$N' = N'_0 + N'_1 + \cdots + N'_{m-1} \le N \le N'' = N''_0 + N''_1 + \cdots + N''_{m-1}. \qquad (90)$$

Exercise 92 proves that the standard set $Z' = S_{N'}$ has exactly N'_a elements with nth coordinate equal to a, for each a; and by the duality between α and β, the standard set $Z'' = S_{N''}$ likewise has exactly N''_a elements with nth coordinate a. Finally, therefore,

$$M_{m-1} = |Z_n(m-1)| \ge |Z'_n(m-1)| = N_{m-1},$$
$$M_0 = |Z_n(0)| \le |Z''_n(0)| = N_0,$$

because $Z' \subseteq Z \subseteq Z''$ by (90). By (81) we also have $|X^\circ| \le |Z^\circ|$. ∎

Now we are ready to prove Theorems K and M, which are in fact special cases of a substantially more general theorem of Clements and Lindström that applies to arbitrary multisets [*J. Combinatorial Theory* **7** (1969), 230–238]:

Corollary C. *If A is a set of N t-multicombinations contained in the multiset $U = \{s_0 \cdot 0, s_1 \cdot 1, \ldots, s_d \cdot d\}$, where $s_0 \geq s_1 \geq \cdots \geq s_d$, then*

$$|\partial A| \geq |\partial P_{Nt}| \qquad \text{and} \qquad |\varrho A| \geq |\varrho Q_{Nt}|, \tag{91}$$

where P_{Nt} denotes the N lexicographically smallest multicombinations $d_t \ldots d_2 d_1$ of U, and Q_{Nt} denotes the N lexicographically largest.

Proof. Multicombinations of U can be represented as points $x_1 \ldots x_n$ of the torus $T(m_1, \ldots, m_n)$, where $n = d + 1$ and $m_j = s_{n-j} + 1$; we let x_j be the number of occurrences of $n - j$. This correspondence preserves lexicographic order. For example, if $U = \{0, 0, 0, 1, 1, 2, 3\}$, its 3-multicombinations are

$$000, \ 100, \ 110, \ 200, \ 210, \ 211, \ 300, \ 310, \ 311, \ 320, \ 321, \tag{92}$$

in lexicographic order, and the corresponding points $x_1 x_2 x_3 x_4$ are

$$0003, 0012, 0021, 0102, 0111, 0120, 1002, 1011, 1020, 1101, 1110. \tag{93}$$

Let T_w be the points of the torus that have weight $x_1 + \cdots + x_n = w$. Then every allowable set A of t-multicombinations is a subset of T_t. Furthermore — and this is the main point — the spread of $T_0 \cup T_1 \cup \cdots \cup T_{t-1} \cup A$ is

$$
\begin{aligned}
(T_0 \cup T_1 \cup \cdots \cup T_{t-1} \cup A)^+ &= T_0^+ \cup T_1^+ \cup \cdots \cup T_{t-1}^+ \cup A^+ \\
&= T_0 \cup T_1 \cup \cdots \cup T_t \cup \varrho A. \tag{94}
\end{aligned}
$$

Thus the upper shadow ϱA is simply $(T_0 \cup T_1 \cup \cdots \cup T_{t-1} \cup A)^+ \cap T_{t+1}$, and Theorem W tells us in essence that $|A| = N$ implies $|\varrho A| \geq |\varrho(S_{M+N} \cap T_t)|$, where $M = |T_0 \cup \cdots \cup T_{t-1}|$. Hence, by the definition of cross order, $S_{M+N} \cap T_t$ consists of the lexicographically largest N t-multicombinations, namely Q_{Nt}.

The proof that $|\partial A| \geq |\partial P_{Nt}|$ now follows by complementation (see exercise 94). ∎

EXERCISES

1. [*M23*] Explain why Golomb's rule (8) makes all sets $\{c_1, \ldots, c_t\} \subseteq \{0, \ldots, n-1\}$ correspond uniquely to multisets $\{e_1, \ldots, e_t\} \subseteq \{\infty \cdot 0, \ldots, \infty \cdot n - t\}$.

2. [*16*] What path in an 11×13 grid corresponds to the bit string (13)?

▶ **3.** [*21*] (R. R. Fenichel, 1968.) Show that the compositions $q_t + \cdots + q_1 + q_0$ of s into $t + 1$ nonnegative parts can be generated in lexicographic order by a simple loopless algorithm.

4. [*16*] Show that every composition $q_t \ldots q_0$ of s into $t + 1$ nonnegative parts corresponds to a composition $r_s \ldots r_0$ of t into $s + 1$ nonnegative parts. What composition corresponds to 10224000001010 under this correspondence?

▶ **5.** [*20*] What is a good way to generate all of the integer solutions to the following systems of inequalities?

a) $n > x_t \geq x_{t-1} > x_{t-2} \geq x_{t-3} > \cdots > x_1 \geq 0$, when t is odd.

b) $n \gg x_t \gg x_{t-1} \gg \cdots \gg x_2 \gg x_1 \gg 0$, where $a \gg b$ means $a \geq b + 2$.

6. [*M22*] How often is each step of Algorithm T performed?

7. [*22*] Design an algorithm that runs through the "dual" combinations $b_s \ldots b_2 b_1$ in *decreasing* lexicographic order (see (5) and Table 1). Like Algorithm T, your algorithm should avoid redundant assignments and unnecessary searching.

8. [*M23*] Design an algorithm that generates all (s,t)-combinations $a_{n-1} \ldots a_1 a_0$ lexicographically in bitstring form. The total running time should be $O\left(\binom{n}{t}\right)$, assuming that $st > 0$.

9. [*M26*] When all (s,t)-combinations $a_{n-1} \ldots a_1 a_0$ are listed in lexicographic order, let $2A_{st}$ be the total number of bit changes between adjacent strings. For example, $A_{33} = 25$ because there are respectively

$$2+2+2+4+2+2+4+2+2+6+2+2+4+2+2+4+2+2 = 50$$

bit changes between the 20 strings in Table 1.
  a) Show that $A_{st} = \min(s,t) + A_{(s-1)t} + A_{s(t-1)}$ when $st > 0$; $A_{st} = 0$ when $st = 0$.
  b) Prove that $A_{st} < 2\binom{s+t}{t}$.

▶ **10.** [*21*] The "World Series" of baseball is traditionally a competition in which the American League champion (A) plays the National League champion (N) until one of them has beaten the other four times. What is a good way to list all possible scenarios AAAA, AAANA, AAANNA, ..., NNNN? What is a simple way to assign consecutive integers to those scenarios?

11. [*19*] Which of the scenarios in exercise 10 occurred most often during the 1900s? Which of them never occurred? [*Hint:* World Series scores are easily found on the Internet.]

12. [*HM32*] A set V of n-bit vectors that is closed under addition modulo 2 is called a *binary vector space*.
  a) Prove that every such V contains 2^t elements, for some integer t, and can be represented as the set $\{x_1 \alpha_1 \oplus \cdots \oplus x_t \alpha_t \mid 0 \le x_1, \ldots, x_t \le 1\}$ where the vectors $\alpha_1, \ldots, \alpha_t$ form a "canonical basis" with the following property: There is a t-combination $c_t \ldots c_2 c_1$ of $\{0, 1, \ldots, n-1\}$ such that, if α_k is the binary vector $a_{k(n-1)} \ldots a_{k1} a_{k0}$, we have

$$a_{kc_j} = [j = k] \quad \text{for } 1 \le j, k \le t; \qquad a_{kl} = 0 \quad \text{for } 0 \le l < c_k, 1 \le k \le t.$$

For example, the canonical bases with $n = 9$, $t = 4$, and $c_4 c_3 c_2 c_1 = 7641$ have the general form

$$\begin{aligned}
\alpha_1 &= *\,0\,0\,*\,0\,*\,*\,1\,0, \\
\alpha_2 &= *\,0\,0\,*\,1\,0\,0\,0\,0, \\
\alpha_3 &= *\,0\,1\,0\,0\,0\,0\,0\,0, \\
\alpha_4 &= *\,1\,0\,0\,0\,0\,0\,0\,0;
\end{aligned}$$

there are 2^8 ways to replace the eight asterisks by 0s and/or 1s, and each of these defines a canonical basis. We call t the dimension of V.
  b) How many t-dimensional spaces are possible with n-bit vectors?
  c) Design an algorithm to generate all canonical bases $(\alpha_1, \ldots, \alpha_t)$ of dimension t. *Hint:* Let the associated combinations $c_t \ldots c_1$ increase lexicographically as in Algorithm L.
  d) What is the 1000000th basis visited by your algorithm when $n = 9$ and $t = 4$?

13. [*25*] A one-dimensional *Ising configuration* of length n, weight t, and energy r, is a binary string $a_{n-1} \ldots a_0$ such that $\sum_{j=0}^{n-1} a_j = t$ and $\sum_{j=1}^{n-1} b_j = r$, where $b_j =$

$a_j \oplus a_{j-1}$. For example, $a_{12} \ldots a_0 = 1100100100011$ has weight 6 and energy 6, since $b_{12} \ldots b_1 = 010110110010$.

Design an algorithm to generate all such configurations, given n, t, and r.

14. [*26*] When the binary strings $a_{n-1} \ldots a_1 a_0$ of (s, t)-combinations are generated in lexicographic order, we sometimes need to change $2 \min(s, t)$ bits to get from one combination to the next. For example, 011100 is followed by 100011 in Table 1. Therefore we apparently cannot hope to generate all combinations with a loopless algorithm unless we visit them in some other order.

Show, however, that there actually is a way to compute the lexicographic successor of a given combination in $O(1)$ steps, if each combination is represented indirectly in a doubly linked list as follows: There are arrays $l[0], \ldots, l[n]$ and $r[0], \ldots, r[n]$ such that $l[r[j]] = j$ for $0 \leq j \leq n$. If $x_0 = l[0]$ and $x_j = l[x_{j-1}]$ for $0 < j < n$, then $a_j = [x_j > s]$ for $0 \leq j < n$.

15. [*M22*] Use the fact that dual combinations $b_s \ldots b_2 b_1$ occur in reverse lexicographic order to prove that the sum $\binom{b_s}{s} + \cdots + \binom{b_2}{2} + \binom{b_1}{1}$ has a simple relation to the sum $\binom{c_t}{t} + \cdots + \binom{c_2}{2} + \binom{c_1}{1}$.

16. [*M21*] What is the millionth combination generated by Algorithm L when t is (a) 2? (b) 3? (c) 4? (d) 5? (e) 1000000?

17. [*HM25*] Given N and t, what is a good way to compute the combinatorial representation (20)?

▶ **18.** [*20*] What binary tree do we get when the binomial tree T_n is represented by "right child" and "left sibling" pointers as in exercise 2.3.2–5?

19. [*21*] Instead of labeling the branches of the binomial tree T_4 as shown in (22), we could label each node with the bit string of its corresponding combination:

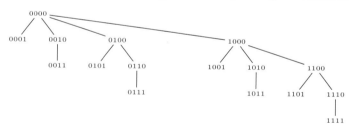

If T_∞ has been labeled in this way, suppressing leading zeros, preorder is the same as the ordinary increasing order of binary notation; so the millionth node turns out to be 11110100001000111111. But what is the millionth node of T_∞ in *postorder*?

20. [*M20*] Find generating functions g and h such that Algorithm F finds exactly $[z^N] g(z)$ feasible combinations and sets $t \leftarrow t + 1$ exactly $[z^N] h(z)$ times.

21. [*M22*] Prove the alternating combination law (30).

22. [*M23*] What is the millionth revolving-door combination visited by Algorithm R when t is (a) 2? (b) 3? (c) 4? (d) 5? (e) 1000000?

23. [*M23*] Suppose we augment Algorithm R by setting $j \leftarrow t + 1$ in step R1, and $j \leftarrow 1$ if R3 goes directly to R2. Find the probability distribution of j, and its average value. What does this imply about the running time of the algorithm?

▶ **24.** [*M25*] (W. H. Payne, 1974.) Continuing the previous exercise, let j_k be the value of j on the kth visit by Algorithm R. Show that $|j_{k+1} - j_k| \leq 2$, and explain how to make the algorithm loopless by exploiting this property.

25. [*M35*] Let $c_t \ldots c_2 c_1$ and $c'_t \ldots c'_2 c'_1$ be the Nth and N'th combinations generated by the revolving-door method, Algorithm R. If the set $C = \{c_t, \ldots, c_2, c_1\}$ has $m > 0$ elements not in $C' = \{c'_t, \ldots, c'_2, c'_1\}$, prove that $|N - N'| > \sum_{k=1}^{m-1} \binom{2k}{k-1}$.

26. [*26*] Do elements of the *ternary* reflected Gray code have properties similar to the revolving-door Gray code Γ_{st}, if we extract only the n-tuples $a_{n-1} \ldots a_1 a_0$ such that (a) $a_{n-1} + \cdots + a_1 + a_0 = t$? (b) $\{a_{n-1}, \ldots, a_1, a_0\} = \{r \cdot 0, s \cdot 1, t \cdot 2\}$?

▶ **27.** [*25*] Show that there is a simple way to generate all combinations of *at most t* elements of $\{0, 1, \ldots, n-1\}$, using only Gray-code-like transitions $0 \leftrightarrow 1$ and $01 \leftrightarrow 10$. (In other words, each step should either insert a new element, delete an element, or shift an element by ± 1.) For example,

$$0000,\ 0001,\ 0011,\ 0010,\ 0110,\ 0101,\ 0100,\ 1100,\ 1010,\ 1001,\ 1000$$

is one such sequence when $n = 4$ and $t = 2$. *Hint:* Think of Chinese rings.

28. [*M21*] True or false: A listing of (s,t)-combinations $a_{n-1} \ldots a_1 a_0$ in bitstring form is in genlex order if and only if the corresponding index-form listings $b_s \ldots b_2 b_1$ (for the 0s) and $c_t \ldots c_2 c_1$ (for the 1s) are both in genlex order.

▶ **29.** [*M28*] (P. J. Chase.) Given a string on the symbols +, -, and 0, say that an *R-block* is a substring of the form $-^{k+1}$ that is preceded by 0 and not followed by -; an *L-block* is a substring of the form $+-^k$ that is followed by 0; in both cases $k \geq 0$. For example, the string $\boxed{+}00++-++\boxed{+-}000\boxed{-}$ has two L-blocks and one R-block, shown in gray. Notice that blocks cannot overlap.

We form the *successor* of such a string as follows, whenever at least one block is present: Replace the rightmost $0-^{k+1}$ by $-+^k 0$, if the rightmost block is an R-block; otherwise replace the rightmost $+-^k 0$ by $0+^{k+1}$. Also negate the first sign, if any, that appears to the right of the block that has been changed. For example,

$$-\boxed{+}00++- \;\to\; -0\boxed{+}0\boxed{-}+- \;\to\; -0\boxed{+-}0\boxed{--} \;\to\; -0+--\boxed{+}0 \;\to\; -0\boxed{+--}0+ \;\to\; -00+++-,$$

where the notation $\alpha \to \beta$ means that β is the successor of α.

a) What strings have no blocks (and therefore no successor)?

b) Can there be a cycle of strings with $\alpha_0 \to \alpha_1 \to \cdots \to \alpha_{k-1} \to \alpha_0$?

c) Prove that if $\alpha \to \beta$ then $-\beta \to -\alpha$, where "$-$" means "negate all the signs." (Therefore every string has at most one predecessor.)

d) Show that if $\alpha_0 \to \alpha_1 \to \cdots \to \alpha_k$ and $k > 0$, the strings α_0 and α_k do not have all their 0s in the same positions. (Therefore, if α_0 has s signs and t zeros, k must be less than $\binom{s+t}{t}$.)

e) Prove that every string α with s signs and t zeros belongs to exactly one chain $\alpha_0 \to \alpha_1 \to \cdots \to \alpha_{\binom{s+t}{t}-1}$.

30. [*M32*] The previous exercise defines 2^s ways to generate all combinations of s 0s and t 1s, via the mapping $+ \mapsto 0$, $- \mapsto 0$, and $0 \mapsto 1$. Show that each of these ways is a homogeneous genlex sequence, definable by an appropriate recurrence. Is Chase's sequence (37) a special case of this general construction?

31. [*M23*] How many genlex listings of (s,t)-combinations are possible in (a) bitstring form $a_{n-1} \ldots a_1 a_0$? (b) index-list form $c_t \ldots c_2 c_1$?

▶ **32.** [*M32*] How many of the genlex listings of (s,t)-combination strings $a_{n-1} \ldots a_1 a_0$ (a) have the revolving-door property? (b) are homogeneous?

33. [*HM33*] How many of the genlex listings in exercise 31(b) are near-perfect?

34. [*M32*] Continuing exercise 33, explain how to find such schemes that are as near as possible to perfection, in the sense that the number of "imperfect" transitions $c_j \leftarrow c_j \pm 2$ is minimized, when s and t are not too large.

35. [*M26*] How many steps of Chase's sequence C_{st} use an imperfect transition?

▶ **36.** [*M21*] Prove that method (39) performs the operation $j \leftarrow j+1$ a total of exactly $\binom{s+t}{t} - 1$ times as it generates all (s,t)-combinations $a_{n-1} \ldots a_1 a_0$, given any genlex scheme for combinations in bitstring form.

▶ **37.** [*27*] What algorithm results when the general genlex method (39) is used to produce (s,t)-combinations $a_{n-1} \ldots a_1 a_0$ in (a) lexicographic order? (b) the revolving-door order of Algorithm R? (c) the homogeneous order of (31)?

38. [*26*] Design a genlex algorithm like Algorithm C for the *reverse* sequence C_{st}^R.

39. [*M21*] When $s = 12$ and $t = 14$, how many combinations precede the bit string 11001001000011111101101010 in Chase's sequence C_{st}? (See (41).)

40. [*M22*] What is the millionth combination in Chase's sequence C_{st}, when $s = 12$ and $t = 14$?

41. [*M27*] Show that there is a permutation $c(0)$, $c(1)$, $c(2)$, $\ldots$ of the nonnegative integers such that the elements of Chase's sequence C_{st} are obtained by complementing the least significant $s + t$ bits of the elements $c(k)$ for $0 \le k < 2^{s+t}$ that have weight $\nu(c(k)) = s$. (Thus the sequence $\bar{c}(0)$, $\ldots$, $\bar{c}(2^n - 1)$ contains, as subsequences, all of the C_{st} for which $s + t = n$, just as Gray binary code $g(0)$, $\ldots$, $g(2^n - 1)$ contains all the revolving-door sequences Γ_{st}.) Explain how to compute the binary representation $c(k) = (\ldots a_2 a_1 a_0)_2$ from the binary representation $k = (\ldots b_2 b_1 b_0)_2$.

42. [*HM34*] Use generating functions of the form $\sum_{s,t} g_{st} w^s z^t$ to analyze each step of Algorithm C.

43. [*20*] Prove or disprove: If $s(x)$ and $p(x)$ denote respectively the successor and predecessor of x in endo-order, then $s(x + 1) = p(x) + 1$.

▶ **44.** [*M21*] Let $C_t(n) - 1$ denote the sequence obtained from $C_t(n)$ by striking out all combinations with $c_1 = 0$, then replacing $c_t \ldots c_1$ by $(c_t - 1) \ldots (c_1 - 1)$ in the combinations that remain. Show that $C_t(n) - 1$ is near-perfect.

45. [*32*] Exploit endo-order and the expansions sketched in (44) to generate the combinations $c_t \ldots c_2 c_1$ of Chase's sequence $C_t(n)$ with a nonrecursive procedure.

▶ **46.** [*33*] Construct a nonrecursive algorithm for the dual combinations $b_s \ldots b_2 b_1$ of Chase's sequence C_{st}, namely for the positions of the zeros in $a_{n-1} \ldots a_1 a_0$.

47. [*26*] Implement the near-perfect multiset permutation method of (46) and (47).

48. [*M21*] Suppose $\alpha_0, \alpha_1, \ldots, \alpha_{N-1}$ is any listing of the permutations of the multiset $\{s_1 \cdot 1, \ldots, s_d \cdot d\}$, where α_k differs from α_{k+1} by the interchange of two elements. Let $\beta_0, \ldots, \beta_{M-1}$ be any revolving-door listing for (s,t)-combinations, where $s = s_0$, $t = s_1 + \cdots + s_d$, and $M = \binom{s+t}{t}$. Then let Λ_j be the list of M elements obtained by starting with $\alpha_j \uparrow \beta_0$ and applying the revolving-door exchanges; here $\alpha \uparrow \beta$ denotes the string obtained by substituting the elements of α for the 1s in β, preserving left-right order. For example, if $\beta_0, \ldots, \beta_{M-1}$ is 0110, 0101, 1100, 1001, 0011, 1010, and if $\alpha_j = 12$, then Λ_j is 0120, 0102, 1200, 1002, 0012, 1020. (The revolving-door listing need *not* be homogeneous.)

Prove that the list (47) contains all permutations of $\{s_0 \cdot 0, s_1 \cdot 1, \ldots, s_d \cdot d\}$, and that adjacent permutations differ from each other by the interchange of two elements.

49. [*HM23*] If q is a primitive mth root of unity, such as $e^{2\pi i/m}$, show that

$$\binom{n}{k}_q = \binom{\lfloor n/m \rfloor}{\lfloor k/m \rfloor} \binom{n \bmod m}{k \bmod m}_q.$$

▶ **50.** [*HM25*] Extend the formula of the previous exercise to q-*multinomial* coefficients

$$\binom{n_1 + \cdots + n_t}{n_1, \ldots, n_t}_q.$$

51. [*25*] Find all Hamiltonian paths in the graph whose vertices are permutations of $\{0, 0, 0, 1, 1, 1\}$ related by adjacent transposition. Which of those paths are equivalent under the operations of interchanging 0s with 1s and/or left-right reflection?

52. [*M37*] Generalizing Theorem P, find a necessary and sufficient condition that all permutations of the multiset $\{s_0 \cdot 0, \ldots, s_d \cdot d\}$ can be generated by adjacent transpositions $a_j a_{j-1} \leftrightarrow a_{j-1} a_j$.

53. [*M46*] (D. H. Lehmer, 1965.) Suppose the N permutations of $\{s_0 \cdot 0, \ldots, s_d \cdot d\}$ cannot be generated by a perfect scheme, because $(N + x)/2$ of them have an even number of inversions, where $x \geq 2$. Is it possible to generate them all with a sequence of $N + x - 2$ adjacent interchanges $a_{\delta_k} \leftrightarrow a_{\delta_k - 1}$ for $1 \leq k < N + x - 1$, where $x - 1$ cases are "spurs" with $\delta_k = \delta_{k-1}$ that take us back to the permutation we've just seen? For example, a suitable sequence $\delta_1 \ldots \delta_{94}$ for the 90 permutations of $\{0, 0, 1, 1, 2, 2\}$, where $x = \binom{2+2+2}{2,2,2}_{-1} = 6$, is $234535432523451\alpha42\alpha^R51\alpha42\alpha^R51\alpha4$, where $\alpha = 45352542345355$, if we start with $a_5 a_4 a_3 a_2 a_1 a_0 = 221100$.

54. [*M40*] For what values of s and t can all (s, t)-combinations be generated if we allow end-around swaps $a_{n-1} \leftrightarrow a_0$ in addition to adjacent interchanges $a_j \leftrightarrow a_{j-1}$?

▶ **55.** [*33*] (Frank Ruskey, 2004.) (a) Show that all (s, t)-combinations $a_{s+t-1} \ldots a_1 a_0$ can be generated efficiently by doing successive rotations $a_j a_{j-1} \ldots a_0 \leftarrow a_{j-1} \ldots a_0 a_j$.
(b) What MMIX instructions will take $(a_{s+t-1} \ldots a_1 a_0)_2$ to its successor, when $s+t < 64$?

56. [*M49*] (Buck and Wiedemann, 1984.) Can all (t, t)-combinations $a_{2t-1} \ldots a_1 a_0$ be generated by repeatedly swapping a_0 with some other element?

▶ **57.** [*22*] (Frank Ruskey.) Can a piano player run through all possible 4-note chords that span at most one octave, changing only one finger at a time? This is the problem of generating all combinations $c_t \ldots c_1$ such that $n > c_t > \cdots > c_1 \geq 0$ and $c_t - c_1 < m$, where $t = 4$ and (a) $m = 8$, $n = 52$ if we consider only the white notes of a piano keyboard; (b) $m = 13$, $n = 88$ if we consider also the black notes.

58. [*20*] Consider the piano player's problem of exercise 57 with the additional condition that the chords don't involve adjacent notes. (In other words, $c_{j+1} > c_j + 1$ for $t > j \geq 1$. Such chords tend to be more harmonious.)

59. [*M25*] Is there a *perfect* solution to the 4-note piano player's problem, in which each step moves a finger to an *adjacent* key?

60. [*23*] Design an algorithm to generate all *bounded* compositions

$$t = r_s + \cdots + r_1 + r_0, \qquad \text{where } 0 \leq r_j \leq m_j \text{ for } s \geq j \geq 0.$$

61. [*32*] Show that all bounded compositions can be generated by changing only two of the parts at each step.

▶ **62.** [*M27*] A *contingency table* is an $m \times n$ matrix of nonnegative integers (a_{ij}) having given row sums $r_i = \sum_{j=1}^{n} a_{ij}$ and column sums $c_j = \sum_{i=1}^{m} a_{ij}$, where $r_1 + \cdots + r_m = c_1 + \cdots + c_n$.

    a) Show that $2 \times n$ contingency tables are equivalent to bounded compositions.

    b) What is the lexicographically largest contingency table for $(r_1, \ldots, r_m; c_1, \ldots, c_n)$, when matrix entries are read row-wise from left to right and top to bottom, namely in the order $(a_{11}, a_{12}, \ldots, a_{1n}, a_{21}, \ldots, a_{mn})$?

    c) What is the lexicographically largest contingency table for $(r_1, \ldots, r_m; c_1, \ldots, c_n)$, when matrix entries are read column-wise from top to bottom and left to right, namely in the order $(a_{11}, a_{21}, \ldots, a_{m1}, a_{12}, \ldots, a_{mn})$?

    d) What is the lexicographically smallest contingency table for $(r_1, \ldots, r_m; c_1, \ldots, c_n)$, in the row-wise and column-wise senses?

    e) Explain how to generate all contingency tables for $(r_1, \ldots, r_m; c_1, \ldots, c_n)$ in lexicographic order.

63. [*M41*] Show that all contingency tables for $(r_1, \ldots, r_m; c_1, \ldots, c_n)$ can be generated by changing exactly four entries of the matrix at each step.

▶ **64.** [*M30*] Construct a genlex Gray cycle for all of the $2^s \binom{s+t}{t}$ *subcubes* that have s digits and t asterisks, using only the transformations $*0 \leftrightarrow 0*$, $*1 \leftrightarrow 1*$, $0 \leftrightarrow 1$. For example, one such cycle when $s = t = 2$ is

$$(00**, 01**, 0*1*, 0**1, 0**0, 0*0*, *00*, *01*, *0*1, *0*0, **00, **01,$$

$$**11, **10, *1*0, *1*1, *11*, *10*, 1*0*, 1**0, 1**1, 1*1*, 11**, 10**).$$

65. [*M40*] Enumerate the total number of genlex Gray paths on subcubes that use only the transformations allowed in exercise 64. How many of those paths are cycles?

▶ **66.** [*22*] Given $n \geq t \geq 0$, show that there is a Gray path through all of the canonical bases $(\alpha_1, \ldots, \alpha_t)$ of exercise 12, changing just one bit at each step. For example, one such path when $n = 3$ and $t = 2$ is

$$\frac{001}{010}, \frac{101}{010}, \frac{101}{110}, \frac{001}{110}, \frac{001}{100}, \frac{011}{100}, \frac{010}{100}.$$

67. [*46*] Consider the Ising configurations of exercise 13 for which $a_0 = 0$. Given n, t, and r, is there a Gray cycle for these configurations in which all transitions have the forms $0^k1 \leftrightarrow 10^k$ or $01^k \leftrightarrow 1^k0$? For example, in the case $n = 9$, $t = 5$, $r = 6$, there is a unique cycle

$$(010101110, 010110110, 011010110, 011011010, 011101010, 010111010).$$

68. [*M01*] If α is a t-combination, what is (a) $\partial^t \alpha$? (b) $\partial^{t+1} \alpha$?

▶ **69.** [*M22*] How large is the smallest set A of t-combinations for which $|\partial A| < |A|$?

70. [*M25*] What is the maximum value of $\kappa_t N - N$, for $N \geq 0$?

71. [*M20*] How many t-cliques can a million-edge graph have?

▶ **72.** [*M22*] Show that if N has the degree-t combinatorial representation (57), there is an easy way to find the degree-s combinatorial representation of the complementary number $M = \binom{s+t}{t} - N$, whenever $N < \binom{s+t}{t}$. Derive (63) as a consequence.

73. [*M23*] (A. J. W. Hilton, 1976.) Let A be a set of s-combinations and B a set of t-combinations, both contained in $U = \{0, \ldots, n-1\}$ where $n \geq s + t$. Show that if A and B are *cross-intersecting*, in the sense that $\alpha \cap \beta \neq \emptyset$ for all $\alpha \in A$ and $\beta \in B$, then so are the sets Q_{Mns} and Q_{Nnt} defined in Theorem K, where $M = |A|$ and $N = |B|$.

74. [*M21*] What are $|\varrho P_{Nt}|$ and $|\varrho Q_{Nnt}|$ in Theorem K?

75. [*M20*] The right-hand side of (60) is not always the degree-$(t-1)$ combinatorial representation of $\kappa_t N$, because $v-1$ might be zero. Show, however, that a positive integer N has at most two representations if we allow $v=0$ in (57), and both of them yield the same value $\kappa_t N$ according to (60). Therefore

$$\kappa_k \kappa_{k+1}\dots\kappa_t N = \binom{n_t}{k-1} + \binom{n_{t-1}}{k-2} + \cdots + \binom{n_v}{k-1+v-t} \qquad \text{for } 1 \le k \le t.$$

76. [*M20*] Find a simple formula for $\kappa_t(N+1) - \kappa_t N$.

▸ **77.** [*M26*] Prove the following properties of the κ functions by manipulating binomial coefficients, without assuming Theorem K:
   a) $\kappa_t(M+N) \le \kappa_t M + \kappa_t N$.
   b) $\kappa_t(M+N) \le \max(\kappa_t M, N) + \kappa_{t-1} N$.
Hint: $\binom{m_t}{t} + \cdots + \binom{m_1}{1} + \binom{n_t}{t} + \cdots + \binom{n_1}{1}$ is equal to $\binom{m_t \vee n_t}{t} + \cdots + \binom{m_1 \vee n_1}{1} + \binom{m_t \wedge n_t}{t} + \cdots + \binom{m_1 \wedge n_1}{1}$, where $\vee$ and $\wedge$ denote max and min.

78. [*M22*] Show that Theorem K follows easily from inequality (b) in the previous exercise. Conversely, both inequalities are simple consequences of Theorem K. *Hint:* Any set A of t-combinations can be written $A = A_1 + A_0 0$, where $A_1 = \{\alpha \in A \mid 0 \notin \alpha\}$.

79. [*M23*] Prove that if $t \ge 2$, we have $M \ge \mu_t N$ if and only if $M + \lambda_{t-1} M \ge N$.

80. [*HM26*] (L. Lovász, 1979.) The function $\binom{x}{t}$ increases monotonically from 0 to ∞ as x increases from $t-1$ to ∞; hence we can define

$$\underline{\kappa}_t N = \binom{x}{t-1}, \qquad \text{if } N = \binom{x}{t} \text{ and } x \ge t-1.$$

Prove that $\kappa_t N \ge \underline{\kappa}_t N$ for all integers $t \ge 1$ and $N \ge 0$. *Hint:* Equality holds when x is an integer.

▸ **81.** [*M27*] Show that the minimum shadow sizes in Theorem M are given by (64).

82. [*HM31*] The Takagi function of Fig. 27 is defined for $0 \le x \le 1$ by the formula

$$\tau(x) = \sum_{k=1}^{\infty} \int_0^x r_k(t)\,dt,$$

where $r_k(t) = (-1)^{\lfloor 2^k t \rfloor}$ is the Rademacher function of Eq. 7.2.1.1–(16).
   a) Prove that $\tau(x)$ is continuous in the interval $[0..1]$, but its derivative does not exist at any point.
   b) Show that $\tau(x)$ is the only continuous function that satisfies

$$\tau(\tfrac{1}{2}x) = \tau(1-\tfrac{1}{2}x) = \tfrac{1}{2}x + \tfrac{1}{2}\tau(x) \qquad \text{for } 0 \le x \le 1.$$

   c) What is the asymptotic value of $\tau(\epsilon)$ when ϵ is small?
   d) Prove that $\tau(x)$ is rational when x is rational.
   e) Find all roots of the equation $\tau(x) = 1/2$.
   f) Find all roots of the equation $\tau(x) = \max_{0 \le x \le 1} \tau(x)$.

83. [*HM46*] Determine the set R of all rational numbers r such that the equation $\tau(x) = r$ has uncountably many solutions. If $\tau(x)$ is rational and x is irrational, is it true that $\tau(x) \in R$? (*Warning:* This problem can be addictive.)

84. [*HM27*] If $T = \binom{2t-1}{t}$, prove the asymptotic formula

$$\kappa_t N - N = \frac{T}{t}\left(\tau\left(\frac{N}{T}\right) + O\left(\frac{(\log t)^3}{t}\right)\right) \qquad \text{for } 0 \leq N \leq T.$$

85. [*HM21*] Relate the functions $\lambda_t N$ and $\mu_t N$ to the Takagi function $\tau(x)$.

86. [*M20*] Prove the law of spread/core duality, $X^{\sim+} = X^{\circ\sim}$.

87. [*M21*] True or false: (a) $X \subseteq Y^\circ$ if and only if $Y^\sim \subseteq X^{\sim\circ}$; (b) $X^{\circ+\circ} = X^\circ$; (c) $\alpha M \leq N$ if and only if $M \leq \beta N$.

88. [*M20*] Explain why cross order is useful, by completing the proof of Lemma S.

89. [*16*] Compute the α and β functions for the $2 \times 2 \times 3$ torus (69).

90. [*M22*] Prove the basic compression lemma, (85).

91. [*M24*] Prove Theorem W for two-dimensional toruses $T(l, m)$, $l \leq m$.

92. [*M28*] Let $x = x_1 \ldots x_{n-1}$ be the Nth element of the torus $T(m_1, \ldots, m_{n-1})$, and let S be the set of all elements of $T(m_1, \ldots, m_{n-1}, m)$ that are $\preceq x_1 \ldots x_{n-1}(m-1)$ in cross order. If N_a elements of S have final component a, for $0 \leq a < m$, prove that $N_{m-1} = N$ and $N_{a-1} = \alpha N_a$ for $1 \leq a < m$, where α is the spread function for standard sets in $T(m_1, \ldots, m_{n-1})$.

93. [*M25*] (a) Find an N for which the conclusion of Theorem W is false when the parameters $m_1, m_2, \ldots, m_n$ have not been sorted into nondecreasing order. (b) Where does the proof of that theorem use the hypothesis that $m_1 \leq m_2 \leq \cdots \leq m_n$?

94. [*M20*] Show that the ∂ half of Corollary C follows from the ϱ half. *Hint:* The complements of the multicombinations (92) with respect to U are 3211, 3210, 3200, 3110, 3100, 3000, 2110, 2100, 2000, 1100, 1000.

95. [*17*] Explain why Theorems K and M follow from Corollary C.

▶ **96.** [*M22*] If S is an infinite sequence $(s_0, s_1, s_2, \ldots)$ of positive integers, let

$$\binom{S(n)}{k} = [z^k] \prod_{j=0}^{n-1}(1 + z + \cdots + z^{s_j});$$

thus $\binom{S(n)}{k}$ is the ordinary binomial coefficient $\binom{n}{k}$ if $s_0 = s_1 = s_2 = \cdots = 1$.

Generalizing the combinatorial number system, show that every nonnegative integer N has a unique representation

$$N = \binom{S(n_t)}{t} + \binom{S(n_{t-1})}{t-1} + \cdots + \binom{S(n_1)}{1}$$

where $n_t \geq n_{t-1} \geq \cdots \geq n_1 \geq 0$ and $\{n_t, n_{t-1}, \ldots, n_1\} \subseteq \{s_0 \cdot 0, s_1 \cdot 1, s_2 \cdot 2, \ldots\}$. Use this representation to give a simple formula for the numbers $|\partial P_{Nt}|$ in Corollary C.

▶ **97.** [*M26*] The text remarked that the vertices of a convex polyhedron can be perturbed slightly so that all of its faces are simplexes. In general, any set of combinations that contains the shadows of all its elements is called a *simplicial complex*; thus C is a simplicial complex if and only if $\alpha \subseteq \beta$ and $\beta \in C$ implies that $\alpha \in C$, if and only if C is an order ideal with respect to set inclusion.

The *size vector* of a simplicial complex C on n vertices is $(N_0, N_1, \ldots, N_n)$ when C contains exactly N_t combinations of size t.

a) What are the size vectors of the five regular solids (the tetrahedron, cube, octahedron, dodecahedron, and icosahedron), when their vertices are slightly tweaked?

b) Construct a simplicial complex with size vector $(1, 4, 5, 2, 0)$.

c) Find a necessary and sufficient condition that a given size vector $(N_0, N_1, \ldots, N_n)$ is feasible.

d) Prove that $(N_0, \ldots, N_n)$ is feasible if and only its "dual" vector $(\overline{N}_0, \ldots, \overline{N}_n)$ is feasible, where we define $\overline{N}_t = \binom{n}{t} - N_{n-t}$.

e) List all feasible size vectors $(N_0, N_1, N_2, N_3, N_4)$ and their duals. Which of them are self-dual?

98. [*30*] Continuing exercise 97, find an efficient way to count the feasible size vectors $(N_0, N_1, \ldots, N_n)$ when $n \le 100$.

99. [*M25*] A *clutter* is a set C of combinations that are incomparable, in the sense that $\alpha \subseteq \beta$ and $\alpha, \beta \in C$ implies $\alpha = \beta$. The size vector of a clutter is defined as in exercise 97.

a) Find a necessary and sufficient condition that $(M_0, M_1, \ldots, M_n)$ is the size vector of a clutter.

b) List all such size vectors in the case $n = 4$.

▶ **100.** [*M30*] (Clements and Lindström.) Let A be a "simplicial multicomplex," a set of submultisets of the multiset U in Corollary C with the property that $\partial A \subseteq A$. How large can the total weight $\nu A = \sum \{|\alpha| \mid \alpha \in A\}$ be when $|A| = N$?

101. [*M25*] If $f(x_1, \ldots, x_n)$ is a Boolean formula, let $F(p)$ be the probability that $f(x_1, \ldots, x_n) = 1$ when each variable x_j independently is 1 with probability p.

a) Calculate $G(p)$ and $H(p)$ for the Boolean formulas $g(w, x, y, z) = wxz \vee wyz \vee xy\bar{z}$, $h(w, x, y, z) = \bar{w}yz \vee xyz$.

b) Show that there is a *monotone* Boolean function $f(w, x, y, z)$ such that $F(p) = G(p)$, but there is no such function with $F(p) = H(p)$. Explain how to test this condition in general.

102. [*HM35*] (F. S. Macaulay, 1927.) A *polynomial ideal* I in the variables $\{x_1 \ldots, x_s\}$ is a set of polynomials closed under the operations of addition, multiplication by a constant, and multiplication by any of the variables. It is called *homogeneous* if it consists of all linear combinations of a set of homogeneous polynomials, namely of polynomials like $xy + z^2$ whose terms all have the same degree. Let N_t be the maximum number of linearly independent elements of degree t in I. For example, if $s = 2$, the set of all $\alpha(x_0, x_1, x_2)(x_0 x_1^2 - 2x_1 x_2^2) + \beta(x_0, x_1, x_2)x_0 x_1 x_2^2$, where α and β run through all possible polynomials in $\{x_0, x_1, x_2\}$, is a homogeneous polynomial ideal with $N_0 = N_1 = N_2 = 0$, $N_3 = 1$, $N_4 = 4$, $N_5 = 9$, $N_6 = 15$, $\ldots$.

a) Prove that for any such ideal I there is another ideal I' in which all homogeneous polynomials of degree t are linear combinations of N_t independent *monomials*. (A monomial is a product of variables, like $x_1^3 x_2 x_5^4$.)

b) Use Theorem M and (64) to prove that $N_{t+1} \ge N_t + \kappa_s N_t$ for all $t \ge 0$.

c) Show that $N_{t+1} > N_t + \kappa_s N_t$ occurs for only finitely many t. (This statement is equivalent to "Hilbert's basis theorem," proved by David Hilbert in *Göttinger Nachrichten* (1888), 450–457; *Math. Annalen* **36** (1890), 473–534.)

▶ **103.** [*M38*] The shadow of a subcube $a_1 \ldots a_n$, where each a_j is either 0 or 1 or $*$, is obtained by replacing some $*$ by 0 or 1. For example,

$$\partial 0*11*0 = \{0011*0, 0111*0, 0*1100, 0*1110\}.$$

Find a set P_{Nst} such that, if A is any set of N subcubes $a_1 \ldots a_n$ having s digits and t asterisks, $|\partial A| \ge |P_{Nst}|$.

104. [*M41*] The *shadow* of a binary string $a_1 \ldots a_n$ is obtained by deleting one of its bits. For example,

$$\partial 110010010 \; = \; \{10010010, \, 11010010, \, 11000010, \, 11001000, \, 11001001\}.$$

Find a set P_{Nn} such that, if A is any set of N binary strings $a_1 \ldots a_n$, $|\partial A| \geq |P_{Nn}|$.

105. [*M20*] A *universal cycle of t-combinations* for $\{0, 1, \ldots, n-1\}$ is a cycle of $\binom{n}{t}$ numbers whose blocks of t consecutive elements run through every t-combination $\{c_1, \ldots, c_t\}$. For example,

$$(0214506132051624315263042536410 3546)$$

is a universal cycle when $t = 3$ and $n = 7$.

Prove that no such cycle is possible unless $\binom{n}{t}$ is a multiple of n.

106. [*M21*] (L. Poinsot, 1809.) Find a "nice" universal cycle of 2-combinations for $\{0, 1, \ldots, 2m\}$. *Hint:* Consider the differences of consecutive elements, mod $(2m + 1)$.

107. [*22*] (O. Terquem, 1849.) Poinsot's theorem implies that all 28 dominoes of a traditional "double-six" set can be arranged in a cycle so that the spots of adjacent dominoes match each other:

How many such cycles are possible?

108. [*M31*] Find universal cycles of 3-combinations for the sets $\{0, \ldots, n-1\}$ when $n \bmod 3 \neq 0$.

109. [*M31*] Find universal cycles of 3-*multicombinations* for $\{0, 1, \ldots, n-1\}$ when $n \bmod 3 \neq 0$ (namely for combinations $d_1 d_2 d_3$ with repetitions permitted). For example,

$$(0001224111233022234413334002444 0113)$$

is such a cycle when $n = 5$.

▶ **110.** [*26*] *Cribbage* is a game played with 52 cards, where each card has a suit (♣, ♢, ♡, or ♠) and a face value (A, 2, 3, 4, 5, 6, 7, 8, 9, 10, J, Q, or K). One feature of the game is to compute the score of a 5-card combination $C = \{c_1, c_2, c_3, c_4, c_5\}$, where one card c_k is called the *starter*. The score is the sum of points computed as follows, for each subset S of C and each choice of k: Let $|S| = s$.

  i) Fifteens: If $\sum \{v(c) \mid c \in S\} = 15$, where $\big(v(\mathtt{A}), v(2), v(3), \ldots, v(9), v(10), v(\mathtt{J}),$ $v(\mathtt{Q}), v(\mathtt{K})\big) = (1, 2, 3, \ldots, 9, 10, 10, 10, 10)$, score two points.

  ii) Pairs: If $s = 2$ and both cards have the same face value, score two points.

  iii) Runs: If $s \geq 3$ and the face values are consecutive, and if C does not contain a run of length $s + 1$, score s points.

  iv) Flushes: If $s = 4$ and all cards of S have the same suit, and if $c_k \notin S$, score $4 + [c_k$ has the same suit as the others].

  v) Nobs: If $s = 1$ and $c_k \notin S$, score 1 if the card is J of the same suit as c_k.

For example, if you hold $\{\mathtt{J}\clubsuit, 5\clubsuit, 5\diamondsuit, 6\heartsuit\}$ and if $4\clubsuit$ is the starter, you score 4×2 for fifteens, 2 for a pair, 2×3 for runs, plus 1 for nobs, totalling 17.

Exactly how many combinations and starter choices lead to a score of x points, for $x = 0, 1, 2, \ldots$?

7.2.1.4. Generating all partitions. Richard Stanley's magnificent book *Enumerative Combinatorics* (1986) begins by discussing The Twelvefold Way, a $2 \times 2 \times 3$ array of basic combinatorial problems that arise frequently in practice (see Table 1). All twelve of Stanley's basic problems can be described in terms of the ways that a given number of balls can be placed into a given number of urns. For example, there are nine ways to put 2 balls into 3 urns if the balls and urns are labeled:

(The order of balls *within* an urn is ignored.) But if the balls are unlabeled, some of these arrangements are indistinguishable, so only six different ways are possible:

   (1)

If the urns are unlabeled, arrangements like ①② and ②①① are essentially the same, hence only two of the original nine arrangements are distinguishable. And if we have three labeled balls, the only distinct ways to place them into three unlabeled urns are

$$\text{(2)}$$

Finally, if neither balls nor urns are labeled, these five possibilities reduce to only three:

$$\text{(3)}$$

The Twelvefold Way considers all arrangements that are possible when balls and urns are labeled or unlabeled, and when the urns may optionally be required to contain at least one ball or at most one ball.

Table 1
THE TWELVEFOLD WAY

balls per urn	unrestricted	≤ 1	≥ 1
n labeled balls, m labeled urns	n-tuples of m things	n-permutations of m things	partitions of $\{1, \ldots, n\}$ into m ordered parts
n unlabeled balls, m labeled urns	n-multicombinations of m things	n-combinations of m things	compositions of n into m parts
n labeled balls, m unlabeled urns	partitions of $\{1, \ldots, n\}$ into $\leq m$ parts	n pigeons into m holes	partitions of $\{1, \ldots, n\}$ into m parts
n unlabeled balls, m unlabeled urns	partitions of n into $\leq m$ parts	n pigeons into m holes	partitions of n into m parts

We've learned about n-tuples, permutations, combinations, and compositions in previous sections of this chapter; and two of the twelve entries in Table 1
are trivial (namely the ones related to "pigeons"). So we can complete our
study of classical combinatorial mathematics by learning about the remaining
five entries in the table, which all involve *partitions*.

> *Let us begin by acknowledging that the word "partition"*
> *has numerous meanings in mathematics.*
> *Any time a division of some object into subobjects is undertaken,*
> *the word partition is likely to pop up.*
> — GEORGE ANDREWS, *The Theory of Partitions* (1976)

Two quite different concepts share the same name: The *partitions of a set*
are the ways to subdivide it into disjoint subsets; thus (2) illustrates the five
partitions of $\{1, 2, 3\}$, namely

$$\{1, 2, 3\}, \quad \{1, 2\}\{3\}, \quad \{1, 3\}\{2\}, \quad \{1\}\{2, 3\}, \quad \{1\}\{2\}\{3\}. \quad (4)$$

And the *partitions of an integer* are the ways to write it as a sum of positive
integers, disregarding order; thus (3) illustrates the three partitions of 3, namely

$$3, \qquad 2 + 1, \qquad 1 + 1 + 1. \qquad (5)$$

We shall follow the common practice of referring to integer partitions as simply
"partitions," without any qualifying adjective; the other kind will be called
"set partitions" in what follows, to make the distinction clear. Both kinds of
partitions are important, so we'll study each of them in turn.

Generating all partitions of an integer. A partition of n can be defined
formally as a sequence of nonnegative integers $a_1 \geq a_2 \geq \cdots$ such that $n = a_1 + a_2 + \cdots$; for example, one partition of 7 has $a_1 = a_2 = 3$, $a_3 = 1$, and
$a_4 = a_5 = \cdots = 0$. The number of nonzero terms is called the number of *parts*,
and the zero terms are usually suppressed. Thus we write $7 = 3 + 3 + 1$, or
simply 331 to save space when the context is clear.

The simplest way to generate all partitions, and one of the fastest, is to visit
them in reverse lexicographic order, starting with 'n' and ending with '$11\ldots1$'.
For example, the partitions of 8 are

$$8, 71, 62, 611, 53, 521, 5111, 44, 431, 422, 4211, 41111, 332, 3311,$$
$$3221, 32111, 311111, 2222, 22211, 221111, 2111111, 11111111, \qquad (6)$$

when listed in this order.

If a partition isn't all 1s, it ends with $(x+1)$ followed by zero or more 1s,
for some $x \geq 1$; therefore the next smallest partition in lexicographic order
is obtained by replacing the suffix $(x+1)1\ldots1$ by $x\ldots xr$ for some appropriate
remainder $r \leq x$. The process is quite efficient if we keep track of the largest subscript q such that $a_q \neq 1$, as suggested by J. K. S. McKay [*CACM* **13** (1970), 52]:

Algorithm P (*Partitions in reverse lexicographic order*). This algorithm generates all partitions $a_1 \geq a_2 \geq \cdots \geq a_m \geq 1$ with $a_1 + a_2 + \cdots + a_m = n$ and $1 \leq m \leq n$, assuming that $n \geq 1$.

P1. [Initialize.] Set $a_0 \leftarrow 0$ and $m \leftarrow 1$.

P2. [Store the final part.] Set $a_m \leftarrow n$ and $q \leftarrow m - [n=1]$.

P3. [Visit.] Visit the partition $a_1 a_2 \ldots a_m$. Then go to P5 if $a_q \neq 2$.

P4. [Change 2 to 1+1.] Set $a_q \leftarrow 1$, $q \leftarrow q - 1$, $m \leftarrow m + 1$, $a_m \leftarrow 1$, and return to P3.

P5. [Decrease a_q.] Terminate the algorithm if $q = 0$. Otherwise set $x \leftarrow a_q - 1$, $a_q \leftarrow x$, $n \leftarrow m - q + 1$, and $m \leftarrow q + 1$.

P6. [Copy x if necessary.] If $n \leq x$, return to step P2. Otherwise set $a_m \leftarrow x$, $m \leftarrow m + 1$, $n \leftarrow n - x$, and repeat this step. ∎

Notice that the operation of going from one partition to the next is particularly easy if a 2 is present; then step P4 simply changes the rightmost 2 to a 1 and appends another 1 at the right. This happy situation is, fortunately, the most common case. For example, nearly 79% of all partitions contain a 2 when $n = 100$.

Another simple algorithm is available when we want to generate all partitions of n into a fixed number of parts. The following method, which was featured in C. F. Hindenburg's 18th-century dissertation [*Infinitinomii Dignitatum Exponentis Indeterminati* (Göttingen, 1779), 73–91], visits the partitions in *colex* order, namely in lexicographic order of the reflected sequence $a_m \ldots a_2 a_1$:

Algorithm H (*Partitions into m parts*). This algorithm generates all integer m-tuples $a_1 \ldots a_m$ such that $a_1 \geq \cdots \geq a_m \geq 1$ and $a_1 + \cdots + a_m = n$, assuming that $n \geq m \geq 2$.

H1. [Initialize.] Set $a_1 \leftarrow n - m + 1$ and $a_j \leftarrow 1$ for $1 < j \leq m$. Also set $a_{m+1} \leftarrow -1$.

H2. [Visit.] Visit the partition $a_1 \ldots a_m$. Then go to H4 if $a_2 \geq a_1 - 1$.

H3. [Tweak a_1 and a_2.] Set $a_1 \leftarrow a_1 - 1$, $a_2 \leftarrow a_2 + 1$, and return to H2.

H4. [Find j.] Set $j \leftarrow 3$ and $s \leftarrow a_1 + a_2 - 1$. Then, if $a_j \geq a_1 - 1$, set $s \leftarrow s + a_j$, $j \leftarrow j + 1$, and repeat until $a_j < a_1 - 1$. (Now $s = a_1 + \cdots + a_{j-1} - 1$.)

H5. [Increase a_j.] Terminate if $j > m$. Otherwise set $x \leftarrow a_j + 1$, $a_j \leftarrow x$, $j \leftarrow j - 1$.

H6. [Tweak $a_1 \ldots a_j$.] While $j > 1$, set $a_j \leftarrow x$, $s \leftarrow s - x$, and $j \leftarrow j - 1$. Finally set $a_1 \leftarrow s$ and return to H2. ∎

For example, when $n = 11$ and $m = 4$ the successive partitions visited are

$$8111, \ 7211, \ 6311, \ 5411, \ 6221, \ 5321, \ 4421, \ 4331, \ 5222, \ 4322, \ 3332. \tag{7}$$

The basic idea is that colex order goes from one partition $a_1 \ldots a_m$ to the next by finding the smallest j such that a_j can be increased without changing $a_{j+1} \ldots a_m$. The new partition $a_1' \ldots a_m'$ will have $a_1' \geq \cdots \geq a_j' = a_j + 1$ and $a_1' + \cdots + a_j' =$

$a_1 + \cdots + a_j$, and these conditions are achievable if and only if $a_j < a_1 - 1$. Furthermore, the smallest such partition $a'_1 \ldots a'_m$ in colex order has $a'_2 = \cdots = a'_j = a_j + 1$.

Step H3 handles the simple case $j = 2$, which is by far the most common. And indeed, the value of j almost always turns out to be quite small; we will prove later that the total running time of Algorithm H is at most a small constant times the number of partitions visited, plus $O(m)$.

Other representations of partitions. We've defined a partition as a sequence of nonnegative integers $a_1 a_2 \ldots$ with $a_1 \geq a_2 \geq \cdots$ and $a_1 + a_2 + \cdots = n$, but we can also regard it as an n-tuple of nonnegative integers $c_1 c_2 \ldots c_n$ such that

$$c_1 + 2c_2 + \cdots + nc_n = n. \tag{8}$$

Here c_j is the number of times the integer j appears in the sequence $a_1 a_2 \ldots$; for example, the partition 331 corresponds to the counts $c_1 = 1$, $c_2 = 0$, $c_3 = 2$, $c_4 = c_5 = c_6 = c_7 = 0$. The number of parts is then $c_1 + c_2 + \cdots + c_n$. A procedure analogous to Algorithm P can readily be devised to generate partitions in part-count form; see exercise 5.

We have already seen the part-count representation implicitly in formulas like Eq. 1.2.9–(38), which expresses the symmetric function

$$h_n = \sum_{N \geq d_n \geq \cdots \geq d_2 \geq d_1 \geq 1} x_{d_1} x_{d_2} \ldots x_{d_n} \tag{9}$$

as

$$\sum_{\substack{c_1, c_2, \ldots, c_n \geq 0 \\ c_1 + 2c_2 + \cdots + nc_n = n}} \frac{S_1^{c_1}}{1^{c_1} c_1!} \frac{S_2^{c_2}}{2^{c_2} c_2!} \cdots \frac{S_n^{c_n}}{n^{c_n} c_n!}, \tag{10}$$

where S_j is the symmetric function $x_1^j + x_2^j + \cdots + x_N^j$. The sum in (9) is essentially taken over all n-multicombinations of N, while the sum in (10) is taken over all partitions of n. Thus, for example, $h_3 = \frac{1}{6}S_1^3 + \frac{1}{2}S_1 S_2 + \frac{1}{3}S_3$, and when $N = 2$ we have

$$x^3 + x^2 y + xy^2 + y^3 = \tfrac{1}{6}(x+y)^3 + \tfrac{1}{2}(x+y)(x^2 + y^2) + \tfrac{1}{3}(x^3 + y^3).$$

Other sums over partitions appear in exercises 1.2.5–21, 1.2.9–10, 1.2.9–11, 1.2.10–12, etc.; for this reason partitions are of central importance in the study of symmetric functions, a class of functions that pervades mathematics in general. [Chapter 7 of Richard Stanley's *Enumerative Combinatorics* **2** (1999) is an excellent introduction to advanced aspects of symmetric function theory.]

Partitions can be visualized in an appealing way by considering an array of n dots, having a_1 dots in the top row and a_2 in the next row, etc. Such an arrangement of dots is called the *Ferrers diagram* of the partition, in honor of N. M. Ferrers [see *Philosophical Mag.* **5** (1853), 199–202]; and the largest square subarray of dots that it contains is called the *Durfee square*, after W. P. Durfee [see *Johns Hopkins Univ. Circular* **2** (December 1882), 23]. For example, the Ferrers diagram of 8887211 is shown with its 4×4 Durfee square in Fig. 28(a).

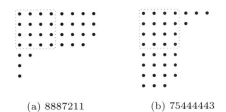

Fig. 28. The Ferrers diagrams and Durfee squares of two conjugate partitions.

(a) 8887211   (b) 75444443

The Durfee square contains k^2 dots when k is the largest subscript such that $a_k \geq k$; we may call k the *trace* of the partition.

If α is any partition $a_1 a_2 \ldots$, its *conjugate* $\alpha^T = b_1 b_2 \ldots$ is obtained by transposing the rows and columns of the corresponding Ferrers diagram. For example, Fig. 28(b) shows that $(8887211)^T = 75444443$. When $\beta = \alpha^T$ we obviously have $\alpha = \beta^T$; the partition β has a_1 parts and α has b_1 parts. Indeed, there's a simple relation between the part-count representation $c_1 \ldots c_n$ of α and the conjugate partition $b_1 b_2 \ldots$, namely

$$b_j - b_{j+1} = c_j \qquad \text{for all } j \geq 1. \tag{11}$$

This relation makes it easy to compute the conjugate of a given partition, or to write it down by inspection (see exercise 6).

The notion of conjugation often explains properties of partitions that would otherwise be quite mysterious. For example, now that we know the definition of α^T, we can easily see that the value of $j - 1$ in step H5 of Algorithm H is just the second-smallest part of the conjugate partition $(a_1 \ldots a_m)^T$. Therefore the average amount of work that needs to be done in steps H4 and H6 is essentially proportional to the average size of the second-smallest part of a random partition whose largest part is m. And we will see below that the second-smallest part is almost always quite small.

Moreover, *Algorithm H produces partitions in lexicographic order of their conjugates*. For example, the respective conjugates of (7) are

$$41111111, \; 4211111, \; 422111, \; 42221, \; 431111,$$
$$43211, \; 4322, \; 4331, \; 44111, \; 4421, \; 443; \tag{12}$$

these are the partitions of $n = 11$ with largest part 4. One way to generate all partitions of n is to start with the trivial partition 'n', then run Algorithm H for $m = 2, 3, \ldots, n$ in turn; this process yields all α in lexicographic order of α^T (see exercise 7). Thus Algorithm H can be regarded as a dual of Algorithm P.

There is at least one more useful way to represent partitions, called the *rim representation*. Suppose we replace the dots of a Ferrers diagram by boxes, thereby obtaining a tableau shape as we did in Section 5.1.4; for example, the partition 8887211 of Fig. 28(a) becomes

$$\tag{13}$$

The right-hand boundary of this shape can be regarded as a path from the lower left corner to the upper right corner of an $n \times n$ square, and we know from Table 7.2.1.3–1 that such a path corresponds to an (n, n)-combination.

For example, (13) corresponds to the 70-bit string

$$0\ldots01001011111010001\ldots1 \;=\; 0^{28}1^10^21^10^11^50^11^10^31^{27}, \tag{14}$$

where we place enough 0s at the beginning and 1s at the end to make exactly n of each. The 0s represent upward steps of the path, and the 1s represent rightward steps. It is easy to see that the bit string defined in this way has exactly n inversions; conversely, every permutation of the multiset $\{n \cdot 0,\ n \cdot 1\}$ that has exactly n inversions corresponds to a partition of n. When the partition has t different parts, its bit string can be written in the form

$$0^{n-q_1-q_2-\cdots-q_t}1^{p_1}0^{q_1}1^{p_2}0^{q_2}\ldots1^{p_t}0^{q_t}1^{n-p_1-p_2-\cdots-p_t}, \tag{15}$$

where the exponents p_j and q_j are positive integers. Then the partition's standard representation is

$$a_1 a_2 \ldots \;=\; (p_1 + \cdots + p_t)^{q_t}(p_1 + \cdots + p_{t-1})^{q_{t-1}} \ldots (p_1)^{q_1}, \tag{16}$$

namely $(1+1+5+1)^3(1+1+5)^1(1+1)^1(1)^2 = 8887211$ in our example.

The number of partitions. Inspired by a question that was posed to him by Philipp Naudé in 1740, Leonhard Euler wrote two fundamental papers in which he counted partitions of various kinds by studying their generating functions [*Commentarii Academiæ Scientiarum Petropolitanæ* **13** (1741), 64–93; *Novi Comment. Acad. Sci. Pet.* **3** (1750), 125–169]. He observed that the coefficient of z^n in the infinite product

$$(1+z+z^2+\cdots+z^j+\cdots)(1+z^2+z^4+\cdots+z^{2k}+\cdots)(1+z^3+z^6+\cdots+z^{3l}+\cdots)\ldots$$

is the number of nonnegative integer solutions to the equation $j+2k+3l+\cdots = n$; and $1 + z^m + z^{2m} + \cdots$ is $1/(1 - z^m)$. Therefore if we write

$$P(z) \;=\; \prod_{m=1}^{\infty} \frac{1}{1 - z^m} \;=\; \sum_{n=0}^{\infty} p(n)z^n, \tag{17}$$

the number of partitions of n is $p(n)$. This function $P(z)$ turns out to have an amazing number of subtle mathematical properties.

For example, Euler discovered that massive cancellation occurs when the denominator of $P(z)$ is multiplied out:

$$(1-z)(1-z^2)(1-z^3)\ldots \;=\; 1 - z - z^2 + z^5 + z^7 - z^{12} - z^{15} + z^{22} + z^{26} - \cdots$$

$$=\; \sum_{-\infty<n<\infty} (-1)^n z^{(3n^2+n)/2}. \tag{18}$$

A combinatorial proof of this remarkable identity, based on Ferrers diagrams, appears in exercise 5.1.1–14; we can also prove it by setting $u = z$ and $v = z^2$ in the even more remarkable identity of Jacobi,

$$\prod_{k=1}^{\infty}(1 - u^k v^{k-1})(1 - u^{k-1}v^k)(1 - u^k v^k) = \sum_{n=-\infty}^{\infty}(-1)^n u^{\binom{n}{2}} v^{\binom{-n}{2}}, \qquad (19)$$

because the left-hand side becomes $\prod_{k=1}^{\infty}(1 - z^{3k-2})(1 - z^{3k-1})(1 - z^{3k})$; see exercise 5.1.1–20. Euler's identity (18) implies that the partition numbers satisfy the recurrence

$$p(n) = p(n-1) + p(n-2) - p(n-5) - p(n-7) + p(n-12) + p(n-15) - \cdots, \quad (20)$$

from which we can compute their values more rapidly than by performing the power series calculations in (17):

$n =$	0	1	2	3	4	5	6	7	8	9	10	11	12	13	14	15
$p(n) =$	1	1	2	3	5	7	11	15	22	30	42	56	77	101	135	176

We know from Section 1.2.8 that solutions to the Fibonacci recurrence $f(n) = f(n-1) + f(n-2)$ grow exponentially, with $f(n) = \Theta(\phi^n)$ when $f(0)$ and $f(1)$ are positive. The additional terms '$- p(n-5) - p(n-7)$' in (20) have a dampening effect on partition numbers, however; in fact, if we were to stop the recurrence there, the resulting sequence would oscillate between positive and negative values. Further terms '$+ p(n-12) + p(n-15)$' reinstate exponential growth.

The actual growth rate of $p(n)$ turns out to be of order $A^{\sqrt{n}}/n$ for a certain constant A. For example, exercise 33 proves directly that $p(n)$ grows at least as fast as $e^{2\sqrt{n}}/n$. And one fairly easy way to obtain a decent *upper* bound is to take logarithms in (17),

$$\ln P(z) = \sum_{m=1}^{\infty} \ln \frac{1}{1 - z^m} = \sum_{m=1}^{\infty}\sum_{n=1}^{\infty} \frac{z^{mn}}{n}, \qquad (21)$$

and then to look at the behavior near $z = 1$ by setting $z = e^{-t}$:

$$\ln P(e^{-t}) = \sum_{m,n \geq 1} \frac{e^{-mnt}}{n} = \sum_{n \geq 1} \frac{1}{n}\frac{1}{e^{tn} - 1} < \sum_{n \geq 1} \frac{1}{n^2 t} = \frac{\zeta(2)}{t}. \qquad (22)$$

Consequently, since $p(n) \leq p(n+1) < p(n+2) < \cdots$ and $e^t > 1$, we have

$$\frac{p(n)}{1 - e^{-t}} < \sum_{k=0}^{\infty} p(k)e^{(n-k)t} = e^{nt} P(e^{-t}) < e^{nt+\zeta(2)/t} \qquad (23)$$

for all $t > 0$. Setting $t = \sqrt{\zeta(2)/n}$ gives

$$p(n) < C e^{2C\sqrt{n}}/\sqrt{n}, \qquad \text{where } C = \sqrt{\zeta(2)} = \pi/\sqrt{6}. \qquad (24)$$

We can obtain more accurate information about the size of $\ln P(e^{-t})$ by using Euler's summation formula (Section 1.2.11.2) or Mellin transforms (Section 5.2.2); see exercise 25. But the methods we have seen so far aren't powerful enough to deduce the precise behavior of $P(e^{-t})$, so it is time for us to add a new weapon to our arsenal of techniques.

Euler's generating function $P(z)$ is ideally suited to the *Poisson summation formula* [*J. École Royale Polytechnique* **12** (1823), 404–509, §63], according to which

$$\sum_{n=-\infty}^{\infty} f(n+\theta) = \lim_{M\to\infty} \sum_{m=-M}^{M} e^{2\pi mi\theta} \int_{-\infty}^{\infty} e^{-2\pi miy} f(y)\, dy, \qquad (25)$$

whenever f is a "well-behaved" function. This formula is based on the fact that the left-hand side is a periodic function of θ, and the right-hand side is the expansion of that function as a Fourier series. The function f is sufficiently nice if, for example, $\int_{-\infty}^{\infty} |f(y)|\, dy < \infty$ and either

i) $f(n+\theta)$ is an analytic function of the complex variable θ in the region $|\Im\theta| \le \epsilon$ for some $\epsilon > 0$ and $0 \le \Re\theta \le 1$, and the left-hand side converges uniformly in that rectangle; or

ii) $f(\theta) = \frac{1}{2}\lim_{\epsilon\to 0}\bigl(f(\theta-\epsilon) + f(\theta+\epsilon)\bigr) = g(\theta) - h(\theta)$ for all real numbers θ, where g and h are monotone increasing and $g(\pm\infty)$, $h(\pm\infty)$ are finite.

[See Peter Henrici, *Applied and Computational Complex Analysis* **2** (New York: Wiley, 1977), Theorem 10.6.2.] Poisson's formula is not a panacea for summation problems of every kind; but when it does apply the results can be spectacular, as we will see.

Let us multiply Euler's formula (18) by $z^{1/24}$ in order to "complete the square":

$$\frac{z^{1/24}}{P(z)} = \sum_{n=-\infty}^{\infty} (-1)^n\, z^{\frac{3}{2}(n+\frac{1}{6})^2}. \qquad (26)$$

Then for all $t > 0$ we have $e^{-t/24}/P(e^{-t}) = \sum_{n=-\infty}^{\infty} f(n)$, where

$$f(y) = e^{-\frac{3}{2}t(y+\frac{1}{6})^2} \cos \pi y; \qquad (27)$$

and this function f qualifies for Poisson's summation formula under both of the criteria (i) and (ii) stated above. Therefore we can try to integrate $e^{-2\pi miy} f(y)$, and for $m = 0$ the result is

$$\int_{-\infty}^{\infty} f(y)\, dy = \sqrt{\frac{\pi}{2t}}\, e^{-\pi^2/6t}. \qquad (28)$$

To this we must add

$$\sum_{m=1}^{\infty} \int_{-\infty}^{\infty} \bigl(e^{2\pi miy} + e^{-2\pi miy}\bigr) f(y)\, dy = 2\sum_{m=1}^{\infty} \int_{-\infty}^{\infty} f(y) \cos 2\pi my\, dy; \qquad (29)$$

again the integral turns out to be doable. And the results (see exercise 27) fit together quite beautifully, giving

$$\frac{e^{-t/24}}{P(e^{-t})} = \sqrt{\frac{2\pi}{t}} \sum_{n=-\infty}^{\infty} (-1)^n e^{-6\pi^2(n+\frac{1}{6})^2/t} = \sqrt{\frac{2\pi}{t}} \frac{e^{-\pi^2/6t}}{P(e^{-4\pi^2/t})}. \qquad (30)$$

Surprise! We have proved another remarkable fact about $P(z)$:

Theorem D. *The generating function* (17) *for partitions satisfies the functional relation*

$$\ln P(e^{-t}) = \frac{\zeta(2)}{t} + \frac{1}{2}\ln\frac{t}{2\pi} - \frac{t}{24} + \ln P(e^{-4\pi^2/t}) \tag{31}$$

when $\Re t > 0$. ∎

This theorem was discovered by Richard Dedekind [*Crelle* **83** (1877), 265–292, §6], who wrote $\eta(\tau)$ for the function $z^{1/24}/P(z)$ when $z = e^{2\pi i\tau}$; his proof was based on a much more complicated theory of elliptic functions. Notice that when t is a small positive number, $\ln P(e^{-4\pi^2/t})$ is *extremely* tiny; for example, when $t = 0.1$ we have $\exp(-4\pi^2/t) \approx 3.5 \times 10^{-172}$. Therefore Theorem D tells us essentially everything we need to know about the value of $P(z)$ when z is near 1.

G. H. Hardy and S. Ramanujan used this knowledge to deduce the asymptotic behavior of $p(n)$ for large n, and their work was extended many years later by Hans Rademacher, who discovered a series that is not only asymptotic but convergent [*Proc. London Math. Soc.* (2) **17** (1918), 75–115; **43** (1937), 241–254]. The Hardy–Ramanujan–Rademacher formula for $p(n)$ is surely one of the most astonishing identities ever discovered; it states that

$$p(n) = \frac{\pi}{2^{5/4}3^{3/4}(n - 1/24)^{3/4}} \sum_{k=1}^{\infty} \frac{A_k(n)}{k} I_{3/2}\left(\sqrt{\frac{2}{3}}\frac{\pi}{k}\sqrt{n - 1/24}\right). \tag{32}$$

Here $I_{3/2}$ denotes the modified spherical Bessel function

$$I_{3/2}(z) = \left(\frac{z}{2}\right)^{3/2} \sum_{k=0}^{\infty} \frac{1}{\Gamma(k + 5/2)} \frac{(z^2/4)^k}{k!} = \sqrt{\frac{2z}{\pi}}\left(\frac{\cosh z}{z} - \frac{\sinh z}{z^2}\right); \tag{33}$$

and the coefficient $A_k(n)$ is defined by the formula

$$A_k(n) = \sum_{h=0}^{k-1} [h \perp k] \exp\left(2\pi i\left(\frac{\sigma(h, k, 0)}{24} - \frac{nh}{k}\right)\right) \tag{34}$$

where $\sigma(h, k, 0)$ is the Dedekind sum defined in Eq. 3.3.3–(16). We have

$$A_1(n) = 1, \qquad A_2(n) = (-1)^n, \qquad A_3(n) = 2\cos\frac{(24n + 1)\pi}{18}, \tag{35}$$

and in general $A_k(n)$ lies between $-k$ and k.

A proof of (32) would take us far afield, but the basic idea is to use the "saddle point method" discussed in Section 7.2.1.5. The term for $k = 1$ is derived from the behavior of $P(z)$ when z is near 1; and the next term is derived from the behavior when z is near -1, where a transformation similar to (31) can be applied. In general, the kth term of (32) takes account of the way $P(z)$ behaves when z approaches $e^{2\pi i h/k}$ for irreducible fractions h/k with denominator k; every kth root of unity is a pole of each of the factors $1/(1 - z^k)$, $1/(1 - z^{2k})$, $1/(1 - z^{3k})$, ... in the infinite product for $P(z)$.

The leading term of (32) can be simplified greatly, if we merely want a rough approximation:

$$p(n) = \frac{e^{\pi\sqrt{2n/3}}}{4n\sqrt{3}}\left(1 + O(n^{-1/2})\right). \qquad (36)$$

Or, if we choose to retain a few more details,

$$p(n) = \frac{e^{\pi\sqrt{2n'/3}}}{4n'\sqrt{3}}\left(1 - \frac{1}{\pi}\sqrt{\frac{3}{2n'}}\right)\left(1 + O(e^{-\pi\sqrt{n/6}})\right), \quad n' = n - \frac{1}{24}. \qquad (37)$$

For example, $p(100)$ has the exact value 190,569,292; formula (36) tells us that $p(100) \approx 1.993 \times 10^8$, while (37) gives the far better estimate 190,568,944.783.

Andrew Odlyzko has observed that, when n is large, the Hardy–Ramanujan–Rademacher formula actually gives a near-optimum way to compute the precise value of $p(n)$, because the arithmetic operations can be carried out in nearly $O(\log p(n)) = O(n^{1/2})$ steps. The first few terms of (32) give the main contribution; then the series settles down to terms that are of order $k^{-3/2}$ and usually of order k^{-2}. Furthermore, about half of the coefficients $A_k(n)$ turn out to be zero (see exercise 28). For example, when $n = 10^6$, the terms for $k = 1$, 2, and 3 are $\approx 1.47 \times 10^{1107}$, 1.23×10^{550}, and -1.23×10^{364}, respectively. The sum of the first 250 terms is $\approx 1471684986\ldots73818.01$, while the true value is $1471684986\ldots73818$; and 123 of those 250 terms are zero.

The number of parts. It is convenient to introduce the notation

$$\left|{n \atop m}\right| \qquad (38)$$

for the number of partitions of n that have exactly m parts. Then the recurrence

$$\left|{n \atop m}\right| = \left|{n-1 \atop m-1}\right| + \left|{n-m \atop m}\right| \qquad (39)$$

holds for all integers m and n, because $\left|{n-1 \atop m-1}\right|$ counts the partitions whose smallest part is 1 and $\left|{n-m \atop m}\right|$ counts the others. (If the smallest part is 2 or more, we can subtract 1 from each part and get a partition of $n - m$ into m parts.) By similar reasoning we can conclude that $\left|{m+n \atop m}\right|$ is the number of partitions of n into *at most* m parts, namely into m nonnegative summands. We also know, by considering Ferrers diagrams, that $\left|{n \atop m}\right|$ is the number of partitions of n whose *largest* part is m. Thus $\left|{n \atop m}\right|$ is a good number to know. The boundary conditions

$$\left|{n \atop 0}\right| = \delta_{n0} \qquad \text{and} \qquad \left|{n \atop m}\right| = 0 \quad \text{for } m < 0 \text{ or } n < 0 \qquad (40)$$

make it easy to tabulate $\left|{n \atop m}\right|$ for small values of the parameters, and we obtain an array of numbers analogous to the familiar triangles for $\binom{n}{m}$, $\left[{n \atop m}\right]$, $\left\{{n \atop m}\right\}$, and $\left\langle{n \atop m}\right\rangle$ that we've seen before; see Table 2. The generating function is

$$\sum_n \left|{n \atop m}\right| z^n = \frac{z^m}{(1-z)(1-z^2)\ldots(1-z^m)}. \qquad (41)$$

Table 2

PARTITION NUMBERS

n	$\left\lvert{n\atop0}\right\rvert$	$\left\lvert{n\atop1}\right\rvert$	$\left\lvert{n\atop2}\right\rvert$	$\left\lvert{n\atop3}\right\rvert$	$\left\lvert{n\atop4}\right\rvert$	$\left\lvert{n\atop5}\right\rvert$	$\left\lvert{n\atop6}\right\rvert$	$\left\lvert{n\atop7}\right\rvert$	$\left\lvert{n\atop8}\right\rvert$	$\left\lvert{n\atop9}\right\rvert$	$\left\lvert{n\atop10}\right\rvert$	$\left\lvert{n\atop11}\right\rvert$
0	1	0	0	0	0	0	0	0	0	0	0	0
1	0	1	0	0	0	0	0	0	0	0	0	0
2	0	1	1	0	0	0	0	0	0	0	0	0
3	0	1	1	1	0	0	0	0	0	0	0	0
4	0	1	2	1	1	0	0	0	0	0	0	0
5	0	1	2	2	1	1	0	0	0	0	0	0
6	0	1	3	3	2	1	1	0	0	0	0	0
7	0	1	3	4	3	2	1	1	0	0	0	0
8	0	1	4	5	5	3	2	1	1	0	0	0
9	0	1	4	7	6	5	3	2	1	1	0	0
10	0	1	5	8	9	7	5	3	2	1	1	0
11	0	1	5	10	11	10	7	5	3	2	1	1

Almost all partitions of n have $\Theta(\sqrt{n}\log n)$ parts. This fact, discovered by P. Erdős and J. Lehner [*Duke Math. J.* **8** (1941), 335–345], has a very instructive proof:

Theorem E. *Let $C = \pi/\sqrt{6}$ and $m = \frac{1}{2C}\sqrt{n}\ln n + x\sqrt{n} + O(1)$. Then*

$$\frac{1}{p(n)}\left\lvert{m+n\atop m}\right\rvert = F(x)\bigl(1 + O(n^{-1/2+\epsilon})\bigr) \tag{42}$$

for all $\epsilon > 0$ and all fixed x as $n \to \infty$, where

$$F(x) = e^{-e^{-Cx}/C}. \tag{43}$$

This function $F(x)$ approaches 0 quite rapidly when $x \to -\infty$, and it rapidly increases to 1 when $x \to +\infty$; so it is a probability distribution function. Figure 29(b) shows that the corresponding density function $f(x) = F'(x)$ is largely concentrated in the region $-2 \le x \le 4$. The values of $\left\lvert{n\atop m}\right\rvert = \left\lvert{m+n\atop m}\right\rvert - \left\lvert{m-1+n\atop m-1}\right\rvert$ are shown in Fig. 29(a) for comparison when $n = 100$; in this case $\frac{1}{2C}\sqrt{n}\ln n \approx 18$.

Proof. We will use the fact that $\left\lvert{m+n\atop m}\right\rvert$ is the number of partitions of n whose largest part is $\le m$. Then, by the principle of inclusion and exclusion, Eq. 1.3.3–(29), we have

$$\left\lvert{m+n\atop m}\right\rvert = p(n) - \sum_{j>m} p(n-j) + \sum_{j_2>j_1>m} p(n-j_1-j_2) - \sum_{j_3>j_2>j_1>m} p(n-j_1-j_2-j_3) + \cdots,$$

because $p(n - j_1 - \cdots - j_r)$ is the number of partitions of n that use each of the parts $\{j_1, \ldots, j_r\}$ at least once. Let us write this as

$$\frac{1}{p(n)}\left\lvert{m+n\atop m}\right\rvert = 1 - \Sigma_1 + \Sigma_2 - \Sigma_3 + \cdots, \qquad \Sigma_r = \sum_{j_r>\cdots>j_1>m} \frac{p(n-j_1-\cdots-j_r)}{p(n)}. \tag{44}$$

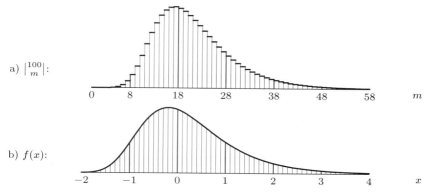

a) $\left|{}^{100}_{m}\right|$:

b) $f(x)$:

Fig. 29. Partitions of n with m parts, when (a) $n = 100$; (b) $n \to \infty$. (See Theorem E.)

In order to evaluate Σ_r we need to have a good estimate of the ratio $p(n - t)/p(n)$. And we're in luck, because Eq. (36) implies that

$$\frac{p(n - t)}{p(n)} = \exp\bigl(2C\sqrt{n - t} - \ln(n - t) + O\bigl((n - t)^{-1/2}\bigr) - 2C\sqrt{n} + \ln n\bigr)$$

$$= \exp\bigl(-Ctn^{-1/2} + O(n^{-1/2+2\epsilon})\bigr) \qquad \text{if } 0 \le t \le n^{1/2+\epsilon}. \qquad (45)$$

Furthermore, if $t \ge n^{1/2+\epsilon}$ we have $p(n - t)/p(n) \le p(n - n^{1/2+\epsilon})/p(n) \approx \exp(-Cn^\epsilon)$, a value that is asymptotically smaller than any power of n. Therefore we may safely use the approximation

$$\frac{p(n - t)}{p(n)} \approx \alpha^t, \qquad\qquad \alpha = \exp(-Cn^{-1/2}), \qquad (46)$$

for all values of $t \ge 0$. For example, we have

$$\Sigma_1 = \sum_{j>m} \frac{p(n - j)}{p(n)} = \frac{\alpha^{m+1}}{1 - \alpha}\bigl(1 + O(n^{-1/2+2\epsilon})\bigr) + \sum_{n \ge j > n^{1/2+\epsilon}} \frac{p(n - j)}{p(n)}$$

$$= \frac{e^{-Cx}}{C}\bigl(1 + O(n^{-1/2+2\epsilon})\bigr) + O(ne^{-Cn^\epsilon}),$$

because $\alpha/(1 - \alpha) = n^{1/2}/C + O(1)$ and $\alpha^m = n^{-1/2}e^{-Cx}$. A similar argument (see exercise 36) proves that, if $r = O(\log n)$,

$$\Sigma_r = \frac{e^{-Crx}}{C^r r!}\bigl(1 + O(n^{-1/2+2\epsilon})\bigr) + O(e^{-n^{\epsilon/2}}). \qquad (47)$$

Finally — and this is a wonderful property of the inclusion-exclusion principle in general — the partial sums of (44) always "bracket" the true value, in the sense that

$$1 - \Sigma_1 + \Sigma_2 - \cdots - \Sigma_{2r-1} \le \frac{1}{p(n)}\left|{}^{m+n}_{m}\right| \le 1 - \Sigma_1 + \Sigma_2 - \cdots - \Sigma_{2r-1} + \Sigma_{2r} \quad (48)$$

for all r. (See exercise 37.) When $2r$ is near $\ln n$ and n is large, the term Σ_{2r} is extremely tiny; therefore we obtain (42), except with 2ϵ in place of ϵ. ∎

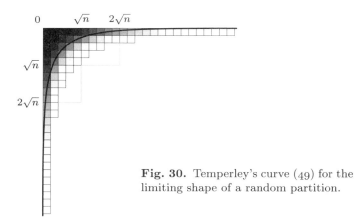

Fig. 30. Temperley's curve (49) for the limiting shape of a random partition.

Theorem E tells us that the largest part of a random partition almost always is $\frac{1}{2C}\sqrt{n}\ln n + O(\sqrt{n})$, and when n is reasonably large the other parts tend to be predictable as well. Suppose, for example, that we take all the partitions of 25 and superimpose their Ferrers diagrams, changing dots to boxes as in the rim representation. Which cells are occupied most often? Figure 30 shows the result: A random partition tends to have a typical shape that approaches a limiting curve as $n \to \infty$.

H. N. V. Temperley [*Proc. Cambridge Philos. Soc.* **48** (1952), 683–697] gave heuristic reasons to believe that most parts a_k of a large random partition $a_1 \ldots a_m$ will satisfy the approximate law

$$e^{-Ck/\sqrt{n}} + e^{-Ca_k/\sqrt{n}} \approx 1, \tag{49}$$

and his formula has subsequently been verified in a strong form. For example, a theorem of Boris Pittel [*Advances in Applied Math.* **18** (1997), 432–488] allows us to conclude that the trace of a random partition is almost always $\frac{\ln 2}{C}\sqrt{n} \approx 0.54\sqrt{n}$, in accordance with (49), with an error of at most $O(\sqrt{n}\ln n)^{1/2}$; thus about 29% of all the Ferrers dots tend to lie in the Durfee square.

If, on the other hand, we look only at partitions of n with m parts, where m is fixed, the limiting shape is rather different: Almost all such partitions have

$$a_k \approx \frac{n}{m}\ln\frac{m}{k}, \tag{50}$$

if m is reasonably large. Figure 31 illustrates the case $n = 50$, $m = 5$. In fact, the same limit holds when m grows with n, but at a slower rate than $\sqrt{n}$ [see Vershik and Yakubovich, *Moscow Math. J.* **1** (2001), 457–468].

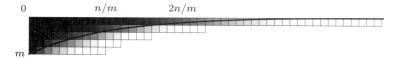

Fig. 31. The limiting shape (50) when there are m parts.

The rim representation of partitions gives us further information about partitions that are *doubly* bounded, in the sense that we not only restrict the number of parts but also the size of each part. A partition that has at most m parts, each of size at most l, fits inside an $m \times l$ box. All such partitions correspond to permutations of the multiset $\{m \cdot 0, l \cdot 1\}$ that have exactly n inversions, and we have studied the inversions of multiset permutations in exercise 5.1.2–16. In particular, that exercise derives a nonobvious formula for the number of ways n inversions can happen:

Theorem C. *The number of partitions of n that have no more than m parts and no part larger than l is*

$$[z^n] \binom{l+m}{m}_z = [z^n] \frac{(1-z^{l+1})}{(1-z)} \frac{(1-z^{l+2})}{(1-z^2)} \cdots \frac{(1-z^{l+m})}{(1-z^m)}. \tag{51}$$

This result is due to A. Cauchy, *Comptes Rendus Acad. Sci.* **17** (Paris, 1843), 523–531. Notice that when $l \to \infty$ the numerator becomes simply 1. An interesting combinatorial proof of a more general result appears in exercise 39 below. ∎

Analysis of the algorithms. Now we know more than enough about the quantitative aspects of partitions to deduce the behavior of Algorithm P quite precisely. Suppose steps P1, ..., P6 of that algorithm are executed respectively $T_1(n), \ldots, T_6(n)$ times. We obviously have $T_1(n) = 1$ and $T_3(n) = p(n)$; furthermore Kirchhoff's law tells us that $T_2(n) = T_5(n)$ and $T_4(n) + T_5(n) = T_3(n)$. We get to step P4 once for each partition that contains a 2; and this is clearly $p(n-2)$.

Thus the only possible mystery about the running time of Algorithm P is the number of times we must perform step P6, which loops back to itself. A moment's thought, however, reveals that the algorithm stores a value ≥ 2 into the array $a_1 a_2 \ldots$ only in steps P2 and P6; and every such value is eventually decreased by 1, either in step P4 or step P5. Therefore

$$T_2''(n) + T_6(n) = p(n) - 1, \tag{52}$$

where $T_2''(n)$ is the number of times step P2 sets a_m to a value ≥ 2. Let $T_2(n) = T_2'(n) + T_2''(n)$, so that $T_2'(n)$ is the number of times step P2 sets $a_m \leftarrow 1$. Then $T_2'(n) + T_4(n)$ is the number of partitions that end in 1, hence

$$T_2'(n) + T_4(n) = p(n-1). \tag{53}$$

Aha! We've found enough equations to determine all of the required quantities:

$$\bigl(T_1(n), \ldots, T_6(n)\bigr) =$$
$$\bigl(1, \; p(n) - p(n-2), \; p(n), \; p(n-2), \; p(n) - p(n-2), \; p(n-1) - 1\bigr). \tag{54}$$

And from the asymptotics of $p(n)$ we also know the average amount of computation per partition:

$$\left(\frac{T_1(n)}{p(n)}, \ldots, \frac{T_6(n)}{p(n)}\right) = \left(0, \; \frac{2C}{\sqrt{n}}, \; 1, \; 1 - \frac{2C}{\sqrt{n}}, \; \frac{2C}{\sqrt{n}}, \; 1 - \frac{C}{\sqrt{n}}\right) + O\left(\frac{1}{n}\right), \tag{55}$$

where $C = \pi/\sqrt{6} \approx 1.283$. (See exercise 45.) The total number of memory accesses per partition therefore comes to only $4 - 3C/\sqrt{n} + O(1/n)$.

> *Whoever wants to go about generating all partitions*
> *not only immerses himself in immense labor,*
> *but also must take pains to keep fully attentive,*
> *so as not to be grossly deceived.*
> — LEONHARD EULER, *De Partitione Numerorum* (1750)

Algorithm H is more difficult to analyze, but we can at least prove a decent upper bound on its running time. The key quantity is the value of j, the smallest subscript for which $a_j < a_1 - 1$. The successive values of j when $m = 4$ and $n = 11$ are $(2, 2, 2, 3, 2, 2, 3, 4, 2, 3, 5)$, and we have observed that $j = b_{l-1} + 1$ when $b_1 \ldots b_l$ is the conjugate partition $(a_1 \ldots a_m)^T$. (See (7) and (12).) Step H3 singles out the case $j = 2$, because this case is not only the most common, it is also especially easy to handle.

Let $c_m(n)$ be the accumulated total value of $j - 1$, summed over all of the $\left|{n \atop m}\right|$ partitions generated by Algorithm H. For example, $c_4(11) = 1 + 1 + 1 + 2 + 1 + 1 + 2 + 3 + 1 + 2 + 4 = 19$. We can regard $c_m(n)/\left|{n \atop m}\right|$ as a good indication of the running time per partition, because the time to perform the most costly steps, H4 and H6, is roughly proportional to $j - 2$. This ratio $c_m(n)/\left|{n \atop m}\right|$ is *not* bounded, because $c_m(m) = m$ while $\left|{m \atop m}\right| = 1$. But the following theorem shows that Algorithm H is efficient nonetheless:

Theorem H. *The cost measure $c_m(n)$ for Algorithm H is at most $3\left|{n \atop m}\right| + m$.*

Proof. We can readily verify that $c_m(n)$ satisfies the same recurrence as $\left|{n \atop m}\right|$, namely

$$c_m(n) = c_{m-1}(n-1) + c_m(n-m), \qquad \text{for } m, n \geq 1, \tag{56}$$

if we artificially define $c_m(n) = 1$ when $1 \leq n < m$; see (39). But the boundary conditions are now different:

$$c_m(0) = [m > 0]; \qquad c_0(n) = 0. \tag{57}$$

Table 3 shows how $c_m(n)$ behaves when m and n are small.

To prove the theorem, we will actually prove a stronger result,

$$c_m(n) \leq 3\left|{n \atop m}\right| + 2m - n - 1 \qquad \text{for } n \geq m \geq 2. \tag{58}$$

Exercise 50 shows that this inequality holds when $m \leq n \leq 2m$, so the proof will be complete if we can prove it when $n > 2m$. In the latter case we have

$$
\begin{aligned}
c_m(n) &= c_1(n-m) + c_2(n-m) + c_3(n-m) + \cdots + c_m(n-m) \\
&\leq 1 + \left(3\left|{n-m \atop 2}\right| + 3 - n + m\right) + \left(3\left|{n-m \atop 3}\right| + 5 - n + m\right) + \cdots \\
&\qquad\qquad\qquad + \left(3\left|{n-m \atop m}\right| + 2m - 1 - n + m\right) \\
&= 3\left|{n-m \atop 1}\right| + 3\left|{n-m \atop 2}\right| + \cdots + 3\left|{n-m \atop m}\right| - 3 + m^2 - (m-1)(n-m) \\
&= 3\left|{n \atop m}\right| + 2m^2 - m - (m-1)n - 3
\end{aligned}
$$

by induction; and $2m^2 - m - (m-1)n - 3 \leq 2m - n - 1$ because $n \geq 2m + 1$. ∎

Table 3

COSTS IN ALGORITHM H

n	$c_0(n)$	$c_1(n)$	$c_2(n)$	$c_3(n)$	$c_4(n)$	$c_5(n)$	$c_6(n)$	$c_7(n)$	$c_8(n)$	$c_9(n)$	$c_{10}(n)$	$c_{11}(n)$
0	0	1	1	1	1	1	1	1	1	1	1	1
1	0	1	1	1	1	1	1	1	1	1	1	1
2	0	1	2	1	1	1	1	1	1	1	1	1
3	0	1	2	3	1	1	1	1	1	1	1	1
4	0	1	3	3	4	1	1	1	1	1	1	1
5	0	1	3	4	4	5	1	1	1	1	1	1
6	0	1	4	6	5	5	6	1	1	1	1	1
7	0	1	4	7	7	6	6	7	1	1	1	1
8	0	1	5	8	11	8	7	7	8	1	1	1
9	0	1	5	11	12	12	9	8	8	9	1	1
10	0	1	6	12	16	17	13	10	9	9	10	1
11	0	1	6	14	19	21	18	14	11	10	10	11

*A Gray code for partitions. When partitions are generated in part-count form $c_1 \ldots c_n$ as in exercise 5, at most four of the c_j values change at each step. But we might prefer to minimize the changes to the individual parts, generating partitions in such a way that the successor of $a_1 a_2 \ldots a_n$ is always obtained by simply setting $a_j \leftarrow a_j + 1$ and $a_k \leftarrow a_k - 1$ for some j and k, as in the "revolving door" algorithms of Section 7.2.1.3. It turns out that this is always possible; in fact, there is a unique way to do it when $n = 6$:

$$111111,\ 21111,\ 3111,\ 2211,\ 222,\ 321,\ 33,\ 42,\ 411,\ 51,\ 6. \tag{59}$$

And in general, the $\left|\begin{smallmatrix} m+n \\ m \end{smallmatrix}\right|$ partitions of n into at most m parts can always be generated by a suitable Gray path.

Notice that $\alpha \to \beta$ is an allowable transition from one partition to another if and only if we get the Ferrers diagram for β by moving just one dot in the Ferrers diagram for α. Therefore $\alpha^T \to \beta^T$ is also an allowable transition. It follows that every Gray code for partitions into at most m parts corresponds to a Gray code for partitions into parts that do not exceed m. We shall work with the latter constraint.

The total number of Gray codes for partitions is vast: There are 52 when $n = 7$, and 652 when $n = 8$; there are 298,896 when $n = 9$, and 2,291,100,484 when $n = 10$. But no really simple construction is known. The reason is probably that a few partitions have only two neighbors, namely the partitions $d^{n/d}$ when $1 < d < n$ and d is a divisor of n. Such partitions must be preceded and followed by $\{(d+1)d^{n/d-2}(d-1),\ d^{n/d-1}(d-1)1\}$, and this requirement seems to rule out any simple recursive approach.

Carla D. Savage [*J. Algorithms* **10** (1989), 577–595] found a way to surmount the difficulties with only a modest amount of complexity. Let

$$\mu(m, n) = \overbrace{m\ m\ \ldots\ m}^{\lfloor n/m \rfloor}\ (n \bmod m) \tag{60}$$

be the lexicographically largest partition of n with parts $\leq m$; our goal will be to construct recursively defined Gray paths $L(m, n)$ and $M(m, n)$ from the partition 1^n to $\mu(m, n)$, where $L(m, n)$ runs through all partitions whose parts are bounded by m while $M(m, n)$ runs through those partitions and a few more: $M(m, n)$ also includes partitions whose largest part is $m + 1$, provided that the other parts are all strictly less than m. For example, $L(3, 8)$ is 11111111, 2111111, 311111, 221111, 22211, 2222, 3221, 32111, 3311, 332, while $M(3, 8)$ is

$$11111111, \; 2111111, \; 221111, \; 22211, \; 2222, \; 3221,$$
$$3311, \; 32111, \; 311111, \; 41111, \; 4211, \; 422, \; 332; \tag{61}$$

the additional partitions starting with 4 will give us "wiggle room" in other parts of the recursion. We will define $L(m, n)$ for all $n \geq 0$, but $M(m, n)$ only for $n > 2m$.

The following construction, illustrated for $m = 5$ to simplify the notation, *almost* works:

$$L(5) = \begin{Bmatrix} L(3) \\ 4L(\infty)^R \\ 5L(\infty) \end{Bmatrix} \text{ if } n \leq 7; \quad \begin{Bmatrix} L(3) \\ 4L(2)^R \\ 5L(2) \\ 431 \\ 44 \\ 53 \end{Bmatrix} \text{ if } n = 8; \quad \begin{Bmatrix} M(4) \\ 54L(4)^R \\ 55L(5) \end{Bmatrix} \text{ if } n \geq 9; \tag{62}$$

$$M(5) = \begin{Bmatrix} L(4) \\ 5L(4)^R \\ 6L(3) \\ 64L(\infty)^R \\ 55L(\infty) \end{Bmatrix} \text{ if } 11 \leq n \leq 13; \quad \begin{Bmatrix} L(4) \\ 5M(4)^R \\ 6L(4) \\ 554L(4)^R \\ 555L(5) \end{Bmatrix} \text{ if } n \geq 14. \tag{63}$$

Here the parameter n in $L(m, n)$ and $M(m, n)$ has been omitted because it can be deduced from the context; each L or M is supposed to generate partitions of whatever amount remains after previous parts have been subtracted. Thus, for example, (63) specifies that

$$M(5, 14) \;=\; L(4, 14), \; 5M(4, 9)^R, \; 6L(4, 8), \; 554L(4, 0)^R, \; 555L(5, -1);$$

the sequence $L(5, -1)$ is actually empty, and $L(4, 0)$ is the empty string, so the final partition of $M(5, 14)$ is $554 = \mu(5, 14)$ as it should be. The notation $L(\infty)$ stands for $L(\infty, n) = L(n, n)$, the Gray path of all partitions of n, starting with 1^n and ending with n^1.

In general, $L(m)$ and $M(m)$ are defined for all $m \geq 3$ by essentially the same rules, if we replace the digits 2, 3, 4, 5, and 6 in (62) and (63) by $m{-}3$, $m{-}2$, $m{-}1$, m, and $m{+}1$, respectively. The ranges $n \leq 7$, $n = 8$, $n \geq 9$ become $n \leq 2m - 3$, $n = 2m - 2$, $n \geq 2m - 1$; the ranges $11 \leq n \leq 13$ and $n \geq 14$ become $2m + 1 \leq n \leq 3m - 2$ and $n \geq 3m - 1$. The sequences $L(0)$, $L(1)$, $L(2)$ have obvious definitions because the paths are unique when $m \leq 2$. The sequence $M(2)$ is 1^n, 21^{n-2}, 31^{n-3}, 221^{n-4}, 2221^{n-6}, $\ldots$, $\mu(2, n)$ for $n \geq 5$.

Theorem S. *Gray paths $L'(m,n)$ for $m, n \geq 0$ and $M'(m,n)$ for $n \geq 2m+1 \geq 5$ exist for all partitions with the properties described above, except in the case $L'(4,6)$. Furthermore, L' and M' obey the mutual recursions* (62) *and* (63) *except in a few cases.*

Proof. We noted above that (62) and (63) *almost* work; the reader may verify that the only glitch occurs in the case $L(4,6)$, when (62) gives

$$L(4,6) = L(2,6), \ 3L(1,3)^R, \ 4L(1,2), \ 321, \ 33, \ 42$$
$$= 111111, \ 21111, \ 2211, \ 222, \ 3111, \ 411, \ 321, \ 33, \ 42. \qquad (64)$$

If $m > 4$, we're OK because the transition from the end of $L(m-2, 2m-2)$ to the beginning of $(m-1)L(m-3, m-1)^R$ is from $(m-2)(m-2)2$ to $(m-1)(m-3)2$. There is no satisfactory path $L(4,6)$, because all Gray codes through those nine partitions must end with either 411, 33, 3111, 222, or 2211.

In order to neutralize this anomaly we need to patch the definitions of $L(m,n)$ and $M(m,n)$ at eight places where the "buggy subroutine" $L(4,6)$ is invoked. One simple way is to make the following definitions:

$$L'(4,6) = 111111, 21111, 3111, 411, 321, 33, 42;$$
$$L'(3,5) = 11111, 2111, 221, 311, 32. \qquad (65)$$

Thus, we omit 222 and 2211 from $L(4,6)$; we also reprogram $L(3,5)$ so that 2111 is adjacent to 221. Then exercise 60 shows that it is always easy to "splice in" the two partitions that are missing from $L(4,6)$. ∎

EXERCISES

▶ **1.** [*M21*] Give formulas for the total number of possibilities in each problem of The Twelvefold Way. For example, the number of n-tuples of m things is m^n. (Use the notation (38) when appropriate, and be careful to make your formulas correct even when $m = 0$ or $n = 0$.)

▶ **2.** [*20*] Show that a small change to step H1 yields an algorithm that will generate all partitions of n into *at most* m parts.

3. [*M17*] A partition $a_1 + \cdots + a_m$ of n into m parts $a_1 \geq \cdots \geq a_m$ is *optimally balanced* if $|a_i - a_j| \leq 1$ for $1 \leq i, j \leq m$. Prove that there is exactly one such partition, whenever $n \geq m \geq 1$, and give a simple formula that expresses the jth part a_j as a function of j, m, and n.

4. [*M22*] (Gideon Ehrlich, 1974.) What is the lexicographically smallest partition of n in which all parts are $\geq r$? For example, when $n = 19$ and $r = 5$ the answer is 766.

▶ **5.** [*23*] Design an algorithm that generates all partitions of n in the part-count form $c_1 \ldots c_n$ of (8). Generate them in colex order, namely in the lexicographic order of $c_n \ldots c_1$, which is equivalent to lexicographic order of the corresponding partitions $a_1 a_2 \ldots$. For efficiency, maintain also a table of links $l_0 l_1 \ldots l_n$ so that, if the distinct values of k for which $c_k > 0$ are $k_1 < \cdots < k_t$, we have

$$l_0 = k_1, \quad l_{k_1} = k_2, \quad \ldots, \quad l_{k_{t-1}} = k_t, \quad l_{k_t} = 0.$$

(Thus the partition 331 would be represented by $c_1 \ldots c_7 = 1020000$, $l_0 = 1$, $l_1 = 3$, and $l_3 = 0$; the other links l_2, l_4, l_5, l_7 can be set to any convenient values.)

6. [20] Design an algorithm to compute $b_1 b_2 \ldots = (a_1 a_2 \ldots)^T$, given $a_1 a_2 \ldots$.

7. [M20] Suppose $a_1 \ldots a_n$ and $a'_1 \ldots a'_n$ are partitions of n with $a_1 \geq \cdots \geq a_n \geq 0$ and $a'_1 \geq \cdots \geq a'_n \geq 0$, and let their respective conjugates be $b_1 \ldots b_n = (a_1 \ldots a_n)^T$, $b'_1 \ldots b'_n = (a'_1 \ldots a'_n)^T$. Show that $b_1 \ldots b_n < b'_1 \ldots b'_n$ if and only if $a_n \ldots a_1 < a'_n \ldots a'_1$.

8. [15] When $(p_1 \ldots p_t, q_1 \ldots q_t)$ is the rim representation of a partition $a_1 a_2 \ldots$ as in (15) and (16), what is the conjugate partition $(a_1 a_2 \ldots)^T = b_1 b_2 \ldots$?

9. [22] If $a_1 a_2 \ldots a_m$ and $b_1 b_2 \ldots b_m = (a_1 a_2 \ldots a_m)^T$ are conjugate partitions, show that the multisets $\{a_1 + 1, a_2 + 2, \ldots, a_m + m\}$ and $\{b_1 + 1, b_2 + 2, \ldots, b_m + m\}$ are equal.

10. [21] Two simple kinds of binary trees are sometimes helpful for reasoning about partitions: (a) a tree that includes all partitions of all integers, and (b) a tree that includes all partitions of a given integer n, illustrated here for $n = 8$:

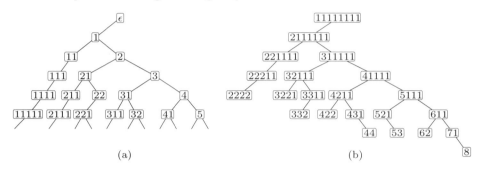

(a)   (b)

Deduce the general rules underlying these constructions. What order of tree traversal corresponds to lexicographic order of the partitions?

11. [M22] How many ways are there to pay one euro, using coins worth 1, 2, 5, 10, 20, 50, and/or 100 cents? What if you are allowed to use at most two of each coin?

▶ **12.** [M21] (L. Euler, 1750.) Use generating functions to prove that the number of ways to partition n into *distinct* parts is the number of ways to partition n into *odd* parts. For example, $5 = 4 + 1 = 3 + 2$; $5 = 3 + 1 + 1 = 1 + 1 + 1 + 1 + 1$.

[*Note:* The next two exercises use combinatorial techniques to prove extensions of this famous theorem.]

▶ **13.** [M22] (F. Franklin, 1882.) Find a one-to-one correspondence between partitions of n that have exactly k parts repeated more than once and partitions of n that have exactly k even parts. (The case $k = 0$ corresponds to Euler's result.)

▶ **14.** [M28] (J. J. Sylvester, 1882.) Find a one-to-one correspondence between partitions of n into distinct parts $a_1 > a_2 > \cdots > a_m$ that have exactly k "gaps" where $a_j > a_{j+1} + 1$, and partitions of n into odd parts that have exactly $k + 1$ different values. (For example, when $k = 0$ this construction proves that the number of ways to write n as a sum of consecutive integers is the number of odd divisors of n.)

15. [M20] (J. J. Sylvester.) Find a generating function for the number of partitions that are *self-conjugate* (namely, partitions such that $\alpha = \alpha^T$).

16. [M21] Find the generating function for partitions of trace k, and sum it on k to obtain a nontrivial identity.

17. [*M26*] A *joint partition* of n is a pair of sequences $(a_1, \ldots, a_r;\ b_1, \ldots, b_s)$ of positive integers for which we have

$$a_1 \geq \cdots \geq a_r, \quad b_1 > \cdots > b_s, \quad \text{and} \quad a_1 + \cdots + a_r + b_1 + \cdots + b_s = n.$$

Thus it is an ordinary partition if $s = 0$, and a partition into distinct parts if $r = 0$.

a) Find a simple formula for the generating function $\sum u^{r+s} v^s z^n$, summed over all joint partitions of n with r ordinary parts a_i and s distinct parts b_j.

b) Similarly, find a simple formula for $\sum v^s z^n$ when the sum is over all joint partitions that have exactly $r + s = t$ total parts, given the value of t.

c) What identity do you deduce?

▶ **18.** [*M23*] (Doron Zeilberger.) Show that there is a one-to-one correspondence between pairs of integer sequences $(a_1, a_2, \ldots, a_r;\ b_1, b_2, \ldots, b_s)$ such that

$$a_1 \geq a_2 \geq \cdots \geq a_r, \quad b_1 > b_2 > \cdots > b_s,$$

and pairs of integer sequences $(c_1, c_2, \ldots, c_{r+s};\ d_1, d_2, \ldots, d_{r+s})$ such that

$$c_1 \geq c_2 \geq \cdots \geq c_{r+s}, \quad d_j \in \{0, 1\} \quad \text{for } 1 \leq j \leq r + s,$$

related by the multiset equations

$$\{a_1, a_2, \ldots, a_r\} = \{c_j \mid d_j = 0\} \quad \text{and} \quad \{b_1, b_2, \ldots, b_s\} = \{c_j + r + s - j \mid d_j = 1\}.$$

Consequently we obtain the interesting identity

$$\sum_{\substack{a_1 \geq \cdots \geq a_r > 0 \\ b_1 > \cdots > b_s > 0}} u^{r+s} v^s z^{a_1 + \cdots + a_r + b_1 + \cdots + b_s} = \sum_{\substack{c_1 \geq \cdots \geq c_t > 0 \\ d_1, \ldots, d_t \in \{0,1\}}} u^t v^{d_1 + \cdots + d_t} z^{c_1 + \cdots + c_t + (t-1)d_1 + \cdots + d_{t-1}}.$$

19. [*M21*] (E. Heine, 1847.) Prove the four-parameter identity

$$\prod_{m=1}^{\infty} \frac{(1 - wxz^m)(1 - wyz^m)}{(1 - wz^m)(1 - wxyz^m)} = \sum_{k=0}^{\infty} \frac{w^k(x-1)(x-z) \ldots (x - z^{k-1})(y-1)(y-z) \ldots (y - z^{k-1})z^k}{(1-z)(1-z^2) \ldots (1-z^k)(1-wz)(1-wz^2) \ldots (1-wz^k)}.$$

Hint: Carry out the sum over either k or l in the formula

$$\sum_{k,l \geq 0} u^k v^l z^{kl} \frac{(z - az)(z - az^2) \ldots (z - az^k)}{(1-z)(1-z^2) \ldots (1-z^k)} \frac{(z - bz)(z - bz^2) \ldots (z - bz^l)}{(1-z)(1-z^2) \ldots (1-z^l)}$$

and consider the simplifications that occur when $b = auz$.

▶ **20.** [*M21*] Approximately how long does it take to compute a table of the partition numbers $p(n)$ for $1 \leq n \leq N$, using Euler's recurrence (20)?

21. [*M21*] (L. Euler.) Let $q(n)$ be the number of partitions into distinct parts. What is a good way to compute $q(n)$ if you already know the values of $p(1), \ldots, p(n)$?

22. [*HM21*] (L. Euler.) Let $\sigma(n)$ be the sum of all positive divisors of the positive integer n. Thus, $\sigma(n) = n + 1$ when n is prime, and $\sigma(n)$ can be significantly larger than n when n is highly composite. Prove that, in spite of this rather chaotic behavior, $\sigma(n)$ satisfies almost the same recurrence (20) as the partition numbers:

$$\sigma(n) = \sigma(n-1) + \sigma(n-2) - \sigma(n-5) - \sigma(n-7) + \sigma(n-12) + \sigma(n-15) - \cdots$$

for $n \geq 1$, except that when a term on the right is '$\sigma(0)$' the value 'n' is used instead. For example, $\sigma(11) = 1 + 11 = \sigma(10) + \sigma(9) - \sigma(6) - \sigma(4) = 18 + 13 - 12 - 7$; $\sigma(12) = 1 + 2 + 3 + 4 + 6 + 12 = \sigma(11) + \sigma(10) - \sigma(7) - \sigma(5) + 12 = 12 + 18 - 8 - 6 + 12$.

23. [*HM25*] Use Jacobi's triple product identity (19) to prove another formula that he discovered:

$$\prod_{k=1}^{\infty}(1-z^k)^3 = 1-3z+5z^3-7z^6+9z^{10}-\cdots = \sum_{n=0}^{\infty}(-1)^n(2n+1)z^{\binom{n+1}{2}}.$$

24. [*M26*] (S. Ramanujan, 1919.) Let $A(z)=\prod_{k=1}^{\infty}(1-z^k)^4$.

a) Prove that $[z^n]\,A(z)$ is a multiple of 5 when $n \bmod 5 = 4$.
b) Prove that $[z^n]\,A(z)B(z)^5$ has the same property, if B is any power series with integer coefficients.
c) Therefore $p(n)$ is a multiple of 5 when $n \bmod 5 = 4$.

25. [*HM27*] Improve on (22) by using (a) Euler's summation formula and (b) Mellin transforms to estimate $\ln P(e^{-t})$. *Hint:* The dilogarithm function $\mathrm{Li}_2(x) = x/1^2 + x^2/2^2 + x^3/3^2 + \cdots$ satisfies $\mathrm{Li}_2(x) + \mathrm{Li}_2(1-x) = \zeta(2) - (\ln x)\ln(1-x)$.

26. [*HM22*] In exercises 5.2.2–44 and 5.2.2–51 we studied two ways to prove that

$$\sum_{k=1}^{\infty} e^{-k^2/n} = \frac{1}{2}(\sqrt{\pi n}-1) + O(n^{-M}) \qquad \text{for all } M > 0.$$

Show that Poisson's summation formula gives a much stronger result.

27. [*HM23*] Evaluate (29) and complete the calculations leading to Theorem D.

28. [*HM42*] (D. H. Lehmer.) Show that the Hardy–Ramanujan–Rademacher coefficients $A_k(n)$ defined in (34) have the following remarkable properties:

a) If k is odd, then $A_{2k}(km + 4n + (k^2-1)/8) = A_2(m)A_k(n)$.
b) If p is prime, $p^e > 2$, and $k \perp 2p$, then

$$A_{p^e k}(k^2 m + p^{2e} n - (k^2 + p^{2e} - 1)/24) = (-1)^{[p^e=4]} A_{p^e}(m)A_k(n).$$

In this formula $k^2 + p^{2e} - 1$ is a multiple of 24 if p or k is divisible by 2 or 3; otherwise division by 24 should be done modulo $p^e k$.

c) If p is prime, $|A_{p^e}(n)| < 2^{[p>2]}p^{e/2}$.
d) If p is prime, $A_{p^e}(n) \neq 0$ if and only if $1 - 24n$ is a quadratic residue modulo p and either $e = 1$ or $24n \bmod p \neq 1$.
e) The probability that $A_k(n) = 0$, when k is divisible by exactly t primes ≥ 5 and n is a random integer, is approximately $1 - 2^{-t}$.

▶ **29.** [*M16*] Generalizing (41), evaluate the sum $\sum_{a_1 \geq a_2 \geq \cdots \geq a_m \geq 1} z_1^{a_1} z_2^{a_2} \ldots z_m^{a_m}$.

30. [*M17*] Find closed forms for the sums

$$\text{(a)} \quad \sum_{k \geq 0} \left| \begin{matrix} n - km \\ m - 1 \end{matrix} \right| \qquad \text{and} \qquad \text{(b)} \quad \sum_{k \geq 0} \left| \begin{matrix} n \\ m - k \end{matrix} \right|$$

(which are finite, because the terms being summed are zero when k is large).

31. [*M24*] (A. De Morgan, 1843.) Show that $\left|{n \atop 2}\right| = \lfloor n/2 \rfloor$ and $\left|{n \atop 3}\right| = \lfloor (n^2+6)/12 \rfloor$; find a similar formula for $\left|{n \atop 4}\right|$.

32. [*M15*] Prove that $\left|{n \atop m}\right| \leq p(n-m)$ for all $m, n \geq 0$. When does equality hold?

33. [*HM20*] Use the fact that there are exactly $\binom{n-1}{m-1}$ *compositions* of n into m parts, Eq. 7.2.1.3–(9), to prove a lower bound on $\left|{n \atop m}\right|$. Then set $m = \lfloor \sqrt{n} \rfloor$ to obtain an elementary lower bound on $p(n)$.

▶ **34.** [*HM21*] Show that $\left|{n - m(m-1)/2 \atop m}\right|$ is the number of partitions of n into m distinct parts. Consequently

$$\left|{n \atop m}\right| = \frac{n^{m-1}}{m!\,(m-1)!}\left(1 + O\left(\frac{m^3}{n}\right)\right) \qquad \text{when } m \le n^{1/3}.$$

35. [*HM21*] In the Erdős–Lehner probability distribution (43), what value of x is (a) most probable? (b) the median? (c) the mean? (d) What is the standard deviation?

36. [*HM24*] Prove the key estimate (47) that is needed in Theorem E.

37. [*M22*] Prove the inclusion-exclusion bracketing lemma (48), by analyzing how many times a partition that has exactly q different parts exceeding m is counted in the rth partial sum.

38. [*M20*] What is the generating function for the partitions of n that have exactly m parts, and largest part l?

▶ **39.** [*M25*] (F. Franklin.) Generalizing Theorem C, show that, for $0 \le k \le m$,

$$[z^n]\,\frac{(1 - z^{l+1}) \ldots (1 - z^{l+k})}{(1 - z)(1 - z^2) \ldots (1 - z^m)}$$

is the number of partitions $a_1 a_2 \ldots$ of n into m or fewer parts with the property that $a_1 \le a_{k+1} + l$.

40. [*M22*] (A. Cauchy.) What is the generating function for partitions into m parts, all *distinct* and less than l?

41. [*HM42*] Extend the Hardy–Ramanujan–Rademacher formula (32) to obtain a convergent series for partitions of n into at most m parts, with no part exceeding l.

42. [*HM42*] Find the limiting shape, analogous to (49), for random partitions of n into at most $\theta\sqrt{n}$ parts, with no part exceeding $\varphi\sqrt{n}$, assuming that $\theta\varphi > 1$.

43. [*M21*] Given n and k, how many partitions of n have $a_1 > a_2 > \cdots > a_k$?

▶ **44.** [*M22*] How many partitions of n have their two smallest parts equal?

45. [*HM21*] Compute the asymptotic value of $p(n-1)/p(n)$, with relative error $O(n^{-2})$.

46. [*M20*] In the text's analysis of Algorithm P, which is larger, $T_2'(n)$ or $T_2''(n)$?

▶ **47.** [*HM22*] (A. Nijenhuis and H. S. Wilf, 1975.) The following simple algorithm, based on a table of the partition numbers $p(0)$, $p(1)$, ..., $p(n)$, generates a random partition of n using the part-count representation $c_1 \ldots c_n$ of (8). Prove that it produces each partition with equal probability.

N1. [Initialize.] Set $m \leftarrow n$ and $c_1 \ldots c_n \leftarrow 0 \ldots 0$.

N2. [Done?] Terminate if $m = 0$.

N3. [Generate.] Generate a random integer M in the range $0 \le M < mp(m)$.

N4. [Choose parts.] Set $s \leftarrow 0$. Then for $j = 1, 2, \ldots, n$ and for $k = 1, 2, \ldots, \lfloor m/j \rfloor$, repeatedly set $s \leftarrow s + kp(m - jk)$ until $s > M$.

N5. [Update.] Set $c_k \leftarrow c_k + j$, $m \leftarrow m - jk$, and return to N2. ∎

Hint: Step N4, which is based on the identity

$$\sum_{j=1}^{m}\sum_{k=1}^{\lfloor m/j \rfloor} kp(m - jk) = mp(m),$$

chooses each particular pair of values (j, k) with probability $kp(m - jk)/(mp(m))$.

48. [*HM40*] Analyze the running time of the algorithm in the previous exercise.

▶ **49.** [*HM26*] (a) What is the generating function $F(z)$ for the sum of the smallest parts of all partitions of n? (The series begins $z + 3z^2 + 5z^3 + 9z^4 + 12z^5 + \cdots$.)

(b) Find the asymptotic value of $[z^n] F(z)$, with relative error $O(n^{-1})$.

50. [*HM33*] Let $c(m) = c_m(2m)$ in the recurrence (56), (57).

a) Prove that $c_m(m + k) = m - k + c(k)$ for $0 \le k \le m$.

b) Consequently (58) holds for $m \le n \le 2m$ if $c(m) < 3p(m)$ for all m.

c) Show that $c(m) - m$ is the sum of the second-smallest parts of all partitions of m.

d) Find a one-to-one correspondence between all partitions of n with second-smallest part k and all partitions of numbers $\le n$ with smallest part $k + 1$.

e) Describe the generating function $\sum_{m \ge 0} c(m) z^m$.

f) Conclude that $c(m) < 3p(m)$ for all $m \ge 0$.

51. [*M46*] Make a detailed analysis of Algorithm H.

▶ **52.** [*M21*] What is the millionth partition generated by Algorithm P when $n = 64$? *Hint:* $p(64) = 1741630 = 1000000 + \left|{77 \atop 13}\right| + \left|{60 \atop 10}\right| + \left|{47 \atop 8}\right| + \left|{35 \atop 5}\right| + \left|{27 \atop 3}\right| + \left|{22 \atop 2}\right| + \left|{18 \atop 1}\right| + \left|{15 \atop 0}\right|$.

▶ **53.** [*M21*] What is the millionth partition generated by Algorithm H when $m = 32$ and $n = 100$? *Hint:* $999999 = \left|{80 \atop 12}\right| + \left|{66 \atop 11}\right| + \left|{50 \atop 7}\right| + \left|{41 \atop 6}\right| + \left|{33 \atop 5}\right| + \left|{26 \atop 4}\right| + \left|{21 \atop 4}\right|$.

▶ **54.** [*M30*] The partition $\alpha = a_1 a_2 \ldots$ is said to *majorize* the partition $\beta = b_1 b_2 \ldots$, written $\alpha \succeq \beta$ or $\beta \preceq \alpha$, if $a_1 + \cdots + a_k \ge b_1 + \cdots + b_k$ for all $k \ge 0$.

a) True or false: $\alpha \succeq \beta$ implies $\alpha \ge \beta$ (lexicographically).

b) True or false: $\alpha \succeq \beta$ implies $\beta^T \succeq \alpha^T$.

c) Show that any two partitions of n have a greatest lower bound $\alpha \wedge \beta$ such that $\alpha \succeq \gamma$ and $\beta \succeq \gamma$ if and only if $\alpha \wedge \beta \succeq \gamma$. Explain how to compute $\alpha \wedge \beta$.

d) Similarly, explain how to compute a least upper bound $\alpha \vee \beta$ such that $\gamma \succeq \alpha$ and $\gamma \succeq \beta$ if and only if $\gamma \succeq \alpha \vee \beta$.

e) If α has l parts and β has m parts, how many parts do $\alpha \wedge \beta$ and $\alpha \vee \beta$ have?

f) True or false: If α has distinct parts and β has distinct parts, then so do $\alpha \wedge \beta$ and $\alpha \vee \beta$.

▶ **55.** [*M37*] Continuing the previous exercise, say that α *covers* β if $\alpha \succeq \beta$, $\alpha \ne \beta$, and $\alpha \succeq \gamma \succeq \beta$ implies $\gamma = \alpha$ or $\gamma = \beta$. For example, Fig. 32 illustrates the covering relations between partitions of the number 12.

a) Let us write $\alpha \vartriangleright \beta$ if $\alpha = a_1 a_2 \ldots$ and $\beta = b_1 b_2 \ldots$ are partitions for which $b_k = a_k - [k = l] + [k = l + 1]$ for all $k \ge 1$ and some $l \ge 1$. Prove that α covers β if and only if $\alpha \vartriangleright \beta$ or $\beta^T \vartriangleright \alpha^T$.

b) Show that there is an easy way to tell if α covers β by looking at the rim representations of α and β.

c) Let $n = \binom{n_2}{2} + \binom{n_1}{1}$ where $n_2 > n_1 \ge 0$. Show that no partition of n covers more than $n_2 - 2$ partitions.

d) Say that the partition μ is *minimal* if there is no partition λ with $\mu \vartriangleright \lambda$. Prove that μ is minimal if and only if μ^T has distinct parts.

e) Suppose $\alpha = \alpha_0 \vartriangleright \alpha_1 \vartriangleright \cdots \vartriangleright \alpha_k$ and $\alpha = \alpha'_0 \vartriangleright \alpha'_1 \vartriangleright \cdots \vartriangleright \alpha'_{k'}$, where α_k and $\alpha'_{k'}$ are minimal partitions. Prove that $k = k'$ and $\alpha_k = \alpha'_{k'}$.

f) Explain how to compute the lexicographically smallest partition into distinct parts that majorizes a given partition α.

g) Describe λ_n, the lexicographically smallest partition of n into distinct parts. What is the length of all paths $n^1 = \alpha_0 \vartriangleright \alpha_1 \vartriangleright \cdots \vartriangleright \lambda_n^T$?

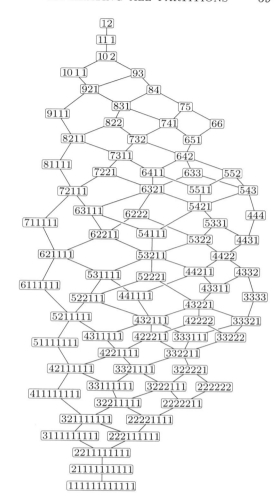

Fig. 32. The majorization lattice for partitions of 12. (See exercises 54–58.)

h) What are the lengths of the longest and shortest paths of the form $n^1 = \alpha_0, \alpha_1,$ $\ldots, \alpha_l = 1^n$, where α_j covers α_{j+1} for $0 \le j < l$?

▶ **56.** [*M27*] Design an algorithm to generate all partitions α such that $\lambda \preceq \alpha \preceq \mu$, given partitions λ and μ with $\lambda \preceq \mu$.

Note: Such an algorithm has numerous applications. For example, to generate all partitions that have m parts and no part exceeding l, we can let λ be the smallest such partition, namely $\lceil n/m \rceil \ldots \lfloor n/m \rfloor$ as in exercise 3, and let μ be the largest, namely $\left((n-m+1)1^{m-1}\right) \wedge \left(l^{\lfloor n/l \rfloor}(n \bmod l)\right)$. Similarly, according to a well-known theorem of H. G. Landau [*Bull. Math. Biophysics* **15** (1953), 143–148], the partitions of $\binom{m}{2}$ such that

$$\left\lfloor \frac{m}{2} \right\rfloor^{\lfloor m/2 \rfloor} \left\lfloor \frac{m-1}{2} \right\rfloor^{\lceil m/2 \rceil} \preceq \alpha \preceq (m-1)(m-2)\ldots 21$$

are the possible "score vectors" of a round-robin tournament, namely the partitions $a_1 \ldots a_m$ such that the jth strongest player wins a_j games.

57. [*M22*] Suppose a matrix (a_{ij}) of 0s and 1s has row sums $r_i = \sum_j a_{ij}$ and column sums $c_j = \sum_i a_{ij}$. Then $\lambda = r_1 r_2 \ldots$ and $\mu = c_1 c_2 \ldots$ are partitions of $n = \sum_{i,j} a_{ij}$. Prove that such a matrix exists if and only if $\lambda \preceq \mu^T$.

58. [*M23*] (*Symmetrical means.*) Let $\alpha = a_1 \ldots a_m$ and $\beta = b_1 \ldots b_m$ be partitions of n. Prove that the inequality

$$\frac{1}{m!} \sum x_{p_1}^{a_1} \ldots x_{p_m}^{a_m} \geq \frac{1}{m!} \sum x_{p_1}^{b_1} \ldots x_{p_m}^{b_m}$$

holds for all nonnegative values of the variables $(x_1, \ldots, x_m)$, where the sums range over all $m!$ permutations of $\{1, \ldots, m\}$, if and only if $\alpha \succeq \beta$. (For example, this inequality reduces to $(y_1 + \cdots + y_n)/n \geq (y_1 \ldots y_n)^{1/n}$ in the special case $m = n$, $\alpha = n0 \ldots 0$, $\beta = 11 \ldots 1$, $x_j = y_j^{1/n}$.)

59. [*M22*] The Gray path (59) is symmetrical in the sense that the reversed sequence 6, 51, ..., 111111 is the same as conjugate sequence $(111111)^T$, $(21111)^T$, ..., $(6)^T$. Find all Gray paths $\alpha_1, \ldots, \alpha_{p(n)}$ that are symmetrical in this way.

60. [*23*] Complete the proof of Theorem S by modifying the definitions of $L(m, n)$ and $M(m, n)$ in all places where $L(4, 6)$ is called in (62) and (63).

61. [*26*] Implement a partition-generation scheme based on Theorem S, always specifying the two parts that have changed between visits.

62. [*46*] Prove or disprove: For all sufficiently large integers n and $3 \leq m < n$ such that $n \bmod m \neq 0$, and for all partitions α of n with $a_1 \leq m$, there is a Gray path for all partitions with parts $\leq m$, beginning at 1^n and ending at α, unless $\alpha = 1^n$ or $\alpha = 21^{n-2}$.

63. [*47*] For which partitions λ and μ is there a Gray code through all partitions α such that $\lambda \preceq \alpha \preceq \mu$?

▶ **64.** [*32*] (*Binary partitions.*) Design a loopless algorithm that visits all partitions of n into powers of 2, where each step replaces $2^k + 2^k$ by 2^{k+1} or vice versa.

65. [*23*] It is well known that every commutative group of m elements can be represented as a discrete torus $T(m_1, \ldots, m_n)$ with the addition operation of 7.2.1.3–(66), where $m = m_1 \ldots m_n$ and m_j is a multiple of m_{j+1} for $1 \leq j < n$. For example, when $m = 360 = 2^3 \cdot 3^2 \cdot 5^1$ there are six such groups, corresponding to the factorizations $(m_1, m_2, m_3) = (30, 6, 2)$, $(60, 6, 1)$, $(90, 2, 2)$, $(120, 3, 1)$, $(180, 2, 1)$, and $(360, 1, 1)$.

Explain how to generate all such factorizations systematically with an algorithm that changes exactly two of the factors m_j at each step.

▶ **66.** [*M25*] (*P-partitions.*) Instead of insisting that $a_1 \geq a_2 \geq \cdots$, suppose we want to consider all nonnegative compositions of n that satisfy a given *partial* order. For example, P. A. MacMahon observed that all solutions to the "up-down" inequalities $a_4 \leq a_2 \geq a_3 \leq a_1$ can be divided into five nonoverlapping types:

$$a_1 \geq a_2 \geq a_3 \geq a_4; \quad a_1 \geq a_2 \geq a_4 > a_3;$$

$$a_2 > a_1 \geq a_3 \geq a_4; \quad a_2 > a_1 \geq a_4 > a_3; \quad a_2 \geq a_4 > a_1 \geq a_3.$$

Each of these types is easily enumerated since, for example, $a_2 > a_1 \geq a_4 > a_3$ is equivalent to $a_2 - 2 \geq a_1 - 1 \geq a_4 - 1 \geq a_3$; the number of solutions with $a_3 \geq 0$ and $a_1 + a_2 + a_3 + a_4 = n$ is the number of partitions of $n - 1 - 2 - 0 - 1$ into at most four parts.

Explain how to solve a general problem of this kind: Given any partial order relation $\prec$ on m elements, consider all m-tuples $a_1 \ldots a_m$ with the property that $a_j \geq a_k$

when $j \prec k$. Assuming that the subscripts have been chosen so that $j \prec k$ implies $j \leq k$, show that all of the desired m-tuples fall into exactly N classes, one for each of the outputs of the topological sorting algorithm 7.2.1.2V. What is the generating function for all such $a_1 \ldots a_m$ that are nonnegative and sum to n? How could you generate them all?

67. [*M25*] (P. A. MacMahon, 1886.) A *perfect partition* of n is a multiset that has exactly $n+1$ submultisets, and these multisets are partitions of the integers $0, 1, \ldots, n$. For example, the multisets $\{1,1,1,1,1\}$, $\{2,2,1\}$, and $\{3,1,1\}$ are perfect partitions of 5.
   Explain how to construct the perfect partitions of n that have fewest elements.

68. [*M23*] What partition of n into m parts has the largest product $a_1 \ldots a_m$, when (a) m is given; (b) m is arbitrary?

69. [*M30*] Find all $n < 10^9$ such that the equation $x_1 + x_2 + \cdots + x_n = x_1 x_2 \ldots x_n$ has only one solution in positive integers $x_1 \geq x_2 \geq \cdots \geq x_n$. (There is, for example, only one solution when $n = 2$, 3, or 4; but $5 + 2 + 1 + 1 + 1 = 5 \cdot 2 \cdot 1 \cdot 1 \cdot 1$ and $3 + 3 + 1 + 1 + 1 = 3 \cdot 3 \cdot 1 \cdot 1 \cdot 1$ and $2 + 2 + 2 + 1 + 1 = 2 \cdot 2 \cdot 2 \cdot 1 \cdot 1$.)

70. [*M30*] ("Bulgarian solitaire.") Take n cards and divide them arbitrarily into one or more piles. Then repeatedly remove one card from each pile and form a new pile.
   Show that if $n = 1 + 2 + \cdots + m$, this process always reaches a self-repeating state with piles of sizes $\{m, m-1, \ldots, 1\}$. For example, if $n = 10$ and if we start with piles whose sizes are $\{3, 3, 2, 2\}$, we get the sequence of partitions

$$3322 \rightarrow 42211 \rightarrow 5311 \rightarrow 442 \rightarrow 3331 \rightarrow 4222 \rightarrow 43111 \rightarrow 532 \rightarrow 4321 \rightarrow 4321 \rightarrow \cdots.$$

What cycles of states are possible for other values of n?

71. [*M46*] Continuing the previous problem, what is the maximum number of steps that can occur before n-card Bulgarian solitaire reaches a cyclic state?

72. [*M25*] Suppose we write down all partitions of n, for example

$$6, \; 51, \; 42, \; 411, \; 33, \; 321, \; 3111, \; 222, \; 2211, \; 21111, \; 111111$$

when $n = 6$, and change each jth occurrence of k to j:

$$1, \; 11, \; 11, \; 112, \; 12, \; 111, \; 1123, \; 123, \; 1212, \; 11234, \; 123456.$$

a) Prove that this operation yields a permutation of the individual elements.
b) How many times does the element k appear altogether?

7.2.1.5. Generating all set partitions.

Now let's shift gears and concentrate on a rather different kind of partition. The *partitions of a set* are the ways to regard that set as a union of nonempty, disjoint subsets called *blocks*. For example, we listed the five essentially different partitions of $\{1, 2, 3\}$ at the beginning of the previous section, in 7.2.1.4–(2) and 7.2.1.4–(4). Those five partitions can also be written more compactly in the form

$$123, \quad 12|3, \quad 13|2, \quad 1|23, \quad 1|2|3, \tag{1}$$

using a vertical line to separate one block from another. In this list the elements of each block could have been written in any order, and so could the blocks themselves, because '13|2' and '31|2' and '2|13' and '2|31' all represent the same partition. But we can standardize the representation by agreeing, for example, to list the elements of each block in increasing order, and to arrange the blocks in increasing order of their smallest elements. With this convention the partitions of $\{1, 2, 3, 4\}$ are

$$1234, \; 123|4, \; 124|3, \; 12|34, \; 12|3|4, \; 134|2, \; 13|24, \; 13|2|4,$$
$$14|23, \; 1|234, \; 1|23|4, \; 14|2|3, \; 1|24|3, \; 1|2|34, \; 1|2|3|4, \tag{2}$$

obtained by placing 4 among the blocks of (1) in all possible ways.

Set partitions arise in many different contexts. Political scientists and economists, for example, often see them as "coalitions"; computer system designers may consider them to be "cache-hit patterns" for memory accesses; poets know them as "rhyme schemes" (see exercises 34–37). We saw in Section 2.3.3 that any *equivalence relation* between objects — namely any binary relation that is reflexive, symmetric, and transitive — defines a partition of those objects into so-called "equivalence classes." Conversely, every set partition defines an equivalence relation: If Π is a partition of $\{1, 2, \ldots, n\}$ we can write

$$j \equiv k \quad (\text{modulo } \Pi) \tag{3}$$

whenever j and k belong to the same block of Π.

One of the most convenient ways to represent a set partition inside a computer is to encode it as a *restricted growth string*, namely as a string $a_1 a_2 \ldots a_n$ in which we have

$$a_1 = 0 \quad \text{and} \quad a_{j+1} \leq 1 + \max(a_1, \ldots, a_j) \text{ for } 1 \leq j < n. \tag{4}$$

The idea is to set $a_j = a_k$ if and only if $j \equiv k$, and to choose the smallest available number for a_j whenever j is smallest in its block. For example, the restricted growth strings for the fifteen partitions in (2) are respectively

$$0000, \; 0001, \; 0010, \; 0011, \; 0012, \; 0100, \; 0101, \; 0102,$$
$$0110, \; 0111, \; 0112, \; 0120, \; 0121, \; 0122, \; 0123. \tag{5}$$

This convention suggests the following simple generation scheme, due to George Hutchinson [*CACM* **6** (1963), 613–614]:

Algorithm H (*Restricted growth strings in lexicographic order*). Given $n \geq 2$, this algorithm generates all partitions of $\{1, 2, \ldots, n\}$ by visiting all strings $a_1 a_2 \ldots a_n$ that satisfy the restricted growth condition (4). We maintain an auxiliary array $b_1 b_2 \ldots b_n$, where $b_{j+1} = 1 + \max(a_1, \ldots, a_j)$; the value of b_n is actually kept in a separate variable, m, for efficiency.

H1. [Initialize.] Set $a_1 \ldots a_n \leftarrow 0 \ldots 0$, $b_1 \ldots b_{n-1} \leftarrow 1 \ldots 1$, and $m \leftarrow 1$.

H2. [Visit.] Visit the restricted growth string $a_1 \ldots a_n$, which represents a partition into $m + [a_n = m]$ blocks. Then go to H4 if $a_n = m$.

H3. [Increase a_n.] Set $a_n \leftarrow a_n + 1$ and return to H2.

H4. [Find j.] Set $j \leftarrow n - 1$; then, while $a_j = b_j$, set $j \leftarrow j - 1$.

H5. [Increase a_j.] Terminate if $j = 1$. Otherwise set $a_j \leftarrow a_j + 1$.

H6. [Zero out $a_{j+1} \ldots a_n$.] Set $m \leftarrow b_j + [a_j = b_j]$ and $j \leftarrow j + 1$. Then, while $j < n$, set $a_j \leftarrow 0$, $b_j \leftarrow m$, and $j \leftarrow j + 1$. Finally set $a_n \leftarrow 0$ and go back to H2. ∎

Exercise 47 proves that steps H4–H6 are rarely necessary, and that the loops in H4 and H6 are almost always short. A linked-list variant of this algorithm appears in exercise 2.

Gray codes for set partitions. One way to pass quickly through all set partitions is to change just one digit of the restricted growth string $a_1 \ldots a_n$ at each step, because a change to a_j simply means that element j moves from one block to another. An elegant way to arrange such a list was proposed by Gideon Ehrlich [*JACM* **20** (1973), 507–508]: We can successively append the digits

$$0, \ m, \ m-1, \ \ldots, \ 1 \qquad \text{or} \qquad 1, \ \ldots, \ m-1, \ m, \ 0 \qquad (6)$$

to each string $a_1 \ldots a_{n-1}$ in the list for partitions of $n - 1$ elements, where $m = 1 + \max(a_1, \ldots, a_{n-1})$, alternating between the two cases. Thus the list '00, 01' for $n = 2$ becomes '000, 001, 011, 012, 010' for $n = 3$; and that list becomes

$$\begin{aligned}
&0000, \ 0001, \ 0011, \ 0012, \ 0010, \ 0110, \ 0112, \ 0111, \\
&\quad 0121, \ 0122, \ 0123, \ 0120, \ 0100, \ 0102, \ 0101
\end{aligned} \qquad (7)$$

when we extend it to the case $n = 4$. Exercise 14 shows that Ehrlich's scheme leads to a simple algorithm that achieves this Gray-code order without doing much more work than Algorithm H.

Suppose, however, that we aren't interested in *all* of the partitions; we might want only the ones that have exactly m blocks. Can we run through this smaller collection of restricted growth strings, still changing only one digit at a time? Yes; a very pretty way to generate such a list has been discovered by Frank Ruskey [*Lecture Notes in Comp. Sci.* **762** (1993), 205–206]. He defined two such sequences, A_{mn} and A'_{mn}, both of which start with the lexicographically smallest m-block string $0^{n-m}01\ldots(m-1)$. The difference between them, if $n > m + 1$, is that A_{mn} ends with $01\ldots(m-1)0^{n-m}$ while A'_{mn} ends with $0^{n-m-1}01\ldots(m-1)0$. Here are Ruskey's recursive rules, when $1 < m < n$:

$$A_{m(n+1)} = \begin{cases} A_{(m-1)n}(m-1), A_{mn}^R(m-1), \ldots, A_{mn}^R 1, A_{mn} 0, & \text{if } m \text{ is even;} \\ A'_{(m-1)n}(m-1), A_{mn}(m-1), \ldots, A_{mn}^R 1, A_{mn} 0, & \text{if } m \text{ is odd;} \end{cases} \qquad (8)$$

$$A'_{m(n+1)} = \begin{cases} A'_{(m-1)n}(m-1), A_{mn}(m-1), \ldots, A_{mn} 1, A_{mn}^R 0, & \text{if } m \text{ is even;} \\ A_{(m-1)n}(m-1), A_{mn}^R(m-1), \ldots, A_{mn} 1, A_{mn}^R 0, & \text{if } m \text{ is odd.} \end{cases} \qquad (9)$$

Of course the base cases are simply one-element lists,

$$A_{1n} = A'_{1n} = \{0^n\} \qquad \text{and} \qquad A_{nn} = \{01\ldots(n-1)\}. \qquad (10)$$

With these definitions the $\{^5_3\} = 25$ partitions of $\{1,2,3,4,5\}$ into three blocks are

$$00012,\ 00112,\ 01112,\ 01012,\ 01002,\ 01102,\ 00102,$$
$$00122,\ 01122,\ 01022,\ 01222,\ 01212,\ 01202,$$
$$01201,\ 01211,\ 01221,\ 01021,\ 01121,\ 00121,$$
$$00120,\ 01120,\ 01020,\ 01220,\ 01210,\ 01200. \tag{11}$$

(See exercise 17 for an efficient implementation.)

In Ehrlich's scheme (7) the rightmost digits of $a_1 \ldots a_n$ vary most rapidly, but in Ruskey's scheme most of the changes occur near the left. In both cases, however, each step affects just one digit a_j, and the changes are quite simple: Either a_j changes by ± 1, or it jumps between the two extreme values 0 and $1 + \max(a_1, \ldots, a_{j-1})$. Under the same constraints, the sequence A'_{1n}, A'_{2n}, $\ldots$, A'_{nn} runs through *all* partitions, in increasing order of the number of blocks.

The number of set partitions. We've seen that there are 5 partitions of $\{1,2,3\}$ and 15 of $\{1,2,3,4\}$. A quick way to compute these counts was discovered by C. S. Peirce, who presented the following triangle of numbers in the *American Journal of Mathematics* **3** (1880), page 48:

$$
\begin{array}{cccccc}
1 \\
2 & 1 \\
5 & 3 & 2 \\
15 & 10 & 7 & 5 \\
52 & 37 & 27 & 20 & 15 \\
203 & 151 & 114 & 87 & 67 & 52
\end{array}
\tag{12}
$$

Here the entries ϖ_{n1}, ϖ_{n2}, $\ldots$, ϖ_{nn} of the nth row obey the simple recurrence

$$\varpi_{nk} = \varpi_{(n-1)k} + \varpi_{n(k+1)} \text{ if } 1 \le k < n; \qquad \varpi_{nn} = \varpi_{(n-1)1} \text{ if } n > 1; \tag{13}$$

and $\varpi_{11} = 1$. Peirce's triangle has many remarkable properties, some of which are surveyed in exercises 26–31. For example, ϖ_{nk} is the number of partitions of $\{1, 2, \ldots, n\}$ in which k is the smallest of its block.

The entries on the diagonal and in the first column of Peirce's triangle, which tell us the total number of set partitions, are commonly known as *Bell numbers*, because E. T. Bell wrote several influential papers about them [*AMM* **41** (1934), 411–419; *Annals of Math.* **35** (1934), 258–277; **39** (1938), 539–557]. We shall denote Bell numbers by ϖ_n, following the lead of Louis Comtet, in order to avoid confusion with the Bernoulli numbers B_n. The first few cases are

$$
\begin{array}{llllllllllll}
n = & 0 & 1 & 2 & 3 & 4 & 5 & 6 & 7 & 8 & 9 & 10 & 11 & 12 \\
\varpi_n = & 1 & 1 & 2 & 5 & 15 & 52 & 203 & 877 & 4140 & 21147 & 115975 & 678570 & 4213597
\end{array}
$$

Notice that this sequence grows rapidly, but not as fast as $n!$; we will prove below that $\varpi_n = \Theta(n/\log n)^n$.

The Bell numbers $\varpi_n = \varpi_{n1}$ for $n \ge 0$ must satisfy the recurrence formula

$$\varpi_{n+1} = \varpi_n + \binom{n}{1}\varpi_{n-1} + \binom{n}{2}\varpi_{n-2} + \cdots = \sum_k \binom{n}{k}\varpi_{n-k}, \tag{14}$$

because every partition of $\{1, \ldots, n+1\}$ is obtained by choosing k elements of $\{1, \ldots, n\}$ to put in the block containing $n+1$ and by partitioning the remaining elements in ϖ_{n-k} ways, for some k. This recurrence, found by Yoshisuke Matsunaga in the 18th century (see Section 7.2.1.7), leads to a nice generating function,

$$\Pi(z) = \sum_{n=0}^{\infty} \varpi_n \frac{z^n}{n!} = e^{e^z - 1}, \qquad (15)$$

discovered by W. A. Whitworth [*Choice and Chance*, 3rd edition (1878), 3.XXIV]. For if we multiply both sides of (14) by $z^n/n!$ and sum on n we get

$$\Pi'(z) = \sum_{n=0}^{\infty} \varpi_{n+1} \frac{z^n}{n!} = \left(\sum_{k=0}^{\infty} \frac{z^k}{k!}\right)\left(\sum_{m=0}^{\infty} \varpi_m \frac{z^m}{m!}\right) = e^z \Pi(z),$$

and (15) is the solution to this differential equation with $\Pi(0) = 1$.

The numbers ϖ_n had been studied for many years because of their curious properties related to this formula, long before Whitworth pointed out their combinatorial connection with set partitions. For example, we have

$$\varpi_n = \frac{n!}{e} [z^n] e^{e^z} = \frac{n!}{e} [z^n] \sum_{k=0}^{\infty} \frac{e^{kz}}{k!} = \frac{1}{e} \sum_{k=0}^{\infty} \frac{k^n}{k!} \qquad (16)$$

[*Mat. Sbornik* **3** (1868), 62; **4** (1869), 39; G. Dobiński, *Archiv der Math. und Physik* **61** (1877), 333–336; **63** (1879), 108–110]. Christian Kramp discussed the expansion of e^{e^z} in *Der polynomische Lehrsatz*, ed. by C. F. Hindenburg (Leipzig: 1796), 112–113; he mentioned two ways to compute the coefficients, namely either to use (14) or to use a summation of $p(n)$ terms, one for each ordinary partition of n. (See Arbogast's formula, exercise 1.2.5–21. Kramp, who came close to discovering that formula, seemed to prefer his partition-based method, not realizing that it would require more than polynomial time as n got larger and larger; and he computed 116015, not 115975, for the coefficient of z^{10}.)

*Asymptotic estimates. We can learn how fast ϖ_n grows by using one of the most basic principles of complex residue theory: If the power series $\sum_{k=0}^{\infty} a_k z^k$ converges whenever $|z| < r$, then

$$a_{n-1} = \frac{1}{2\pi i} \oint \frac{a_0 + a_1 z + a_2 z^2 + \cdots}{z^n} \, dz, \qquad (17)$$

if the integral is taken along a simple closed path that goes counterclockwise around the origin and stays inside the circle $|z| = r$. Let $f(z) = \sum_{k=0}^{\infty} a_k z^{k-n}$ be the integrand. We're free to choose any such path, but special techniques often apply when the path goes through a point z_0 at which the derivative $f'(z_0)$ is zero, because we have

$$f(z_0 + \epsilon e^{i\theta}) = f(z_0) + \frac{f''(z_0)}{2} \epsilon^2 e^{2i\theta} + O(\epsilon^3) \qquad (18)$$

in the vicinity of such a point. If, for example, $f(z_0)$ and $f''(z_0)$ are real and positive, say $f(z_0) = u$ and $f''(z_0) = 2v$, this formula says that the value of

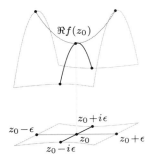

Fig. 33. The behavior of an analytic function near a saddle point.

$f(z_0 \pm \epsilon)$ is approximately $u + v\epsilon^2$ while $f(z_0 \pm i\epsilon)$ is approximately $u - v\epsilon^2$. If z moves from $z_0 - i\epsilon$ to $z_0 + i\epsilon$, the value of $f(z)$ rises to a maximum value u, then falls again; but the larger value $u + v\epsilon^2$ occurs both to the left and to the right of this path. In other words, a mountaineer who goes hiking on the complex plane, when the altitude at point z is $\Re f(z)$, encounters a "pass" at z_0; the terrain looks like a saddle at that point. The overall integral of $f(z)$ will be the same if taken around any path, but a path that doesn't go through the pass won't be as nice because it will have to cancel out some higher values of $f(z)$ that could have been avoided. Therefore we tend to get best results by choosing a path that goes through z_0, in the direction of increasing imaginary part. This important technique, due to P. Debye [*Math. Annalen* **67** (1909), 535–558], is called the "saddle point method."

Let's get familiar with the saddle point method by starting with an example for which we already know the answer:

$$\frac{1}{(n-1)!} = \frac{1}{2\pi i} \oint \frac{e^z}{z^n} \, dz. \tag{19}$$

Our goal is to find a good approximation for the value of the integral on the right when n is large. It will be convenient to deal with $f(z) = e^z/z^n$ by writing it as $e^{g(z)}$ where $g(z) = z - n \ln z$; then the saddle point occurs where $g'(z_0) = 1 - n/z_0$ is zero, namely at $z_0 = n$. If $z = n + it$ we have

$$g(z) = g(n) + \sum_{k=2}^{\infty} \frac{g^{(k)}(n)}{k!} (it)^k$$

$$= n - n \ln n - \frac{t^2}{2n} + \frac{it^3}{3n^2} + \frac{t^4}{4n^3} - \frac{it^5}{5n^4} + \cdots$$

because $g^{(k)}(z) = (-1)^k (k-1)! \, n/z^k$ when $k \geq 2$. Let's integrate $f(z)$ on a rectangular path from $n - im$ to $n + im$ to $-n + im$ to $-n - im$ to $n - im$:

$$\frac{1}{2\pi i} \oint \frac{e^z}{z^n} \, dz = \frac{1}{2\pi} \int_{-m}^{m} f(n + it) \, dt + \frac{1}{2\pi i} \int_{n}^{-n} f(t + im) \, dt$$

$$+ \frac{1}{2\pi} \int_{m}^{-m} f(-n + it) \, dt + \frac{1}{2\pi i} \int_{-n}^{n} f(t - im) \, dt.$$

Clearly $|f(z)| \le 2^{-n} f(n)$ on the last three sides of this path if we choose $m = 2n$, because $|e^z| = e^{\Re z}$ and $|z| \ge \max(\Re z, \Im z)$; so we're left with

$$\frac{1}{2\pi i} \oint \frac{e^z}{z^n}\, dz = \frac{1}{2\pi} \int_{-m}^{m} e^{g(n+it)}\, dt + O\left(\frac{ne^n}{2^n n^n}\right).$$

Now we fall back on a technique that we've used several times before — for example to derive Eq. 5.1.4–(53): If $\hat{f}(t)$ is a good approximation to $f(t)$ when $t \in A$, and if the sums $\sum_{t \in B \setminus A} f(t)$ and $\sum_{t \in C \setminus A} \hat{f}(t)$ are both small, then $\sum_{t \in C} \hat{f}(t)$ is a good approximation to $\sum_{t \in B} f(t)$. The same idea applies to integrals as well as sums. [This general method, introduced by Laplace in 1782, is often called "trading tails"; see *CMath* §9.4.] If $|t| \le n^{1/2+\epsilon}$ we have

$$e^{g(n+it)} = \exp\left(g(n) - \frac{t^2}{2n} + \frac{it^3}{3n^2} + \cdots\right)$$

$$= \frac{e^n}{n^n} \exp\left(-\frac{t^2}{2n} + \frac{it^3}{3n^2} + \frac{t^4}{4n^3} + O(n^{5\epsilon-3/2})\right)$$

$$= \frac{e^n}{n^n} e^{-t^2/(2n)}\left(1 + \frac{it^3}{3n^2} + \frac{t^4}{4n^3} - \frac{t^6}{18n^4} + O(n^{9\epsilon-3/2})\right).$$

And when $|t| > n^{1/2+\epsilon}$ we have

$$|e^{g(n+it)}| < |f(n + in^{1/2+\epsilon})| = \frac{e^n}{n^n} \exp\left(-\frac{n}{2}\ln(1 + n^{2\epsilon-1})\right) = O\left(\frac{e^{n-n^{-2\epsilon}/2}}{n^n}\right).$$

Furthermore the incomplete gamma function

$$\int_{n^{1/2+\epsilon}}^{\infty} e^{-t^2/(2n)} t^k\, dt = 2^{(k-1)/2} n^{(k+1)/2}\, \Gamma\left(\frac{k+1}{2}, \frac{n^{2\epsilon}}{2}\right) = O(n^{O(1)} e^{-n^{2\epsilon}/2})$$

is negligible. Thus we can trade tails and obtain the approximation

$$\frac{1}{2\pi i} \oint \frac{e^z}{z^n}\, dz = \frac{e^n}{2\pi n^n} \int_{-\infty}^{\infty} e^{-t^2/(2n)}\left(1 + \frac{it^3}{3n^2} + \frac{t^4}{4n^3} - \frac{t^6}{18n^4} + O(n^{9\epsilon-3/2})\right) dt$$

$$= \frac{e^n}{2\pi n^n}\left(I_0 + \frac{i}{3n^2} I_3 + \frac{1}{4n^3} I_4 - \frac{1}{18n^4} I_6 + O(n^{9\epsilon-3/2})\right),$$

where $I_k = \int_{-\infty}^{\infty} e^{-t^2/(2n)} t^k\, dt$. Of course $I_k = 0$ when k is odd. Otherwise we can evaluate I_k by using the well-known fact that

$$\int_{-\infty}^{\infty} e^{-at^2} t^{2l}\, dt = \frac{\Gamma\big((2l+1)/2\big)}{a^{(2l+1)/2}} = \frac{\sqrt{2\pi}}{(2a)^{(2l+1)/2}} \prod_{j=1}^{l} (2j-1) \qquad (20)$$

when $a > 0$; see exercise 39. Putting everything together gives us, for all $\epsilon > 0$, the asymptotic estimate

$$\frac{1}{(n-1)!} = \frac{e^n}{\sqrt{2\pi}\, n^{n-1/2}}\left(1 + 0 + \frac{3}{4n} - \frac{15}{18n} + O(n^{9\epsilon-3/2})\right); \qquad (21)$$

this result agrees perfectly with Stirling's approximation, which we derived by quite different methods in 1.2.11.2–(19). Further terms in the expansion of

$g(n + it)$ would allow us to prove that the true error in (21) is only $O(n^{-2})$, because the same procedure yields an asymptotic series of the general form $e^n/(\sqrt{2\pi}n^{n-1/2})(1 + c_1/n + c_2/n^2 + \cdots + c_m/n^m + O(n^{-m-1}))$ for all m.

Our derivation of this result has glossed over an important technicality: The function $\ln z$ is not single-valued along the path of integration, because it grows by $2\pi i$ when we loop around the origin. Indeed, this fact underlies the basic mechanism that makes the residue theorem work. But our reasoning was valid because the ambiguity of the logarithm does not affect the integrand $f(z) = e^z/z^n$ when n is an integer. Furthermore, if n were not an integer, we could have adapted the argument and kept it rigorous by choosing to carry out the integral (19) along a path that starts at $-\infty$, circles the origin counterclockwise and returns to $-\infty$. That would have given us Hankel's integral for the gamma function, Eq. 1.2.5–(17); we could thereby have derived the asymptotic formula

$$\frac{1}{\Gamma(x)} = \frac{1}{2\pi i} \oint \frac{e^z}{z^x}\, dz = \frac{e^x}{\sqrt{2\pi}\, x^{x-1/2}}\left(1 - \frac{1}{12x} + O(x^{-2})\right), \qquad (22)$$

valid for all real x as $x \to \infty$.

So the saddle point method seems to work — although it isn't the simplest way to get this particular result. Let's apply it now to deduce the approximate size of the Bell numbers:

$$\frac{\varpi_{n-1}}{(n-1)!} = \frac{1}{2\pi i e} \oint e^{g(z)}\, dz, \qquad g(z) = e^z - n\ln z. \qquad (23)$$

A saddle point now occurs at the point $z_0 = \xi > 0$, where

$$\xi e^\xi = n. \qquad (24)$$

(We should actually write $\xi(n)$ to indicate that ξ depends on n; but that would clutter up the formulas below.) Let's assume for the moment that a little bird has told us the value of ξ. Then we want to integrate on a path where $z = \xi + it$, and we have

$$g(\xi + it) = e^\xi - n\left(\ln\xi - \frac{(it)^2}{2!}\frac{\xi + 1}{\xi^2} - \frac{(it)^3}{3!}\frac{\xi^2 - 2!}{\xi^3} - \frac{(it)^4}{4!}\frac{\xi^3 + 3!}{\xi^4} + \cdots\right).$$

By integrating on a suitable rectangular path, we can prove as above that the integral in (23) is well approximated by

$$\int_{-n^{\epsilon-1/2}}^{n^{\epsilon-1/2}} e^{g(\xi)-na_2t^2-nia_3t^3+na_4t^4+\cdots}\, dt, \qquad a_k = \frac{\xi^{k-1}+(-1)^k(k-1)!}{k!\,\xi^k}; \qquad (25)$$

see exercise 43. Noting that $a_k t^k$ is $O(n^{k\epsilon-k/2})$ inside this integral, we obtain an asymptotic expansion of the form

$$\varpi_{n-1} = \frac{e^{e^\xi-1}(n-1)!}{\xi^{n-1}\sqrt{2\pi n(\xi+1)}}\left(1 + \frac{b_1}{n} + \frac{b_2}{n^2} + \cdots + \frac{b_m}{n^m} + O\left(\frac{\log n}{n}\right)^{m+1}\right), \qquad (26)$$

where $(\xi + 1)^{3k}b_k$ is a polynomial of degree $4k$ in ξ. (See exercise 44.) For example,

$$b_1 = -\frac{2\xi^4 - 3\xi^3 - 20\xi^2 - 18\xi + 2}{24(\xi+1)^3};\qquad(27)$$

$$b_2 = \frac{4\xi^8 - 156\xi^7 - 695\xi^6 - 696\xi^5 + 1092\xi^4 + 2916\xi^3 + 1972\xi^2 - 72\xi + 4}{1152(\xi+1)^6}.\qquad(28)$$

Stirling's approximation (21) can be used in (26) to prove that

$$\varpi_{n-1} = \exp\left(n\left(\xi - 1 + \frac{1}{\xi}\right) - \xi - \frac{1}{2}\ln(\xi+1) - 1 - \frac{\xi}{12n} + O\left(\frac{\log n}{n}\right)^2\right);\quad(29)$$

and exercise 45 proves the similar formula

$$\varpi_n = \exp\left(n\left(\xi - 1 + \frac{1}{\xi}\right) - \frac{1}{2}\ln(\xi+1) - 1 - \frac{\xi}{12n} + O\left(\frac{\log n}{n}\right)^2\right).\qquad(30)$$

Consequently we have $\varpi_n/\varpi_{n-1} \approx e^\xi = n/\xi$. More precisely,

$$\frac{\varpi_{n-1}}{\varpi_n} = \frac{\xi}{n}\left(1 + O\left(\frac{1}{n}\right)\right).\qquad(31)$$

But what is the asymptotic value of ξ? The definition (24) implies that

$$\xi = \ln n - \ln\xi = \ln n - \ln(\ln n - \ln\xi)$$

$$= \ln n - \ln\ln n + O\left(\frac{\log\log n}{\log n}\right);\qquad(32)$$

and we can go on in this vein, as shown in exercise 49. But the asymptotic series for ξ developed in this way never gives better accuracy than $O(1/(\log n)^m)$ for larger and larger m; so it is hugely inaccurate when multiplied by n in formula (29) for ϖ_{n-1} or formula (30) for ϖ_n.

Thus if we want to use (29) or (30) to calculate good numerical approximations to Bell numbers, our best strategy is to start by computing a good numerical value for ξ, without using a slowly convergent series. Newton's rootfinding method, discussed in the remarks preceding Algorithm 4.7N, yields the efficient iterative scheme

$$\xi_0 = \ln n,\qquad \xi_{k+1} = \frac{\xi_k}{\xi_k + 1}(1 + \xi_0 - \ln\xi_k),\qquad(33)$$

which converges rapidly to the correct value. For example, when $n = 100$ the fifth iterate

$$\xi_5 = 3.38563\,01402\,90050\,18488\,82443\,64529\,72686\,74917-\qquad(34)$$

is already correct to 40 decimal places. Using this value in (29) gives us successive approximations

$$(1.6176088053\ldots, 1.6187421339\ldots, 1.6187065391\ldots, 1.6187060254\ldots) \times 10^{114}$$

when we take terms up to b_0, b_1, b_2, b_3 into account; the true value of ϖ_{99} is the 115-digit integer $16187060274460\ldots20741$.

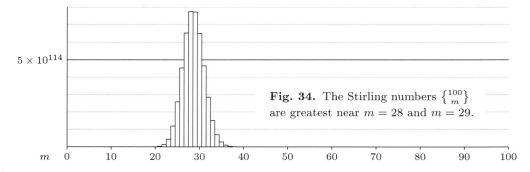

5×10^{114}

Fig. 34. The Stirling numbers $\left\{ {100 \atop m} \right\}$ are greatest near $m = 28$ and $m = 29$.

m 0   10   20   30   40   50   60   70   80   90   100

Now that we know the number of set partitions ϖ_n, let's try to figure out how many of them have exactly m blocks. It turns out that nearly all partitions of $\{1, \ldots, n\}$ have roughly $n/\xi = e^\xi$ blocks, with about ξ elements per block. For example, Fig. 34 shows a histogram of the numbers $\left\{ {n \atop m} \right\}$ when $n = 100$ and $e^\xi \approx 29.54$.

We can investigate the size of $\left\{ {n \atop m} \right\}$ by applying the saddle point method to formula 1.2.9–(23), which states that

$$\left\{ {n \atop m} \right\} = \frac{n!}{m!} [z^n] (e^z - 1)^m = \frac{n!}{m!} \frac{1}{2\pi i} \oint e^{m \ln(e^z - 1) - (n+1) \ln z} \, dz. \qquad (35)$$

Let $\alpha = (n+1)/m$. The function $g(z) = \alpha^{-1} \ln(e^z - 1) - \ln z$ has a saddle point at $\sigma > 0$ when

$$\frac{\sigma}{1 - e^{-\sigma}} = \alpha. \qquad (36)$$

Notice that $\alpha > 1$ for $1 \le m \le n$. This special value σ is given by

$$\sigma = \alpha - \beta, \qquad \beta = T(\alpha e^{-\alpha}), \qquad (37)$$

where T is the tree function of Eq. 2.3.4.4–(30). Indeed, β is the value between 0 and 1 for which we have

$$\beta e^{-\beta} = \alpha e^{-\alpha}; \qquad (38)$$

the function $x e^{-x}$ increases from 0 to e^{-1} when x increases from 0 to 1, then it decreases to 0 again. Therefore β is uniquely defined, and we have

$$e^\sigma = \frac{\alpha}{\beta}. \qquad (39)$$

All such pairs α and β are obtainable by using the inverse formulas

$$\alpha = \frac{\sigma e^\sigma}{e^\sigma - 1}, \qquad \beta = \frac{\sigma}{e^\sigma - 1}; \qquad (40)$$

for example, the values $\alpha = \ln 4$ and $\beta = \ln 2$ correspond to $\sigma = \ln 2$.

We can show as above that the integral in (35) is asymptotically equivalent to an integral of $e^{(n+1)g(z)} \, dz$ over the path $z = \sigma + it$. (See exercise 58.) Exercise 56 proves that the Taylor series about $z = \sigma$,

$$g(\sigma + it) = g(\sigma) - \frac{t^2(1 - \beta)}{2\sigma^2} - \sum_{k=3}^{\infty} \frac{(it)^k}{k!} g^{(k)}(\sigma), \qquad (41)$$

has the property that

$$|g^{(k)}(\sigma)| < 2(k-1)!\,(1-\beta)/\sigma^k \qquad \text{for all } k > 0. \qquad (42)$$

Therefore we can conveniently remove a factor of $N = (n+1)(1-\beta)$ from the power series $(n+1)g(z)$, and the saddle point method leads to the formula

$$\left\{ {n \atop m} \right\} = \frac{n!}{m!} \frac{1}{(\alpha - \beta)^{n-m}\beta^m \sqrt{2\pi N}} \left(1 + \frac{b_1}{N} + \frac{b_2}{N^2} + \cdots + \frac{b_l}{N^l} + O\left(\frac{1}{N^{l+1}}\right) \right) \quad (43)$$

as $N \to \infty$, where $(1 - \beta)^{2k} b_k$ is a polynomial in α and β. (The quantity $(\alpha - \beta)^{n-m}\beta^m$ in the denominator comes from the fact that $(e^\sigma - 1)^m/\sigma^n = (\alpha/\beta - 1)^m/(\alpha - \beta)^n$, by (37) and (39).) For example,

$$b_1 = \frac{6 - \beta^3 - 4\alpha\beta^2 - \alpha^2\beta}{8(1 - \beta)} - \frac{5(2 - \beta^2 - \alpha\beta)^2}{24(1 - \beta)^2}. \qquad (44)$$

Exercise 57 proves that $N \to \infty$ if and only if $n - m \to \infty$. An asymptotic expansion for $\left\{ {n \atop m} \right\}$ similar to (43), but somewhat more complicated, was first obtained by Leo Moser and Max Wyman, *Duke Math. J.* **25** (1957), 29–43.

Formula (43) looks a bit scary because it is designed to apply over the entire range of block counts m. Significant simplifications are possible when m is relatively small or relatively large (see exercises 60 and 61); but the simplified formulas don't give accurate results in the important cases when $\left\{ {n \atop m} \right\}$ is largest. Let's look at those crucial cases more closely now, so that we can account for the sharp peak illustrated in Fig. 34.

Let $\xi e^\xi = n$ as in (24), and suppose $m = \exp(\xi + r/\sqrt{n}) = ne^{r/\sqrt{n}}/\xi$; we will assume that $|r| \le n^\epsilon$, so that m is near e^ξ. The leading term of (43) can be rewritten

$$\frac{n!}{m!} \frac{1}{(\alpha - \beta)^{n-m}\beta^m \sqrt{2\pi(n+1)(1-\beta)}} =$$

$$\frac{m^n}{m!} \frac{(n+1)!}{(n+1)^{n+1}} \frac{e^{n+1}}{\sqrt{2\pi(n+1)}} \left(1 - \frac{\beta}{\alpha}\right)^{m-n} \frac{e^{-\beta m}}{\sqrt{1-\beta}}, \qquad (45)$$

and Stirling's approximation for $(n+1)!$ is evidently ripe for cancellation in the midst of this expression. With the help of computer algebra we find

$$\frac{m^n}{m!} = \frac{1}{\sqrt{2\pi}} \exp\left(n\left(\xi - 1 + \frac{1}{\xi}\right) - \frac{1}{2}\left(\xi + r^2 + \frac{r^2}{\xi}\right) \right.$$

$$\left. - \left(\frac{r}{2} + \frac{r^3}{6} + \frac{r^3}{3\xi}\right)\frac{1}{\sqrt{n}} + O(n^{4\epsilon - 1}) \right);$$

and the relevant quantities related to α and β are

$$\frac{\beta}{\alpha} = \frac{\xi}{n} + \frac{r\xi^2}{n\sqrt{n}} + O(\xi^3 n^{2\epsilon-2});$$

$$e^{-\beta m} = \exp\left(-\xi - \frac{r\xi^2}{\sqrt{n}} + O(\xi^3 n^{2\epsilon-1})\right);$$

$$\left(1 - \frac{\beta}{\alpha}\right)^{m-n} = \exp\left(\xi - 1 + \frac{r(\xi^2 - \xi - 1)}{\sqrt{n}} + O(\xi^3 n^{2\epsilon-1})\right).$$

Therefore the overall result is

$$\left\{\genfrac{}{}{0pt}{}{n}{e^{\xi+r/\sqrt{n}}}\right\} = \frac{1}{\sqrt{2\pi}} \exp\left(n\left(\xi - 1 + \frac{1}{\xi}\right) - \frac{\xi}{2} - 1\right.$$
$$\left. - \frac{\xi+1}{2\xi}\left(r + \frac{3\xi(2\xi+3) + (\xi+2)r^2}{6(\xi+1)\sqrt{n}}\right)^2 + O(\xi^3 n^{4\epsilon-1})\right). \quad (46)$$

The squared expression on the last line is zero when

$$r = -\frac{\xi(2\xi+3)}{2(\xi+1)\sqrt{n}} + O(\xi^2 n^{-3/2});$$

thus the maximum occurs when the number of blocks is

$$m = \frac{n}{\xi} - \frac{3+2\xi}{2+2\xi} + O\left(\frac{\xi}{n}\right). \quad (47)$$

By comparing (47) to (30) we see that the largest Stirling number $\left\{\genfrac{}{}{0pt}{}{n}{m}\right\}$ for a given value of n is approximately equal to $\xi\varpi_n/\sqrt{2\pi n}$.

The saddle point method applies to problems that are considerably more difficult than the ones we have considered here. Excellent expositions of advanced techniques can be found in several books: N. G. de Bruijn, *Asymptotic Methods in Analysis* (1958), Chapters 5 and 6; F. W. J. Olver, *Asymptotics and Special Functions* (1974), Chapter 4; R. Wong, *Asymptotic Approximations of Integrals* (2001), Chapters 2 and 7.

Random set partitions. The sizes of blocks in a partition of $\{1, \ldots, n\}$ constitute by themselves an ordinary partition of the number n. Therefore we might wonder what sort of partition they are likely to be. Figure 30 in Section 7.2.1.4 showed the result of superimposing the Ferrers diagrams of all $p(25) = 1958$ partitions of 25; those partitions tended to follow the symmetrical curve of Eq. 7.2.1.4–(49). By contrast, Fig. 35 shows what happens when we superimpose the corresponding diagrams of all $\varpi_{25} \approx 4.6386 \times 10^{18}$ partitions of the set $\{1, \ldots, 25\}$. Evidently the "shape" of a random set partition is quite different from the shape of a random integer partition.

This change is due to the fact that some integer partitions occur only a few times as block sizes of set partitions, while others are extremely common. For example, the partition $n = 1 + 1 + \cdots + 1$ arises in only one way, but if n is

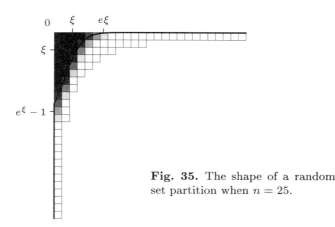

Fig. 35. The shape of a random set partition when $n = 25$.

even the partition $n = 2 + 2 + \cdots + 2$ arises in $(n-1)(n-3)\ldots(1)$ ways. When $n = 25$, the integer partition

$$25 = 4 + 4 + 3 + 3 + 3 + 2 + 2 + 2 + 1 + 1$$

actually occurs in more than 2% of all possible set partitions. (This particular partition turns out to be most common in the case $n = 25$. The answer to exercise 1.2.5–21 explains that exactly

$$\frac{n!}{c_1!\, 1!^{c_1}\, c_2!\, 2!^{c_2} \ldots c_n!\, n!^{c_n}} \tag{48}$$

set partitions correspond to the integer partition $n = c_1 \cdot 1 + c_2 \cdot 2 + \cdots + c_n \cdot n$.)

We can easily determine the average number of k-blocks in a random partition of $\{1, \ldots, n\}$: If we write out all ϖ_n of the possibilities, every particular k-element block occurs exactly ϖ_{n-k} times. Therefore the average number is

$$\binom{n}{k} \frac{\varpi_{n-k}}{\varpi_n}. \tag{49}$$

An extension of Eq. (31) above, proved in exercise 64, shows moreover that

$$\frac{\varpi_{n-k}}{\varpi_n} = \left(\frac{\xi}{n}\right)^k \left(1 + \frac{k\xi(k\xi + k + 1)}{2(\xi+1)^2 n} + O\left(\frac{k^3}{n^2}\right)\right) \qquad \text{if } k \leq n^{2/3}, \tag{50}$$

where ξ is defined in (24). Therefore if, say, $k \leq n^\epsilon$, formula (49) simplifies to

$$\frac{n^k}{k!} \left(\frac{\xi}{n}\right)^k \left(1 + O\left(\frac{1}{n}\right)\right) = \frac{\xi^k}{k!} \left(1 + O(n^{2\epsilon - 1})\right). \tag{51}$$

There are, on average, about ξ blocks of size 1, and $\xi^2/2!$ blocks of size 2, etc.

The variance of these quantities is small (see exercise 65), and it turns out that a random partition behaves essentially as if the number of k-blocks were a Poisson deviate with mean $\xi^k/k!$. The smooth curve shown in Fig. 35 runs through the points $(f(k), k)$ in Ferrers-like coordinates, where

$$f(k) = \xi^{k+1}/(k+1)! + \xi^{k+2}/(k+2)! + \xi^{k+3}/(k+3)! + \cdots \tag{52}$$

is the approximate distance from the top line corresponding to block size $k \geq 0$. (This curve becomes more nearly vertical when n is larger.)

The largest block tends to contain approximately $e\xi$ elements. Furthermore, the probability that the block containing element 1 has size less than $\xi + a\sqrt{\xi}$ approaches the probability that a normal deviate is less than a. [See John Haigh, *J. Combinatorial Theory* **A13** (1972), 287–295; V. N. Sachkov, *Probabilistic Methods in Combinatorial Analysis* (1997), Chapter 4, translated from a Russian book published in 1978; Yu. Yakubovich, *J. Mathematical Sciences* **87** (1997), 4124–4137, translated from a Russian paper published in 1995; B. Pittel, *J. Combinatorial Theory* **A79** (1997), 326–359.]

A nice way to generate random partitions of $\{1, 2, \ldots, n\}$ was introduced by A. J. Stam in the *Journal of Combinatorial Theory* **A35** (1983), 231–240: Let M be a random integer that takes the value m with probability

$$p_m = \frac{m^n}{e\,m!\,\varpi_n}; \tag{53}$$

these probabilities sum to 1 because of (16). Once M has been chosen, generate a random n-tuple $X_1 X_2 \ldots X_n$, where each X_j is uniformly and independently distributed between 0 and $M - 1$. Then let $i \equiv j$ in the partition if and only if $X_i = X_j$. This procedure works because each k-block partition is obtained with probability $\sum_{m \geq 0} (m^{\underline{k}}/m^n) p_m = 1/\varpi_n$.

For example, if $n = 25$ we have

$p_4 \approx .00000372$	$p_9 \approx .15689865$	$p_{14} \approx .04093663$	$p_{19} \approx .00006068$
$p_5 \approx .00019696$	$p_{10} \approx .21855285$	$p_{15} \approx .01531445$	$p_{20} \approx .00001094$
$p_6 \approx .00313161$	$p_{11} \approx .21526871$	$p_{16} \approx .00480507$	$p_{21} \approx .00000176$
$p_7 \approx .02110279$	$p_{12} \approx .15794784$	$p_{17} \approx .00128669$	$p_{22} \approx .00000026$
$p_8 \approx .07431024$	$p_{13} \approx .08987171$	$p_{18} \approx .00029839$	$p_{23} \approx .00000003$

and the other probabilities are negligible. So we can usually get a random partition of 25 elements by looking at a random 25-digit integer in radix 9, 10, 11, or 12. The number M can be generated using 3.4.1–(3); it tends to be approximately $n/\xi = e^\xi$ (see exercise 67).

*Partitions of a multiset. The partitions of an integer and the partitions of a set are just the extreme cases of a far more general problem, the partitions of a multiset. Indeed, the partitions of n are essentially the same as the partitions of $\{1, 1, \ldots, 1\}$, where there are n 1s.

From this standpoint there are essentially $p(n)$ different multisets with n elements. For example, five different cases of multiset partitions arise when $n = 4$:

$$1234,\ 123|4,\ 124|3,\ 12|34,\ 12|3|4,\ 134|2,\ 13|24,\ 13|2|4,$$
$$14|23,\ 14|2|3,\ 1|234,\ 1|23|4,\ 1|24|3,\ 1|2|34,\ 1|2|3|4;$$
$$1123,\ 112|3,\ 113|2,\ 11|23,\ 11|2|3,\ 123|1,\ 12|13,\ 12|1|3,\ 13|1|2,\ 1|1|23,\ 1|1|2|3;$$
$$1122,\ 112|2,\ 11|22,\ 11|2|2,\ 122|1,\ 12|12,\ 12|1|2,\ 1|1|22,\ 1|1|2|2;$$
$$1112,\ 111|2,\ 112|1,\ 11|12,\ 11|1|2,\ 12|1|1,\ 1|1|1|2;$$
$$1111,\ 111|1,\ 11|11,\ 11|1|1,\ 1|1|1|1. \tag{54}$$

When the multiset contains m distinct elements, with n_1 of one kind, n_2 of another, $\ldots$, and n_m of the last, we write $p(n_1, n_2, \ldots, n_m)$ for the total number of partitions. Thus the examples in (54) show that

$$p(1,1,1,1) = 15, \quad p(2,1,1) = 11, \quad p(2,2) = 9, \quad p(3,1) = 7, \quad p(4) = 5. \quad (55)$$

Partitions with $m = 2$ are often called "bipartitions"; those with $m = 3$ are "tripartitions"; and in general these combinatorial objects are known as *multi-partitions*. The study of multipartitions was inaugurated long ago by P. A. MacMahon [*Philosophical Transactions* **181** (1890), 481–536; **217** (1917), 81–113; *Proc. Cambridge Philos. Soc.* **22** (1925), 951–963]; but the subject is so vast that many unsolved problems remain. In the remainder of this section and in the exercises below we shall take a glimpse at some of the most interesting and instructive aspects of the theory that have been discovered so far.

In the first place it is important to notice that multipartitions are essentially the partitions of *vectors* with nonnegative integer components, namely the ways to decompose such a vector as a sum of such vectors. For example, the nine partitions of $\{1, 1, 2, 2\}$ listed in (54) are the same as the nine partitions of the bipartite column vector $\frac{2}{2}$, namely

$$\frac{2}{2}, \quad \frac{2\,0}{1\,1}, \quad \frac{2\,0}{0\,2}, \quad \frac{2\,0\,0}{0\,1\,1}, \quad \frac{1\,1}{2\,0}, \quad \frac{1\,1}{1\,1}, \quad \frac{1\,1\,0}{1\,0\,1}, \quad \frac{1\,1\,0}{0\,0\,2}, \quad \frac{1\,1\,0\,0}{0\,0\,1\,1}. \quad (56)$$

(We drop the + signs for brevity, as in the case of one-dimensional integer partitions.) Each partition can be written in canonical form if we list its parts in nonincreasing lexicographic order.

A simple algorithm suffices to generate the partitions of any given multiset. In the following procedure we represent partitions on a stack that contains triples of elements (c, u, v), where c denotes a component number, $u > 0$ denotes the yet-unpartitioned amount remaining in component c, and $v \le u$ denotes the c component of the current part. Triples are actually kept in three arrays $(c_0, c_1, \ldots)$, $(u_0, u_1, \ldots)$, and $(v_0, v_1, \ldots)$ for convenience, and a "stack frame" array $(f_0, f_1, \ldots)$ is also maintained so that the $(l+1)$st vector of the partition consists of elements f_l through $f_{l+1} - 1$ in the c, u, and v arrays. For example, the following arrays would represent the bipartition $\frac{3\,2\,2\,1\,1\,0\,0}{1\,2\,0\,1\,1\,3\,1}$:

j	0	1	2	3	4	5	6	7	8	9	10
c_j	1	2	1	2	1	1	2	1	2	2	2
u_j	9	9	6	8	4	2	6	1	5	4	1
v_j	3	1	2	2	2	1	1	1	1	3	1

$$f_0 = 0 \quad f_1 = 2 \quad f_2 = 4 \quad f_3 = 5 \quad f_4 = 7 \quad f_5 = 9 \quad f_6 = 10 \quad f_7 = 11 \quad (57)$$

Algorithm M (*Multipartitions in decreasing lexicographic order*). Given a multiset $\{n_1 \cdot 1, \ldots, n_m \cdot m\}$, this algorithm visits all of its partitions using arrays $f_0 f_1 \ldots f_n$, $c_0 c_1 \ldots c_n$, $u_0 u_1 \ldots u_n$, and $v_0 v_1 \ldots v_n$ as described above, where $n = n_1 + \cdots + n_m$. We assume that $m > 0$ and $n_1, \ldots, n_m > 0$.

M1. [Initialize.] Set $c_j \leftarrow j + 1$ and $u_j \leftarrow v_j \leftarrow n_{j+1}$ for $0 \leq j < m$; also set $f_0 \leftarrow a \leftarrow l \leftarrow 0$ and $f_1 \leftarrow b \leftarrow m$. (In the following steps, the current stack frame runs from a to $b - 1$, inclusive.)

M2. [Subtract v from u.] (At this point we want to find all partitions of the vector u in the current frame, into parts that are lexicographically $\leq v$. First we will use v itself.) Set $j \leftarrow a$ and $k \leftarrow b$. Then while $j < b$ do the following: Set $u_k \leftarrow u_j - v_j$, and if $u_k \geq v_j$ set $c_k \leftarrow c_j$, $v_k \leftarrow v_j$, $k \leftarrow k+1$, $j \leftarrow j + 1$. But if u_k is less than v_j after it has been decreased, the action changes: First set $c_k \leftarrow c_j$, $v_k \leftarrow u_k$, and $k \leftarrow k + 1$ if u_k was nonzero; then set $j \leftarrow j + 1$. While $j < b$, set $u_k \leftarrow u_j - v_j$, $c_k \leftarrow c_j$, $v_k \leftarrow u_k$, and $k \leftarrow k + 1$ if $u_j \neq v_j$; then again $j \leftarrow j + 1$, until $j = b$.

M3. [Push if nonzero.] If $k > b$, set $a \leftarrow b$, $b \leftarrow k$, $l \leftarrow l + 1$, $f_{l+1} \leftarrow b$, and return to M2.

M4. [Visit a partition.] Visit the partition represented by the $l + 1$ vectors currently in the stack. (For $0 \leq k \leq l$, the vector has v_j in component c_j, for $f_k \leq j < f_{k+1}$.)

M5. [Decrease v.] Set $j \leftarrow b - 1$, and if $v_j = 0$ set $j \leftarrow j - 1$ until $v_j > 0$. Then if $j = a$ and $v_j = 1$, go to M6. Otherwise set $v_j \leftarrow v_j - 1$, and $v_k \leftarrow u_k$ for $j < k < b$. Return to M2.

M6. [Backtrack.] Terminate if $l = 0$. Otherwise set $l \leftarrow l - 1$, $b \leftarrow a$, $a \leftarrow f_l$, and return to M5. ∎

The key to this algorithm is step M2, which decreases the current residual vector, u, by the largest permissible part, v; that step also decreases v, if necessary, to the lexicographically largest vector $\leq v$ that is less than or equal to the new residual amount in every component.

Let us conclude this section by discussing an amusing connection between multipartitions and the least-significant-digit-first procedure for radix sorting (Algorithm 5.2.5R). The idea is best understood by considering an example. See Table 1, where Step (0) shows nine 4-partite column vectors in lexicographic order. Serial numbers ①–⑨ have been attached at the bottom for identification. Step (1) performs a stable sort of the vectors, bringing their fourth (least significant) entries into decreasing order; similarly, Steps (2), (3), and (4) do a stable sort on the third, second, and top rows. The theory of radix sorting tells us that the original lexicographic order is thereby restored.

Suppose the serial number sequences after these stable sorting operations are respectively α_4, $\alpha_3\alpha_4$, $\alpha_2\alpha_3\alpha_4$, and $\alpha_1\alpha_2\alpha_3\alpha_4$, where the α's are permutations; Table 1 shows the values of α_4, α_3, α_2, and α_1 in parentheses. And now comes the point: Wherever the permutation α_j has a descent, the numbers in row j after sorting must also have a descent, because the sorting is stable. (These descents are indicated by caret marks in the table.) For example, where α_3 has 8 followed by 7, we have 5 followed by 3 in row 3. Therefore the entries $a_1 \ldots a_9$ in row 3 after Step (2) are not an arbitrary partition of their sum; they must satisfy

$$a_1 \geq a_2 \geq a_3 \geq a_4 > a_5 \geq a_6 > a_7 \geq a_8 \geq a_9. \tag{58}$$

Table 1

RADIX SORTING AND MULTIPARTITIONS

Step (0): Original partition	Step (1): Sort row 4	Step (2): Sort row 3
6 5 5 4 3 2 1 0 0	0 6 4 3 5 0 5 2 1	0 6 5 2 5 1 4 3 0
3 2 1 0 4 5 6 4 2	2 3 0 4 2 4 1 5 6	2 3 2 5 1 6 0 4 4
6 6 3 1 1 5 2 0 7	7 6 1 1 6 0 3 5 2	7 6 6 5$_\wedge$3 2$_\wedge$1 1 0
4 2 1 3 3 1 1 2 5	5$_\wedge$4 3 3$_\wedge$2 2$_\wedge$1 1 1	5 4 2 1 1 1 3 3 2
①②③④⑤⑥⑦⑧⑨	⑨①④⑤②⑧③⑥⑦	⑨①②⑥③⑦④⑤⑧

$$\alpha_4 = (\ 9_\wedge 1\ 4\ 5_\wedge 2\ 8_\wedge 3\ 6\ 7\ ) \qquad \alpha_3 = (\ 1\ 2\ 5\ 8_\wedge 7\ 9_\wedge 3\ 4\ 6\ )$$

Step (3): Sort row 2	Step (4): Sort row 1
1 2 3 0 6 0 5 5 4	6 5 5 4$_\wedge$3$_\wedge$2$_\wedge$1 0 0
6$_\wedge$5 4 4$_\wedge$3$_\wedge$2 2 1 0	3 2 1 0 4 5 6 4 2
2 5 1 0 6 7 6 3 1	6 6 3 1 1 5 2 0 7
1 1 3 2 4 5 2 1 3	4 2 1 3 3 1 1 2 5
⑦⑥⑤⑧①⑨②③④	①②③④⑤⑥⑦⑧⑨

$$\alpha_2 = (\ 6_\wedge 4\ 8\ 9_\wedge 2_\wedge 1\ 3\ 5\ 7\ ) \qquad \alpha_1 = (\ 5\ 7\ 8\ 9_\wedge 3_\wedge 2_\wedge 1\ 4\ 6\ )$$

But the numbers $(a_1-2,\ a_2-2,\ a_3-2,\ a_4-2,\ a_5-1,\ a_6-1,\ a_7,\ a_8,\ a_9)$ do form an essentially arbitrary partition of the original sum, minus $(4+6)$. The amount of decrease, $4 + 6$, is the sum of the indices where descents occur; this number is what we called ind α_3, the "index" of α_3, in Section 5.1.1.

Thus we see that any given partition of an m-partite number into at most r parts, with extra zeros added so that the number of columns is exactly r, can be encoded as a sequence of permutations $\alpha_1,\ \dots,\ \alpha_m$ of $\{1,\dots,r\}$ such that the product $\alpha_1 \dots \alpha_m$ is the identity, together with a sequence of ordinary one-dimensional partitions of the numbers $(n_1 - \text{ind}\,\alpha_1,\ \dots,\ n_m - \text{ind}\,\alpha_m)$ into at most r parts. For example, the vectors in Table 1 represent a partition of $(26, 27, 31, 22)$ into 9 parts; the permutations $\alpha_1,\ \dots,\ \alpha_4$ appear in the table, and we have $(\text{ind}\,\alpha_1,\dots,\text{ind}\,\alpha_4) = (15, 10, 10, 11)$; the partitions are respectively

$$26-15 = (322111100), \qquad 27-10 = (332222210),$$
$$31-10 = (544321110), \qquad 22-11 = (221111111).$$

Conversely, any such permutations and partitions will yield a multipartition of $(n_1, \dots, n_m)$. If r and m are small, it can be helpful to consider these $r!^{m-1}$ sequences of one-dimensional partitions when listing or reasoning about multipartitions, especially in the bipartite case. [This construction is due to Basil Gordon, *J. London Math. Soc.* **38** (1963), 459–464.]

A good summary of early work on multipartitions, including studies of partitions into distinct parts and/or strictly positive parts, appears in a paper by M. S. Cheema and T. S. Motzkin, *Proc. Symp. Pure Math.* **19** (Amer. Math. Soc., 1971), 39–70.

EXERCISES

1. [*20*] (G. Hutchinson.) Show that a simple modification to Algorithm H will generate all partitions of $\{1,\dots,n\}$ into *at most* r blocks, given n and $r \geq 2$.

▶ **2.** [*22*] When set partitions are used in practice, we often want to link the elements of each block together. Thus it is convenient to have an array of links $l_1 \ldots l_n$ and an array of headers $h_1 \ldots h_t$ so that the elements of the jth block of a t-block partition are $i_1 > \cdots > i_k$, where

$$i_1 = h_j, \quad i_2 = l_{i_1}, \quad \ldots, \quad i_k = l_{i_{k-1}}, \quad \text{and} \quad l_{i_k} = 0.$$

For example, the representation of $137|25|489|6$ would have $t = 4$, $l_1 \ldots l_9 = 001020348$, and $h_1 \ldots h_4 = 7596$.

Design a variant of Algorithm H that generates partitions using this representation.

3. [*M23*] What is the millionth partition of $\{1, \ldots, 12\}$ generated by Algorithm H?

▶ **4.** [*21*] If $x_1 \ldots x_n$ is any string, let $\rho(x_1 \ldots x_n)$ be the restricted growth string that corresponds to the equivalence relation $j \equiv k \iff x_j = x_k$. Classify each of the five-letter English words in the Stanford GraphBase by applying this ρ function; for example, $\rho(\text{tooth}) = 01102$. How many of the 52 set partitions of five elements are representable by English words in this way? What's the most common word of each type?

5. [*22*] Guess the next elements of the following two sequences: (a) 0, 1, 1, 1, 12, 12, 12, 12, 12, 12, 100, 121, 122, 123, 123, ...; (b) 0, 1, 12, 100, 112, 121, 122, 123, ...

▶ **6.** [*25*] Suggest an algorithm to generate all partitions of $\{1, \ldots, n\}$ in which there are exactly c_1 blocks of size 1, c_2 blocks of size 2, etc.

7. [*M20*] How many permutations $a_1 \ldots a_n$ of $\{1, \ldots, n\}$ have the property that $a_{k-1} > a_k > a_j$ implies $j > k$?

8. [*20*] Suggest a way to generate all permutations of $\{1, \ldots, n\}$ that have exactly m left-to-right minima.

9. [*M20*] How many restricted growth strings $a_1 \ldots a_n$ contain exactly k_j occurrences of j, given the integers $k_0, k_1, \ldots, k_{n-1}$?

10. [*25*] A *semilabeled tree* is an oriented tree in which the leaves are labeled with the integers $\{1, \ldots, k\}$, but the other nodes are unlabeled. Thus there are 15 semilabeled trees with 5 vertices:

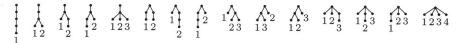

Find a one-to-one correspondence between partitions of $\{1, \ldots, n\}$ and semilabeled trees with $n + 1$ vertices.

▶ **11.** [*28*] We observed in Section 7.2.1.2 that Dudeney's famous problem $\text{send} + \text{more} = \text{money}$ is a "pure" alphametic, namely an alphametic with a unique solution. His puzzle corresponds to a set partition on 13 digit positions, for which the restricted growth string $\rho(\text{sendmoremoney})$ is 0123456145217; and we might wonder how lucky he had to be in order to come up with such a construction. How many restricted growth strings of length 13 define pure alphametics of the form $a_1a_2a_3a_4 + a_5a_6a_7a_8 = a_9a_{10}a_{11}a_{12}a_{13}$?

12. [*M31*] (*The partition lattice.*) If Π and Π' are partitions of the same set, we write $\Pi \preceq \Pi'$ if $x \equiv y$ (modulo Π) whenever $x \equiv y$ (modulo Π'). In other words, $\Pi \preceq \Pi'$ means that Π' is a "refinement" of Π, obtained by partitioning zero or more of the latter's blocks; and Π is a "crudification" or *coalescence* of Π', obtained by merging zero or more blocks together. This partial ordering is easily seen to be a lattice, with

$\Pi \vee \Pi'$ the greatest common refinement of Π and Π', and with $\Pi \wedge \Pi'$ their least common coalescence. For example, the lattice of partitions of $\{1, 2, 3, 4\}$ is

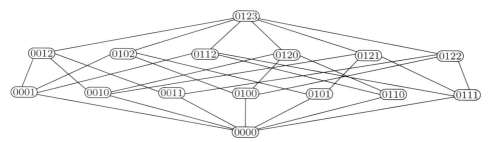

if we represent partitions by restricted growth strings $a_1 a_2 a_3 a_4$; upward paths in this diagram take each partition into its refinements. Partitions with t blocks appear on level t from the bottom, and their descendants form the partition lattice of $\{1, \ldots, t\}$.

a) Explain how to compute $\Pi \vee \Pi'$, given $a_1 \ldots a_n$ and $a'_1 \ldots a'_n$.

b) Explain how to compute $\Pi \wedge \Pi'$, given $a_1 \ldots a_n$ and $a'_1 \ldots a'_n$.

c) When does Π' cover Π in this lattice? (See exercise 7.2.1.4–55.)

d) If Π has t blocks of sizes $s_1, \ldots, s_t$, how many partitions does it cover?

e) If Π has t blocks of sizes $s_1, \ldots, s_t$, how many partitions cover it?

f) True or false: If $\Pi \vee \Pi'$ covers Π, then Π' covers $\Pi \wedge \Pi'$.

g) True or false: If Π' covers $\Pi \wedge \Pi'$, then $\Pi \vee \Pi'$ covers Π.

h) Let $b(\Pi)$ denote the number of blocks of Π. Prove that

$$b(\Pi) + b(\Pi') \leq b(\Pi \vee \Pi') + b(\Pi \wedge \Pi').$$

13. [*M28*] (Stephen C. Milne, 1977.) If A is a set of partitions of $\{1, \ldots, n\}$, its *shadow* ∂A is the set of all partitions Π' such that Π covers Π' for some $\Pi \in A$. (We considered the analogous concept for the subset lattice in 7.2.1.3–(54).)

Let $\Pi_1, \Pi_2, \ldots$ be the partitions of $\{1, \ldots, n\}$ into t blocks, in lexicographic order of their restricted growth strings; and let $\Pi'_1, \Pi'_2, \ldots$ be the $(t-1)$-block partitions, also in lexicographic order. Prove that there is a function $f_{nt}(N)$ such that

$$\partial\{\Pi_1, \ldots, \Pi_N\} = \{\Pi'_1, \ldots, \Pi'_{f_{nt}(N)}\} \qquad \text{for } 0 \leq N \leq \left\{ {n \atop t} \right\}.$$

Hint: The diagram in exercise 12 shows that $(f_{43}(0), \ldots, f_{43}(6)) = (0, 3, 5, 7, 7, 7, 7)$.

14. [*23*] Design an algorithm to generate set partitions in Gray-code order like (7).

15. [*M21*] What is the final partition generated by the algorithm of exercise 14?

16. [*16*] The list (11) is Ruskey's A_{35}; what is A'_{35}?

17. [*26*] Implement Ruskey's Gray code (8) for all m-block partitions of $\{1, \ldots, n\}$.

18. [*M46*] For which n is it possible to generate all restricted growth strings $a_1 \ldots a_n$ in such a way that some a_j changes by ± 1 at each step?

19. [*28*] Prove that there's a Gray code for restricted growth strings in which, at each step, some a_j changes by either ± 1 or ± 2, when (a) we want to generate all ϖ_n strings $a_1 \ldots a_n$; or (b) we want to generate only the $\left\{ {n \atop m} \right\}$ cases with $\max(a_1, \ldots, a_n) = m - 1$.

20. [*17*] If Π is a partition of $\{1, \ldots, n\}$, its conjugate Π^T is defined by the rule

$$ j \equiv k \quad (\text{modulo } \Pi^T) \qquad \Longleftrightarrow \qquad n + 1 - j \equiv n + 1 - k \quad (\text{modulo } \Pi). $$

Suppose Π has the restricted growth string 001010202013; what is the restricted growth string of Π^T?

21. [*M27*] How many partitions of $\{1, \ldots, n\}$ are self-conjugate?

22. [*M23*] If X is a random variable with a given distribution, the expected value of X^n is called the nth *moment* of that distribution. What is the nth moment when X is (a) a Poisson deviate with mean 1 (Eq. 3.4.1–(40))? (b) the number of fixed points of a random permutation of $\{1, \ldots, m\}$, when $m \geq n$ (Eq. 1.3.3–(27))?

23. [*HM30*] If $f(x) = \sum a_k x^k$ is a polynomial, let $f(\varpi)$ stand for $\sum a_k \varpi_k$.

a) Prove the symbolic formula $f(\varpi + 1) = \varpi f(\varpi)$. (For example, if $f(x)$ is the polynomial x^2, this formula states that $\varpi_2 + 2\varpi_1 + \varpi_0 = \varpi_3$.)

b) Similarly, prove that $f(\varpi + k) = \varpi^k f(\varpi)$ for all positive integers k.

c) If p is prime, prove that $\varpi_{n+p} \equiv \varpi_n + \varpi_{n+1}$ (modulo p). *Hint:* Show first that $x^{\underline{p}} \equiv x^p - x$.

d) Consequently $\varpi_{n+N} \equiv \varpi_n$ (modulo p) when $N = p^{p-1} + p^{p-2} + \cdots + p + 1$.

24. [*HM35*] Continuing the previous exercise, prove that the Bell numbers satisfy the periodic law $\varpi_{n+p^{e-1}N} \equiv \varpi_n$ (modulo p^e), if p is an odd prime. *Hint:* Show that

$$ x^{\underline{p^e}} \equiv g_e(x) + 1 \ (\text{modulo } p^e, \ p^{e-1}g_1(x), \ \ldots, \ \text{and } pg_{e-1}(x)), \ \text{where } g_j(x) = (x^p - x - 1)^{p^j}. $$

25. [*M27*] Prove that $\varpi_n / \varpi_{n-1} \leq \varpi_{n+1} / \varpi_n \leq \varpi_n / \varpi_{n-1} + 1$.

▶ **26.** [*M22*] According to the recurrence equations (13), the numbers ϖ_{nk} in Peirce's triangle count the paths from $\boxed{nk}$ to $\boxed{11}$ in the infinite directed graph

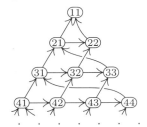

Explain why each path from $\boxed{n1}$ to $\boxed{11}$ corresponds to a partition of $\{1, \ldots, n\}$.

▶ **27.** [*M35*] A "vacillating tableau loop" of order n is a sequence of integer partitions $\lambda_k = a_{k1}a_{k2}a_{k3} \ldots$ with $a_{k1} \geq a_{k2} \geq a_{k3} \geq \cdots$ for $0 \leq k \leq 2n$, such that $\lambda_0 = \lambda_{2n} = e_0$ and $\lambda_k = \lambda_{k-1} + (-1)^k e_{t_k}$ for $1 \leq k \leq 2n$ and for some t_k with $0 \leq t_k \leq n$; here e_t denotes the unit vector $0^{t-1}10^{n-t}$ when $0 < t \leq n$, and e_0 is all zeros.

a) List all the vacillating tableau loops of order 4. [*Hint:* There are 15 altogether.]

b) Prove that exactly ϖ_{nk} vacillating tableau loops of order n have $t_{2k-1} = 0$.

▶ **28.** [*M25*] (*Generalized rook polynomials.*) Consider an arrangement of $a_1 + \cdots + a_m$ square cells in rows and columns, where row k contains cells in columns 1, $\ldots$, a_k. Place zero or more "rooks" into the cells, with at most one rook in each row and at most one in each column. An empty cell is called "free" if there is no rook to its right and no rook below. For example, Fig. 35 shows two such placements, one with four rooks in rows of lengths (3,1,4,1,5,9,2,6,5), and another with nine on a 9×9 square board. Rooks are indicated by solid circles; hollow circles have been placed above and to the left of each rook, thereby leaving the free cells blank.

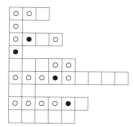 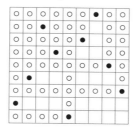

Fig. 35. Rook placements and free cells.

Let $R(a_1, \ldots, a_m)$ be the polynomial in x and y obtained by summing $x^r y^f$ over all legal rook placements, where r is the number of rooks and f is the number of free cells; for example, the left-hand placement in Fig. 35 contributes $x^4 y^{17}$ to the polynomial $R(3, 1, 4, 1, 5, 9, 2, 6, 5)$.

a) Prove that we have $R(a_1, \ldots, a_m) = R(a_1, \ldots, a_{j-1}, a_{j+1}, a_j, a_{j+2}, \ldots, a_m)$; in other words, the order of the row lengths is irrelevant, and we can assume that $a_1 \geq \cdots \geq a_m$ as in a Ferrers diagram like 7.2.1.4–(13).

b) If $a_1 \geq \cdots \geq a_m$ and if $b_1 \ldots b_n = (a_1 \ldots a_m)^T$ is the conjugate partition, prove that $R(a_1, \ldots, a_m) = R(b_1, \ldots, b_n)$.

c) Find a recurrence for evaluating $R(a_1, \ldots, a_m)$ and use it to compute $R(3, 2, 1)$.

d) Generalize Peirce's triangle (12) by changing the addition rule (13) to

$$\varpi_{nk}(x, y) = x \varpi_{(n-1)k}(x, y) + y \varpi_{n(k+1)}(x, y), \qquad 1 \leq k < n.$$

Thus $\varpi_{21}(x, y) = x + y$, $\varpi_{32}(x, y) = x + xy + y^2$, $\varpi_{31}(x, y) = x^2 + 2xy + xy^2 + y^3$, etc. Prove that the resulting quantity $\varpi_{nk}(x, y)$ is the rook polynomial $R(a_1, \ldots, a_{n-1})$ where $a_j = n - j - [j < k]$.

e) The polynomial $\varpi_{n1}(x, y)$ in part (d) can be regarded as a generalized Bell number $\varpi_n(x, y)$, representing paths from ⓝⓘ to ①① in the digraph of exercise 26 that have a given number of "x steps" to the northeast and a given number of "y steps" to the east. Prove that

$$\varpi_n(x, y) = \sum_{a_1 \ldots a_n} x^{n-1-\max(a_1, \ldots, a_n)} y^{a_1 + \cdots + a_n}$$

summed over all restricted growth strings $a_1 \ldots a_n$ of length n.

29. [*M26*] Continuing the previous exercise, let $R_r(a_1, \ldots, a_m) = [x^r] R(a_1, \ldots, a_m)$ be the polynomial in y that enumerates free cells when r rooks are placed.

a) Show that the number of ways to place n rooks on an $n \times n$ board, leaving f cells free, is the number of permutations of $\{1, \ldots, n\}$ that have f inversions. Thus, by Eq. 5.1.1–(8) and exercise 5.1.2–16, we have

$$R_n(\overbrace{n, \ldots, n}^{n}) = n!_y = \prod_{k=1}^{n}(1 + y + \cdots + y^{k-1}).$$

b) What is $R_r(\overbrace{n, \ldots, n}^{m})$, the generating function for r rooks on an $m \times n$ board?

c) If $a_1 \geq \cdots \geq a_m$ and t is a nonnegative integer, prove the general formula

$$\prod_{j=1}^{m} \frac{1 - y^{a_j + m - j + t}}{1 - y} = \sum_{k=0}^{m} \frac{t!_y}{(t - k)!_y} R_{m-k}(a_1, \ldots, a_m).$$

[*Note:* The quantity $t!_y/(t-k)!_y = \prod_{j=0}^{k-1}((1-y^{t-j})/(1-y))$ is zero when $k > t \geq 0$. Thus, for example, when $t = 0$ the right-hand side reduces to $R_m(a_1, \ldots, a_m)$. We can compute $R_m, R_{m-1}, \ldots, R_0$ by successively setting $t = 0, 1, \ldots, m$.]

d) If $a_1 \geq a_2 \geq \cdots \geq a_m \geq 0$ and $a_1' \geq a_2' \geq \cdots \geq a_m' \geq 0$, show that we have $R(a_1, a_2 \ldots, a_m) = R(a_1', a_2', \ldots, a_m')$ if and only if the associated multisets $\{a_1+m, a_2+m-1, \ldots, a_m+1\}$ and $\{a_1'+m, a_2'+m-1, \ldots, a_m'+1\}$ are the same.

30. [*HM30*] The generalized Stirling number $\left\{{n \atop m}\right\}_q$ is defined by the recurrence

$$\left\{{n+1 \atop m}\right\}_q = (1+q+\cdots+q^{m-1})\left\{{n \atop m}\right\}_q + \left\{{n \atop m-1}\right\}_q; \qquad \left\{{0 \atop m}\right\}_q = \delta_{m0}.$$

Thus $\left\{{n \atop m}\right\}_q$ is a polynomial in q; and $\left\{{n \atop m}\right\}_1$ is the ordinary Stirling number $\left\{{n \atop m}\right\}$, because it satisfies the recurrence relation in Eq. 1.2.6–(46).

a) Prove that the generalized Bell number $\varpi_n(x, y) = R(n-1, \ldots, 1)$ of exercise 28(e) has the explicit form

$$\varpi_n(x, y) = \sum_{m=0}^{n} x^{n-m} y^{\binom{m}{2}} \left\{{n \atop m}\right\}_y.$$

b) Show that generalized Stirling numbers also obey the recurrence

$$q^m \left\{{n+1 \atop m+1}\right\}_q = q^n \left\{{n \atop m}\right\}_q + \binom{n}{1} q^{n-1} \left\{{n-1 \atop m}\right\}_q + \cdots = \sum_k \binom{n}{k} q^k \left\{{k \atop m}\right\}_q.$$

c) Find generating functions for $\left\{{n \atop m}\right\}_q$, generalizing 1.2.9–(23) and 1.2.9–(28).

31. [*HM23*] Generalizing (15), show that the elements of Peirce's triangle have a simple generating function, if we compute the sum

$$\sum_{n,k} \varpi_{nk} \frac{w^{n-k}}{(n-k)!} \frac{z^{k-1}}{(k-1)!}.$$

32. [*M22*] Let δ_n be the number of restricted growth strings $a_1 \ldots a_n$ for which the sum $a_1 + \cdots + a_n$ is even minus the number for which $a_1 + \cdots + a_n$ is odd. Prove that

$$\delta_n = (1, 0, -1, -1, 0, 1) \qquad \text{when} \qquad n \bmod 6 = (1, 2, 3, 4, 5, 0).$$

Hint: See exercise 28(e).

33. [*M21*] How many partitions of $\{1, 2, \ldots, n\}$ have $1 \not\equiv 2$, $2 \not\equiv 3$, $\ldots$, $k-1 \not\equiv k$?

34. [*14*] Many poetic forms involve *rhyme schemes*, which are partitions of the lines of a stanza with the property that $j \equiv k$ if and only if line j rhymes with line k. For example, a "limerick" is generally a 5-line poem with certain rhythmic constraints and with a rhyme scheme described by the restricted growth string 00110.

What rhyme schemes were used in the classical *sonnets* by (a) Guittone d'Arezzo (c. 1270)? (b) Petrarch (c. 1350)? (c) Spenser (1595)? (d) Shakespeare (1609)? (e) Elizabeth Barrett Browning (1850)?

35. [*M21*] Let ϖ_n' be the number of schemes for n-line poems that are "completely rhymed," in the sense that every line rhymes with at least one other. Thus we have $\langle \varpi_0', \varpi_1', \varpi_2', \ldots \rangle = \langle 1, 0, 1, 1, 4, 11, 41, \ldots \rangle$. Give a combinatorial proof of the fact that $\varpi_n' + \varpi_{n+1}' = \varpi_n$.

36. [*M22*] Continuing exercise 35, what is the generating function $\sum_n \varpi_n' z^n/n!$?

37. [*M18*] Alexander Pushkin adopted an elaborate structure in his poetic novel *Eugene Onegin* (1833), based not only on "masculine" rhymes in which the sounds of accented final syllables agree with each other (pain–gain, form–warm, pun–fun, bucks–crux), but also on "feminine" rhymes in which one or two unstressed syllables also participate (humor–tumor, tetrameter–pentameter, lecture–conjecture, iguana–piranha). Every stanza of *Eugene Onegin* is a sonnet with the strict scheme 01012233455477, where the rhyme is feminine or masculine according as the digit is even or odd. Several modern translators of Pushkin's novel have also succeeded in retaining the same form in English and German.

> How do I justify this stanza? / These feminine rhymes? My wrinkled muse?
> This whole passé extravaganza? / How can I (careless of time) use
> The dusty bread molds of Onegin / In the brave bakery of Reagan?
> The loaves will surely fail to rise / Or else go stale before my eyes.
> The truth is, I can't justify it. / But as no shroud of critical terms
> Can save my corpse from boring worms, / I may as well have fun and try it.
> If it works, good; and if not, well, / A theory won't postpone its knell.
> — VIKRAM SETH, *The Golden Gate* (1986)

A 14-line poem might have any of $\varpi'_{14} = 24{,}011{,}157$ complete rhyme schemes, according to exercise 35. But how many schemes are possible if we are allowed to specify, for each block, whether its rhyme is to be feminine or masculine?

▶ **38.** [*M30*] Let σ_k be the cyclic permutation $(1, 2, \ldots, k)$. The object of this exercise is to study the sequences $k_1 k_2 \ldots k_n$, called σ-*cycles*, for which $\sigma_{k_1} \sigma_{k_2} \ldots \sigma_{k_n}$ is the identity permutation. For example, when $n = 4$ there are exactly 15 σ-cycles, namely

$$1111, 1122, 1212, 1221, 1333, 2112, 2121, 2211, 2222, 2323, 3133, 3232, 3313, 3331, 4444.$$

a) Find a one-to-one correspondence between partitions of $\{1, 2, \ldots, n\}$ and σ-cycles of length n.
b) How many σ-cycles of length n have $1 \leq k_1, \ldots, k_n \leq m$, given m and n?
c) How many σ-cycles of length n have $k_i = j$, given i, j, and n?
d) How many σ-cycles of length n have $k_1, \ldots, k_n \geq 2$?
e) How many partitions of $\{1, \ldots, n\}$ have $1 \not\equiv 2$, $2 \not\equiv 3$, $\ldots$, $n - 1 \not\equiv n$, and $n \not\equiv 1$?

39. [*HM16*] Evaluate $\int_0^\infty e^{-t^{p+1}} t^q \, dt$ when p and q are nonnegative integers. *Hint:* See exercise 1.2.5–20.

40. [*HM20*] Suppose the saddle point method is used to estimate $[z^{n-1}] e^{cz}$. The text's derivation of (21) from (19) deals with the case $c = 1$; how should that derivation change if c is an arbitrary positive constant?

41. [*HM21*] Solve the previous exercise when $c = -1$.

42. [*HM23*] Use the saddle point method to estimate $[z^{n-1}] e^{z^2}$ with relative error $O(1/n^2)$.

43. [*HM22*] Justify replacing the integral in (23) by (25).

44. [*HM22*] Explain how to compute $b_1, b_2, \ldots$ in (26) from $a_2, a_3, \ldots$ in (25).

▶ **45.** [*HM23*] Show that, in addition to (26), we also have the expansion

$$\varpi_n = \frac{e^{e^\xi - 1} n!}{\xi^n \sqrt{2\pi n (\xi + 1)}} \left(1 + \frac{b'_1}{n} + \frac{b'_2}{n^2} + \cdots + \frac{b'_m}{n^m} + O\left(\frac{1}{n^{m+1}}\right) \right),$$

where $b'_1 = -(2\xi^4 + 9\xi^3 + 16\xi^2 + 6\xi + 2)/(24(\xi + 1)^3)$.

46. [*HM25*] Estimate the value of ϖ_{nk} in Peirce's triangle when $n \to \infty$.

47. [*M21*] Analyze the running time of Algorithm H.

48. [*HM25*] If n is not an integer, the integral in (23) can be taken over a Hankel contour to define a generalized Bell number ϖ_x for all real $x > 0$. Show that, as in (16),

$$\varpi_x = \frac{1}{e} \sum_{k=0}^{\infty} \frac{k^x}{k!}.$$

▶ **49.** [*HM35*] Prove that, for large n, the number ξ defined in Eq. (24) is equal to

$$\ln n - \ln \ln n + \sum_{j,k \geq 0} \begin{bmatrix} j+k \\ j+1 \end{bmatrix} \alpha^j \frac{\beta^k}{k!}, \qquad \alpha = -\frac{1}{\ln n}, \qquad \beta = \frac{\ln \ln n}{\ln n}.$$

▶ **50.** [*HM21*] If $\xi(n)e^{\xi(n)} = n$ and $\xi(n) > 0$, how does $\xi(n+k)$ relate to $\xi(n)$?

51. [*HM27*] Use the saddle point method to estimate $t_n = n! \, [z^n] \, e^{z+z^2/2}$, the number of *involutions* on n elements (aka partitions of $\{1, \ldots, n\}$ into blocks of sizes ≤ 2).

52. [*HM22*] The *cumulants* of a probability distribution are defined in Eq. 1.2.10–(23). What are the cumulants, when the probability that a random integer equals k is (a) $e^{1-e^\xi} \varpi_k \xi^k / k!$? (b) $\sum_j \begin{Bmatrix} k \\ j \end{Bmatrix} e^{e^{-1}-1-j} / k!$?

▶ **53.** [*HM30*] Let $G(z) = \sum_{k=0}^{\infty} p_k z^k$ be the generating function for a discrete probability distribution, converging for $|z| < 1 + \delta$; thus the coefficients p_k are nonnegative, $G(1) = 1$, and the mean and variance are respectively $\mu = G'(1)$ and $\sigma^2 = G''(1) + G'(1) - G'(1)^2$. If $X_1, \ldots, X_n$ are independent random variables having this distribution, the probability that $X_1 + \cdots + X_n = m$ is $[z^m] G(z)^n$, and we often want to estimate this probability when m is near the mean value μn.

Assume that $p_0 \neq 0$ and that no integer $d > 1$ is a common divisor of all subscripts k with $p_k \neq 0$; this assumption means that m does not have to satisfy any special congruence conditions mod d when n is large. Prove that

$$[z^{\mu n + r}] G(z)^n = \frac{e^{-r^2/(2\sigma^2 n)}}{\sigma \sqrt{2\pi n}} + O\left(\frac{1}{n}\right) \qquad \text{as } n \to \infty,$$

when $\mu n + r$ is an integer. *Hint:* Integrate $G(z)^n / z^{\mu n + r}$ on the circle $|z| = 1$.

54. [*HM20*] If α and β are defined by (40), show that their arithmetic and geometric means are respectively $\frac{\alpha+\beta}{2} = s \coth s$ and $\sqrt{\alpha\beta} = s \operatorname{csch} s$, where $s = \sigma/2$.

55. [*HM20*] Suggest a good way to compute the number β needed in (43).

▶ **56.** [*HM26*] Let $g(z) = \alpha^{-1} \ln(e^z - 1) - \ln z$ and $\sigma = \alpha - \beta$ as in (37).

a) Prove that $(-\sigma)^{n+1} g^{(n+1)}(\sigma) = n! - \sum_{k=0}^{n} \left\langle {n \atop k} \right\rangle \alpha^k \beta^{n-k}$, where the Eulerian numbers $\left\langle {n \atop k} \right\rangle$ are defined in Section 5.1.3.

b) Prove that $\frac{\beta}{\alpha} n! < \sum_{k=0}^{n} \left\langle {n \atop k} \right\rangle \alpha^k \beta^{n-k} < n!$ for all $\sigma > 0$. *Hint:* See exercise 5.1.3–25.

c) Now verify the inequality (42).

57. [*HM22*] In the notation of (43), prove that (a) $n+1-m < 2N$; (b) $N < 2(n+1-m)$.

58. [*HM31*] Complete the proof of (43) as follows.

a) Show that for all $\sigma > 0$ there is a number $\tau \geq 2\sigma$ such that τ is a multiple of 2π and $|e^{\sigma+it} - 1|/|\sigma + it|$ is monotone decreasing for $0 \leq t \leq \tau$.

b) Prove that $\int_{-\tau}^{\tau} \exp((n+1)g(\sigma+it)) \, dt$ leads to (43).

c) Show that the corresponding integrals over the straight-line paths $z = t \pm i\tau$ for $-n \leq t \leq \sigma$ and $z = -n \pm it$ for $-\tau \leq t \leq \tau$ are negligible.

▶ **59.** [*HM23*] What does (43) predict for the approximate value of $\{{n \atop n}\}$?

60. [*HM25*] (a) Show that the partial sums in the identity

$$\left\{{n \atop m}\right\} = \frac{m^n}{m!} - \frac{(m-1)^n}{1!\,(m-1)!} + \frac{(m-2)^n}{2!\,(m-2)!} - \cdots + (-1)^m \frac{0^n}{m!\,0!}$$

alternately overestimate and underestimate the final value. (b) Conclude that

$$\left\{{n \atop m}\right\} = \frac{m^n}{m!}(1 - O(ne^{-n^\epsilon})) \qquad \text{when } m \le n^{1-\epsilon}.$$

(c) Derive a similar result from (43).

61. [*HM26*] Prove that if $m = n - r$ where $r \le n^\epsilon$ and $\epsilon \le n^{1/2}$, Eq. (43) yields

$$\left\{{n \atop n-r}\right\} = \frac{n^{2r}}{2^r r!}\left(1 + O(n^{2\epsilon-1}) + O\left(\frac{1}{r}\right)\right).$$

62. [*HM40*] Prove rigorously that if $\xi e^\xi = n$, the maximum $\{{n \atop m}\}$ occurs either when $m = \lfloor e^\xi - 1 \rfloor$ or when $m = \lceil e^\xi - 1 \rceil$.

▶ **63.** [*M35*] (J. Pitman.) Prove that there is an elementary way to locate the maximum Stirling numbers, and many similar quantities, as follows: Suppose $0 \le p_j \le 1$.

a) Let $f(z) = (1+p_1(z-1))\dots(1+p_n(1-z))$ and $a_k = [z^k]\,f(z)$; thus a_k is the probability that k heads turn up after n independent coin flips with the respective probabilities $p_1, \dots, p_n$. Prove that $a_{k-1} < a_k$ whenever $k \le \mu = p_1 + \cdots + p_n$, $a_k \ne 0$.

b) Similarly, prove that $a_{k+1} < a_k$ whenever $k \ge \mu$ and $a_k \ne 0$.

c) If $f(x) = a_0 + a_1 x + \cdots + a_n x^n$ is any nonzero polynomial with nonnegative coefficients and with n real roots, prove that $a_{k-1} < a_k$ when $k \le \mu$ and $a_{k+1} < a_k$ when $k \ge \mu$, where $\mu = f'(1)/f(1)$. Therefore if $a_m = \max(a_0, \dots, a_n)$ we must have either $m = \lfloor \mu \rfloor$ or $m = \lceil \mu \rceil$.

d) Under the hypotheses of (c), and with $a_j = 0$ when $j < 0$ or $j > n$, show that there are indices $s \le t$, such that $a_{k+1} - a_k < a_k - a_{k-1}$ if and only if $s \le k \le t$. (Thus, a histogram of the sequence $(a_0, a_1, \dots, a_n)$ is always "bell-shaped.")

e) What do these results tell us about Stirling numbers?

64. [*HM21*] Prove the approximate ratio (50), using (30) and exercise 50.

▶ **65.** [*HM22*] What is the variance of the number of blocks of size k in a random partition of $\{1, \dots, n\}$?

66. [*M46*] What partition of n leads to the most partitions of $\{1, \dots, n\}$?

67. [*HM20*] What are the mean and variance of M in Stam's method (53)?

68. [*20*] How large can the stack get in Algorithm M, when it is generating all $p(n_1, \dots, n_m)$ partitions of $\{n_1 \cdot 1, \dots, n_m \cdot m\}$?

▶ **69.** [*21*] Modify Algorithm M so that it produces only partitions into at most r parts.

▶ **70.** [*M22*] Analyze the number of r-block partitions possible in the n-element multisets (a) $\{0, \dots, 0, 1\}$; (b) $\{1, 2, \dots, n-1, n-1\}$. What is the total, summed over r?

71. [*M20*] How many partitions of $\{n_1 \cdot 1, \dots, n_m \cdot m\}$ have exactly 2 parts?

72. [*M26*] Can $p(n, n)$ be evaluated in polynomial time?

▶ **73.** [*M32*] Can $p(2, \dots, 2)$ be evaluated in polynomial time when there are n 2s?

74. [*M46*] Can $p(n, \dots, n)$ be evaluated in polynomial time when there are n ns?

75. [*HM41*] Find the asymptotic value of $p(n, n)$.

76. [*HM36*] Find the asymptotic value of $p(2, \dots, 2)$ when there are n 2s.

77. [*HM46*] Find the asymptotic value of $p(n, \dots, n)$ when there are n ns.

78. [*20*] What partition of $(15, 10, 10, 11)$ leads to the permutations α_1, α_2, α_3, and α_4 shown in Table 1?

79. [*22*] A sequence u_1, u_2, u_3, ... is called *universal* for partitions of $\{1, \ldots, n\}$ if its subsequences $(u_{m+1}, u_{m+2}, \ldots, u_{m+n})$ for $0 \le m < \varpi_n$ represent all possible set partitions under the convention "$j \equiv k$ if and only if $u_{m+j} = u_{m+k}$." For example, $(0, 0, 0, 1, 0, 2, 2)$ is a universal sequence for partitions of $\{1, 2, 3\}$.

Write a program to find all universal sequences for partitions of $\{1, 2, 3, 4\}$ with the properties that (i) $u_1 = u_2 = u_3 = u_4 = 0$; (ii) the sequence has restricted growth; (iii) $0 \le u_j \le 3$; and (iv) $u_{16} = u_{17} = u_{18} = 0$ (hence the sequence is essentially *cyclic*).

80. [*M28*] Prove that universal cycles for partitions of $\{1, 2, \ldots, n\}$ exist in the sense of the previous exercise whenever $n \ge 4$.

81. [*29*] Find a way to arrange an ordinary deck of 52 playing cards so that the following trick is possible: Five players each cut the deck (applying a cyclic permutation) as often as they like. Then each player takes a card from the top. A magician tells them to look at their cards and to form affinity groups, joining with others who hold the same suit: Everybody with clubs gets together, everybody with diamonds forms another group, and so on. (The Jack of Spades is, however, considered to be a "joker"; its holder, if any, should remain aloof.)

Observing the affinity groups, but not being told any of the suits, the magician can name all five cards, if the cards were suitably arranged in the first place.

82. [*22*] In how many ways can the following 15 dominoes, optionally rotated, be partitioned into three sets of five having the same sum when regarded as fractions?

SECTION 7.2.1.3

1. Given a multiset, form the sequence $e_t \ldots e_2 e_1$ from right to left by listing the distinct elements first, then those that appear twice, then those that appear thrice, etc. Let us set $e_{-j} \leftarrow s - j$ for $0 \leq j \leq s = n - t$, so that every element e_j for $1 \leq j \leq t$ is equal to some element to its right in the sequence $e_t \ldots e_1 e_0 \ldots e_{-s}$. If the first such element is $e_{c_j - s}$, we obtain a solution to (3). Conversely, every solution to (3) yields a unique multiset $\{e_1, \ldots, e_t\}$, because $c_j < s + j$ for $1 \leq j \leq t$.

[A similar correspondence was proposed by E. Catalan: If $0 \leq e_1 \leq \cdots \leq e_t \leq s$, let

$$\{c_1, \ldots, c_t\} = \{e_1, \ldots, e_t\} \cup \{s + j \mid 1 \leq j < t \text{ and } e_j = e_{j+1}\}.$$

See *Mémoires de la Soc. roy. des Sciences de Liège* (2) **12** (1885), *Mélanges Math.*, 3.]

2. Start at the bottom left corner; then go up for each 0, go right for each 1. The result is .

3. In this algorithm, variable r is the least positive index such that $q_r > 0$.

F1. [Initialize.] Set $q_j \leftarrow 0$ for $1 \leq j \leq t$, and $q_0 \leftarrow s$. (We assume that $st > 0$.)

F2. [Visit.] Visit the composition $q_t \ldots q_0$. Go to F4 if $q_0 = 0$.

F3. [Easy case.] Set $q_0 \leftarrow q_0 - 1$, $r \leftarrow 1$, and go to F5.

F4. [Tricky case.] Terminate if $r = t$. Otherwise set $q_0 \leftarrow q_r - 1$, $q_r \leftarrow 0$, $r \leftarrow r + 1$.

F5. [Increase q_r.] Set $q_r \leftarrow q_r + 1$ and return to F2. ∎

[See *CACM* **11** (1968), 430; **12** (1969), 187. The task of generating such compositions in *decreasing* lexicographic order is more difficult.]

4. We can reverse the roles of 0 and 1 in (14), so that $0^{q_t} 10^{q_{t-1}} 1 \ldots 10^{q_1} 10^{q_0} = 1^{r_s} 01^{r_{s-1}} 0 \ldots 01^{r_1} 01^{r_0}$. This gives $0^1 10^0 10^2 10^2 10^4 10^0 10^0 10^0 10^0 10^0 10^1 10^0 10^1 10^0 = 1^0 01^2 01^0 01^1 01^0 01^1 01^0 01^0 01^6 01^2 01^1$. Lexicographic order of $a_{n-1} \ldots a_1 a_0$ corresponds to lexicographic order of $r_s \ldots r_1 r_0$.

Incidentally, there's also a multiset connection: $\{d_t, \ldots, d_1\} = \{r_s \cdot s, \ldots, r_0 \cdot 0\}$. For example, $\{10, 10, 8, 6, 2, 2, 2, 2, 2, 2, 1, 1, 0\} = \{0 \cdot 11, 2 \cdot 10, 0 \cdot 9, 1 \cdot 8, 0 \cdot 7, 1 \cdot 6, 0 \cdot 5, 0 \cdot 4, 0 \cdot 3, 6 \cdot 2, 2 \cdot 1, 1 \cdot 0\}$.

5. (a) Set $x_j = c_j - \lfloor (j-1)/2 \rfloor$ in each t-combination of $n + \lfloor t/2 \rfloor$. (b) Set $x_j = c_j + j + 1$ in each t-combination of $n - t - 2$.

(A similar approach finds all solutions $(x_t, \ldots, x_1)$ to the inequalities $x_{j+1} \geq x_j + \delta_j$ for $0 \leq j \leq t$, given the values of x_{t+1}, $(\delta_t, \ldots, \delta_1)$, and x_0.)

6. Assume that $t > 0$. We get to T3 when $c_1 > 0$; to T5 when $c_2 = c_1 + 1 > 1$; to T4 for $2 \leq j \leq t + 1$ when $c_j = c_1 + j - 1 \geq j$. So the counts are: T1, 1; T2, $\binom{n}{t}$; T3, $\binom{n-1}{t}$; T4, $\binom{n-2}{t-1} + \binom{n-2}{t-2} + \cdots + \binom{n-t-1}{0} = \binom{n-1}{t-1}$; T5, $\binom{n-2}{t-1}$; T6, $\binom{n-1}{t-1} + \binom{n-2}{t-1} - 1$.

7. A procedure slightly simpler than Algorithm T suffices: Assume that $s < n$.

S1. [Initialize.] Set $b_j \leftarrow j + n - s - 1$ for $1 \leq j \leq s$; then set $j \leftarrow 1$.

S2. [Visit.] Visit the combination $b_s \ldots b_2 b_1$. Terminate if $j > s$.

S3. [Decrease b_j.] Set $b_j \leftarrow b_j - 1$. If $b_j < j$, set $j \leftarrow j + 1$ and return to S2.

S4. [Reset $b_{j-1} \ldots b_1$.] While $j > 1$, set $b_{j-1} \leftarrow b_j - 1$, $j \leftarrow j - 1$, and repeat until $j = 1$. Go to S2. ∎

(See S. Dvořák, *Comp. J.* **33** (1990), 188. Notice that if $x_k = n - b_k$ for $1 \le k \le s$, this algorithm runs through all combinations $x_s \dots x_2 x_1$ of $\{1, 2, \dots, n\}$ with $1 \le x_s < \cdots < x_2 < x_1 \le n$, in *increasing* lexicographic order.)

8. A1. [Initialize.] Set $a_n \dots a_0 \leftarrow 0^{s+1} 1^t$, $q \leftarrow t$, $r \leftarrow 0$. (We assume that $0 < t < n$.)

   A2. [Visit.] Visit the combination $a_{n-1} \dots a_1 a_0$. Go to A4 if $q = 0$.

   A3. [Replace $\dots 01^q$ by $\dots 101^{q-1}$.] Set $a_q \leftarrow 1$, $a_{q-1} \leftarrow 0$, $q \leftarrow q - 1$; then if $q = 0$, set $r \leftarrow 1$. Return to A2.

   A4. [Shift block of 1s.] Set $a_r \leftarrow 0$ and $r \leftarrow r + 1$. Then if $a_r = 1$, set $a_q \leftarrow 1$, $q \leftarrow q + 1$, and repeat step A4.

   A5. [Carry to left.] Terminate if $r = n$; otherwise set $a_r \leftarrow 1$.

   A6. [Odd?] If $q > 0$, set $r \leftarrow 0$. Return to A2. ∎

In step A2, q and r point respectively to the rightmost 0 and 1 in $a_{n-1} \dots a_0$. Steps A1, $\dots$, A6 are executed with frequency 1, $\binom{n}{t}$, $\binom{n-1}{t-1}$, $\binom{n}{t} - 1$, $\binom{n-1}{t}$, $\binom{n-1}{t} - 1$.

9. (a) The first $\binom{n-1}{t}$ strings begin with 0 and have $2A_{(s-1)t}$ bit changes; the other $\binom{n-1}{t-1}$ begin with 1 and have $2A_{s(t-1)}$. And $\nu(01^t 0^{s-1} \oplus 10^s 1^{t-1}) = 2 \min(s, t)$.

   (b) Solution 1 (direct): Let $B_{st} = A_{st} + \min(s, t) + 1$. Then

$$B_{st} = B_{(s-1)t} + B_{s(t-1)} + [s = t] \quad \text{when } st > 0; \qquad B_{st} = 1 \quad \text{when } st = 0.$$

Consequently $B_{st} = \sum_{k=0}^{\min(s,t)} \binom{s+t-2k}{s-k}$. If $s \le t$ this is $\le \sum_{k=0}^{s} \binom{s+t-k}{s-k} = \binom{s+t+1}{s} = \binom{s+t}{s} \frac{s+t+1}{t+1} < 2 \binom{s+t}{t}$.

   Solution 2 (indirect): The algorithm in answer 8 makes $2(x + y)$ bit changes when steps (A3, A4) are executed (x, y) times. Thus $A_{st} \le \binom{n-1}{t-1} + \binom{n}{t} - 1 < 2 \binom{n}{t}$.

   [The comment in answer 7.2.1.1–3 therefore applies to combinations as well.]

10. Each scenario corresponds to a $(4, 4)$-combination $b_4 b_3 b_2 b_1$ or $c_4 c_3 c_2 c_1$ in which A wins games $\{8 - b_4, 8 - b_3, 8 - b_2, 8 - b_1\}$ and N wins games $\{8 - c_4, 8 - c_3, 8 - c_2, 8 - c_1\}$, because we can assume that the losing team wins the remaining games in a series of 8. (Equivalently, we can generate all permutations of $\{A, A, A, A, N, N, N, N\}$ and omit the trailing run of As or Ns.) The American League wins if and only if $b_1 \ne 0$, if and only if $c_1 = 0$. The formula $\binom{c_4}{4} + \binom{c_3}{3} + \binom{c_2}{2} + \binom{c_1}{1}$ assigns a unique integer between 0 and 69 to each scenario.

   For example, ANANAA $\Longleftrightarrow a_7 \dots a_1 a_0 = 01010011 \Longleftrightarrow b_4 b_3 b_2 b_1 = 7532 \Longleftrightarrow c_4 c_3 c_2 c_1 = 6410$, and this is the scenario of rank $\binom{6}{4} + \binom{4}{3} + \binom{1}{2} + \binom{0}{1} = 19$ in lexicographic order. (Notice that the term $\binom{c_j}{j}$ will be zero if and only if it corresponds to a trailing N.)

11. AAAA (9 times), NNNN (8), and ANAAA (7) were most common. Exactly 27 of the 70 failed to occur, including all four beginning with NNNA. (We disregard the games that were tied because of darkness, in 1907, 1912, and 1922. The case ANNAAA should perhaps be excluded too, because it occurred only in 1920 as part of ANNAAAA in a best-of-nine series. The scenario NNAAANN occurred for the first time in 2001.)

12. (a) Let V_j be the subspace $\{a_{n-1} \dots a_0 \in V \mid a_k = 0 \text{ for } 0 \le k < j\}$, so that $\{0 \dots 0\} = V_n \subseteq V_{n-1} \subseteq \cdots \subseteq V_0 = V$. Then $\{c_1, \dots, c_t\} = \{c \mid V_c \ne V_{c+1}\}$, and α_k is the unique element $a_{n-1} \dots a_0$ of V with $a_{c_j} = [j = k]$ for $1 \le j \le t$.

   Incidentally, the $t \times n$ matrix corresponding to a canonical basis is said to be in *reduced row-echelon form*. It can be found by a standard "triangulation" algorithm (see exercise 4.6.1–19 and Algorithm 4.6.2N).

(b) The 2-nomial coefficient $\binom{n}{t}_2 = 2^t \binom{n-1}{t}_2 + \binom{n-1}{t-1}_2$ of exercise 1.2.6–58 has the right properties, because $2^t \binom{n-1}{t}_2$ binary vector spaces have $c_t < n-1$ and $\binom{n-1}{t-1}_2$ have $c_t = n - 1$. [In general the number of canonical bases with r asterisks is the number of partitions of r into at most t parts, with no part exceeding $n - t$, and this is $[z^r]\binom{n}{t}_z$ by Eq. 7.2.1.4–(51). See D. E. Knuth, *J. Combinatorial Theory* **10** (1971), 178–180.]

(c) The following algorithm assumes that $n > t > 0$ and that $a_{(t+1)j} = 0$ for $t \leq j \leq n$.

V1. [Initialize.] Set $a_{kj} \leftarrow [j = k - 1]$ for $1 \leq k \leq t$ and $0 \leq j < n$. Also set $q \leftarrow t$, $r \leftarrow 0$.

V2. [Visit.] (At this point we have $a_{k(k-1)} = 1$ for $1 \leq k \leq q$, $a_{(q+1)q} = 0$, and $a_{1r} = 1$.) Visit the canonical basis $(a_{1(n-1)} \ldots a_{11}a_{10}, \ldots, a_{t(n-1)} \ldots a_{t1}a_{t0})$. Go to V4 if $q > 0$.

V3. [Find block of 1s.] Set $q \leftarrow 1, 2, \ldots$, until $a_{(q+1)(q+r)} = 0$. Terminate if $q + r = n$.

V4. [Add 1 to column $q+r$.] Set $k \leftarrow 1$. If $a_{k(q+r)} = 1$, set $a_{k(q+r)} \leftarrow 0$, $k \leftarrow k+1$, and repeat until $a_{k(q+r)} = 0$. Then if $k \leq q$, set $a_{k(q+r)} \leftarrow 1$; otherwise set $a_{q(q+r)} \leftarrow 1$, $a_{q(q+r-1)} \leftarrow 0$, $q \leftarrow q - 1$.

V5. [Shift block right.] If $q = 0$, set $r \leftarrow r+1$. Otherwise, if $r > 0$, set $a_{k(k-1)} \leftarrow 1$ and $a_{k(r+k-1)} \leftarrow 0$ for $1 \leq k \leq q$, then set $r \leftarrow 0$. Go to V2. ∎

Step V2 finds $q > 0$ with probability $1 - (2^{n-t} - 1)/(2^n - 1) \approx 1 - 2^{-t}$, so we could save time by treating this case separately.

(d) Since $999999 = 4\binom{8}{4}_2 + 16\binom{7}{4}_2 + 5\binom{6}{3}_2 + 5\binom{5}{3}_2 + 8\binom{4}{3}_2 + 0\binom{3}{2}_2 + 4\binom{2}{2}_2 + 1\binom{1}{1}_2 + 2\binom{0}{1}_2$, the millionth output has binary columns 4, 16/2, 5, 5, 8/2, 0, 4/2, 1, 2/2, namely

$$\begin{aligned}
\alpha_1 &= 0\,0\,1\,1\,0\,0\,0\,1\,1, \\
\alpha_2 &= 0\,0\,0\,0\,0\,0\,1\,0\,0, \\
\alpha_3 &= 1\,0\,1\,1\,1\,0\,0\,0\,0, \\
\alpha_4 &= 0\,1\,0\,0\,0\,0\,0\,0\,0.
\end{aligned}$$

[*Reference:* E. Calabi and H. S. Wilf, *J. Combinatorial Theory* **A22** (1977), 107–109.]

13. Let $n = s + t$. There are $\binom{s-1}{\lceil(r-1)/2\rceil}\binom{t-1}{\lfloor(r-1)/2\rfloor}$ configurations beginning with 0 and $\binom{s-1}{\lfloor(r-1)/2\rfloor}\binom{t-1}{\lceil(r-1)/2\rceil}$ beginning with 1, because an Ising configuration that begins with 0 corresponds to a composition of s 0s into $\lceil(r+1)/2\rceil$ parts and a composition of t 1s into $\lfloor(r+1)/2\rfloor$ parts. We can generate all such pairs of compositions and weave them into configurations. [See E. Ising, *Zeitschrift für Physik* **31** (1925), 253–258; J. M. S. Simões Pereira, *CACM* **12** (1969), 562.]

14. Start with $l[j] \leftarrow j - 1$ and $r[j - 1] \leftarrow j$ for $1 \leq j \leq n$; $l[0] \leftarrow n$, $r[n] \leftarrow 0$. To get the next combination, assuming that $t > 0$, set $p \leftarrow s$ if $l[0] > s$, otherwise $p \leftarrow r[n] - 1$. Terminate if $p \leq 0$; otherwise set $q \leftarrow r[p]$, $l[q] \leftarrow l[p]$, and $r[l[p]] \leftarrow q$. Then if $r[q] > s$ and $p < s$, set $r[p] \leftarrow r[n]$, $l[r[n]] \leftarrow p$, $r[s] \leftarrow r[q]$, $l[r[q]] \leftarrow s$, $r[n] \leftarrow 0$, $l[0] \leftarrow n$; otherwise set $r[p] \leftarrow r[q]$, $l[r[q]] \leftarrow p$. Finally set $r[q] \leftarrow p$ and $l[p] \leftarrow q$.

[See Korsh and Lipschutz, *J. Algorithms* **25** (1997), 321–335, where the idea is extended to a loopless algorithm for multiset permutations. *Caution:* This exercise, like exercise 7.2.1.1–16, is more academic than practical, because the routine that visits the linked list might need a loop that nullifies any advantage of loopless generation.]

15. (The stated fact is true because lexicographic order of $c_t \ldots c_1$ corresponds to lexicographic order of $a_{n-1} \ldots a_0$, which is reverse lexicographic order of the complementary sequence $1 \ldots 1 \oplus a_{n-1} \ldots a_0$.) By Theorem L, the combination $c_t \ldots c_1$ is visited *before* exactly $\binom{b_s}{s} + \cdots + \binom{b_2}{2} + \binom{b_1}{1}$ others have been visited, and we must have

$$\binom{b_s}{s} + \cdots + \binom{b_1}{1} + \binom{c_t}{t} + \cdots + \binom{c_1}{1} = \binom{s+t}{t} - 1.$$

This general identity can be written

$$\sum_{j=0}^{n-1} x_j \binom{j}{x_0 + \cdots + x_j} + \sum_{j=0}^{n-1} \bar{x}_j \binom{j}{\bar{x}_0 + \cdots + \bar{x}_j} = \binom{n}{x_0 + \cdots + x_{n-1}} - 1$$

when each x_j is 0 or 1, and $\bar{x}_j = 1 - x_j$; it follows also from the equation

$$x_n \binom{n}{x_0 + \cdots + x_n} + \bar{x}_n \binom{n}{\bar{x}_0 + \cdots + \bar{x}_n} = \binom{n+1}{x_0 + \cdots + x_n} - \binom{n}{x_0 + \cdots + x_{n-1}}.$$

16. Since $999999 = \binom{1414}{2} + \binom{1008}{1} = \binom{182}{3} + \binom{153}{2} + \binom{111}{1} = \binom{71}{4} + \binom{56}{3} + \binom{36}{2} + \binom{14}{1} = \binom{43}{5} + \binom{32}{4} + \binom{21}{3} + \binom{15}{2} + \binom{6}{1}$, the answers are (a) 1414 1008; (b) 182 153 111; (c) 71 56 36 14; (d) 43 32 21 15 6; (e) 1000000 999999 ... 2 0.

17. By Theorem L, n_t is the largest integer such that $N \geq \binom{n_t}{t}$; the remaining terms are the degree-$(t-1)$ representation of $N - \binom{n_t}{t}$.

A simple sequential method for $t > 1$ starts with $x = 1$, $c = t$, and sets $c \leftarrow c+1$, $x \leftarrow xc/(c-t)$ zero or more times until $x > N$; then we complete the first phase by setting $x \leftarrow x(c-t)/c$, $c \leftarrow c-1$, at which point we have $x = \binom{c}{t} \leq N < \binom{c+1}{t}$. Set $n_t \leftarrow c$, $N \leftarrow N-x$; terminate with $n_1 \leftarrow N$ if $t = 2$; otherwise set $x \leftarrow xt/c$, $t \leftarrow t-1$, $c \leftarrow c-1$; while $x > N$ set $x \leftarrow x(c-t)/c$, $c \leftarrow c-1$; repeat. This method requires $O(n)$ arithmetic operations if $N < \binom{n}{t}$, so it is suitable unless t is small and N is large.

When $t = 2$, exercise 1.2.4–41 tells us that $n_2 = \lfloor \sqrt{2N+2} + \frac{1}{2} \rfloor$. In general, n_t is $\lfloor x \rfloor$ where x is the largest root of $x^t = t!\,N$; this root can be approximated by reverting the series $y = (x^t)^{1/t} = x - \frac{1}{2}(t-1) + \frac{1}{24}(t^2-1)x^{-1} + \cdots$ to get $x = y + \frac{1}{2}(t-1) + \frac{1}{24}(t^2-1)/y + O(y^{-3})$. Setting $y = (t!\,N)^{1/t}$ in this formula gives a good approximation, after which we can check that $\binom{\lfloor x \rfloor}{t} \leq N < \binom{\lfloor x \rfloor + 1}{t}$ or make a final adjustment. [See A. S. Fraenkel and M. Mor, *Comp. J.* **26** (1983), 336–343.]

18. A complete binary tree of $2^n - 1$ nodes is obtained, with an extra node at the top, like the "tree of losers" in replacement selection sorting (Fig. 63 in Section 5.4.1). Therefore explicit links aren't necessary; the right child of node k is node $2k+1$, and the left sibling is node $2k$, for $1 \leq k < 2^{n-1}$.

This representation of a binomial tree has the curious property that node $k = (0^a 1 \alpha)_2$ corresponds to the combination whose binary string is $0^a 1 \alpha^R$.

19. It is $\mathrm{post}(1000000)$, where $\mathrm{post}(n) = 2^k + \mathrm{post}(n - 2^k + 1)$ if $2^k \leq n < 2^{k+1}$, and $\mathrm{post}(0) = 0$. So it is 11110100001001000100.

20. $f(z) = (1 + z^{w_{n-1}}) \ldots (1 + z^{w_1})/(1-z)$, $g(z) = (1 + z^{w_0})f(z)$, $h(z) = z^{w_0}f(z)$.

21. The rank of $c_t \ldots c_2 c_1$ is $\binom{c_t+1}{t} - 1$ minus the rank of $c_{t-1} \ldots c_2 c_1$. [See H. Lüneburg, *Abh. Math. Sem. Hamburg* **52** (1982), 208–227.]

22. Since $999999 = \binom{1415}{2} - \binom{406}{1} = \binom{183}{3} - \binom{98}{2} + \binom{21}{1} = \binom{72}{4} - \binom{57}{3} + \binom{32}{2} - \binom{27}{1} = \binom{44}{5} - \binom{40}{4} + \binom{33}{3} - \binom{13}{2} + \binom{3}{1}$, the answers are (a) 1414 405; (b) 182 97 21; (c) 71 56 31 26; (d) 43 39 32 12 3; (e) 1000000 999999 999998 999996 ... 0.

23. There are $\binom{n-r}{t-r}$ combinations with $j > r$, for $r = 1, 2, \ldots, t$. (If $r = 1$ we have $c_2 = c_1 + 1$; if $r = 2$ we have $c_1 = 0, c_2 = 1$; if $r = 3$ we have $c_1 = 0, c_2 = 1, c_4 = c_3 + 1$; etc.) Thus the mean is $\left(\binom{n}{t} + \binom{n-1}{t-1} + \cdots + \binom{n-t}{0}\right)/\binom{n}{t} = \binom{n+1}{t}/\binom{n}{t} = (n+1)/(n+1-t)$. The average running time per step is approximately proportional to this quantity; thus the algorithm is quite fast when t is small, but slow if t is near n.

24. In fact $j_k - 2 \le j_{k+1} \le j_k + 1$ when $j_k \equiv t$ (modulo 2) and $j_k - 1 \le j_{k+1} \le j_k + 2$ when $j_k \not\equiv t$, because R5 is performed only when $c_i = i - 1$ for $1 \le i < j$.

Thus we could say, "If $j \ge 4$, set $j \leftarrow j - 1 - [j \text{ odd}]$ and go to R5" at the end of R2, if t is odd; "If $j \ge 3$, set $j \leftarrow j - 1 - [j \text{ even}]$ and go to R5" if t is even. The algorithm will then be loopless, since R4 and R5 will be performed at most twice per visit.

25. Assume that $N > N'$ and $N - N'$ is minimum; furthermore let t and c_t be minimum, subject to those assumptions. Then $c_t > c'_t$.

If there is an element $x \notin C \cup C'$ with $0 \le x < c_t$, map each t-combination of $C \cup C'$ by changing $j \mapsto j - 1$ for $j > x$; or, if there is an element $x \in C \cap C'$, map each t-combination that contains x into a $(t-1)$-combination by omitting x and changing $j \mapsto x - j$ for $j < x$. In either case the mapping preserves alternating lexicographic order; hence $N - N'$ must exceed the number of combinations between the images of C and C'. But c_t is minimum, so no such x can exist. Consequently $t = m$ and $c_t = 2m - 1$.

Now if $c'_m < c_m - 1$, we could decrease $N - N'$ by increasing c'_m. Therefore $c'_m = 2m - 2$, and the problem has been reduced to finding the *maximum* of $\text{rank}(c_{m-1} \ldots c_1) - \text{rank}(c'_{m-1} \ldots c'_1)$, where rank is calculated as in (30).

Let $f(s, t) = \max(\text{rank}(b_s \ldots b_1) - \text{rank}(c_t \ldots c_1))$ over all $\{b_s, \ldots, b_1, c_t \ldots, c_1\} = \{0, \ldots, s + t - 1\}$. Then $f(s, t)$ satisfies the curious recurrence

$$f(s, 0) = f(0, t) = 0; \qquad f(1, t) = t;$$
$$f(s, t) = \binom{s+t-1}{s} + \max(f(t-1, s-1), f(s-2, t)) \quad \text{if } st > 0 \text{ and } s > 1.$$

When $s + t = 2u + 2$ the solution turns out to be

$$f(s, t) = \binom{2u+1}{t-1} + \sum_{j=1}^{u-r}\binom{2u+1-2j}{r} + \sum_{j=0}^{r-1}\binom{2j+1}{j}, \qquad r = \min(s-2, t-1),$$

with the maximum occurring at $f(t-1, s-1)$ when $s \le t$ and at $f(s-2, t)$ when $s \ge t+2$.

Therefore the minimum $N - N'$ occurs for

$$C = \{2m - 1\} \cup \{2m - 2 - x \mid 1 \le x \le 2m - 2, \ x \bmod 4 \le 1\},$$
$$C' = \{2m - 2\} \cup \{2m - 2 - x \mid 1 \le x \le 2m - 2, \ x \bmod 4 \ge 2\};$$

and it equals $\binom{2m-1}{m-1} - \sum_{k=0}^{m-2}\binom{2k+1}{k} = 1 + \sum_{k=1}^{m-1}\binom{2k}{k-1}$. [See A. J. van Zanten, *IEEE Trans.* **IT-37** (1991), 1229–1233.]

26. (a) Yes: The first is $0^{n-\lceil t/2 \rceil}1^{t \bmod 2}2^{\lfloor t/2 \rfloor}$ and the last is $2^{\lfloor t/2 \rfloor}1^{t \bmod 2}0^{n-\lceil t/2 \rceil}$; transitions are substrings of the forms $02^a 1 \leftrightarrow 12^a 0$, $02^a 2 \leftrightarrow 12^a 1$, $10^a 1 \leftrightarrow 20^a 0$, $10^a 2 \leftrightarrow 20^a 1$.

(b) No: If $s = 0$ there is a big jump from $02^t 0^{r-1}$ to $20^r 2^{t-1}$.

27. The following procedure extracts all combinations $c_1 \ldots c_k$ of Γ_n that have weight $\le t$: Begin with $k \leftarrow 0$ and $c_0 \leftarrow n$. Visit $c_1 \ldots c_k$. If k is even and $c_k = 0$, set $k \leftarrow k - 1$; if k is even and $c_k > 0$, set $c_k \leftarrow c_k - 1$ if $k = t$, otherwise $k \leftarrow k + 1$ and $c_k \leftarrow 0$. On the other hand if k is odd and $c_k + 1 = c_{k-1}$, set $k \leftarrow k - 1$ and

$c_k \leftarrow c_{k+1}$ (but terminate if $k = 0$); if k is odd and $c_k + 1 < c_{k-1}$, set $c_k \leftarrow c_k + 1$ if $k = t$, otherwise $k \leftarrow k + 1$, $c_k \leftarrow c_{k-1}$, $c_{k-1} \leftarrow c_k + 1$. Repeat.

(This loopless algorithm reduces to that of exercise 7.2.1.1–12(b) when $t = n$, with slight changes of notation.)

28. True. Bit strings $a_{n-1} \ldots a_0 = \alpha\beta$ and $a'_{n-1} \ldots a'_0 = \alpha\beta'$ correspond to index lists $(b_s \ldots b_1 = \theta\chi, c_t \ldots c_1 = \phi\psi)$ and $(b'_s \ldots b'_1 = \theta\chi', c'_t \ldots c'_1 = \phi\psi')$ such that everything between $\alpha\beta$ and $\alpha\beta'$ begins with α if and only if everything between $\theta\chi$ and $\theta\chi'$ begins with θ and everything between $\phi\psi$ and $\phi\psi'$ begins with ϕ. For example, if $n = 10$, the prefix $\alpha = 01101$ corresponds to prefixes $\theta = 96$ and $\phi = 875$.

(But just having $c_t \ldots c_1$ in genlex order is a much weaker condition. For example, *every* such sequence is genlex when $t = 1$.)

29. (a) $-^k 0^{l+1}$ or $-^k 0^{l+1} +\pm^m$ or $\pm^k$, for $k, l, m \geq 0$.

(b) No; the successor is always smaller in balanced ternary notation.

(c) For all α and all $k, l, m \geq 0$ we have $\alpha 0 -^{k+1} 0^l +\pm^m \to \alpha -+^k 0^{l+1} -\pm^m$ and $\alpha +-^k 0^{l+1} +\pm^m \to \alpha 0 +^{k+1} 0^l -\pm^m$; also $\alpha 0 -^{k+1} 0^l \to \alpha -+^k 0^{l+1}$ and $\alpha +-^k 0^{l+1} \to \alpha 0 +^{k+1} 0^l$.

(d) Let the jth sign of α_i be $(-1)^{a_{ij}}$, and let it be in position b_{ij}. Then we have $(-1)^{a_{ij} + b_{i(j-1)}} = (-1)^{a_{(i+1)j} + b_{(i+1)(j-1)}}$ for $0 \leq i < k$ and $1 \leq j \leq t$, if we let $b_{i0} = 0$.

(e) By parts (a), (b), and (c), α belongs to some chain $\alpha_0 \to \cdots \to \alpha_k$, where α_k is final (has no successor) and α_0 is initial (has no predecessor). By part (d), every such chain has at most $\binom{s+t}{t}$ elements. But there are 2^s final strings, by (a), and there are $2^s \binom{s+t}{t}$ strings with s signs and t zeros; so k must be $\binom{s+t}{t} - 1$.

Reference: SICOMP **2** (1973), 128–133.

30. Assume that $t > 0$. Initial strings are the negatives of final strings. Let σ_j be the initial string $0^t -\tau_j$ for $0 \leq j < 2^{s-1}$, where the kth character of τ_j for $1 \leq k < s$ is the sign of $(-1)^{a_k}$ when j is the binary number $(a_{s-1} \ldots a_1)_2$; thus $\sigma_0 = 0^t -++ \ldots +$, $\sigma_1 = 0^t --+ \ldots +$, $\ldots$, $\sigma_{2^{s-1}-1} = 0^t --- \ldots -$. Let ρ_j be the final string obtained by inserting -0^t after the first (possibly empty) run of minus signs in τ_j; thus $\rho_0 = -0^t ++ \ldots +$, $\rho_1 = --0^t + \ldots +$, $\ldots$, $\rho_{2^{s-1}-1} = -- \ldots -0^t$. We also let $\sigma_{2^{s-1}} = \sigma_0$ and $\rho_{2^{s-1}} = \rho_0$. Then we can prove by induction that the chain beginning with σ_j ends with ρ_j when t is even, with ρ_{j-1} when t is odd, for $1 \leq j \leq 2^{s-1}$. Therefore the chain beginning with $-\rho_j$ ends with $-\sigma_j$ or $-\sigma_{j+1}$.

Let $A_j(s, t)$ be the sequence of (s, t)-combinations derived by mapping the chain that starts with σ_j, and let $B_j(s, t)$ be the analogous sequence derived from $-\rho_j$. Then, for $1 \leq j \leq 2^{s-1}$, the reverse sequence $A_j(s,t)^R$ is $B_j(s, t)$ when t is even, $B_{j-1}(s, t)$ when t is odd. The corresponding recurrences when $st > 0$ are

$$A_j(s,t) = \begin{cases} 1A_j(s, t-1), \; 0A_{\lfloor (2^{s-1}-1-j)/2 \rfloor}(s-1, t)^R, & \text{if } j + t \text{ is even;} \\ 1A_j(s, t-1), \; 0A_{\lfloor j/2 \rfloor}(s-1, t), & \text{if } j + t \text{ is odd;} \end{cases}$$

and when $st > 0$ all 2^{s-1} of these sequences are distinct.

Chase's sequence C_{st} is $A_{\lfloor 2^s/3 \rfloor}(s, t)$, and $\widehat{C}_{st}$ is $A_{\lfloor 2^{s-1}/3 \rfloor}(s, t)$. Incidentally, the homogeneous sequence K_{st} of (31) is $A_{2^{s-1} - [t \text{ even}]}(s, t)^R$.

31. (a) $2^{\binom{s+t}{t} - 1}$ solves the recurrence $f(s,t) = 2f(s-1, t) f(s, t-1)$ when $f(s, 0) = f(0, t) = 1$. (b) Now $f(s, t) = (s+1)! f(s, t-1) \ldots f(0, t-1)$ has the solution

$$(s+1)!^t \, s!^{\binom{t}{2}} (s-1)!^{\binom{t+1}{3}} \ldots 2!^{\binom{s+t-2}{s}} = \prod_{r=1}^s (r+1)!^{\binom{s+t-1-r}{t-2} + [r=s]}.$$

32. (a) No simple formula seems to exist, but the listings can be counted for small s and t by systematically computing the number of genlex paths that run through all weight-t strings from a given starting point to a given ending point via revolving-door moves. The totals for $s + t \le 6$ are

$$
\begin{array}{ccccccccccccc}
 & & & & & & 1 & & & & & & \\
 & & & & & 1 & & 1 & & & & & \\
 & & & & 1 & & 2 & & 1 & & & & \\
 & & & 1 & & 4 & & 4 & & 1 & & & \\
 & & 1 & & 8 & & 20 & & 8 & & 1 & & \\
 & 1 & & 16 & & 160 & & 160 & & 16 & & 1 & \\
1 & & 32 & & 2264 & & 17152 & & 2264 & & 32 & & 1
\end{array}
$$

and $f(4,4) = 95{,}304{,}112{,}865{,}280$; $f(5,5) \approx 5.92646 \times 10^{48}$. [This class of combination generators was first studied by G. Ehrlich, *JACM* **20** (1973), 500–513, but he did not attempt to enumerate them.]

(b) By extending the proof of Theorem N, one can show that all such listings or their reversals must run from $1^t 0^s$ to $0^a 1^t 0^{s-a}$ for some a, $1 \le a \le s$. Moreover, the number n_{sta} of possibilities, given s, t, and a with $st > 0$, satisfies $n_{1t1} = 1$ and

$$
n_{sta} = \begin{cases}
n_{s(t-1)1}\, n_{(s-1)t(a-1)}, & \text{if } a > 1; \\
n_{s(t-1)2}\, n_{(s-1)t1} + \cdots + n_{s(t-1)s}\, n_{(s-1)t(s-1)}, & \text{if } a = 1 < s.
\end{cases}
$$

This recurrence has the remarkable solution $n_{sta} = 2^{m(s,t,a)}$, where

$$
m(s,t,a) = \begin{cases}
\binom{s+t-3}{t} + \binom{s+t-5}{t-2} + \cdots + \binom{s-1}{2}, & \text{if } t \text{ is even;} \\
\binom{s+t-3}{t} + \binom{s+t-5}{t-2} + \cdots + \binom{s}{3} + s - a - [a<s], & \text{if } t \text{ is odd.}
\end{cases}
$$

33. Consider first the case $t = 1$: The number of near-perfect paths from i to $j > i$ is $f(j - i - [i>0] - [j<n-1])$, where $\sum_j f(j) z^j = 1/(1 - z - z^3)$. (By coincidence, the same sequence $f(j)$ arises in Caron's polyphase merge on 6 tapes, Table 5.4.2–2.) The sum over $0 \le i < j < n$ is $3f(n) + f(n-1) + f(n-2) + 2 - n$; and we must double this, to cover cases with $j > i$.

When $t > 1$ we can construct $\binom{n}{t} \times \binom{n}{t}$ matrices that tell how many genlex listings begin and end with particular combinations. The entries of these matrices are sums of products of matrices for the case $t - 1$, summed over all paths of the type considered for $t = 1$. The totals for $s + t \le 6$ turn out to be

$$
\begin{array}{ccccccc}
 & & & 1 & & & \\
 & & 1 & & 1 & & \\
 & & 1 & 2 & 1 & & \\
 & 1 & 6 & 2 & 1 & & \\
 & 1 & 12 & 10 & 2 & 1 & \\
1 & 20 & 44 & 10 & 2 & 1 & \\
1 & 34 & 238 & 68 & 10 & 2 & 1
\end{array}
\qquad
\begin{array}{ccccccc}
 & & & 1 & & & \\
 & & 1 & & 1 & & \\
 & & 1 & 2 & 1 & & \\
 & 1 & 2 & 0 & 1 & & \\
 1 & 2 & 2 & 0 & 1 & & \\
1 & 2 & 0 & 0 & 0 & 1 & \\
1 & 2 & 6 & 0 & 0 & 0 & 1
\end{array}
$$

where the right-hand triangle shows the number of *cycles*, $g(s,t)$. Further values include $f(4,4) = 17736$; $f(5,5) = 9{,}900{,}888{,}879{,}984$; $g(4,4) = 96$; $g(5,5) = 30{,}961{,}456{,}320$.

There are exactly 10 such schemes when $s = 2$ and $n \ge 4$. For example, when $n = 7$ they run from 43210 to 65431 or 65432, or from 54321 to 65420 or 65430 or 65432, or the reverse.

34. The minimum can be computed as in the previous answer, but using min-plus matrix multiplication $c_{ij} = \min_k(a_{ik} + b_{kj})$ instead of ordinary matrix multiplication $c_{ij} = \sum_k a_{ik}b_{kj}$. (When $s = t = 5$, the genlex path in Fig. 26(e) with only 49 imperfect transitions is essentially unique. There is a genlex cycle for $s = t = 5$ that has only 55 imperfections.)

35. From the recurrences (35) we have $a_{st} = b_{s(t-1)} + [s > 1][t > 0] + a_{(s-1)t}$, $b_{st} = a_{s(t-1)} + a_{(s-1)t}$; consequently $a_{st} = b_{st} + [s > 1][t\,\text{odd}]$ and $a_{st} = a_{s(t-1)} + a_{(s-1)t} + [s > 1][t\,\text{odd}]$. The solution is

$$a_{st} = \sum_{k=0}^{t/2} \binom{s+t-2-2k}{s-2} - [s > 1][t\,\text{even}];$$

this sum is approximately $s/(s + 2t)$ times $\binom{s+t}{t}$.

36. Consider the binary tree with root node (s, t) and with recursively defined subtrees rooted at $(s-1, t)$ and $(s, t-1)$ whenever $st > 0$; the node (s, t) is a leaf if $st = 0$. Then the subtree rooted at (s, t) has $\binom{s+t}{t}$ leaves, corresponding to all (s, t)-combinations $a_{n-1} \ldots a_1 a_0$. Nodes on level l correspond to prefixes $a_{n-1} \ldots a_{n-l}$, and leaves on level l are combinations with $r = n - l$.

Any genlex algorithm for combinations $a_{n-1} \ldots a_1 a_0$ corresponds to preorder traversal of such a tree, after the children of the $\binom{s+t}{t} - 1$ branch nodes have been ordered in any desired way; that, in fact, is why there are $2^{\binom{s+t}{t}-1}$ such genlex schemes (exercise 31(a)). And the operation $j \leftarrow j + 1$ is performed exactly once per branch node, namely after both children have been processed.

Incidentally, exercise 7.2.1.2–6(a) implies that the average value of r is $s/(t + 1) + t/(s+1)$, which can be $\Omega(n)$; thus the extra time needed to keep track of r is worthwhile.

37. (a) In the lexicographic case we needn't maintain the w_j table, since a_j is active for $j \geq r$ if and only if $a_j = 0$. After setting $a_j \leftarrow 1$ and $a_{j-1} \leftarrow 0$ there are two cases to consider if $j > 1$: If $r = j$, set $r \leftarrow j - 1$; otherwise set $a_{j-2} \ldots a_0 \leftarrow 0^r 1^{j-1-r}$ and $r \leftarrow j - 1 - r$ (or $r \leftarrow j$ if r was $j - 1$).

(b) Now the transitions to be handled when $j > 1$ are to change $a_j \ldots a_0$ as follows: $01^r \rightarrow 1101^{r-2}$, $010^r \rightarrow 10^{r+1}$, $010^a 1^r \rightarrow 110^{a+1}1^{r-1}$, $10^r \rightarrow 010^{r-1}$, $110^r \rightarrow 010^{r-1}1$, $10^a 1^r \rightarrow 0^a 1^{r+1}$; these six cases are easily distinguished. The value of r should change appropriately.

(c) Again the case $j = 1$ is trivial. Otherwise $01^a 0^r \rightarrow 101^{a-1}0^r$; $0^a 1^r \rightarrow 10^a 1^{r-1}$; $101^a 0^r \rightarrow 01^{a+1}0^r$; $10^a 1^r \rightarrow 0^a 1^{r+1}$; and there is also an ambiguous case, which can occur only if $a_{n-1} \ldots a_{j+1}$ contains at least one 0: Let $k > j$ be minimal with $a_k = 0$. Then $10^r \rightarrow 010^{r-1}$ if k is odd, $10^r \rightarrow 0^r 1$ if k is even.

38. The same algorithm works, except that (i) step C1 sets $a_{n-1} \ldots a_0 \leftarrow 01^t 0^{s-1}$ if n is odd or $s = 1$, $a_{n-1} \ldots a_0 \leftarrow 001^t 0^{s-2}$ if n is even and $s > 1$, with an appropriate value of r; (ii) step C3 interchanges the roles of even and odd; (iii) step C5 goes to C4 also if $j = 1$.

39. In general, start with $r \leftarrow 0$, $j \leftarrow s + t - 1$, and repeat the following steps until $st = 0$:

$$r \leftarrow r + [w_j = 0]\binom{j}{s - a_j}, \quad s \leftarrow s - [a_j = 0], \quad t \leftarrow t - [a_j = 1], \quad j \leftarrow j - 1.$$

Then r is the rank of $a_{n-1} \ldots a_1 a_0$. So the rank of 1100100100001111110110101010 is $\binom{23}{12} + \binom{22}{11} + \binom{21}{9} + \binom{17}{8} + \binom{16}{7} + \binom{14}{5} + \binom{13}{3} + \binom{12}{3} + \binom{11}{3} + \binom{10}{3} + \binom{9}{3} + \binom{8}{3} + \binom{4}{3} + \binom{3}{1} + \binom{1}{0} = 2390131$.

40. We start with $N \leftarrow 999999$, $v \leftarrow 0$, and repeat the following steps until $st = 0$: If $v = 0$, set $t \leftarrow t - 1$ and $a_{s+t} \leftarrow 1$ if $N < \binom{s+t-1}{s}$, otherwise set $N \leftarrow N - \binom{s+t-1}{s}$, $v \leftarrow (s+t) \bmod 2$, $s \leftarrow s - 1$, $a_{s+t} \leftarrow 0$. If $v = 1$, set $v \leftarrow (s+t) \bmod 2$, $s \leftarrow s - 1$, and $a_{s+t} \leftarrow 0$ if $N < \binom{s+t-1}{t}$, otherwise set $N \leftarrow N - \binom{s+t-1}{t}$, $t \leftarrow t - 1$, $a_{s+t} \leftarrow 1$. Finally if $s = 0$, set $a_{t-1} \ldots a_0 \leftarrow 1^t$; if $t = 0$, set $a_{s-1} \ldots a_0 \leftarrow 0^s$. The answer is $a_{25} \ldots a_0 = 11101001111110101001000001$.

41. Let $c(0)$, $\ldots$, $c(2^n - 1) = C_n$ where $C_{2n} = 0C_{2n-1}$, $1C_{2n-1}$; $C_{2n+1} = 0C_{2n}$, $1\widehat{C}_{2n}$; $\widehat{C}_{2n} = 1C_{2n-1}$, $0\widehat{C}_{2n-1}$; $\widehat{C}_{2n+1} = 1\widehat{C}_{2n}$, $0\widehat{C}_{2n}$; $C_0 = \widehat{C}_0 = \epsilon$. Then $a_j \oplus b_j = b_{j+1} \& (b_{j+2} \mid (b_{j+3} \& (b_{j+4} \mid \cdots)))$ if j is even, $b_{j+1} \mid (b_{j+2} \& (b_{j+3} \mid (b_{j+4} \& \cdots)))$ if j is odd. Curiously we also have the inverse relation $c((\ldots a_4 \bar{a}_3 a_2 \bar{a}_1 a_0)_2) = (\ldots b_4 \bar{b}_3 b_2 \bar{b}_1 b_0)_2$.

42. Equation (40) shows that the left context $a_{n-1} \ldots a_{l+1}$ does not affect the behavior of the algorithm on $a_{l-1} \ldots a_0$ if $a_l = 0$ and $l > r$. Therefore we can analyze Algorithm C by counting combinations that end with certain bit patterns, and it follows that the number of times each operation is performed can be represented as $[w^s z^t] p(w, z)/(1 - w^2)^2 (1 - z^2)^2 (1 - w - z)$ for an appropriate polynomial $p(w, z)$.

For example, the algorithm goes from C5 to C4 once for each combination that ends with $01^{2a+1} 01^{2b+1}$ or has the form $1^{a+1} 01^{2b+1}$, for integers $a, b \geq 0$; the corresponding generating functions are $w^2 z^2/(1 - z^2)^2 (1 - w - z)$ and $w(z^2 + z^3)/(1 - z^2)^2$.

Here are the polynomials $p(w, z)$ for key operations. Let $W = 1 - w^2$, $Z = 1 - z^2$.

C3 $\rightarrow$ C4: $wzW(1+wz)(1-w-z^2)$;   C5$(r \leftarrow 1)$: $w^2 z W^2 Z(1-wz-z^2)$;
C3 $\rightarrow$ C5: $wzW(w+z)(1-wz-z^2)$;   C5$(r \leftarrow j-1)$: $w^2 z^3 W^2(1-wz-z^2)$;
C3 $\rightarrow$ C6: $w^2 z^2 W(w+z)$;   C6$(j = 1)$: $w^2 z W^2 Z$;
C3 $\rightarrow$ C7: $w^2 z W(1+wz)$;   C6$(r \leftarrow j-1)$: $w^2 z^3 W^2$;
C4$(j = 1)$: $wzW^2 Z(1-w-z^2)$;   C6$(r \leftarrow j)$: $w^3 z^2 W Z$;
C4$(r \leftarrow j-1)$: $w^3 z W Z(1-w-z^2)$;   C7 $\rightarrow$ C6: $w^2 z W^2$;
C4$(r \leftarrow j)$: $wz^2 W^2(1+z-2wz-z^2-z^3)$;   C7$(r \leftarrow j)$: $w^4 z W Z$;
C5 $\rightarrow$ C4: $wz^2 W^2(1-wz-z^2)$;   C7$(r \leftarrow j-2)$: $w^3 z^2 W^2$.
C5$(r \leftarrow j-2)$: $w^4 z W Z(1-wz-z^2)$;

The asymptotic value is $\binom{s+t}{t} (p(1 - x, x)/(2x - x^2)^2 (1 - x^2)^2 + O(n^{-1}))$, for fixed $0 < x < 1$, if $t = xn + O(1)$ as $n \to \infty$. Thus we find, for example, that the four-way branching in step C3 takes place with relative frequencies $x + x^2 - x^3 : 1 : x : 1 + x - x^2$.

Incidentally, the number of cases with j odd exceeds the number of cases with j even by

$$\sum_{k,l \geq 1} \binom{s+t-2k-2l}{s-2k} [2k + 2l \leq s + t] + [s \text{ odd}][t \text{ odd}],$$

in *any* genlex scheme that uses (39). This quantity has the interesting generating function $wz/(1 + w)(1 + z)(1 - w - z)$.

43. The identity is true for all nonnegative integers x, except when $x = 1$.

44. In fact, $C_t(n) - 1 = \widehat{C}_t(n - 1)^R$, and $\widehat{C}_t(n) - 1 = C_t(n - 1)^R$. (Hence $C_t(n) - 2 = C_t(n - 2)$, etc.)

45. In the following algorithm, r is the least subscript with $c_r \geq r$.

CC1. [Initialize.] Set $c_j \leftarrow n - t - 1 + j$ and $z_j \leftarrow 0$ for $1 \leq j \leq t + 1$. Also set $r \leftarrow 1$. (We assume that $0 < t < n$.)

CC2. [Visit.] Visit the combination $c_t \ldots c_2 c_1$. Then set $j \leftarrow r$.

CC3. [Branch.] Go to CC5 if $z_j \neq 0$.

CC4. [Try to decrease c_j.] Set $x \leftarrow c_j + (c_j \bmod 2) - 2$. If $x \geq j$, set $c_j \leftarrow x$, $r \leftarrow 1$; otherwise if $c_j = j$, set $c_j \leftarrow j - 1$, $z_j \leftarrow c_{j+1} - ((c_{j+1} + 1) \bmod 2)$, $r \leftarrow j$; otherwise if $c_j < j$, set $c_j \leftarrow j$, $z_j \leftarrow c_{j+1} - ((c_{j+1} + 1) \bmod 2)$, $r \leftarrow \max(1, j - 1)$; otherwise set $c_j \leftarrow x$, $r \leftarrow j$. Return to CC2.

CC5. [Try to increase c_j.] Set $x \leftarrow c_j + 2$. If $x < z_j$, set $c_j \leftarrow x$; otherwise if $x = z_j$ and $z_{j+1} \neq 0$, set $c_j \leftarrow x - (c_{j+1} \bmod 2)$; otherwise set $z_j \leftarrow 0$, $j \leftarrow j + 1$, and go to CC3 (but terminate if $j > t$). If $c_1 > 0$, set $r \leftarrow 1$; otherwise set $r \leftarrow j - 1$. Return to CC2. ∎

46. Equation (40) implies that $u_k = (b_j + k + 1) \bmod 2$ when j is minimal with $b_j > k$. Then (37) and (38) yield the following algorithm, where we assume for convenience that $3 \leq s < n$.

CB1. [Initialize.] Set $b_j \leftarrow j - 1$ for $1 \leq j \leq s$; also set $z \leftarrow s + 1$, $b_z \leftarrow 1$. (When subsequent steps examine the value of z, it is the smallest index such that $b_z \neq z - 1$.)

CB2. [Visit.] Visit the dual combination $b_s \ldots b_2 b_1$.

CB3. [Branch.] If b_2 is odd: Go to CB4 if $b_2 \neq b_1 + 1$, otherwise to CB5 if $b_1 > 0$, otherwise to CB6 if b_z is odd. Go to CB9 if b_2 is even and $b_1 > 0$. Otherwise go to CB8 if $b_{z+1} = b_z + 1$, otherwise to CB7.

CB4. [Increase b_1.] Set $b_1 \leftarrow b_1 + 1$ and return to CB2.

CB5. [Slide b_1 and b_2.] If b_3 is odd, set $b_1 \leftarrow b_1 + 1$ and $b_2 \leftarrow b_2 + 1$; otherwise set $b_1 \leftarrow b_1 - 1$, $b_2 \leftarrow b_2 - 1$, $z \leftarrow 3$. Go to CB2.

CB6. [Slide left.] If z is odd, set $z \leftarrow z - 2$, $b_{z+1} \leftarrow z + 1$, $b_z \leftarrow z$; otherwise set $z \leftarrow z - 1$, $b_z \leftarrow z$. Go to CB2.

CB7. [Slide b_z.] If b_{z+1} is odd, set $b_z \leftarrow b_z + 1$ and terminate if $b_z \geq n$; otherwise set $b_z \leftarrow b_z - 1$, then if $b_z < z$ set $z \leftarrow z + 1$. To CB2.

CB8. [Slide b_z and b_{z+1}.] If b_{z+2} is odd, set $b_z \leftarrow b_{z+1}$, $b_{z+1} \leftarrow b_z + 1$, and terminate if $b_{z+1} \geq n$. Otherwise set $b_{z+1} \leftarrow b_z$, $b_z \leftarrow b_z - 1$, then if $b_z < z$ set $z \leftarrow z + 2$. To CB2.

CB9. [Decrease b_1.] Set $b_1 \leftarrow b_1 - 1$, $z \leftarrow 2$, and return to CB2. ∎

Notice that this algorithm is *loopless*. Chase gave a similar procedure for the sequence $\widehat{C}^R_{st}$ in *Cong. Num.* **69** (1989), 233–237. It is truly amazing that this algorithm defines precisely the complements of the indices $c_t \ldots c_1$ produced by the algorithm in the previous exercise.

47. We can, for example, use Algorithm C and its reverse (exercise 38), with w_j replaced by a d-bit number whose bits represent activity at different levels of the recursion. Separate pointers $r_0, r_1, \ldots, r_{d-1}$ are needed to keep track of the r-values on each level. (Many other solutions are possible.)

48. There are permutations $\pi_1, \ldots, \pi_M$ such that the kth element of Λ_j is $\pi_k \alpha_j \uparrow \beta_{k-1}$. And $\pi_k \alpha_j$ runs through all permutations of $\{s_1 \cdot 1, \ldots, s_d \cdot d\}$ as j varies from 0 to $N - 1$.

Historical note: The first publication of a homogeneous revolving-door scheme for (s, t)-combinations was by Éva Török, *Matematikai Lapok* **19** (1968), 143–146, who was motivated by the generation of multiset permutations. Many authors have subsequently relied on the homogeneity condition for similar constructions, but this exercise shows that homogeneity is not necessary.

49. We have $\lim_{z \to q}(z^{km+r} - 1)/(z^{lm+r} - 1) = 1$ when $0 < r < m$, and the limit is $\lim_{z \to q}(kmz^{km-1})/(lmz^{lm-1}) = k/l$ when $r = 0$. So we can pair up factors of the numerator $\prod_{n-k < a \leq n}(z^a - 1)$ with factors of the denominator $\prod_{0 < b \leq k}(z^b - 1)$ when $a \equiv b$ (modulo m).

Notes: This formula was discovered by G. Olive, *AMM* **72** (1965), 619. In the special case $m = 2$, $q = -1$, the second factor vanishes only when n is even and k is odd. The formula $\binom{n}{k}_q = \binom{n}{n-k}_q$ holds for all $n \geq 0$, but $\binom{\lfloor n/m \rfloor}{\lfloor k/m \rfloor}$ is *not* always equal to $\binom{\lfloor n/m \rfloor}{\lfloor (n-k)/m \rfloor}$. We do, however, have $\lfloor k/m \rfloor + \lfloor (n-k)/m \rfloor = \lfloor n/m \rfloor$ in the case when $n \bmod m \geq k \bmod m$; otherwise the second factor is zero.

50. The stated coefficient is zero when $n_1 \bmod m + \cdots + n_t \bmod m \geq m$. Otherwise it equals

$$\binom{\lfloor (n_1 + \cdots + n_t)/m \rfloor}{\lfloor n_1/m \rfloor, \ldots, \lfloor n_t/m \rfloor} \binom{(n_1 + \cdots + n_t) \bmod m}{n_1 \bmod m, \ldots, n_t \bmod m}_q,$$

by Eq. 1.2.6–(43); here each upper index is the sum of the lower indices.

51. All paths clearly run between 000111 and 111000, since those vertices have degree 1. Fourteen total paths reduce to four under the stated equivalences. The path in (50), which is equivalent to itself under reflection-and-reversal, can be described by the delta sequence $A = 3452132523414354123$; the other three classes are $B = 3452541453414512543$, $C = 3452541453252154123$, $D = 3452134145341432543$. D. H. Lehmer found path C [*AMM* **72** (1965), Part II, 36–46]; D is essentially the path constructed by Eades, Hickey, and Read.

(Incidentally, perfect schemes aren't really rare, although they seem to be difficult to construct systematically. The case $(s, t) = (3, 5)$ has 4,050,046 of them.)

52. We may assume that each s_j is nonzero and that $d > 1$. Then the difference between permutations with an even and odd number of inversions is $\binom{\lfloor (s_0 + \cdots + s_d)/2 \rfloor}{\lfloor s_0/2 \rfloor, \ldots, \lfloor s_d/2 \rfloor} \geq 2$, by exercise 50, unless at least two of the multiplicities s_j are odd.

Conversely, if at least two multiplicities are odd, a general construction by G. Stachowiak [*SIAM J. Discrete Math.* **5** (1992), 199–206] shows that a perfect scheme exists. Indeed, his construction applies to a variety of topological sorting problems; in the special case of multisets it gives a Hamiltonian cycle in all cases with $d > 1$ and $s_0 s_1$ odd, except when $d = 2$, $s_0 = s_1 = 1$, and s_2 is even.

53. See *AMM* **72** (1965), Part II, 36–46.

54. Assuming that $st \neq 0$, a Hamiltonian path exists if and only if s and t are not both even; a Hamiltonian cycle exists if and only if, in addition, ($s \neq 2$ and $t \neq 2$) or $n = 5$. [T. C. Enns, *Discrete Math.* **122** (1993), 153–165.]

55. [Solution by Aaron Williams.] The sequence $0^s 1^t$, W_{st} has the correct properties if

$$W_{st} = 0W_{(s-1)t}, \ 1W_{s(t-1)}, \ 10^s 1^{t-1}, \quad \text{for } st > 0; \qquad W_{0t} = W_{s0} = \emptyset.$$

And there is an amazingly efficient, *loopless* implementation: Assume that $t > 0$.

W1. [Initialize.] Set $n \leftarrow s + t$, $a_j \leftarrow 1$ for $0 \leq j < t$, and $a_j \leftarrow 0$ for $t \leq i \leq n$. Also set $j \leftarrow k \leftarrow t - 1$. (This is tricky, but it works.)

W2. [Visit.] Visit the (s, t)-combination $a_{n-1} \ldots a_1 a_0$.

W3. [Zero out a_j.] Set $a_j \leftarrow 0$ and $j \leftarrow j + 1$.

W4. [Easy case?] If $a_j = 1$, set $a_k \leftarrow 1$, $k \leftarrow k + 1$, and return to W2.

W5. [Wrap around.] Terminate if $j = n$. Otherwise set $a_j \leftarrow 1$. Then if $k > 0$, set $a_k \leftarrow 1$, $a_0 \leftarrow 0$, $j \leftarrow 1$, and $k \leftarrow 0$. Return to W2. ∎

After the second visit, j is the smallest index with $a_j a_{j-1} = 10$, and k is smallest with $a_k = 0$. The easy case occurs exactly $\binom{s+t-1}{s} - 1$ times; the condition $k = 0$ occurs in step W5 exactly $\binom{s+t-2}{t} + \delta_{t1}$ times. Curiously, if N has the combinatorial representation (57), the combination of rank N in Algorithm L has rank $N - t + \binom{n_v}{v-1} + v - 1$ in Algorithm W. [*Lecture Notes in Comp. Sci.* **3595** (2005), 570–576.]

(b) `SET bits,(1<<t)-1`   (This program assumes that $s > 0$ and $t > 0$.)

```
1H PUSHJ $0,Visit
   ADDU $0,bits,1; AND $0,$0,bits
   SUBU $1,$0,1; XOR $1,$0,$1
   ADDU $0,$1,1; AND $1,$1,bits
   AND $0,$0,bits; ODIF $0,$0,1
   SUBU $1,$1,$0; ADDU bits,bits,$1
   SRU $0,bits,s+t; PBZ $0,1B
```

$\text{Visit } \mathtt{bits} = (a_{s+t-1}\ldots a_1 a_0)_2.$
$\text{Set } \$0 \leftarrow \mathtt{bits}\ \&\ (\mathtt{bits}+1).$
$\text{Set } \$1 \leftarrow \$0 \oplus (\$0 - 1).$
$\text{Set } \$0 \leftarrow \$1 + 1,\ \$1 \leftarrow \$1\ \&\ \mathtt{bits}.$
$\text{Set } \$0 \leftarrow (\$0\ \&\ \mathtt{bits}) \dotminus 1.$
$\text{Set } \mathtt{bits} \leftarrow \mathtt{bits} + \$1 - \$0.$
$\text{Repeat unless } a_{s+t} = 1.\quad\blacksquare$

56. [*Discrete Math.* **48** (1984), 163–171.] This problem is equivalent to the "middle levels conjecture," which states that there is a Gray path through all binary strings of length $2t - 1$ and weights $\{t - 1, t\}$. In fact, such strings can almost certainly be generated by a delta sequence of the special form $\alpha_0 \alpha_1 \ldots \alpha_{2t-2}$ where the elements of α_k are those of α_0 shifted by k, modulo $2t - 1$. For example, when $t = 3$ we can start with $a_5 a_4 a_3 a_2 a_1 a_0 = 000111$ and repeatedly swap $a_0 \leftrightarrow a_\delta$, where δ runs through the cycle $(4134\ 5245\ 1351\ 2412\ 3523)$. The middle levels conjecture is known to be true for $t \le 15$ [see I. Shields and C. D. Savage, *Cong. Num.* **140** (1999), 161–178].

57. Yes; there is a near-perfect genlex solution for all m, n, and t when $n \ge m > t$. One such scheme, in bitstring notation, is $1 A_{(m-t)(t-1)} 0^{n-m}$, $01 A_{(m-t)(t-1)} 0^{n-m-1}$, $\ldots$, $0^{n-m} 1 A_{(m-t)(t-1)}$, $0^{n-m+1} 1 A_{(m-1-t)(t-1)}$, $\ldots$, $0^{n-t} 1 A_{0(t-1)}$, using the sequences A_{st} of (35).

58. Solve the previous problem with m and n reduced by $t - 1$, then add $j - 1$ to each c_j. (Case (a), which is particularly simple, was probably known to Czerny.)

59. The generating function $G_{mnt}(z) = \sum g_{mntk} z^k$ for the number g_{mntk} of chords reachable in k steps from $0^{n-t} 1^t$ satisfies $G_{mmt}(z) = \binom{m}{t}_z$ and $G_{m(n+1)t}(z) = G_{mnt}(z) + z^{tn-(t-1)m} \binom{m-1}{t-1}_z$, because the latter term accounts for cases with $c_t = n$ and $c_1 > n - m$. A perfect scheme is possible only if $|G_{mnt}(-1)| \le 1$. But if $n \ge m > t \ge 2$, this condition holds only when $m = t + 1$ or $(n - t)t$ is odd, by (49). So there is no perfect solution when $t = 4$ and $m > 5$. (Many chords have only two neighbors when $n = t + 2$, so one can easily rule out that case. All cases with $n \ge m > 5$ and $t = 3$ apparently do have perfect paths when n is even.)

60. The following solution uses lexicographic order, taking care to ensure that the average amount of computation per visit is bounded. We may assume that $s t m_s \ldots m_0 \neq 0$ and $t \le m_s + \cdots + m_1 + m_0$.

Q1. [Initialize.] Set $q_j \leftarrow 0$ for $s \ge j \ge 1$, and $x = t$.

Q2. [Distribute.] Set $j \leftarrow 0$. Then while $x > m_j$, set $q_j \leftarrow m_j$, $x \leftarrow x - m_j$, $j \leftarrow j + 1$, and repeat until $x \le m_j$. Finally set $q_j \leftarrow x$.

Q3. [Visit.] Visit the bounded composition $q_s + \cdots + q_1 + q_0$.

Q4. [Pick up the rightmost units.] If $j = 0$, set $x \leftarrow q_0 - 1$, $j \leftarrow 1$. Otherwise if $q_0 = 0$, set $x \leftarrow q_j - 1$, $q_j \leftarrow 0$, and $j \leftarrow j + 1$. Otherwise go to Q7.

Q5. [Full?] Terminate if $j > s$. Otherwise if $q_j = m_j$, set $x \leftarrow x + m_j$, $q_j \leftarrow 0$, $j \leftarrow j + 1$, and repeat this step.

Q6. [Increase q_j.] Set $q_j \leftarrow q_j + 1$. Then if $x = 0$, set $q_0 \leftarrow 0$ and return to Q3. (In that case $q_{j-1} = \cdots = q_0 = 0$.) Otherwise go to Q2.

Q7. [Increase and decrease.] (Now $q_i = m_i$ for $j > i \geq 0$.) While $q_j = m_j$, set $j \leftarrow j + 1$ and repeat until $q_j < m_j$ (but terminate if $j > s$). Then set $q_j \leftarrow q_j + 1$, $j \leftarrow j - 1$, $q_j \leftarrow q_j - 1$. If $q_0 = 0$, set $j \leftarrow 1$. Return to Q3. ∎

For example, if $m_s = \cdots = m_0 = 9$, the successors of the composition $3+9+9+7+0+0$ are $4+0+0+6+9+9$, $4+0+0+7+8+9$, $4+0+0+7+9+8$, $4+0+0+8+7+9$, ...

61. Let $F_s(t) = \emptyset$ if $t < 0$ or $t > m_s + \cdots + m_0$; otherwise let $F_0(t) = t$, and

$$F_s(t) = 0 + F_{s-1}(t), \ 1 + F_{s-1}(t-1)^R, \ 2 + F_{s-1}(t-2), \ \ldots, \ m_s + F_{s-1}(t - m_s)^{R^{m_s}}$$

when $s > 0$. This sequence can be shown to have the required properties; it is, in fact, equivalent to the compositions defined by the homogeneous sequence K_{st} of (31) under the correspondence of exercise 4, when restricted to the subsequence defined by the bounds m_s, ..., m_0. [See T. Walsh, *J. Combinatorial Math. and Combinatorial Computing* **33** (2000), 323–345, who has implemented it looplessly.]

62. (a) A $2 \times n$ contingency table with row sums r and $c_1 + \cdots + c_n - r$ is equivalent to solving $r = a_1 + \cdots + a_n$ with $0 \leq a_1 \leq c_1, \ldots, 0 \leq a_n \leq c_n$.

(b) We can compute it sequentially by setting $a_{ij} \leftarrow \min(r_i - a_{i1} - \cdots - a_{i(j-1)}, c_j - a_{1j} - \cdots - a_{(i-1)j})$ for $j = 1, \ldots, n$, for $i = 1, \ldots, m$. Alternatively, if $r_1 \leq c_1$, set $a_{11} \leftarrow r_1, a_{12} \leftarrow \cdots \leftarrow a_{1n} \leftarrow 0$, and do the remaining rows with c_1 decreased by r_1; if $r_1 > c_1$, set $a_{11} \leftarrow c_1, a_{21} \leftarrow \cdots \leftarrow a_{m1} \leftarrow 0$, and do the remaining columns with r_1 decreased by c_1. The second approach shows that at most $m + n - 1$ of the entries are nonzero. We can also write down the explicit formula

$$a_{ij} = \max(0, \min(r_i, c_j, r_1 + \cdots + r_i - c_1 - \cdots - c_{j-1}, c_1 + \cdots + c_j - r_1 - \cdots - r_{i-1})).$$

(c) The same matrix is obtained as in (b).

(d) Reverse left and right in (b) and (c); in both cases the answer is

$$a_{ij} = \max(0, \min(r_i, c_j, r_{i+1} + \cdots + r_m - c_1 - \cdots - c_{j-1}, c_1 + \cdots + c_j - r_i - \cdots - r_m)).$$

(e) Here we choose, say, row-wise order: Generate the first row just as for bounded compositions of r_1, with bounds $(c_1, \ldots, c_n)$; and for each row $(a_{11}, \ldots, a_{1n})$, generate the remaining rows recursively in the same way, but with the column sums $(c_1 - a_{11}, \ldots, c_n - a_{1n})$. Most of the action takes place on the bottom two rows, but when a change is made to an earlier row the later rows must be re-initialized.

63. If a_{ij} and a_{kl} are positive, we obtain another contingency table by setting $a_{ij} \leftarrow a_{ij} - 1, a_{il} \leftarrow a_{il} + 1, a_{kj} \leftarrow a_{kj} + 1, a_{kl} \leftarrow a_{kl} - 1$. We want to show that the graph G whose vertices are the contingency tables for $(r_1, \ldots, r_m; c_1, \ldots, c_n)$, adjacent if they can be obtained from each other by such a transformation, has a Hamiltonian path.

When $m = n = 2$, G is a simple path. When $m = 2$ and $n = 3$, G has a two-dimensional structure from which we can see that every vertex is the starting point of at least two Hamiltonian paths, having distinct endpoints. When $m = 2$ and $n \geq 4$ we can show, inductively, that G actually has Hamiltonian paths from any vertex to any other.

When $m \geq 3$ and $n \geq 3$, we can reduce the problem from m to $m - 1$ as in answer 62(e), if we are careful not to "paint ourselves into a corner." Namely, we must avoid reaching a state where the nonzero entries of the bottom two rows have the form $\left(\begin{smallmatrix} 1 & a & 0 \\ 0 & b & c \end{smallmatrix}\right)$ for some $a, b, c > 0$ and a change to row $m - 2$ forces this to become $\left(\begin{smallmatrix} 0 & a & 1 \\ 0 & b & c \end{smallmatrix}\right)$. The previous round of changes to rows $m-1$ and m can avoid such a trap unless $c=1$ and it begins with $\left(\begin{smallmatrix} 0 & a+1 & 0 \\ 1 & b-1 & 1 \end{smallmatrix}\right)$ or $\left(\begin{smallmatrix} 1 & a-1 & 1 \\ 0 & b+1 & 0 \end{smallmatrix}\right)$. But that situation can be avoided too.

(A genlex method based on exercise 61 would be considerably simpler, and it almost always would make only four changes per step. But it would occasionally need to update $2\min(m,n)$ entries at a time.)

64. When $x_1\ldots x_s$ is a binary string and A is a list of subcubes, let $A\oplus x_1\ldots x_s$ denote replacing the digits $(a_1,\ldots,a_s)$ in each subcube of A by $(a_1\oplus x_1,\ldots,a_s\oplus x_s)$, from left to right. For example, $0*1**10\oplus 1010 = 1*1**00$. Then the following mutual recursions define a Gray cycle, because A_{st} gives a Gray path from 0^s*^t to $10^{s-1}*^t$ and B_{st} gives a Gray path from 0^s*^t to $*01^{s-1}*^{t-1}$, when $st>0$:

$$A_{st} = 0B_{(s-1)t},\ *A_{s(t-1)}\oplus 001^{s-2},\ 1B^R_{(s-1)t};$$

$$B_{st} = 0A_{(s-1)t},\ 1B_{(s-1)t}\oplus 010^{s-2},\ *A_{s(t-1)}\oplus 1^s.$$

The strings 001^{s-2} and 010^{s-2} are simply 0^s when $s<2$; A_{s0} is Gray binary code; $A_{0t}=B_{0t}=*^t$. (Incidentally, the somewhat simpler construction

$$G_{st} = *G_{s(t-1)},\ a_t G_{(s-1)t},\ a_{t-1}G^R_{(s-1)t},\qquad a_t = t \bmod 2,$$

defines a pleasant Gray *path* from $*^t 0^s$ to $a_{t-1}*^t 0^{s-1}$.)

65. If a path P is considered equivalent to P^R and to $P\oplus x_1\ldots x_s$, the total number can be computed systematically as in exercise 33, with the following results for $s+t\leq 6$:

paths							cycles						
1							1						
1	1						1	1					
1	2	1					1	1	1				
1	3	3	1				1	1	1	1			
1	5	10	4	1			1	2	1	1	1		
1	6	36	35	5	1		1	2	3	1	1	1	
1	9	310	4630	218	6	1	1	3	46	4	1	1	1

In general there are $t+1$ paths when $s=1$ and $\binom{\lceil s/2\rceil+2}{2}-(s \bmod 2)$ when $t=1$. The cycles for $s\leq 2$ are unique. When $s=t=5$ there are approximately 6.869×10^{170} paths and 2.495×10^{70} cycles.

66. Let $G(n,0)=\epsilon$; $G(n,t)=\emptyset$ when $n<t$; and for $1\leq t\leq n$, let $G(n,t)$ be

$$\hat{g}(0)G(n-1,t),\ \hat{g}(1)G(n-1,t)^R,\ \ldots,\ \hat{g}(2^t-1)G(n-1,t)^R,\ \hat{g}(2^t-1)G(n-1,t-1),$$

where $\hat{g}(k)$ is a t-bit column containing the Gray binary number $g(k)$ with its least significant bit at the top. In this general formula we implicitly add a row of zeros below the bases of $G(n-1,t-1)$.

This remarkable rule gives ordinary Gray binary code when $t=1$, omitting $0\ldots00$. A cyclic Gray code is impossible because $\binom{n}{t}_2$ is odd.

67. A Gray path for compositions corresponding to Algorithm C implies that there is a path in which all transitions are $0^k1^l\leftrightarrow 1^l0^k$ with $\min(k,l)\leq 2$. Perhaps there is, in fact, a cycle with $\min(k,l)=1$ in each transition.

68. (a) $\{\emptyset\}$; (b) $\emptyset$.

69. The least N with $\kappa_t N < N$ is $\binom{2t-1}{t}+\binom{2t-3}{t-1}+\cdots+\binom{1}{1}+1=\frac{1}{2}(\binom{2t}{t}+\binom{2t-2}{t-1}+\cdots+\binom{0}{0}+1)$, because $\binom{n}{t-1}\leq\binom{n}{t}$ if and only if $n\geq 2t-1$.

70. From the identity

$$\kappa_t\left(\binom{2t-3}{t}+N'\right)-\left(\binom{2t-3}{t}+N'\right) = \kappa_t\left(\binom{2t-2}{t}+N'\right)-\left(\binom{2t-2}{t}+N'\right) = \binom{2t-2}{t}\frac{1}{t-1}+\kappa_{t-1}N'-N'$$

when $N' < \binom{2t-3}{t}$, we conclude that the maximum is $\binom{2t-2}{t}\frac{1}{t} + \binom{2t-4}{t-1}\frac{1}{t-2}+\cdots+\binom{2}{2}\frac{1}{1}$, and it occurs at 2^{t-1} values of N when $t > 1$.

71. Let C_t be the t-cliques. The first $\binom{1414}{t} + \binom{1009}{t-1}$ t-combinations visited by Algorithm L define a graph on 1415 vertices with 1000000 edges. If $|C_t|$ were larger, $|\partial^{t-2}C_t|$ would exceed 1000000. Thus the single graph defined by $P_{(1000000)2}$ has the maximum number of t-cliques for all $t \geq 2$.

72. $M = \binom{m_s}{s} + \cdots + \binom{m_u}{u}$ for $m_s > \cdots > m_u \geq u \geq 1$, where $\{m_s,\ldots,m_u\} = \{s+t-1,\ldots,n_v\}\setminus\{n_t,\ldots,n_{v+1}\}$. (Compare with exercise 15, which gives $\binom{s+t}{t}-1-N$.)

If $\alpha = a_{n-1}\ldots a_0$ is the bit string corresponding to the combination $n_t\ldots n_1$, then v is 1 plus the number of trailing 1s in α, and u is the length of the rightmost run of 0s. For example, when $\alpha = 1010001111$ we have $s = 4$, $t = 6$, $M = \binom{8}{4} + \binom{7}{3}$, $u = 3$, $N = \binom{9}{6} + \binom{7}{5}$, $v = 5$.

73. A and B are cross-intersecting $\iff \alpha \not\subseteq U \setminus \beta$ for all $\alpha \in A$ and $\beta \in B \iff A \cap \partial^{n-s-t}B^- = \emptyset$, where $B^- = \{U\setminus\beta \mid \beta \in B\}$ is a set of $(n-t)$-combinations. Since $Q^-_{\bar{N}nt} = P_{N(n-t)}$, we have $|\partial^{n-s-t}B^-| \geq |\partial^{n-s-t}P_{N(n-t)}|$, and $\partial^{n-s-t}P_{N(n-t)} = P_{N's}$ where $N' = \kappa_{s+1}\ldots\kappa_{n-t}N$. Thus if A and B are cross-intersecting we have $M + N' \leq |A| + |\partial^{n-s-t}B^-| \leq \binom{n}{s}$, and $Q_{Mns} \cap P_{N's} = \emptyset$.

Conversely, if $Q_{Mns} \cap P_{N's} \neq \emptyset$ we have $\binom{n}{s} < M + N' \leq |A| + |\partial^{n-s-t}B^-|$, so A and B cannot be cross-intersecting.

74. $|\varrho Q_{Nnt}| = \kappa_{n-t}N$ (see exercise 94). Also, arguing as in (58) and (59), we find $\varrho P_{N5} = (n-1)P_{N5} \cup \cdots \cup 10P_{N5} \cup \{543210,\ldots,987654\}$ in that particular case; and $|\varrho P_{Nt}| = (n+1-n_t)N + \binom{n_t+1}{t+1}$ in general.

75. The identity $\binom{n+1}{k} = \binom{n}{k} + \binom{n-1}{k-1} + \cdots + \binom{n-k}{0}$, Eq. 1.2.6–(10), gives another representation if $n_v > v$. But (60) is unaffected, since we have $\binom{n+1}{k-1} = \binom{n}{k-1} + \binom{n-1}{k-2} + \cdots + \binom{n-k+1}{0}$.

76. Represent $N+1$ by adding $\binom{v-1}{v-1}$ to (57); then use the previous exercise to deduce that $\kappa_t(N+1) - \kappa_t N = \binom{v-1}{v-2} = v - 1$.

77. [D. E. Daykin, *Nanta Math.* **8**, 2 (1975), 78–83.] We work with extended representations $M = \binom{m_t}{t} + \cdots + \binom{m_u}{u}$ and $N = \binom{n_t}{t} + \cdots + \binom{n_v}{v}$ as in exercise 75, calling them *improper* if the final index u or v is zero. Call N *flexible* if it has both proper and improper representations, that is, if $n_v > v > 0$.

(a) Given an integer S, find $M + N$ such that $M + N = S$ and $\kappa_t M + \kappa_t N$ is minimum, with M as large as possible. If $N = 0$, we're done. Otherwise the max-min operation preserves both $M + N$ and $\kappa_t M + \kappa_t N$, so we can assume that $v \geq u \geq 1$ in the proper representations of M and N. If N is inflexible, $\kappa_t(M + 1) + \kappa_t(N - 1) = (\kappa_t M + u - 1) + (\kappa_t N - v) < \kappa_t M + \kappa_t N$, by exercise 76; therefore N must be flexible. But then we can apply the max-min operation to M and the improper representation of N, increasing M: Contradiction.

This proof shows that equality holds if and only if $MN = 0$, a fact that was noted in 1927 by F. S. Macaulay.

(b) Now we try to minimize $\max(\kappa_t M, N) + \kappa_{t-1}N$ when $M + N = S$, this time representing N as $\binom{n_{t-1}}{t-1} + \cdots + \binom{n_v}{v}$. The max-min operation can still be used if $n_{t-1} < m_t$; leaving m_t unchanged, it preserves $M + N$ and $\kappa_t M + \kappa_{t-1}N$ as well as the relation $\kappa_t M > N$. We arrive at a contradiction as in (a) if $N \neq 0$, so we can assume that $n_{t-1} \geq m_t$.

If $n_{t-1} > m_t$ we have $N > \kappa_t M$ and also $\lambda_t N > M$; hence $M + N < \lambda_t N + N = \binom{n_{t-1}+1}{t} + \cdots + \binom{n_v+1}{v}$, and we have $\kappa_t(M + N) \leq \kappa_t(\lambda_t N + N) = N + \kappa_{t-1}N$.

Finally if $n_{t-1} = m_t = a$, let $M = \binom{a}{t}+M'$ and $N = \binom{a}{t-1}+N'$. Then $\kappa_t(M+N) = \binom{a+1}{t-1} + \kappa_{t-1}(M' + N')$, $\kappa_t M = \binom{a}{t-1} + \kappa_{t-1}M'$, and $\kappa_{t-1}N = \binom{a}{t-2} + \kappa_{t-2}N'$; the result follows by induction on t.

78. [J. Eckhoff and G. Wegner, *Periodica Math. Hung.* **6** (1975), 137–142; A. J. W. Hilton, *Periodica Math. Hung.* **10** (1979), 25–30.] Let $M = |A_1|$ and $N = |A_0|$; we can assume that $t > 0$ and $N > 0$. Then $|\partial A| = |\partial A_1 \cup A_0| + |\partial A_0| \geq \max(|\partial A_1|, |A_0|) + |\partial A_0| \geq \max(\kappa_t M, N) + \kappa_{t-1}N \geq \kappa_t(M + N) = |P_{|A|t}|$, by induction on $m + n + t$.

Conversely, let $A_1 = P_{Mt} + 1$ and $A_0 = P_{N(t-1)} + 1$; this notation means, for example, that $\{210, 320\} + 1 = \{321, 431\}$. Then $\kappa_t(M + N) \leq |\partial A| = |\partial A_1 \cup A_0| + |(\partial A_0)0| = \max(\kappa_t M, N) + \kappa_{t-1}N$, because $\partial A_1 = P_{(\kappa_t M)(t-1)} + 1$. [Schützenberger observed in 1959 that $\kappa_t(M + N) \leq \kappa_t M + \kappa_{t-1}N$ if and only if $\kappa_t M \geq N$.]

For the first inequality, let A and B be disjoint sets of t-combinations with $|A| = M$, $|\partial A| = \kappa_t M$, $|B| = N$, $|\partial B| = \kappa_t N$. Then $\kappa_t(M + N) = \kappa_t|A \cup B| \leq |\partial(A \cup B)| = |\partial A \cup \partial B| = |\partial A| + |\partial B| = \kappa_t M + \kappa_t N$.

79. In fact, $\mu_t(M + \lambda_{t-1}M) = M$, and $\mu_t N + \lambda_{t-1}\mu_t N = N + (n_2 - n_1)[v = 1]$ when N is given by (57).

80. If $N > 0$ and $t > 1$, represent N as in (57) and let $N = N_0 + N_1$, where

$$N_0 = \binom{n_t - 1}{t} + \cdots + \binom{n_v - 1}{v}, \qquad N_1 = \binom{n_t - 1}{t - 1} + \cdots + \binom{n_v - 1}{v - 1}.$$

Let $N_0 = \binom{y}{t}$ and $N_1 = \binom{z}{t-1}$. Then, by induction on t and $\lfloor x \rfloor$, we have $\binom{x}{t} = N_0 + \kappa_t N_0 \geq \binom{y}{t} + \binom{y}{t-1} = \binom{y+1}{t}$; $N_1 = \binom{x}{t} - \binom{y}{t} \geq \binom{x}{t} - \binom{x-1}{t} = \binom{x-1}{t-1}$; and $\kappa_t N = N_1 + \kappa_{t-1}N_1 \geq \binom{z}{t-1} + \binom{z}{t-2} = \binom{z+1}{t-1} \geq \binom{x}{t-1}$.

[Lovász actually proved a stronger result; see exercise 1.2.6–66. We have, similarly, $\mu_t N \geq \binom{x-1}{t-1}$; see Björner, Frankl, and Stanley, *Combinatorica* **7** (1987), 27–28.]

81. For example, if the largest element of $\widehat{P}_{N5}$ is 66433, we have

$$\widehat{P}_{N5} = \{00000, \ldots, 55555\} \cup \{60000, \ldots, 65555\} \cup \{66000, \ldots, 66333\} \cup \{66400, \ldots, 66433\}$$

so $N = \binom{10}{5} + \binom{9}{4} + \binom{6}{3} + \binom{5}{2}$. Its lower shadow is

$$\partial\widehat{P}_{N5} = \{0000, \ldots, 5555\} \cup \{6000, \ldots, 6555\} \cup \{6600, \ldots, 6633\} \cup \{6640, \ldots, 6643\},$$

of size $\binom{9}{4} + \binom{8}{3} + \binom{5}{2} + \binom{4}{1}$.

If the smallest element of Q_{N95} is 66433, we have

$$\widehat{Q}_{N95} = \{99999, \ldots, 70000\} \cup \{66666, \ldots, 66500\} \cup \{66444, \ldots, 66440\} \cup \{66433\}$$

so $N = \left(\binom{13}{9}+\binom{12}{8}+\binom{11}{7}\right) + \left(\binom{8}{6}+\binom{7}{5}\right) + \binom{5}{4} + \binom{3}{3}$. Its upper shadow is

$$\varrho\widehat{Q}_{N95} = \{999999, \ldots, 700000\} \cup \{666666, \ldots, 665000\}$$
$$\cup \{664444, \ldots, 664400\} \cup \{664333, \ldots, 664330\},$$

of size $\left(\binom{14}{9}+\binom{13}{8}+\binom{12}{7}\right) + \left(\binom{9}{6}+\binom{8}{5}\right) + \binom{6}{4} + \binom{4}{3} = N + \kappa_9 N$. The size, t, of each combination is essentially irrelevant, as long as $N \leq \binom{s+t}{t}$; for example, the smallest element of $\widehat{Q}_{N98}$ is 99966433 in the case we have considered.

82. (a) The derivative would have to be $\sum_{k>0} r_k(x)$, but that series diverges.

[Informally, the graph of $\tau(x)$ shows "pits" of relative magnitude 2^{-k} at all odd multiples of 2^{-k}. Takagi's original publication, in *Proc. Physico-Math. Soc. Japan* (2) **1** (1903), 176–177, has been translated into English in his *Collected Papers* (Iwanami Shoten, 1973).]

(b) Since $r_k(1-t) = (-1)^{\lceil 2^k t \rceil}$ when $k > 0$, we have $\int_0^{1-x} r_k(t)\,dt = \int_x^1 r_k(1-u)\,du = -\int_x^1 r_k(u)\,du = \int_0^x r_k(u)\,du$. The second equation follows from the fact that $r_k(\frac{1}{2}t) = r_{k-1}(t)$. Part (d) shows that these two equations suffice to define $\tau(x)$ when x is rational.

(c) Since $\tau(2^{-a}x) = a2^{-a}x + 2^{-a}\tau(x)$ for $0 \le x \le 1$, we have $\tau(\epsilon) = a\epsilon + O(\epsilon)$ when $2^{-a-1} \le \epsilon \le 2^{-a}$. Therefore $\tau(\epsilon) = \epsilon \lg \frac{1}{\epsilon} + O(\epsilon)$ for $0 < \epsilon \le 1$.

(d) Suppose $0 \le p/q \le 1$. If $p/q \le 1/2$ we have $\tau(p/q) = p/q + \tau(2p/q)/2$; otherwise $\tau(p/q) = (q-p)/q + \tau(2(q-p)/q)/2$. Therefore we can assume that q is odd. When q is odd, let $p' = p/2$ when p is even, $p' = (q-p)/2$ when p is odd. Then $\tau(p/q) = 2\tau(p'/q) - 2p'/q$ for $0 < p < q$; this system of $q-1$ equations has a unique solution. For example, the values for $q = 3, 4, 5, 6, 7$ are 2/3, 2/3; 1/2, 1/2, 1/2; 8/15, 2/3, 2/3, 8/15; 1/2, 2/3, 1/2, 2/3, 1/2; 22/49, 30/49, 32/49, 32/49, 30/49, 22/49.

(e) The solutions $< \frac{1}{2}$ are $x = \frac{1}{4}, \frac{1}{4} - \frac{1}{16}, \frac{1}{4} - \frac{1}{16} - \frac{1}{64}, \frac{1}{4} - \frac{1}{16} - \frac{1}{64} - \frac{1}{256}, \ldots, \frac{1}{6}$.

(f) The value $\frac{2}{3}$ is achieved for $x = \frac{1}{2} \pm \frac{1}{8} \pm \frac{1}{32} \pm \frac{1}{128} \pm \cdots$, an uncountable set.

83. Given any integers $q > p > 0$, consider paths from 0 in the digraph

$$
\begin{array}{ccccccccccc}
0 & \leftarrow & 1 & \leftarrow & 2 & \leftarrow & 3 & \leftarrow & 4 & \leftarrow & 5 & \leftarrow & \cdots \\
& & \updownarrow & & \updownarrow & & \updownarrow & & \updownarrow & & \updownarrow & & \updownarrow \\
& & 1 & \rightarrow & 2 & \rightarrow & 3 & \rightarrow & 4 & \rightarrow & 5 & \rightarrow & 6 & \rightarrow & \cdots
\end{array}
$$

Compute an associated value v, starting with $v \leftarrow -p$; horizontal moves change $v \leftarrow 2v$, vertical moves from node a change $v \leftarrow 2(qa - v)$. The path stops if we reach a node twice with the same value v. Transitions are not allowed to upper node a if $v \le -q$ or $v \ge qa$ at that node; they are not allowed to lower node a with $v \le 0$ or $v \ge q(a+1)$. These restrictions force most steps of the path. (Node a in the upper row means, "Solve $\tau(x) = ax - v/q$"; in the lower row it means, "Solve $\tau(x) = v/q - ax$.") Empirical tests suggest that all such paths are finite. The equation $\tau(x) = p/q$ then has solutions $x = x_0$ defined by the sequence $x_0, x_1, x_2, \ldots$ where $x_k = \frac{1}{2}x_{k+1}$ on a horizontal step and $x_k = 1 - \frac{1}{2}x_{k+1}$ on a vertical step; eventually $x_k = x_j$ for some $j < k$. If $j > 0$ and if q is not a power of 2, these are all the solutions to $\tau(x) = p/q$ when $x > 1/2$.

For example, this procedure establishes that $\tau(x) = 1/5$ and $x > 1/2$ only when x is $83581/87040$; the only path yields $x_0 = 1 - \frac{1}{2}x_1$, $x_1 = \frac{1}{2}x_2$, $\ldots$, $x_{18} = \frac{1}{2}x_{19}$, and $x_{19} = x_{11}$. There are, similarly, just two values $x > 1/2$ with $\tau(x) = 3/5$, having denominator $2^{46}(2^{56} - 1)/3$.

Moreover, it appears that all cycles in the digraph that pass through node 0 define values of p and q such that $\tau(x) = p/q$ has uncountably many solutions. Such values are, for example, 2/3, 8/15, 8/21, corresponding to the cycles (01), (0121), (012321). The value 32/63 corresponds to (012121) and also to (012101234545454321), as well as to two other paths that do not return to 0.

84. [Frankl, Matsumoto, Ruzsa, and Tokushige, *J. Combinatorial Theory* **A69** (1995), 125–148.] If $a \le b$ we have

$$
\binom{2t-1-b}{t-a} \Big/ T = t^a(t-1)^{b-a}/(2t-1)^b = 2^{-b}(1 + f(a,b)t^{-1} + O(b^4/t^2)),
$$

where $f(a,b) = a(1+b) - a^2 - b(1+b)/4 = f(a+1,b) - b + 2a$. Therefore if N has the combinatorial representation (57), and if we set $n_j = 2t - 1 - b_j$, we have

$$\frac{t}{T}\left(\kappa_t N - N\right) = \frac{b_t}{2^{b_t}} + \frac{b_{t-1} - 2}{2^{b_{t-1}}} + \frac{b_{t-2} - 4}{2^{b_{t-2}}} + \cdots + \frac{O(\log t)^3}{t},$$

the terms being negligible when b_j exceeds $2 \lg t$. And one can show that

$$\tau\left(\sum_{j=0}^{l} 2^{-e_j}\right) = \sum_{j=0}^{l} (e_j - 2j) 2^{-e_j}.$$

85. $N - \lambda_{t-1} N$ has the same asymptotic form as $\kappa_t N - N$, by (63), since $\tau(x) = \tau(1-x)$. So does $2\mu_t N - N$, up to $O(T(\log t)^3/t^2)$, because $\binom{2t-1-b}{t-a} = 2\binom{2t-2-b}{t-a}(1 + O(\log t)/t)$ when $b < 2 \lg t$.

86. $x \in X^{\circ \sim} \iff \bar{x} \notin X^{\circ} \iff \bar{x} \notin X$ or $\bar{x} \notin X + e_1$ or $\cdots$ or $\bar{x} \notin X + e_n \iff x \in X^{\sim}$ or $x \in X^{\sim} - e_1$ or $\cdots$ or $x \in X^{\sim} - e_n \iff x \in X^{\sim +}$.

87. All three are true, using the fact that $X \subseteq Y^{\circ}$ if and only if $X^+ \subseteq Y$: (a) $X \subseteq Y^{\circ} \iff X^{\sim} \supseteq Y^{\circ \sim} = Y^{\sim +} \iff Y^{\sim} \subseteq X^{\sim \circ}$. (b) $X^+ \subseteq X^+ \implies X \subseteq X^{+\circ}$; hence $X^{\circ} \subseteq X^{\circ + \circ}$. Also $X^{\circ} \subseteq X^{\circ} \implies X^{\circ +} \subseteq X$; hence $X^{\circ + \circ} \subseteq X^{\circ}$. (c) $\alpha M \leq N \iff S_M^+ \subseteq S_N \iff S_M \subseteq S_N^{\circ} \iff M \leq \beta N$.

88. If $\nu x < \nu y$ then $\nu(x - e_k) < \nu(y - e_j)$, so we can assume that $\nu x = \nu y$ and that $x > y$ in lexicographic order. We must have $y_j > 0$; otherwise $\nu(y - e_j)$ would exceed $\nu(x - e_k)$. If $x_i = y_i$ for $1 \leq i \leq j$, clearly $k > j$ and $x - e_k \prec y - e_j$. Otherwise $x_i > y_i$ for some $i \leq j$; again we have $x - e_k \prec y - e_j$, unless $x - e_k = y - e_j$.

89. From the table

$j =$	0	1	2	3	4	5	6	7	8	9	10	11
$e_j + e_1 =$	e_1	e_0	e_4	e_5	e_2	e_3	e_8	e_9	e_6	e_7	e_{11}	e_{10}
$e_j + e_2 =$	e_2	e_4	e_0	e_6	e_1	e_8	e_3	e_{10}	e_5	e_{11}	e_7	e_9
$e_j + e_3 =$	e_3	e_5	e_6	e_7	e_8	e_9	e_{10}	e_0	e_{11}	e_1	e_2	e_4

we find $(\alpha 0, \alpha 1, \ldots, \alpha 12) = (0, 4, 6, 7, 8, 9, 10, 11, 11, 12, 12, 12, 12)$; $(\beta 0, \beta 1, \ldots, \beta 12) = (0, 0, 0, 0, 1, 1, 2, 3, 4, 5, 6, 8, 12)$.

90. Let $Y = X^+$ and $Z = C_k X$, and let $N_a = |X_k(a)|$ for $0 \leq a < m_k$. Then

$$|Y| = \sum_{a=0}^{m_k - 1} |Y_k(a)| = \sum_{a=0}^{m_k - 1} |(X_k(a - 1) + e_k) \cup (X_k(a) + E_k(0))|$$

$$\geq \sum_{a=0}^{m_k - 1} \max(N_{a-1}, \alpha N_a),$$

where $a - 1$ stands for $(a - 1) \bmod m_k$ and the α function comes from the $(n - 1)$-dimensional torus, because $|X_k(a) + E_k(0)| \geq \alpha N_a$ by induction. Also

$$|Z^+| = \sum_{a=0}^{m_k - 1} |Z_k^+(a)| = \sum_{a=0}^{m_k - 1} |(Z_k(a - 1) + e_k) \cup (Z_k(a) + E_k(0))|$$

$$= \sum_{a=0}^{m_k - 1} \max(N_{a-1}, \alpha N_a),$$

because both $Z_k(a - 1) + e_k$ and $Z_k(a) + E_k(0)$ are standard in $n - 1$ dimensions.

91. Let there be N_a points in row a of a totally compressed array, where row 0 is at the bottom; thus $l = N_{-1} \geq N_0 \geq \cdots \geq N_{m-1} \geq N_m = 0$. We show first that there is an optimum X for which the "bad" condition $N_a = N_{a+1}$ never occurs except when $N_a = 0$ or $N_a = l$. For if a is the smallest bad subscript, suppose $N_{a-1} > N_a = N_{a+1} = \cdots = N_{a+k} > N_{a+k+1}$. Then we can always decrease N_{a+k} by 1 and add 1 to some N_b for $b \leq a$ without increasing $|X^+|$, except in cases where $k = 1$ and $N_{a+2} = N_{a+1} - 1$ and $N_b = N_a + a - b < l$ for $0 \leq b \leq a$. Exploring such cases further, if $N_{c+1} < N_c = N_{c-1}$ for some $c > a + 1$, we can set $N_c \leftarrow N_c - 1$ and $N_a \leftarrow N_a + 1$, thereby either decreasing a or increasing N_0. Otherwise we can find a subscript d such that $N_c = N_{a+1} + a + 1 - c > 0$ for $a < c < d$, and either $N_d = 0$ or $N_d < N_{d-1} - 1$. Then it is OK to decrease N_c by 1 for $a < c < d$ and subsequently to increase N_b by 1 for $0 \leq b < d - a - 1$. (It is important to note that if $N_d = 0$ we have $N_0 \geq d - 1$; hence $d = m$ implies $l = m$.)

Repeating such transformations until $N_a > N_{a+1}$ whenever $N_a \neq l$ and $N_{a+1} \neq 0$, we reach situation (86), and the proof can be completed as in the text.

92. Let $x + k$ denote the lexicographically smallest element of $T(m_1, \ldots, m_{n-1})$ that exceeds x and has weight $\nu x + k$, if any such element exists. For example, if $m_1 = m_2 = m_3 = 4$ and $x = 211$, we have $x + 1 = 212$, $x + 2 = 213$, $x + 3 = 223$, $x + 4 = 233$, $x + 5 = 333$, and $x + 6$ does not exist; in general, $x + k + 1$ is obtained from $x + k$ by increasing the rightmost component that can be increased. If $x + k = (m_1 - 1, \ldots, m_{n-1} - 1)$, let us set $x + k + 1 = x + k$. Then if $S(k)$ is the set of all elements of $T(m_1, \ldots, m_{n-1})$ that are $\preceq x + k$, we have $S(k + 1) = S(k)^+$. Furthermore, the elements of S that end in a are those whose first $n - 1$ components are in $S(m - 1 - a)$.

The result of this exercise can be stated more intuitively: As we generate n-dimensional standard sets S_1, S_2, $\ldots$, the $(n - 1)$-dimensional standard sets on each layer become spreads of each other just after each point is added to layer $m - 1$. Similarly, they become cores of each other just before each point is added to layer 0.

93. (a) Suppose the parameters are $2 \leq m'_1 \leq m'_2 \leq \cdots \leq m'_n$ when sorted properly, and let k be minimal with $m_k \neq m'_k$. Then take $N = 1 + \text{rank}(0, \ldots, 0, m'_k - 1, 0, \ldots, 0)$. (We must assume that $\min(m_1, \ldots, m_n) \geq 2$, since parameters equal to 1 can be placed anywhere.)

(b) Only in the proof for $n = 2$, buried inside the answer to exercise 91. That proof is incorporated by induction when n is larger.

94. Complementation reverses lexicographic order and changes ϱ to ∂.

95. For Theorem K, let $d = n - 1$ and $s_0 = \cdots = s_d = 1$. For Theorem M, let $d = s$ and $s_0 = \cdots = s_d = t + 1$.

96. In such a representation, N is the number of t-multicombinations of $\{s_0 \cdot 0, s_1 \cdot 1, s_2 \cdot 2, \ldots\}$ that precede $n_t n_{t-1} \ldots n_1$ in lexicographic order, because the generalized coefficient $\binom{S(n)}{t}$ counts the multicombinations whose leftmost component is $< n$.

If we truncate the representation by stopping at the rightmost nonzero term $\binom{S(n_v)}{v}$, we obtain a nice generalization of (60):

$$|\partial P_{Nt}| = \binom{S(n_t)}{t - 1} + \binom{S(n_{t-1})}{t - 2} + \cdots + \binom{S(n_v)}{v - 1}.$$

[See G. F. Clements, *J. Combinatorial Theory* **A37** (1984), 91–97. The inequalities $s_0 \geq s_1 \geq \cdots \geq s_d$ are needed for the validity of Corollary C, but not for the calculation of $|\partial P_{Nt}|$. Some terms $\binom{S(n_k)}{k}$ for $t \geq k > v$ may be zero. For example, when $N = 1$, $t = 4$, $s_0 = 3$, and $s_1 = 2$, we have $N = \binom{S(1)}{4} + \binom{S(1)}{3} = 0 + 1$.]

97. (a) The tetrahedron has four vertices, six edges, four faces: $(N_0, \ldots, N_4) = (1, 4, 6, 4, 1)$. The octahedron, similarly, has $(N_0, \ldots, N_6) = (1, 6, 8, 8, 0, 0, 0)$, and the icosahedron has $(N_0, \ldots, N_{12}) = (1, 12, 30, 20, 0, \ldots, 0)$. The hexahedron, aka the 3-cube, has eight vertices, 12 edges, and six square faces; perturbation breaks each square face into two triangles and introduces new edges, so we have $(N_0, \ldots, N_8) = (1, 8, 18, 12, 0, \ldots, 0)$. Finally, the perturbed pentagonal faces of the dodecahedron lead to $(N_0, \ldots, N_{20}) = (1, 20, 54, 36, 0, \ldots, 0)$.

(b) $\{210, 310\} \cup \{10, 20, 21, 30, 31\} \cup \{0, 1, 2, 3\} \cup \{\epsilon\}$.

(c) $0 \le N_t \le \binom{n}{t}$ for $0 \le t \le n$ and $N_{t-1} \ge \kappa_t N_t$ for $1 \le t \le n$. The second condition is equivalent to $\lambda_{t-1} N_{t-1} \ge N_t$ for $1 \le t \le n$, if we define $\lambda_0 1 = \infty$. These conditions are necessary for Theorem K, and sufficient if $A = \bigcup P_{N_t t}$.

(d) The complements of the elements not in a simplicial complex, namely the sets $\big\{\, \{0, \ldots, n-1\} \setminus \alpha \mid \alpha \notin C \,\big\}$, form a simplicial complex. (We can also verify that the necessary and sufficient condition holds: $N_{t-1} \ge \kappa_t N_t \iff \lambda_{t-1} N_{t-1} \ge N_t \iff \kappa_{n-t+1} \overline{N}_{n-t+1} \le \overline{N}_{n-t}$, because $\kappa_{n-t} \overline{N}_{n-t+1} = \binom{n}{t} - \lambda_{t-1} N_{t-1}$ by exercise 94.)

(e) $00000 \leftrightarrow 14641$; $10000 \leftrightarrow 14640$; $11000 \leftrightarrow 14630$; $12000 \leftrightarrow 14620$; $13000 \leftrightarrow 14610$; $14000 \leftrightarrow 14600$; $12100 \leftrightarrow 14520$; $13100 \leftrightarrow 14510$; $14100 \leftrightarrow 14500$; $13200 \leftrightarrow 14410$; $14200 \leftrightarrow 14400$; $13300 \leftrightarrow 14400$; and the self-dual cases 14300, 13310.

98. The following procedure by S. Linusson [*Combinatorica* **19** (1999), 255–266], who considered also the more general problem for multisets, is considerably faster than a more obvious approach. Let $L(n, h, l)$ count feasible vectors with $N_t = \binom{n}{t}$ for $0 \le t \le l$, $N_{t+1} < \binom{n}{t+1}$, and $N_t = 0$ for $t > h$. Then $L(n, h, l) = 0$ unless $-1 \le l \le h \le n$; also $L(n, h, h) = L(n, h, -1) = 1$, and $L(n, n, l) = L(n, n-1, l)$ for $l < n$. When $n > h \ge l \ge 0$ we can compute $L(n, h, l) = \sum_{j=l}^{h} L(n-1, h, j) L(n-1, j-1, l-1)$, a recurrence that follows from Theorem K. (Each size vector corresponds to the complex $\bigcup P_{N_t t}$, with $L(n-1, h, j)$ representing combinations that do not contain the maximum element $n-1$ and $L(n-1, j-1, l-1)$ representing those that do.) Finally the grand total is $L(n) = \sum_{l=1}^{n} L(n, n, l)$.

We have $L(0)$, $L(1)$, $L(2)$, $\ldots$ = 2, 3, 5, 10, 26, 96, 553, 5461, 100709, 3718354, 289725509, $\ldots$; $L(100) \approx 3.2299 \times 10^{1842}$.

99. The maximal elements of a simplicial complex form a clutter; conversely, the combinations contained in elements of a clutter form a simplicial complex. Thus the two concepts are essentially equivalent.

(a) If $(M_0, M_1, \ldots, M_n)$ is the size vector of a clutter, then $(N_0, N_1, \ldots, N_n)$ is the size vector of a simplicial complex if $N_n = M_n$ and $N_t = M_t + \kappa_{t+1} N_{t+1}$ for $0 \le t < n$. Conversely, every such $(N_0, \ldots, N_n)$ yields an $(M_0, \ldots, M_n)$ if we use the lexicographically first N_t t-combinations. [G. F. Clements extended this result to general multisets in *Discrete Math.* **4** (1973), 123–128.]

(b) In the order of answer 97(e) they are 00000, 00001, 10000, 00040, 01000, 00030, 02000, 00120, 03000, 00310, 04000, 00600, 00100, 00020, 01100, 00210, 02100, 00500, 00200, 00110, 01200, 00400, 00300, 01010, 01300, 00010. Notice that $(M_0, \ldots, M_n)$ is feasible if and only if $(M_n, \ldots, M_0)$ is feasible, so we have a different sort of duality in this interpretation.

100. Represent A as a subset of $T(m_1, \ldots, m_n)$ as in the proof of Corollary C. Then the maximum value of νA is obtained when A consists of the N lexicographically smallest points $x_1 \ldots x_n$.

The proof starts by reducing to the case that A is compressed, in the sense that its t-multicombinations are $P_{|A \cap T_t| t}$ for each t. Then if y is the largest element $\in A$

and if x is the smallest element $\notin A$, we prove that $x < y$ implies $\nu x > \nu y$, hence $\nu(A \setminus \{y\} \cup \{x\}) > \nu A$. For if $\nu x = \nu y - k$ we could find an element of $\partial^k y$ that is greater than x, contradicting the assumption that A is compressed.

101. (a) In general, $F(p) = N_0 p^n + N_1 p^{n-1}(1-p) + \cdots + N_n(1-p)^n$ when $f(x_1, \ldots, x_n)$ is satisfied by exactly N_t binary strings $x_1 \ldots x_n$ of weight t. Thus we find $G(p) = p^4 + 3p^3(1-p) + p^2(1-p)^2$; $H(p) = p^4 + p^3(1-p) + p^2(1-p)^2$.

(b) A monotone formula f is equivalent to a simplicial complex C under the correspondence $f(x_1, \ldots, x_n) = 1 \iff \{j - 1 \mid x_j = 0\} \in C$. Therefore the functions $f(p)$ of monotone Boolean functions are those that satisfy the condition of exercise 97(c), and we obtain a suitable function by choosing the lexicographically last N_{n-t} t-combinations (which are complements of the first N_s s-combinations): $\{3210\}$, $\{321, 320, 310\}$, $\{32\}$ gives $f(w, x, y, z) = wxyz \lor xyz \lor wyz \lor wxz \lor yz = wxz \lor yz$.

M. P. Schützenberger observed that we can find the parameters N_t easily from $f(p)$ by noting that $f(1/(1+u)) = (N_0 + N_1 u + \cdots + N_n u^n)/(1+u)^n$. One can show that $H(p)$ is not equivalent to a monotone formula in any number of variables, because $(1 + u + u^2)/(1+u)^4 = (N_0 + N_1 u + \cdots + N_n u^n)/(1+u)^n$ implies that $N_1 = n - 3$, $N_2 = \binom{n-3}{2} + 1$, and $\kappa_2 N_2 = n - 2$.

But the task of deciding this question is not so simple in general. For example, the function $(1 + 5u + 5u^2 + 5u^3)/(1+u)^5$ does not match any monotone formula in five variables, because $\kappa_3 5 = 7$; but it equals $(1 + 6u + 10u^2 + 10u^3 + 5u^4)/(1+u)^6$, which works fine with six.

102. (a) Choose N_t linearly independent polynomials of degree t in I; order their terms lexicographically, and take linear combinations so that the lexicographically smallest terms are distinct monomials. Let I' consist of all multiples of those monomials.

(b) Each monomial of degree t in I' is essentially a t-multicombination; for example, $x_1^3 x_2 x_5^4$ corresponds to 55552111. If M_t is the set of independent monomials for degree t, the ideal property is equivalent to saying that $M_{t+1} \supseteq \varrho M_t$.

In the given example, $M_3 = \{x_0 x_1^2\}$; $M_4 = \varrho M_3 \cup \{x_0 x_1 x_2^2\}$; $M_5 = \varrho M_4 \cup \{x_1 x_2^4\}$, since $x_2^2(x_0 x_1^2 - 2x_1 x_2^2) - x_1(x_0 x_1 x_2^2) = -2x_1 x_2^4$; and $M_{t+1} = \varrho M_t$ thereafter.

(c) By Theorem M we can assume that $M_t = \widehat{Q}_{Mst}$. Let $N_t = \binom{n_{ts}}{s} + \cdots + \binom{n_{t2}}{2} + \binom{n_{t1}}{1}$, where $s + t \geq n_{ts} > \cdots > n_{t2} > n_{t1} \geq 0$; then $n_{ts} = s + t$ if and only if $n_{t(s-1)} = s - 2$, ..., $n_{t1} = 0$. Furthermore we have

$$N_{t+1} \geq N_t + \kappa_s N_t = \binom{n_{ts} + [n_{ts} \geq s]}{s} + \cdots + \binom{n_{t2} + [n_{t2} \geq 2]}{2} + \binom{n_{t1} + [n_{t1} \geq 1]}{1}.$$

Therefore the sequence $(n_{ts} - t - \infty[n_{ts} < s], \ldots, n_{t2} - t - \infty[n_{t2} < 2], n_{t1} - t - \infty[n_{t1} < 1])$ is lexicographically nondecreasing as t increases, where we insert '$-\infty$' in components that have $n_{tj} = j - 1$. Such a sequence cannot increase infinitely many times without exceeding the maximum value $(s, -\infty, \ldots, -\infty)$, by exercise 1.2.1–15(d).

103. Let P_{Nst} be the first N elements of a sequence determined as follows: For each binary string $x = x_{s+t-1} \ldots x_0$, in lexicographic order, write down $\binom{\nu x}{t}$ subcubes by changing t of the 1s to $*$s in all possible ways, in lexicographic order (considering $1 < *$). For example, if $x = 0101101$ and $t = 2$, we generate the subcubes $0101*0*$, $010*10*$, $010**01$, $0*0110*$, $0*01*01$, $0*0*101$.

[See B. Lindström, *Arkiv för Mat.* **8** (1971), 245–257; a generalization analogous to Corollary C appears in K. Engel, *Sperner Theory* (Cambridge Univ. Press, 1997), Theorem 8.1.1.]

104. The first N strings in cross order have the desired property. [T. N. Danh and D. E. Daykin, *J. London Math. Soc.* (2) **55** (1997), 417–426.]

Notes: Beginning with the observation that the "1-shadow" of the N lexicographically first strings of weight t (namely the strings obtained by deleting 1 bits only) consists of the first $\mu_t N$ strings of weight t, R. Ahlswede and N. Cai extended the Danh–Daykin theorem to allow insertion, deletion, and/or transposition of bits [*Combinatorica* **17** (1997), 11–29; *Applied Math. Letters* **11**, 5 (1998), 121–126]. Uwe Leck has proved that no total ordering of *ternary strings* has the analogous minimum-shadow property [Preprint 98/6 (Univ. Rostock, 1998), 6 pages].

105. Every number must occur the same number of times in the cycle. Equivalently, $\binom{n-1}{t-1}$ must be a multiple of t. This necessary condition appears to be sufficient as well, provided that n is not too small with respect to t; but such a result may well be true yet impossible to prove. [See Chung, Graham, and Diaconis, *Discrete Math.* **110** (1992), 55–57.]

The next few exercises consider the cases $t = 2$ and $t = 3$, for which elegant results are known. Similar but more complicated results have been derived for $t = 4$ and $t = 5$, and the case $t = 6$ has been partially resolved. The case $(n, t) = (12, 6)$ is currently the smallest for which the existence of a universal cycle is unknown.

106. Let the differences mod $(2m+1)$ be $1, 2, \ldots, m, 1, 2, \ldots, m, \ldots$, repeated $2m+1$ times; for example, the cycle for $m = 3$ is (013602561450346235124). This works because $1 + \cdots + m = \binom{m+1}{2}$ is relatively prime to $2m + 1$. [*J. École Polytechnique* **4**, Cahier 10 (1810), 16–48.]

107. The seven doubles ■■, ■··■, $\ldots$, ■■■■ can be inserted in 3^7 ways into any universal cycle of 3-combinations for $\{0, 1, 2, 3, 4, 5, 6\}$. The number of such universal cycles is the number of Eulerian trails of the complete graph K_7, which can be shown to be $129{,}976{,}320$ if we regard $(a_0 a_1 \ldots a_{20})$ as equivalent to $(a_1 \ldots a_{20} a_0)$ but not to the reverse-order cycle $(a_{20} \ldots a_1 a_0)$. So the answer is $284{,}258{,}211{,}840$.

[This problem was first solved in 1859 by M. Reiss, whose method was so complicated that people doubted the result; see *Nouvelles Annales de Mathématiques* **8** (1849), 74; **11** (1852), 115; *Annali di Matematica Pura ed Applicata* (2) **5** (1871–1873), 63–120. A considerably simpler solution, confirming Reiss's claim, was found by P. Jolivald and G. Tarry, who also enumerated the Eulerian trails of K_9; see *Comptes Rendus Association Française pour l'Avancement des Sciences* **15**, part 2 (1886), 49–53; É. Lucas, *Récréations Mathématiques* **4** (1894), 123–151. Brendan D. McKay and Robert W. Robinson found an approach that is better still, enabling them to continue the enumeration through K_{21} by using the fact that the number of trails is

$$(m - 1)!^{2m+1} \, [z_0^{2m} z_1^{2m-2} \ldots z_{2m}^{2m-2}] \, \det(a_{jk}) \prod_{1 \le j < k \le 2m} (z_j^2 + z_k^2),$$

where $a_{jk} = -1/(z_j^2 + z_k^2)$ when $j \ne k$; $a_{jj} = -1/(2z_j^2) + \sum_{0 \le k \le 2m} 1/(z_j^2 + z_k^2)$; see *Combinatorics, Probability, and Computing* **7** (1998), 437–449.]

C. Flye Sainte-Marie, in L'*Intermédiaire des Mathématiciens* **1** (1894), 164–165, noted that the Eulerian trails of K_7 include 2×720 that have 7-fold symmetry under permutation of $\{0, 1, \ldots, 6\}$ (namely Poinsot's cycle and its reverse), plus 32×1680 with 3-fold symmetry, plus 25778×5040 cycles that are asymmetric.

108. No solution is possible for $n < 7$, except in the trivial case $n = 4$. When $n = 7$ there are $12{,}255{,}208 \times 7!$ universal cycles, not considering $(a_0 a_1 \ldots a_{34})$ to be the same as $(a_1 \ldots a_{34} a_0)$, including cases with 5-fold symmetry like the example cycle in exercise 105.

When $n \geq 8$ we can proceed systematically as suggested by B. Jackson in *Discrete Math.* **117** (1993), 141–150; see also G. Hurlbert, *SIAM J. Disc. Math.* **7** (1994), 598–604: Put each 3-combination into the "standard cyclic order" $c_1 c_2 c_3$ where $c_2 = (c_1 + \delta) \bmod n$, $c_3 = (c_2 + \delta') \bmod n$, $0 < \delta, \delta' < n/2$, and either $\delta = \delta'$ or $\max(\delta, \delta') < n - \delta - \delta' \neq (n-1)/2$ or $(1 < \delta < n/4$ and $\delta' = (n-1)/2)$ or $(\delta = (n-1)/2$ and $1 < \delta' < n/4)$. For example, when $n = 8$ the allowable values of (δ, δ') are $(1,1)$, $(1,2)$, $(1,3)$, $(2,1)$, $(2,2)$, $(3,1)$, $(3,3)$; when $n = 11$ they are $(1,1)$, $(1,2)$, $(1,3)$, $(1,4)$, $(2,1)$, $(2,2)$, $(2,3)$, $(2,5)$, $(3,1)$, $(3,2)$, $(3,3)$, $(4,1)$, $(4,4)$, $(5,2)$, $(5,5)$. Then construct the digraph with vertices (c, δ) for $0 \leq c < n$ and $1 \leq \delta < n/2$, and with arcs $(c_1, \delta) \to (c_2, \delta')$ for every combination $c_1 c_2 c_3$ in standard cyclic order. This digraph is connected and balanced, so it has an Eulerian trail by Theorem 2.3.4.2D. (The peculiar rules about $(n-1)/2$ make the digraph connected when n is odd. The Eulerian trail can be chosen to have n-fold symmetry when $n = 8$, but not when $n = 12$.)

109. When $n = 1$ the cycle (000) is trivial; when $n = 2$ there is no cycle; and there are essentially only two when $n = 4$, namely $(0001112223330 2021313)$ and $(0001112 0203332221313)$. When $n \geq 5$, let the multicombination $d_1 d_2 d_3$ be in standard cyclic order if $d_2 = (d_1 + \delta - 1) \bmod n$, $d_3 = (d_2 + \delta' - 1) \bmod n$, and (δ, δ') is allowable for $n + 3$ in the previous answer. Construct the digraph with vertices (d, δ) for $0 \leq d < n$ and $1 \leq \delta < (n+3)/2$, and with arcs $(d_1, \delta) \to (d_2, \delta')$ for every multicombination $d_1 d_2 d_3$ in standard cyclic order; then find an Eulerian trail.

Perhaps a universal cycle of t-multicombinations exists for $\{0, 1, \ldots, n-1\}$ if and only if a universal cycle of t-combinations exists for $\{0, 1, \ldots, n + t - 1\}$.

110. A nice way to check for runs is to compute the numbers $b(S) = \sum \{2^{p(c)} \mid c \in S\}$ where $(p(\texttt{A}), \ldots, p(\texttt{K})) = (1, \ldots, 13)$; then set $l \leftarrow b(S) \,\&\, -b(S)$ and check that $b(S) + l = l \ll s$, and also that $((l \ll s) \mid (l \gg 1)) \,\&\, a = 0$, where $a = 2^{p(c_1)} \mid \cdots \mid 2^{p(c_5)}$. The values of $b(S)$ and $\sum \{v(c) \mid c \in S\}$ are easily maintained as S runs through all 31 nonempty subsets in Gray-code order. The answers are $(1009008, 99792, 2813796, 505008, 2855676, 697508, 1800268, 751324, 1137236, 361224, 388740, 51680, 317340, 19656, 90100, 9168, 58248, 11196, 2708, 0, 8068, 2496, 444, 356, 3680, 0, 0, 0, 76, 4)$ for $x = (0, \ldots, 29)$; thus the mean score is ≈ 4.769 and the variance is ≈ 9.768.

> *Hands without points are sometimes facetiously called nineteen,*
> *as that number cannot be made by the cards.*
> — G. H. DAVIDSON, *Dee's Hand-Book of Cribbage* (1839)

Note: A four-card flush is not allowed in the "crib." Then the distribution is a bit easier to compute, and it turns out to be $(1022208, 99792, 2839800, 508908, 2868960, 703496, 1787176, 755320, 1118336, 358368, 378240, 43880, 310956, 16548, 88132, 9072, 57288, 11196, 2264, 0, 7828, 2472, 444, 356, 3680, 0, 0, 0, 76, 4)$; the mean and variance decrease to approximately 4.735 and 9.667.

SECTION 7.2.1.4

1.

m^n	$m^{\underline{n}}$	$m!\,{n \brace m}$
$\binom{m+n-1}{n}$	$\binom{m}{n}$	$\binom{n-1}{n-m}$
${n \brace 0}+\cdots+{n \brace m}$	$[m \geq n]$	${n \brace m}$
$\left\lvert {m+n \atop m} \right\rvert$	$[m \geq n]$	$\left\lvert {n \atop m} \right\rvert$

2. In general, given any integers $x_1 \geq \cdots \geq x_m$, we obtain all integer m-tuples $a_1 \ldots a_m$ such that $a_1 \geq \cdots \geq a_m$, $a_1 + \cdots + a_m = x_1 + \cdots + x_m$, and $a_m \ldots a_1 \geq x_m \ldots x_1$ by initializing $a_1 \ldots a_m \leftarrow x_1 \ldots x_m$ and $a_{m+1} \leftarrow x_m - 2$. In particular, if c is any integer constant, we obtain all integer m-tuples such that $a_1 \geq \cdots \geq a_m \geq c$ and $a_1 + \cdots + a_m = n$ by initializing $a_1 \leftarrow n - mc + c$, $a_j \leftarrow c$ for $1 < j \leq m$, and $a_{m+1} \leftarrow c - 2$, assuming that $n \geq cm$.

3. $a_j = \lfloor (n + m - j)/m \rfloor = \lceil (n + 1 - j)/m \rceil$, for $1 \leq j \leq m$; see *CMath* §3.4.

4. We must have $a_m \geq a_1 - 1$; therefore $a_j = \lfloor (n + m - j)/m \rfloor$ for $1 \leq j \leq m$, where m is the largest integer with $\lfloor n/m \rfloor \geq r$, namely $m = \lfloor n/r \rfloor$.

5. [See Eugene M. Klimko, *BIT* **13** (1973), 38–49.]

  C1. [Initialize.] Set $c_0 \leftarrow 1$, $c_1 \leftarrow n$, $c_2 \ldots c_n \leftarrow 0 \ldots 0$, $l_0 \leftarrow 1$, $l_1 \leftarrow 0$. (We assume that $n > 0$.)

  C2. [Visit.] Visit the partition represented by part counts $c_1 \ldots c_n$ and links $l_0 l_1 \ldots l_n$.

  C3. [Branch.] Set $j \leftarrow l_0$ and $k \leftarrow l_j$. If $c_j = 1$, go to C6; otherwise, if $j > 1$, go to C5.

  C4. [Change 1+1 to 2.] Set $c_1 \leftarrow c_1 - 2$, $c_2 \leftarrow c_2 + 1$. Then if $c_1 = 0$, set $l_0 \leftarrow 2$, and set $l_2 \leftarrow l_1$ if $k \neq 2$. If $c_1 > 0$ and $k \neq 2$, set $l_2 \leftarrow l_1$ and $l_1 \leftarrow 2$. Return to C2.

  C5. [Change $j \cdot c_j$ to $(j{+}1) + 1 + \cdots + 1$.] Set $c_1 \leftarrow j(c_j - 1) - 1$ and go to C7.

  C6. [Change $k \cdot c_k + j$ to $(k{+}1) + 1 + \cdots + 1$.] Terminate if $k = 0$. Otherwise set $c_j \leftarrow 0$; then set $c_1 \leftarrow k(c_k - 1) + j - 1$, $j \leftarrow k$, and $k \leftarrow l_k$.

  C7. [Adjust links.] If $c_1 > 0$, set $l_0 \leftarrow 1$, $l_1 \leftarrow j + 1$; otherwise set $l_0 \leftarrow j + 1$. Then set $c_j \leftarrow 0$ and $c_{j+1} \leftarrow c_{j+1} + 1$. If $k \neq j + 1$, set $l_{j+1} \leftarrow k$. Return to C2. ∎

Notice that this algorithm is *loopless*; but it isn't really faster than Algorithm P. Steps C4, C5, and C6 are performed respectively $p(n - 2)$, $2p(n) - p(n + 1) - p(n - 2)$, and $p(n + 1) - p(n)$ times; thus step C4 is most important when n is large. (See exercise 45 and the detailed analysis by Fenner and Loizou in *Acta Inf.* **16** (1981), 237–252.)

6. Set $k \leftarrow a_1$ and $j \leftarrow 1$. Then, while $k > a_{j+1}$, set $b_k \leftarrow j$ and $k \leftarrow k - 1$ until $k = a_{j+1}$. If $k > 0$, set $j \leftarrow j + 1$ and repeat until $k = 0$. (We have used (11) in the dual form $a_j - a_{j+1} = d_j$, where $d_1 \ldots d_n$ is the part-count representation of $b_1 b_2 \ldots$. Notice that the running time of this algorithm is essentially proportional to $a_1 + b_1$, the length of the output plus the length of the input.)

7. We have $b_1 \ldots b_n = n^{a_n} (n-1)^{a_{n-1} - a_n} \ldots 1^{a_1 - a_2} 0^{n - a_1}$, by the dual of (11).

8. Transposing the Ferrers diagram corresponds to reflecting and complementing the bit string (15). So we simply interchange and reverse the p's and q's, getting the partition $b_1 b_2 \ldots = (q_t + \cdots + q_1)^{p_1} (q_t + \cdots + q_2)^{p_2} \ldots (q_t)^{p_t}$.

9. By induction: If $a_k = l - 1$ and $b_l = k - 1$, increasing a_k and b_l preserves equality.

10. (a) The left child of each node is obtained by appending '1'. The right child is obtained by increasing the rightmost digit; this child exists if and only if the parent node ends with unequal digits. All partitions of n appear on level n in lexicographic order.

(b) The left child is obtained by changing '11' to '2'; it exists if and only if the parent node contains at least two 1s. The right child is obtained by deleting a 1 and increasing the smallest part that exceeds 1; it exists if and only if there is at least one 1 and the smallest larger part appears exactly once. All partitions of n into m parts appear on level $n - m$ in lexicographic order; preorder of the entire tree gives lexicographic order of the whole. [T. I. Fenner and G. Loizou, *Comp. J.* **23** (1980), 332–337.]

11. $[z^{100}] \, 1/((1-z)(1-z^2)(1-z^5)(1-z^{10})(1-z^{20})(1-z^{50})(1-z^{100})) = 4563$; and $[z^{100}] \, (1+z+z^2)(1+z^2+z^4)\dots(1+z^{100}+z^{200}) = 7$. [See G. Pólya, *AMM* **63** (1956), 689–697.] In the infinite series $\prod_{k \geq 1}(1 + z^k + z^{2k})(1 + z^{2k} + z^{4k})(1 + z^{5k} + z^{10k})$, the coefficient of z^{10^n} is $2^{n+1} - 1$, and the coefficient of $z^{10^n - 1}$ is 2^n.

12. To prove that $(1 + z)(1 + z^2)(1 + z^3)\dots = 1/((1-z)(1-z^3)(1-z^5)\dots)$, write the left-hand side as

$$\frac{(1 - z^2)}{(1 - z)} \frac{(1 - z^4)}{(1 - z^2)} \frac{(1 - z^6)}{(1 - z^3)} \dots$$

and cancel common factors from numerator and denominator. Alternatively, replace z by z^1, z^3, z^5, $\dots$ in the identity $(1 + z)(1 + z^2)(1 + z^4)(1 + z^8)\dots = 1/(1 - z)$ and multiply the results together. [*Novi Comment. Acad. Sci. Pet.* **3** (1750), 125–169, §47.]

13. Map the partition $c_1 \cdot 1 + c_2 \cdot 2 + \cdots$ into $\lfloor c_1/2 \rfloor \cdot 2 + \lfloor c_2/2 \rfloor \cdot 4 + \cdots + r_1 \cdot 1 + r_3 \cdot 3 + \cdots$, where $r_m = (c_m \bmod 2) + 2(c_{2m} \bmod 2) + 4(c_{4m} \bmod 2) + \cdots$. [*Johns Hopkins Univ. Circular* **2** (1882), 72.]

14. Sylvester's correspondence is best understood as a diagram in which the dots of the odd permutation are centered and divided into disjoint hooks. For example, the partition $17 + 15 + 15 + 9 + 9 + 9 + 9 + 5 + 5 + 3 + 3$, having five different odd parts, corresponds via the diagram

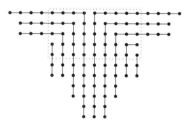

to the all-distinct partition $19 + 18 + 16 + 13 + 12 + 9 + 5 + 4 + 3$ with four gaps.

Conversely, a partition into $2t$ distinct nonnegative parts can be written uniquely in the form $(a_1 + b_1 - 1) + (a_1 + b_2 - 2) + (a_2 + b_2 - 3) + (a_2 + b_3 - 4) + \cdots + (a_{t-1} + b_t - 2t + 2) + (a_t + b_t - 2t + 1) + (a_t + b_{t+1} - 2t)$ where $a_1 \geq a_2 \geq \cdots \geq a_t \geq t$ and $b_1 \geq b_2 \geq \cdots \geq b_t \geq b_{t+1} = t$. It corresponds to $(2a_1 - 1) + \cdots + (2a_t - 1) + (2A_1 - 1) + \cdots + (2A_r - 1)$, where $A_1 + \cdots + A_r$ is the conjugate of $(b_1 - t) + \cdots + (b_t - t)$. The value of t is essentially the size of a "Durfee rectangle."

The relevant odd-parts partitions when $n = 10$ are $9 + 1$, $7 + 3$, $7 + 1 + 1 + 1$, $5 + 5$, $5 + 3 + 1 + 1$, $5 + 1 + 1 + 1 + 1 + 1$, $3 + 3 + 3 + 1$, $3 + 3 + 1 + 1 + 1 + 1$, $3 + 1 + \cdots + 1$, $1 + \cdots + 1$, corresponding respectively to the distinct-parts partitions $6 + 4$, $5 + 4 + 1$,

$7 + 3$, $4 + 3 + 2 + 1$, $6 + 3 + 1$, $8 + 2$, $5 + 3 + 2$, $7 + 2 + 1$, $9 + 1$, 10. [See Sylvester's remarkable paper in *Amer. J. Math.* **5** (1882), 251–330; **6** (1883), 334–336.]

15. Every self-conjugate partition of trace k corresponds to a partition of n into k distinct odd parts ("hooks"). Therefore we can write the generating function either as the product $(1+z)(1+z^3)(1+z^5)\dots$ or as the sum $1+z^1/(1-z^2)+z^4/((1-z^2)(1-z^4))+z^9/((1-z^2)(1-z^4)(1-z^6))+\cdots$. [*Johns Hopkins Univ. Circular* **3** (1883), 42–43.]

16. The Durfee square contains k^2 dots, and the remaining dots correspond to two independent partitions with largest part $\leq k$. Thus, if we use w to count parts and z to count dots, we find

$$\prod_{m=1}^{\infty} \frac{1}{1-wz^m} = \sum_{k=0}^{\infty} \frac{w^k z^{k^2}}{(1-z)(1-z^2)\dots(1-z^k)(1-wz)(1-wz^2)\dots(1-wz^k)}.$$

[This impressive-looking formula turns out to be just the special case $x = y = 0$ of the even more impressive identity of exercise 19.]

17. (a) $\left((1+uvz)(1+uvz^2)(1+uvz^3)\dots\right)/\left((1-uz)(1-uz^2)(1-uz^3)\dots\right)$.

(b) A joint partition can be represented by a generalized Ferrers diagram in which we merge all the parts together, putting a_i above b_j if $a_i \geq b_j$, then mark the rightmost dot of each b_j. For example, the joint partition $(8,8,5;\ 9,7,5,2)$ has the diagram illustrated here, with marked dots shown as '$\blacklozenge$'. Marks appear only in corners; thus the transposed diagram corresponds to another joint partition, which in this case is $(7,6,6,4,3;\ 7,6,4,1)$. [See J. T. Joichi and D. Stanton, *Pacific J. Math.* **127** (1987), 103–120; S. Corteel and J. Lovejoy, *Trans. Amer. Math. Soc.* **356** (2004), 1623–1635; Igor Pak, "Partition bijections, a survey," to appear in *The Ramanujan Journal*.)

Every joint partition with $t > 0$ parts corresponds in this way to a "conjugate" in which the largest part is t. And the generating function for such joint partitions is $\left((1+vz)\dots(1+vz^{t-1})\right)/\left((1-z)\dots(1-z^t)\right)$ times $(vz^t + z^t)$, where vz^t corresponds to the case that $b_1 = t$, and z^t corresponds to the case that $r = 0$ or $b_1 < t$).

(c) Thus we obtain a form of the general z-nomial theorem in answer 1.2.6–58:

$$\frac{(1+uvz)}{(1-uz)}\frac{(1+uvz^2)}{(1-uz^2)}\frac{(1+uvz^3)}{(1-uz^3)}\cdots = \sum_{t=0}^{\infty} \frac{(1+v)}{(1-z)}\frac{(1+vz)}{(1-z^2)}\cdots\frac{(1+vz^{t-1})}{(1-z^t)}u^t z^t.$$

18. The equations obviously determine the a's and b's when the c's and d's are given, so we want to show that the c's and d's are uniquely determined from the a's and b's. The following algorithm determines the c's and d's from right to left:

A1. [Initialize.] Set $i \leftarrow r$, $j \leftarrow s$, $k \leftarrow 0$, and $a_0 \leftarrow b_0 \leftarrow \infty$.

A2. [Branch.] Stop if $i + j = 0$. Otherwise go to A4 if $a_i \geq b_j - k$.

A3. [Absorb a_i.] Set $c_{i+j} \leftarrow a_i$, $d_{i+j} \leftarrow 0$, $i \leftarrow i - 1$, $k \leftarrow k + 1$, and return to A2.

A4. [Absorb b_j.] Set $c_{i+j} \leftarrow b_j - k$, $d_{i+j} \leftarrow 1$, $j \leftarrow j - 1$, $k \leftarrow k + 1$, and return to A2. ∎

There's also a left-to-right method:

B1. [Initialize.] Set $i \leftarrow 1$, $j \leftarrow 1$, $k \leftarrow r + s$, and $a_{r+1} \leftarrow b_{s+1} \leftarrow -\infty$.

B2. [Branch.] Stop if $k = 0$. Otherwise set $k \leftarrow k - 1$, then go to B4 if $a_i \leq b_j - k$.

B3. [Absorb a_i.] Set $c_{i+j-1} \leftarrow a_i$, $d_{i+j-1} \leftarrow 0$, $i \leftarrow i + 1$, and return to B2.

B4. [Absorb b_j.] Set $c_{i+j-1} \leftarrow b_j - k$, $d_{i+j-1} \leftarrow 1$, $j \leftarrow j+1$, and return to B2. ∎

In both cases the branching is forced and the resulting sequence satisfies $c_1 \geq \cdots \geq c_{r+s}$. Notice that $c_{r+s} = \min(a_r, b_s)$ and $c_1 = \max(a_1, b_1 - r - s + 1)$.

We have thereby proved the identity of exercise 17(c) in a different way. Extensions of this idea lead to a combinatorial proof of Ramanujan's "remarkable formula with many parameters,"

$$\sum_{n=-\infty}^{\infty} w^n \prod_{k=0}^{\infty} \frac{1 - bz^{k+n}}{1 - az^{k+n}} = \prod_{k=0}^{\infty} \frac{(1-a^{-1}bz^k)(1-a^{-1}w^{-1}z^{k+1})(1-awz^k)(1-z^{k+1})}{(1-a^{-1}bw^{-1}z^k)(1-a^{-1}z^{k+1})(1-az^k)(1-wz^k)}.$$

[*References:* G. H. Hardy, *Ramanujan* (1940), Eq. (12.12.2); D. Zeilberger, *Europ. J. Combinatorics* **8** (1987), 461–463; A. J. Yee, *J. Comb. Theory* **A105** (2004), 63–77.]

19. [*Crelle* **34** (1847), 285–328.] By exercise 17(c), the hinted sum over k is

$$\left(\sum_{l \geq 0} v^l \frac{(z-bz)\ldots(z-bz^l)}{(1-z)\ldots(1-z^l)} \frac{(1-uz)\ldots(1-uz^l)}{(1-auz)\ldots(1-auz^l)} \right) \cdot \prod_{m=1}^{\infty} \frac{1 - auz^m}{1 - uz^m};$$

and the sum over l is similar but with $u \leftrightarrow v$, $a \leftrightarrow b$, $k \leftrightarrow l$. Furthermore the sum over both k and l reduces to

$$\prod_{m=1}^{\infty} \frac{(1 - uvz^{m+1})(1 - auz^m)}{(1 - uz^m)(1 - vz^m)}$$

when $b = auz$. Now let $u = wxy$, $v = 1/(yz)$, $a = 1/x$, and $b = wyz$; equate this infinite product to the sum over l.

20. To get $p(n)$ we need to add or subtract approximately $\sqrt{8n/3}$ of the previous entries, and most of those entries are $\Theta(\sqrt{n})$ bits long. Therefore $p(n)$ is computed in $\Theta(n)$ steps and the total time is $\Theta(n^2)$.

(A straightforward use of (17) would take $\Theta(n^{5/2})$ steps.)

21. Since $\sum_{n=0}^{\infty} q(n)z^n = (1+z)(1+z^2)\ldots$ is equal to $(1-z^2)(1-z^4)\ldots P(z) = (1 - z^2 - z^4 + z^{10} + z^{14} - z^{24} - \cdots)P(z)$, we have

$$q(n) = p(n) - p(n-2) - p(n-4) + p(n-10) + p(n-14) - p(n-24) - \cdots.$$

[There is also a "pure recurrence" in the q's alone, analogous to the recurrence for $\sigma(n)$ in the next exercise.]

22. From (21) we have $\sum_{n=1}^{\infty} \sigma(n)z^n = \sum_{m,n \geq 1} m z^{mn} = z\frac{d}{dz}\ln P(z) = (z + 2z^2 - 5z^5 - 7z^7 + \cdots)/(1 - z - z^2 + z^5 + z^7 + \cdots)$. [*Bibliothèque Impartiale* **3** (1751), 10–31.]

23. Set $u = w$ and $v = z/w$ to get

$$\prod_{k=1}^{\infty}(1 - z^k w)(1 - z^k/w)(1 - z^k) = \sum_{n=-\infty}^{\infty} (-1)^n w^n z^{n(n+1)/2}/(1-w)$$

$$= \sum_{n=0}^{\infty}(-1)^n(w^{-n} - w^{n+1})z^{n(n+1)/2}/(1-w)$$

$$= \sum_{n=0}^{\infty}(-1)^n(w^{-n} + \cdots + w^n)z^{n(n+1)/2}.$$

These manipulations are legitimate when $|z| < 1$ and w is near 1. Now set $w = 1$.

[See §57 of Sylvester's paper cited in answer 14. Jacobi's proof is in §66 of his monograph *Fundamenta Nova Theoriæ Functionum Ellipticarum* (1829).]

24. (a) By (18) and exercise 23, $[z^n]\, A(z) = \sum (-1)^{j+k} (2k+1)[3j^2 + j + k^2 + k = 2n]$, summed over all integers j and k. When $n \bmod 5 = 4$, the contributions all have $j \bmod 5 = 4$ and $k \bmod 5 = 2$; but then $(2k+1) \bmod 5 = 0$.

(b) $B(z)^p \equiv B(z^p)$ (modulo p) when p is prime, by Eq. 4.6.2–(5).

(c) Take $B(z) = P(z)$, since $A(z) = P(z)^{-4}$. [*Proc. Cambridge Philos. Soc.* **19** (1919), 207–210. A similar proof shows that $p(n)$ is a multiple of 7 when $n \bmod 7 = 5$. Ramanujan went on to obtain the beautiful formulas $p(5n+4)/5 = [z^n]\, P(z)^6/P(z^5)$; $p(7n+5)/7 = [z^n]\,(P(z)^4/P(z^7)^3 + 7zP(z)^8/P(z^7)^7)$. Atkin and Swinnerton-Dyer, in *Proc. London Math. Soc.* (3) **4** (1953), 84–106, showed that the partitions of $5n+4$ and $7n+5$ can be divided into equal-size classes according to the respective values of (largest part − number of parts) mod 5 or mod 7, as conjectured by F. Dyson. A slightly more complicated combinatorial statistic proves also that $p(n) \bmod 11 = 0$ when $n \bmod 11 = 6$; see F. G. Garvan, *Trans. Amer. Math. Soc.* **305** (1988), 47–77.]

25. [The hint can be proved by differentiating both sides of the stated identity. It is the special case $y = 1 - x$ of a beautiful formula discovered by N. H. Abel in 1826:

$$\mathrm{Li}_2(x) + \mathrm{Li}_2(y) = \mathrm{Li}_2\left(\frac{x}{1-y}\right) + \mathrm{Li}_2\left(\frac{y}{1-x}\right) - \mathrm{Li}_2\left(\frac{xy}{(1-x)(1-y)}\right) - \ln(1-x)\ln(1-y).$$

See Abel's *Œuvres Complètes* **2** (Christiania: Grøndahl, 1881), 189–193.]

(a) Let $f(x) = \ln(1/(1 - e^{-xt}))$. Then $\int_1^x f(x)\, dx = -\mathrm{Li}_2(e^{-tx})/t$ and $f^{(n)}(x) = (-t)^n e^{tx} \sum_k \left\langle {n-1 \atop k} \right\rangle e^{ktx}/(e^{tx} - 1)^n$, so Euler's summation formula gives $\mathrm{Li}_2(e^{-t})/t + \frac{1}{2}\ln(1/(1 - e^{-t})) + O(1) = (\zeta(2) + t\ln(1 - e^{-t}) - \mathrm{Li}_2(1 - e^{-t}))/t - \frac{1}{2}\ln t + O(1) = \zeta(2)/t + \frac{1}{2}\ln t + O(1)$, as $t \to 0$.

(b) We have $\sum_{m,n\geq 1} e^{-mnt}/n = \frac{1}{2\pi i}\sum_{m,n\geq 1} \int_{1-i\infty}^{1+i\infty} (mnt)^{-z}\Gamma(z)\, dz/n$, which sums to $\frac{1}{2\pi i}\int_{1-i\infty}^{1+i\infty} \zeta(z+1)\zeta(z)t^{-z}\Gamma(z)\, dz$. The pole at $z = 1$ gives $\zeta(2)/t$; the double pole at $z = 0$ gives $-\zeta(0)\ln t + \zeta'(0) = \frac{1}{2}\ln t - \frac{1}{2}\ln 2\pi$; the pole at $z = -1$ gives $-\zeta(-1)\zeta(0)t = B_2 B_1 t = -t/24$. Zeros of $\zeta(z+1)\zeta(z)$ cancel the other poles of $\Gamma(z)$, so the result is $\ln P(e^{-t}) = \zeta(2)/t + \frac{1}{2}\ln(t/2\pi) - t/24 + O(t^M)$ for arbitrarily large M.

26. Let $F(n) = \sum_{k=1}^{\infty} e^{-k^2/n}$. We can use (25) either with $f(x) = e^{-x^2/n}[x>0] + \frac{1}{2}\delta_{x0}$, or with $f(x) = e^{-x^2/n}$ for all x because $2F(n) + 1 = \sum_{k=-\infty}^{\infty} e^{-k^2/n}$. Let's choose the latter alternative; then the right-hand side of (25), for $\theta = 0$, is the rapidly convergent

$$\lim_{M\to\infty} \sum_{m=-M}^{M} \int_{-\infty}^{\infty} e^{-2\pi miy - y^2/n}\, dy = \sum_{m=-\infty}^{\infty} e^{-\pi^2 m^2 n^2} \int_{-\infty}^{\infty} e^{-u^2/n}\, du$$

if we substitute $u = y + \pi mni$; and the integral is $\sqrt{\pi n}$. [This result is formula (15) on page 420 of Poisson's original paper.]

27. Let $g_n = \sqrt{\pi/6t}\, e^{-n^2\pi^2/6t} \cos\frac{n\pi}{6}$. Then $\int_{-\infty}^{\infty} f(y)\cos 2\pi my\, dy = g_{2m+1} + g_{2m-1}$, so we have

$$\frac{e^{-t/24}}{P(e^{-t})} = g_1 + g_{-1} + 2\sum_{m=1}^{\infty} (g_{2m+1} + g_{2m-1}) = 2\sum_{m=-\infty}^{\infty} g_{2m+1}.$$

The terms g_{6n+1} and g_{-6n-1} combine to give the nth term of (30). [See M. I. Knopp, *Modular Functions in Analytic Number Theory* (1970), Chapter 3.]

28. (a,b,c,d) See *Trans. Amer. Math. Soc.* **43** (1938), 271–295. In fact, Lehmer found explicit formulas for $A_{p^e}(n)$, in terms of the Jacobi symbol of exercise 4.5.4–23:

$$A_{2^e}(n) = (-1)^e \left(\frac{-1}{m}\right) 2^{e/2} \sin \frac{4\pi m}{2^{e+3}}, \qquad \text{if } (3m)^2 \equiv 1 - 24n \text{ (modulo } 2^{e+3}\text{)};$$

$$A_{3^e}(n) = (-1)^{e+1} \left(\frac{m}{3}\right) \frac{2}{\sqrt{3}} 3^{e/2} \sin \frac{4\pi m}{3^{e+1}}, \quad \text{if } (8m)^2 \equiv 1 - 24n \text{ (modulo } 3^{e+1}\text{)};$$

$$A_{p^e}(n) = \begin{cases} 2\left(\dfrac{3}{p^e}\right) p^{e/2} \cos \dfrac{4\pi m}{p^e}, & \text{if } (24m)^2 \equiv 1 - 24n \text{ (modulo } p^e\text{), } p \geq 5, \\ & \text{and } 24n \bmod p \neq 1; \\ \left(\dfrac{3}{p^e}\right) p^{e/2} [e=1], & \text{if } 24n \bmod p = 1 \text{ and } p \geq 5. \end{cases}$$

(e) If $n = 2^a 3^b p_1^{e_1} \dots p_t^{e_t}$ for $3 < p_1 < \dots < p_t$ and $e_1 \dots e_t \neq 0$, the probability that $A_k(n) \neq 0$ is $2^{-t}(1 + (-1)^{[e_1=1]}/p_1) \dots (1 + (-1)^{[e_t=1]}/p_t)$.

29. $z_1 z_2 \dots z_m / ((1 - z_1)(1 - z_1 z_2) \dots (1 - z_1 z_2 \dots z_m))$.

30. (a) $\left|{n+1 \atop m}\right|$ and (b) $\left|{m+n \atop m}\right|$, by (39).

31. *First solution* [Marshall Hall, Jr., *Combinatorial Theory* (1967), §4.1]: From the recurrence (39), we can show directly that, for $0 \leq r < k!$, there is a polynomial $f_{k,r}(n) = n^{k-1}/(k!(k-1)!) + O(n^{k-2})$ such that $\left|{n \atop k}\right| = f_{n, n \bmod k!}(n)$.

Second solution: Since $(1 - z) \dots (1 - z^m) = \prod_{p \perp q} (1 - e^{2\pi i p/q} z)^{\lfloor m/q \rfloor}$, where the product is over all reduced fractions p/q with $0 \leq p < q$, the coefficient of z^n in (41) can be expressed as a sum of roots of unity times polynomials in n, namely as $\sum_{p \perp q} e^{2\pi i p n/q} f_{pq}(n)$ where $f_{pq}(n)$ is a polynomial of degree less than m/q. Thus there exist constants such that $\left|{n \atop 2}\right| = a_1 n + a_2 + (-1)^n a_3$; $\left|{n \atop 3}\right| = b_1 n^2 + b_2 n + b_3 + (-1)^n b_4 + \omega^n b_5 + \omega^{-n} b_6$, where $\omega = e^{2\pi i/3}$; etc. The constants are determined by the values for small n, and the first two cases are

$$\left|{n \atop 2}\right| = \frac{1}{2} n - \frac{1}{4} + \frac{1}{4}(-1)^n; \qquad \left|{n \atop 3}\right| = \frac{1}{12} n^2 - \frac{7}{72} - \frac{1}{8}(-1)^n + \frac{1}{9}\omega^n + \frac{1}{9}\omega^{-n}.$$

It follows that $\left|{n \atop 3}\right|$ is the nearest integer to $n^2/12$. Similarly, $\left|{n \atop 4}\right|$ is the nearest integer to $(n^3 + 3n^2 - 9n\,[n\,\text{odd}])/144$.

[Exact formulas for $\left|{n \atop 2}\right|$, $\left|{n \atop 3}\right|$, and $\left|{n \atop 4}\right|$, without the simplification of floor functions, were first found by G. F. Malfatti, *Memorie di Mat. e Fis. Società Italiana* **3** (1786), 571–663. W. J. A. Colman, in *Fibonacci Quarterly* **21** (1983), 272–284, showed that $\left|{n \atop 5}\right|$ is the nearest integer to $(n^4 + 10n^3 + 10n^2 - 75n - 45n(-1)^n)/2880$, and gave similar formulas for $\left|{n \atop 6}\right|$ and $\left|{n \atop 7}\right|$.]

32. Since $\left|{m+n \atop m}\right| \leq p(n)$, with equality if and only if $m \geq n$, we have $\left|{n \atop m}\right| \leq p(n - m)$ with equality if and only if $2m \geq n$.

33. A partition into m parts corresponds to at most $m!$ compositions; hence $\binom{n-1}{m-1} \leq m! \left|{n \atop m}\right|$. Consequently $p(n) \geq (n - 1)!/((n - m)!\, m!\, (m - 1)!)$, and when $m = \sqrt{n}$ Stirling's approximation proves that $\ln p(n) \geq 2\sqrt{n} - \ln n - \frac{1}{2} - \ln 2\pi$.

34. $a_1 > a_2 > \dots > a_m > 0$ if and only if $a_1 - m + 1 \geq a_2 - m + 2 \geq \dots \geq a_m \geq 1$. And partitions into m distinct parts correspond to $m!$ compositions. Thus, by the previous answer, we have

$$\frac{1}{m!} \binom{n-1}{m-1} \leq \left|{n \atop m}\right| \leq \frac{1}{m!} \binom{n + m(m-1)/2}{m-1}.$$

[See H. Gupta, *Proc. Indian Acad. Sci.* **A16** (1942), 101–102. A detailed asymptotic formula for $\left|{n\atop m}\right|$ when $n = \Theta(m^3)$ appears in exercise 3.3.2–30.]

35. (a) $x = \frac{1}{C}\ln\frac{1}{C} \approx -0.194$.

(b) $x = \frac{1}{C}\ln\frac{1}{C} - \frac{1}{C}\ln\ln 2 \approx 0.092$; in general we have $x = \frac{1}{C}\left(\ln\frac{1}{C} - \ln\ln\frac{1}{F(x)}\right)$.

(c) $\int_{-\infty}^{\infty} x\,dF(x) = \int_0^\infty (Cu)^{-2}(\ln u)e^{-1/(Cu)}\,du = -\frac{1}{C}\int_0^\infty(\ln C + \ln v)e^{-v}\,dv = (\gamma - \ln C)/C \approx 0.256$.

(d) Similarly, $\int_{-\infty}^\infty x^2 e^{-Cx}\exp(-e^{-Cx}/C)\,dx = (\gamma^2 + \zeta(2) - 2\gamma\ln C + (\ln C)^2)/C^2 \approx 1.0656$. So the variance is $\zeta(2)/C^2 = 1$, exactly(!).

[The probability distribution $e^{-e^{(a-x)/b}}$ is commonly called the Fisher–Tippett distribution; see *Proc. Cambridge Phil. Soc.* **24** (1928), 180–190.]

36. The sum over $j_r - (m + r - 1) \geq \cdots \geq j_2 - (m + 1) \geq j_1 - m \geq 1$ gives

$$\Sigma_r = \sum_t \left|{t - rm - r(r-1)/2 \atop r}\right| \frac{p(n-t)}{p(n)}$$

$$= \frac{\alpha}{1-\alpha}\frac{\alpha^2}{1-\alpha^2}\cdots\frac{\alpha^r}{1-\alpha^r}\alpha^{rm}\bigl(1 + O(n^{-1/2+2\epsilon})\bigr) + E$$

$$= \frac{n^{-1/2}}{\alpha^{-1}-1}\frac{n^{-1/2}}{\alpha^{-2}-1}\cdots\frac{n^{-1/2}}{\alpha^{-r}-1}\exp(-Crx + O(rn^{-1/2+2\epsilon})) + E,$$

where E is an error term that accounts for the cases $t > n^{1/2+\epsilon}$. The leading factor $n^{-1/2}/(\alpha^{-j}-1)$ is $\frac{1}{jC}(1 + O(jn^{-1/2}))$. And it is easy to verify that $E = O(n^{\log n}e^{-Cn^\epsilon})$, even if we use the crude upper bound $\left|{t - rm - r(r-1)/2 \atop r}\right| \leq t^r$, because

$$\sum_{t \geq xN} t^r e^{-t/N} = O\left(\int_{xN}^\infty t^r e^{-t/N}\,dt\right) = O(N^{r+1}x^r e^{-x}/(1 - r/x)),$$

where $N = \Theta(\sqrt n)$, $x = \Theta(n^\epsilon)$, $r = O(\log n)$.

37. Such a partition is counted once in Σ_0, q times in Σ_1, $\binom{q}{2}$ times in Σ_2, ...; so it is counted exactly $\sum_{j=0}^r (-1)^j\binom{q}{j} = (-1)^r\binom{q-1}{r}$ times in the partial sum that ends with $(-1)^r\Sigma_r$. This count is at most δ_{q0} when r is odd, at least δ_{q0} when r is even. [A similar argument shows that the generalized principle of exercise 1.3.3–26 also has this bracketing property. *Reference:* C. Bonferroni, *Pubblicazioni del Reale Istituto Superiore de Scienze Economiche e Commerciale di Firenze* **8** (1936), 3–62.]

38. $z^{l+m-1}\binom{l+m-2}{m-1}_z = z^{l+m-1}(1 - z^l)\ldots(1 - z^{l+m-2})/((1 - z)\ldots(1 - z^{m-1}))$.

39. If $\alpha = a_1\ldots a_m$ is a partition with at most m parts, let $f(\alpha) = \infty$ if $a_1 \leq l$, otherwise $f(\alpha) = \min\{j \mid a_1 > l + a_{j+1}\}$. Let g_k be the generating function for partitions with $f(\alpha) > k$. Partitions with $f(\alpha) = k < \infty$ are characterized by the inequalities

$$a_1 \geq a_2 \geq \cdots \geq a_k \geq a_1 - l > a_{k+1} \geq \cdots \geq a_{m+1} = 0.$$

Thus $a_1 a_2\ldots a_m = (b_k + l + 1)(b_1 + 1)\ldots(b_{k-1} + 1)b_{k+1}\ldots b_m$, where $f(b_1\ldots b_m) \geq k$; and the converse is also true. It follows that $g_k = g_{k-1} - z^{l+k}g_{k-1}$.

[See *American J. Math.* **5** (1882), 254–257.]

40. $z^{m(m+1)/2}\binom{l}{m}_z = (z - z^l)(z^2 - z^l)\ldots(z^m - z^l)/((1 - z)(1 - z^2)\ldots(1 - z^m))$. This formula is essentially the z-nomial theorem of exercise 1.2.6–58.

41. See G. Almkvist and G. E. Andrews, *J. Number Theory* **38** (1991), 135–144.

42. A. Vershik [*Functional Anal. Applic.* **30** (1996), 90–105, Theorem 4.7] has stated the formula

$$\frac{1 - e^{-c\varphi}}{1 - e^{-c(\theta+\varphi)}} e^{-ck/\sqrt{n}} + \frac{1 - e^{-c\theta}}{1 - e^{-c(\theta+\varphi)}} e^{-ca_k/\sqrt{n}} \approx 1,$$

where the constant c must be chosen as a function of θ and φ so that the area of the shape is n. This constant c is negative if $\theta\varphi < 2$, positive if $\theta\varphi > 2$; the shape reduces to a straight line

$$\frac{k}{\theta\sqrt{n}} + \frac{a_k}{\varphi\sqrt{n}} \approx 1$$

when $\theta\varphi = 2$. If $\varphi = \infty$ we have $c = \sqrt{\mathrm{Li}_2(t)}$ where t satisfies $\theta = (\ln \frac{1}{1-t})/\sqrt{\mathrm{Li}_2(t)}$.

43. We have $a_1 > a_2 > \cdots > a_k$ if and only if the conjugate partition includes each of the the parts $1, 2, \ldots, k-1$ at least once. The number of such partitions is $p(n - k(k-1)/2)$; this total includes $\left|\begin{smallmatrix} n-(k-1)(k-2)/2 \\ k-1 \end{smallmatrix}\right|$ cases with $a_k = 0$.

44. Assume that $n > 0$. The number with smallest parts *unequal* (or with only one part) is $p(n+1) - p(n)$, the number of partitions of $n+1$ that don't end in 1, because we get the former from the latter by changing the smallest part. Therefore the answer is $2p(n) - p(n+1)$. [See R. J. Boscovich, *Giornale de' Letterati* (Rome, 1748), 15. The number of partitions whose smallest *three* parts are equal is $3p(n) - p(n+1) - 2p(n+2) + p(n+3)$; similar formulas can be derived for other constraints on the smallest parts.]

45. By Eq. (37) we have $p(n-j)/p(n) = 1 - Cjn^{-1/2} + (C^2j^2 + 2j)/(2n) - (8C^3j^3 + 60Cj^2 + Cj + 12C^{-1}j)/(48n^{3/2}) + O(j^4n^{-2})$.

46. If $n > 1$, $T_2'(n) = p(n-1) - p(n-2) \le p(n) - p(n-1) = T_2''(n)$, because $p(n) - p(n-1)$ is the number of partitions of n that don't end in 1; every such partition of $n - 1$ yields one for n if we increase the largest part. But the difference is rather small: $(T_2''(n) - T_2'(n))/p(n) = C^2/n + O(n^{-3/2})$.

47. The identity in the hint follows by differentiating (21); see exercise 22. The probability of obtaining the part-counts $c_1 \ldots c_n$ when $c_1 + 2c_2 + \cdots + nc_n = n$ is

$$\Pr(c_1 \ldots c_n) = \sum_{k=1}^{n} \sum_{j=1}^{c_k} \frac{kp(n-jk)}{np(n)} \Pr(c_1 \ldots c_{k-1}(c_k-j)c_{k+1} \ldots c_n)$$

$$= \sum_{k=1}^{n} \sum_{j=1}^{c_k} \frac{k}{np(n)} = \frac{1}{p(n)},$$

by induction on n. [*Combinatorial Algorithms* (Academic Press, 1975), Chapter 10.]

48. The probability that j has a particular fixed value in step N5 is $6/(\pi^2 j^2) + O(n^{-1/2})$, and the average value of jk is order $\sqrt{n}$. The average time spent in step N4 is $\Theta(n)$, so the average running time is of order $n^{3/2}$. (A more precise analysis would be desirable.)

49. (a) We have $F(z) = \sum_{k=1}^{\infty} F_k(z)$, where $F_k(z)$ is the generating function for all partitions whose smallest part is $\ge k$, namely $1/((1 - z^k)(1 - z^{k+1})\ldots) - 1$.

  (b) Let $f_k(n) = [z^n] F_k(z)/p(n)$. Then $f_1(n) = 1$; $f_2(n) = 1 - p(n-1)/p(n) = Cn^{-1/2} + O(n^{-1})$; $f_3(n) = (p(n) - p(n-1) - p(n-2) + p(n-3))/p(n) = 2C^2n^{-1} + O(n^{-3/2})$; and $f_4(n) = 6C^3n^{-3/2} + O(n^{-2})$. (See exercise 45.) It turns out that $f_{k+1}(n) = k! C^k n^{-k/2} + O(n^{-(k+1)/2})$; in particular, $f_5(n) = O(n^{-2})$. Hence $f_5(n) + \cdots + f_n(n) = O(n^{-1})$, because $f_{k+1}(n) \le f_k(n)$.

  Adding everything up yields $[z^n] F(z) = p(n)(1 + C/\sqrt{n} + O(n^{-1}))$.

50. (a) $c_m(m + k) = c_{m-1}(m - 1 + k) + c_m(k) = m - 1 - k + c(k) + 1$ by induction when $0 \le k < m$.

(b) Because $\left|{m+k \atop m}\right| = p(k)$ for $0 \le k \le m$.

(c) When $n = 2m$, Algorithm H essentially generates the partitions of m, and we know that $j - 1$ is the second-smallest part in the conjugate of the partition just generated — except when $j - 1 = m$, just after the partition $1 \ldots 1$ whose conjugate has only one part.

(d) If all parts of α exceed k, let $\alpha k^{q+1} j$ correspond to $\alpha (k+1)$.

(e) The generating function $G_k(z)$ for all partitions whose second-smallest part is $\ge k$ is $(z + \cdots + z^{k-1}) F_k(z) + F_k(z) - z^k/(1-z) = F_{k+1}(z)/(1-z)$, where $F_k(z)$ is defined in the previous exercise. Consequently $C(z) = (F(z) - F_1(z))/(1 - z) + z/(1 - z)^2$.

(f) We can show as in the previous exercise that $[z^n] G_k(n)/p(n) = O(n^{-k/2})$ for $k \le 5$; hence $c(m)/p(m) = 1 + O(m^{-1/2})$. The ratios $(c(m) + 1)/p(m)$, which are readily computed for small m, reach a maximum of 2.6 at $m = 7$ and decrease steadily thereafter. So a rigorous attention to asymptotic error bounds will complete the proof.

Note: B. Fristedt [*Trans. Amer. Math. Soc.* **337** (1993), 703–735] has proved, among other things, that the number of k's in a random partition of n is greater than $Cx\sqrt{n}$ with asymptotic probability e^{-x}.

52. In lexicographic order, $\left|{64+13 \atop 13}\right|$ partitions of 64 have $a_1 \le 13$; $\left|{50+10 \atop 10}\right|$ of them have $a_1 = 14$ and $a_2 \le 10$; etc. Therefore, by the hint, the partition $14\ 11\ 9\ 6\ 4\ 3\ 2\ 1^{15}$ is preceded by exactly $p(64) - 1000000$ partitions in lexicographic order, making it the millionth in *reverse* lexicographic order.

53. As in the previous answer, $\left|{80 \atop 12}\right|$ partitions of 100 have $a_1 = 32$ and $a_2 \le 12$, etc.; so the lexicographically millionth partition in which $a_1 = 32$ is $32\ 13\ 12\ 8\ 7\ 6\ 5\ 5\ 1^{12}$. Algorithm H produces its conjugate, namely $20\ 8\ 8\ 8\ 6\ 5\ 4\ 3\ 3\ 3\ 3\ 2\ 1^{19}$.

54. (a) Obviously true. This question was just a warmup.

(b) True, but not so obvious. If $\alpha^T = a_1' a_2' \ldots$ we have

$$a_1 + \cdots + a_k + a_1' + \cdots + a_k' \le n - kl \qquad \text{when } k \le a_l'$$

by considering the Ferrers diagram, with equality when $k = a_l'$. Thus if $\alpha \succeq \beta$ and $a_1' + \cdots + a_l' > b_1' + \cdots + b_l'$ for some l, with l minimum, we have $n - kl = b_1 + \cdots + b_k + b_1' + \cdots + b_l' < a_1 + \cdots + a_k + a_1' + \cdots + a_l' \le n - kl$ when $k = b_l'$, a contradiction.

(c) The recurrence $c_k = \min(a_1 + \cdots + a_k, b_1 + \cdots + b_k) - (c_1 + \cdots + c_{k-1})$ clearly defines a greatest lower bound, if $c_1 c_2 \ldots$ is a partition. And it is; for if $c_1 + \cdots + c_k = a_1 + \cdots + a_k$ we have $0 \le \min(a_{k+1}, b_{k+1}) \le c_{k+1} \le a_{k+1} \le a_k = c_k - (c_1 + \cdots + c_{k-1}) - (a_1 + \cdots + a_{k-1}) \le c_k$.

(d) $\alpha \vee \beta = (\alpha^T \wedge \beta^T)^T$. (Double conjugation is needed because a max-oriented recurrence analogous to the one in part (c) can fail.)

(e) $\alpha \wedge \beta$ has $\max(l, m)$ parts and $\alpha \vee \beta$ has $\min(l, m)$ parts. (Consider the first components of their conjugates.)

(f) True for $\alpha \wedge \beta$, by the derivation in part (c). False for $\alpha \vee \beta$ (although true in Fig. 32); for example, $(17\ 16\ 5\ 4\ 3\ 2) \vee (17\ 9\ 8\ 7\ 6) = (17\ 16\ 5\ 5\ 4)$.

Reference: T. Brylawski, *Discrete Mathematics* **6** (1973), 201–219.

55. (a) If $\alpha \rhd \beta$ and $\alpha \succeq \gamma \succeq \beta$, where $\gamma = c_1 c_2 \ldots$, we have $a_1 + \cdots + a_k = c_1 + \cdots + c_k = b_1 + \cdots + b_k$ for all k except $k = l$ and $k = l + 1$; thus α covers β. Therefore β^T covers α^T.

Conversely, if $\alpha \succeq \beta$ and $\alpha \ne \beta$ we can find $\gamma \succeq \beta$ such that $\alpha \rhd \gamma$ or $\gamma^T \rhd \alpha^T$, as follows: Find the smallest k with $a_k > b_k$, and the smallest l with $a_k > a_{l+1}$. If

$a_l > a_{l+1}+1$, define $\gamma = c_1 c_2 \ldots$ by $c_k = a_k - [k\,{=}\,l] + [k\,{=}\,l+1]$. If $a_l = a_{l+1}+1$, find the smallest l' with $a_{l+1} > a_{l'+1}$ and let $c_k = a_k - [k\,{=}\,l'] + [k\,{=}\,l'+1]$ if $a_{l'} > a_{l'+1}+1$, otherwise $c_k = a_k - [k\,{=}\,l] + [k\,{=}\,l'+1]$.

(b) Consider α and β to be strings of n 0s and n 1s, as in (15). Then $\alpha \vdash \beta$ if and only if $\alpha \to \beta$, and $\beta^T \vdash \alpha^T$ if and only if $\alpha \Rightarrow \beta$, where '$\to$' denotes replacing a substring of the form 011^q10 by 101^q01 and '$\Rightarrow$' denotes replacing a substring of the form 010^q10 by 100^q01, for some $q \geq 0$.

(c) A partition covers at most $[a_1 > a_2] + \cdots + [a_{m-1} > a_m] + [a_m \geq 2]$ others. The partition $\alpha = (n_2+n_1-1)(n_2-2)(n_2-3)\ldots21$ maximizes this quantity in the case $a_m = 1$; cases with $a_m \geq 2$ give no improvement. (The conjugate partition, namely $(n_2-1)(n_2-2)\ldots21^{n_1+1}$, is just as good. Therefore both α and α^T are also *covered by* the maximum number of others.)

(d) Equivalently, consecutive parts of μ differ by at most 1, and the smallest part is 1; the rim representation has no consecutive 1s.

(e) Use rim representations and replace $\vdash$ by the relation $\to$. If $\alpha \to \alpha_1$ and $\alpha \to \alpha_1'$ we can easily show the existence of a string β such that $\alpha_1 \to \beta$ and $\alpha_1' \to \beta$; for example,

$$011^q1011^r10 \; {\nearrow}^{\;101^q0111^r10}_{\;\searrow_{\;011^q1101^r01}} \; {}^{\searrow}_{\;\nearrow} \; 101^q1011^r01.$$

Let $\beta = \beta_2 \vdash \cdots \vdash \beta_m$ where β_m is minimal. Then, by induction on $\max(k, k')$, we have $k = m$ and $\alpha_k = \beta_m$; also $k' = m$ and $\alpha_{k'}' = \beta_m$.

(f) Set $\beta \leftarrow \alpha^T$; then repeatedly set $\beta \leftarrow \beta'$ until β is minimal, using any convenient partition β' such that $\beta \vdash \beta'$. The desired partition is β^T.

Proof: Let $\mu(\alpha)$ be the common value $\alpha_k = \alpha_{k'}'$ in part (e); we must prove that $\alpha \succeq \beta$ implies $\mu(\alpha) \succeq \mu(\beta)$. There is a sequence $\alpha = \alpha_0, \ldots, \alpha_k = \beta$ where $\alpha_j \to \alpha_{j+1}$ or $\alpha_j \Rightarrow \alpha_{j+1}$ for $0 \leq j < k$. If $\alpha_0 \to \alpha_1$ we have $\mu(\alpha) = \mu(\alpha_1)$; thus it suffices to prove that $\alpha \Rightarrow \beta$ and $\alpha \to \alpha'$ implies $\alpha' \succeq \mu(\beta)$. But we have, for example,

$$010^q1011^r10 \; {\nearrow\!\!\!\nearrow}^{\;100^q0111^r10}_{\;\searrow_{\;010^q1101^r01 \,\to\, 010^{q-1}10011^r01}} \; {}^{\searrow}_{\;\nearrow\!\!\!\nearrow} \; 100^q1011^r01$$

because we may assume that $q > 0$; and the other cases are similar.

(g) The parts of λ_n are $a_k = n_2 + [k \leq n_1] - k$ for $1 \leq k < n_2$; the parts of λ_n^T are $b_k = n_2 - k + [n_2 - k < n_1]$ for $1 \leq k \leq n_2$. The algorithm of (f) reaches λ_n^T from n^1 after $\binom{n_2+1}{3} - \binom{n_2-n_1}{2}$ steps, because each step increases $\sum k b_k = \sum \binom{a_k+1}{2}$ by 1.

(h) The path n, $(n-1)1$, $(n-2)2$, $(n-2)11$, $(n-3)21$, $\ldots$, 321^{n-5}, 31^{n-3}, 221^{n-4}, 21^{n-2}, 1^n, of length $2n - 4$ when $n \geq 3$, is shortest.

It can be shown that the longest path has $m = 2\binom{n_2}{3} + n_1(n_2-1)$ steps. One such path has the form $\alpha_0, \ldots, \alpha_k, \ldots, \alpha_l, \ldots, \alpha_m$ where $\alpha_0 = n^1$; $\alpha_k = \lambda_n$; $\alpha_l = \lambda_n^T$; $\alpha_j \vdash \alpha_{j+1}$ for $0 \leq j < l$; and $\alpha_{j+1}^T \vdash \alpha_j^T$ for $k \leq j < m$.

Reference: C. Greene and D. J. Kleitman, *Europ. J. Combinatorics* **7** (1986), 1–10.

56. Suppose $\lambda = u_1 \ldots u_m$ and $\mu = v_1 \ldots v_m$. The following (unoptimized) algorithm applies the theory of exercise 54 to generate the partitions in colex order, maintaining $\alpha = a_1 a_2 \ldots a_m \preceq \mu$ as well as $\alpha^T = b_1 b_2 \ldots b_l \preceq \lambda^T$. To find the successor of α, we first find the largest j such that b_j can be increased. Then we have

$\beta = b_1 \ldots b_{j-1}(b_j{+}1)1 \ldots 1 \preceq \lambda^T$, hence the desired successor is $\beta^T \wedge \mu$. The algorithm maintains auxiliary tables $r_j = b_j + \cdots + b_l$, $s_j = v_1 + \cdots + v_j$, and $t_j = w_j + w_{j+1} + \cdots$, where $\lambda^T = w_1 w_2 \ldots$.

M1. [Initialize.] Set $q \leftarrow 0$, $k \leftarrow u_1$. For $j = 1, \ldots, m$, while $u_{j+1} < k$ set $t_k \leftarrow q \leftarrow q + j$ and $k \leftarrow k - 1$. Then set $q \leftarrow 0$ again, and for $j = 1, \ldots, m$ set $a_j \leftarrow v_j$, $s_j \leftarrow q \leftarrow q + a_j$. Then set $q \leftarrow 0$ yet again, and $k \leftarrow l \leftarrow a_1$. For $j = 1, \ldots, m$, while $a_{j+1} < k$ set $b_k \leftarrow j$, $r_k \leftarrow q \leftarrow q + j$, and $k \leftarrow k - 1$. Finally, set $t_1 \leftarrow 0$, $b_0 \leftarrow 0$, $b_{-1} \leftarrow -1$.

M2. [Visit.] Visit the partition $a_1 \ldots a_m$ and/or its conjugate $b_1 \ldots b_l$.

M3. [Find j.] Let j be the largest integer $< l$ such that $r_{j+1} > t_{j+1}$ and $b_j \neq b_{j-1}$. Terminate the algorithm if $j = 0$.

M4. [Increase b_j.] Set $x \leftarrow r_{j+1} - 1$, $k \leftarrow b_j$, $b_j \leftarrow k + 1$, and $a_{k+1} \leftarrow j$. (The previous value of a_{k+1} was $j - 1$. Now we're going to update $a_1 \ldots a_k$ using essentially the method of exercise 54(c) to distribute x dots into columns $j + 1, j + 2, \ldots$.)

M5. [Majorize.] Set $z \leftarrow 0$ and then do the following for $i = 1, \ldots, k$: Set $x \leftarrow x + j$, $y \leftarrow \min(x, s_i)$, $a_i \leftarrow y - z$, $z \leftarrow y$; if $i = 1$ set $l \leftarrow p \leftarrow a_1$ and $q \leftarrow 0$; if $i > 1$ while $p > a_i$ set $b_p \leftarrow i - 1$, $r_p \leftarrow q \leftarrow q + i - 1$, $p \leftarrow p - 1$. Finally, while $p > j$ set $b_p \leftarrow k$, $r_p \leftarrow q \leftarrow q + k$, $p \leftarrow p - 1$. Return to M2. ∎

57. If $\lambda = \mu^T$ there obviously is only one such matrix, essentially the Ferrers diagram of λ. And the condition $\lambda \preceq \mu^T$ is necessary, for if $\mu^T = b_1 b_2 \ldots$ we have $b_1 + \cdots + b_k = \min(c_1, k) + \min(c_2, k) + \cdots$, and this quantity must not be less than the number of 1s in the first k rows. Finally, if there is a matrix for λ and μ and if λ covers α, we can readily construct a matrix for α and μ by moving a 1 from any specified row to another that has fewer 1s.

Notes: This result is often called the Gale–Ryser theorem, because of well-known papers by D. Gale [*Pacific J. Math.* **7** (1957), 1073–1082] and H. J. Ryser [*Canadian J. Math.* **9** (1957), 371–377]. But the number of 0–1 matrices with row sums λ and column sums μ is the coefficient of the monomial symmetric function $\sum x_{i_1}^{c_1} x_{i_2}^{c_2} \ldots$ in the product of elementary symmetric functions $e_{r_1} e_{r_2} \ldots$, where

$$e_r = [z^r](1 + x_1 z)(1 + x_2 z)(1 + x_3 z) \ldots.$$

In this context the result has been known at least since the 1930s; see D. E. Littlewood's formula for $\prod_{m,n \geq 0}(1 + x_m y_n)$ in *Proc. London Math. Soc.* (2) **40** (1936), 40–70. [Cayley had shown much earlier, in *Philosophical Trans.* **147** (1857), 489–499, that the lexicographic condition $\lambda \leq \mu^T$ is necessary.]

58. [R. F. Muirhead, *Proc. Edinburgh Math. Soc.* **21** (1903), 144–157.] The condition $\alpha \succeq \beta$ is necessary, because we can set $x_1 = \cdots = x_k = x$ and $x_{k+1} = \cdots = x_n = 1$ and let $x \to \infty$. It is sufficient because we need only prove it when α covers β. Then if, say, parts (a_1, a_2) become $(a_1 - 1, a_2 + 1)$, the left-hand side is the right-hand side plus the nonnegative quantity

$$\frac{1}{2m!} \sum x_{p_1}^{a_2} x_{p_2}^{a_2} \ldots x_{p_m}^{a_m} (x_{p_1}^{a_1 - a_2 - 1} - x_{p_2}^{a_1 - a_2 - 1})(x_{p_1} - x_{p_2}).$$

[*Historical notes:* Muirhead's paper is the earliest known appearance of the concept now known as majorization; shortly afterward, an equivalent definition was given by M. O. Lorenz, *Quarterly Publ. Amer. Stat. Assoc.* **9** (1905), 209–219, who was interested in measuring nonuniform distribution of wealth. Yet another equivalent

concept was formulated by I. Schur in *Sitzungsberichte Berliner Math. Gesellschaft*
22 (1923), 9–20. "Majorization" was named by Hardy, Littlewood, and Pólya, who
established its most basic properties in *Messenger of Math.* **58** (1929), 145–152; see
exercise 2.3.4.5–17. An excellent book, *Inequalities* by A. W. Marshall and I. Olkin
(Academic Press, 1979), is entirely devoted to the subject.]

59. The unique paths for $n = 0$, 1, 2, 3, 4, and 6 must have the stated symmetry.
There is one such path for $n = 5$, namely 11111, 2111, 221, 311, 32, 41, 5. And there
are four for $n = 7$:

    1111111, 211111, 22111, 2221, 322, 3211, 31111, 4111, 511, 421, 331, 43, 52, 61, 7;
    1111111, 211111, 22111, 2221, 322, 421, 511, 4111, 31111, 3211, 331, 43, 52, 61, 7;
    1111111, 211111, 31111, 22111, 2221, 322, 3211, 4111, 421, 331, 43, 52, 511, 61, 7;
    1111111, 211111, 31111, 22111, 2221, 322, 421, 4111, 3211, 331, 43, 52, 511, 61, 7.

There are no others, because at least two self-conjugate partitions exist for all $n \geq 8$
(see exercise 16).

60. For $L(6,6)$, use (59); otherwise use $L'(4,6)$ and $L'(3,5)$ everywhere.
    In $M(4, 18)$, insert 444222, 4442211 between 443322 and 4432221.
    In $M(5, 11)$, insert 52211, 5222 between 62111 and 6221.
    In $M(5, 20)$, insert 5542211, 554222 between 5552111 and 555221.
    In $M(6, 13)$, insert 72211, 7222 between 62221 and 6322.
    In $L(4, 14)$, insert 44222, 442211 between 43322 and 432221.
    In $L(5, 15)$, insert 542211, 54222 between 552111 and 55221.
    In $L(7, 12)$, insert 62211, 6222 between 72111 and 7221.

62. The statement holds for $n = 7$, 8, and 9, except in two cases: $n = 8$, $m = 3$,
$\alpha = 3221$; $n = 9$, $m = 4$, $\alpha = 432$.

64. If $n = 2^k q$ where q is odd, let ω_n denote the partition $(2^k)^q$, namely q parts equal
to 2^k. The recursive rule

$$B(n) \;=\; B(n-1)^R 1, \; 2 \times B(n/2)$$

for $n > 0$, where $2 \times B(n/2)$ denotes doubling all parts of $B(n/2)$ (or the empty sequence
if n is odd), defines a pleasant Gray path that begins with $\omega_{n-1}1$ and ends with ω_n, if
we let $B(0)$ be the unique partition of 0. Thus,

$$B(1) = 1; \quad B(2) = 11, 2; \quad B(3) = 21, 111; \quad B(4) = 1111, 211, 22, 4.$$

Among the remarkable properties satisfied by this sequence is the fact that

$$B(n) = (2 \times B(0))1^n, \; (2 \times B(1))1^{n-2}, \; (2 \times B(2))1^{n-4}, \; \ldots, \; (2 \times B(n/2))1^0,$$

when n is even; for example,

$$B(8) = 11111111, 2111111, 221111, 41111, 4211, 22211, 2222, 422, 44, 8.$$

The following algorithm generates $B(n)$ looplessly when $n \geq 2$:

    K1. [Initialize.] Set $c_0 \leftarrow p_0 \leftarrow 0$, $p_1 \leftarrow 1$. If n is even, set $c_1 \leftarrow n$, $t \leftarrow 1$; other-
        wise let $n - 1 = 2^k q$ where q is odd and set $c_1 \leftarrow 1$, $c_2 \leftarrow q$, $p_2 \leftarrow 2^k$, $t \leftarrow 2$.

    K2. [Even visit.] Visit the partition $p_t^{c_t} \ldots p_1^{c_1}$. (Now $c_t + \cdots + c_1$ is even.)

    K3. [Change the largest part.] If $c_t = 1$, split the largest part: If $p_t \neq 2p_{t-1}$, set
        $c_t \leftarrow 2$, $p_t \leftarrow p_t/2$, otherwise set $c_{t-1} \leftarrow c_{t-1} + 2$, $t \leftarrow t - 1$. But if $c_t > 1$,
        merge two of the largest parts: If $c_t = 2$, set $c_t \leftarrow 1$, $p_t \leftarrow 2p_t$, otherwise set
        $c_t \leftarrow c_t - 2$, $c_{t+1} \leftarrow 1$, $p_{t+1} \leftarrow 2p_t$, $t \leftarrow t + 1$.

K4. [Odd visit.] Visit the partition $p_t^{c_t} \ldots p_1^{c_1}$. (Now $c_t + \cdots + c_1$ is odd.)

K5. [Change the next-largest part.] Now we wish to apply the following transformation: "Remove $c_t - [t$ is even$]$ of the largest parts temporarily, then apply step K3, then restore the removed parts." More precisely, there are nine cases: (1a) If c_t is odd and $t = 1$, terminate. (1b1) If c_t is odd, $c_{t-1} = 1$, and $p_{t-1} = 2p_{t-2}$, set $c_{t-2} \leftarrow c_{t-2} + 2$, $c_{t-1} \leftarrow c_t$, $p_{t-1} \leftarrow p_t$, $t \leftarrow t - 1$. (1b2) If c_t is odd, $c_{t-1} = 1$, and $p_{t-1} \neq 2p_{t-2}$, set $c_{t-1} \leftarrow 2$, $p_{t-1} \leftarrow p_{t-1}/2$. (1c1) If c_t is odd, $c_{t-1} = 2$, and $p_t = 2p_{t-1}$, set $c_{t-1} \leftarrow c_t + 1$, $p_{t-1} \leftarrow p_t$, $t \leftarrow t - 1$. (1c2) If c_t is odd, $c_{t-1} = 2$, and $p_t \neq 2p_{t-1}$, set $c_{t-1} \leftarrow 1$, $p_{t-1} \leftarrow 2p_{t-1}$. (1d1) If c_t is odd, $c_{t-1} > 2$, and $p_t = 2p_{t-1}$, set $c_{t-1} \leftarrow c_{t-1} - 2$, $c_t \leftarrow c_t + 1$. (1d2) If c_t is odd, $c_{t-1} > 2$, and $p_t \neq 2p_{t-1}$, set $c_{t+1} \leftarrow c_t$, $p_{t+1} \leftarrow p_t$, $c_t \leftarrow 1$, $p_t \leftarrow 2p_{t-1}$, $c_{t-1} \leftarrow c_{t-1} - 2$, $t \leftarrow t + 1$. (2a) If c_t is even and $p_t = 2p_{t-1}$, set $c_t \leftarrow c_t - 1$, $c_{t-1} \leftarrow c_{t-1} + 2$. (2b) If c_t is even and $p_t \neq 2p_{t-1}$, set $c_{t+1} \leftarrow c_t - 1$, $p_{t+1} \leftarrow p_t$, $c_t \leftarrow 2$, $p_t \leftarrow p_t/2$, $t \leftarrow t + 1$. Return to K2. ∎

[The transformations in K3 and K5 undo themselves when performed twice in a row. This construction is due to T. Colthurst and M. Kleber, "A Gray path on binary partitions," to appear. Euler considered the number of such partitions in §50 of his paper in 1750.]

65. If $p_1^{e_1} \ldots p_r^{e_r}$ is the prime factorization of m, the number of such factorizations is $p(e_1) \ldots p(e_r)$, and we can let $n = \max(e_1, \ldots, e_r)$. Indeed, for each r-tuple $(x_1, \ldots, x_r)$ with $0 \leq x_k < p(e_k)$ we can let $m_j = p_1^{a_{1j}} \ldots p_r^{a_{rj}}$, where $a_{k1} \ldots a_{kn}$ is the $(x_k + 1)$st partition of e_k. Thus we can use a reflected Gray code for r-tuples together with a Gray code for partitions.

66. Let $a_1 \ldots a_m$ be an m-tuple that satisfies the specified inequalities. We can sort it into nonincreasing order $a_{x_1} \geq \cdots \geq a_{x_m}$, where the permutation $x_1 \ldots x_m$ is uniquely determined if we require the sorting to be *stable*; see Eq. 5–(2).

If $j \prec k$, we have $a_j \geq a_k$, hence j appears to the left of k in the permutation $x_1 \ldots x_m$. Therefore $x_1 \ldots x_m$ is one of the permutations output by Algorithm 7.2.1.2V. Moreover, j will be left of k also when $a_j = a_k$ and $j < k$, by stability. Hence a_{x_i} is strictly greater than $a_{x_{i+1}}$ when $x_i > x_{i+1}$ is a "descent."

To generate all the relevant partitions of n, take each topological permutation $x_1 \ldots x_m$ and generate the partitions $y_1 \ldots y_m$ of $n - t$ where t is the *index* of $x_1 \ldots x_m$ (see Section 5.1.1). For $1 \leq j \leq m$ set $a_{x_j} \leftarrow y_j + t_j$, where t_j is the number of descents to the right of x_j in $x_1 \ldots x_m$.

For example, if $x_1 \ldots x_m = 314592687$ we want to generate all cases with $a_3 > a_1 \geq a_4 \geq a_5 \geq a_9 > a_2 \geq a_6 \geq a_8 > a_7$. In this case $t = 1 + 5 + 8 = 14$; so we set $a_1 \leftarrow y_2 + 2$, $a_2 \leftarrow y_6 + 1$, $a_3 \leftarrow y_1 + 3$, $a_4 \leftarrow y_3 + 2$, $a_5 \leftarrow y_4 + 2$, $a_6 \leftarrow y_7 + 1$, $a_7 \leftarrow y_9$, $a_8 \leftarrow y_8 + 1$, and $a_9 \leftarrow y_5 + 2$. The generalized generating function $\sum z_1^{a_1} \ldots z_9^{a_9}$ in the sense of exercise 29 is

$$\frac{z_1^2 z_2 z_3^3 z_4^2 z_5^2 z_6 z_8 z_9^2}{(1 - z_3)(1 - z_3 z_1)(1 - z_3 z_1 z_4)(1 - z_3 z_1 z_4 z_5) \ldots (1 - z_3 z_1 z_4 z_5 z_9 z_2 z_6 z_8 z_7)}.$$

When $\prec$ is any given partial ordering, the ordinary generating function for all such partitions of n is therefore $\sum z^{\mathrm{ind}\,\alpha}/((1-z)(1-z^2) \ldots (1-z^m))$, where the sum is over all outputs α of Algorithm 7.2.1.2V.

[See R. P. Stanley, *Memoirs Amer. Math. Soc.* **119** (1972), for significant extensions and applications of these ideas. See also L. Carlitz, *Studies in Foundations and Combinatorics* (New York: Academic Press, 1978), 101–129, for information about up-down partitions.]

67. If $n + 1 = q_1 \ldots q_r$, where the factors $q_1, \ldots, q_r$ are all ≥ 2, we get a perfect partition $\{(q_1-1) \cdot 1, (q_2-1) \cdot q_1, (q_3-1) \cdot q_1 q_2, \ldots, (q_r-1) \cdot q_1 \ldots q_{r-1}\}$ that corresponds in an obvious way to mixed radix notation. (The order of the factors q_j is significant.)

Conversely, all perfect partitions arise in this way. Suppose the multiset $M = \{k_1 \cdot p_1, \ldots, k_m \cdot p_m\}$ is a perfect partition, where $p_1 < \cdots < p_m$; then we must have $p_j = (k_1+1) \ldots (k_{j-1}+1)$ for $1 \leq j \leq m$, because p_j is the smallest sum of a submultiset of M that is not a submultiset of $\{k_1 \cdot p_1, \ldots, k_{j-1} \cdot p_{j-1}\}$.

The perfect partitions of n with fewest elements occur if and only if the q_j are all prime, because $pq - 1 > (p-1) + (q-1)$ whenever $p > 1$ and $q > 1$. Thus, for example, the minimal perfect partitions of 11 correspond to the ordered factorizations $2 \cdot 2 \cdot 3$, $2 \cdot 3 \cdot 2$, and $3 \cdot 2 \cdot 2$. *Reference: Quarterly Journal of Mathematics* **21** (1886), 367–373.

68. (a) If $a_i + 1 \leq a_j - 1$ for some i and j we can change $\{a_i, a_j\}$ to $\{a_i+1, a_j-1\}$, thereby increasing the product by $a_j - a_i - 1 > 0$. Thus the optimum occurs only in the optimally balanced partition of exercise 3. [L. Oettinger and J. Derbès, *Nouv. Ann. Math.* **18** (1859), 442; **19** (1860), 117–118.]

(b) No part is 1; and if $a_j \geq 4$ we can change it to $2 + (a_j-2)$ without decreasing the product. Thus we can assume that all parts are 2 or 3. We get an improvement by changing $2 + 2 + 2$ to $3 + 3$, hence there are at most two 2s. The optimum therefore is $3^{n/3}$ when $n \bmod 3$ is 0; $4 \cdot 3^{(n-4)/3} = 3^{(n-4)/3} \cdot 2 \cdot 2 = (4/3^{4/3})3^{n/3}$ when $n \bmod 3$ is 1; $3^{(n-2)/3} \cdot 2 = (2/3^{2/3})3^{n/3}$ when $n \bmod 3$ is 2. [O. Meißner, *Mathematisch-naturwissenschaftliche Blätter* **4** (1907), 85.]

69. All $n > 2$ have the solution $(n, 2, 1, \ldots, 1)$. We can "sieve out" the other cases $\leq N$ by starting with $s_2 \ldots s_N \leftarrow 1 \ldots 1$ and then setting $s_{ak-b} \leftarrow 0$ whenever $ak - b \leq N$, where $a = x_1 \ldots x_t - 1$, $b = x_1 + \cdots + x_t - t - 1$, $k \geq x_1 \geq \cdots \geq x_t$, and $a > 1$, because $k + x_1 + \cdots + x_t + (ak - b - t - 1) = kx_1 \ldots x_t$. The sequence $(x_1, \ldots, x_t)$ needs to be considered only when $(x_1 \ldots x_t - 1)x_1 - (x_1 + \cdots + x_t) < N - t$; we can also continue to decrease N so that $s_N = 1$. In this way only $(32766, 1486539, 254887, 1511, 937, 478, 4)$ sequences $(x_1, \ldots, x_t)$ need to be tried when N is initially 2^{30}, and the only survivors turn out to be 2, 3, 4, 6, 24, 114, 174, and 444. [See E. Trost, *Elemente der Math.* **11** (1956), 135; M. Misiurewicz, *Elemente der Math.* **21** (1966), 90.]

Notes: No new survivors are likely as $N \to \infty$, but a new idea will be needed to rule them out. The simplest sequences $(x_1, \ldots, x_t) = (3)$ and $(2, 2)$ already exclude all $n > 5$ with $n \bmod 6 \neq 0$; this fact can be used to speed up the computation by a factor of 6. The sequences (6) and (3, 2) exclude 40% of the remainder (namely all n of the forms $5k - 4$ and $5k - 2$); the sequences (8), (4, 2), and (2, 2, 2) exclude 3/7 of the remainder; the sequences with $t = 1$ imply that $n - 1$ must be prime; the sequences in which $x_1 \ldots x_t = 2^r$ exclude about $p(r)$ residues of $n \bmod (2^r - 1)$; sequences in which $x_1 \ldots x_t$ is the product of r distinct primes will exclude about ϖ_r residues of $n \bmod (x_1 \ldots x_t - 1)$.

70. Each step takes one partition of n into another, so we must eventually reach a repeating cycle. Many partitions simply perform a cyclic shift on each northeast-to-southwest diagonal of the Ferrers diagram, changing it

$$
\begin{array}{c}
\text{from}
\end{array}
\quad
\begin{array}{cccccc}
x_1 & x_2 & x_4 & x_7 & x_{11} & x_{16} \cdots \\
x_3 & x_5 & x_8 & x_{12} & x_{17} & x_{23} \cdots \\
x_6 & x_9 & x_{13} & x_{18} & x_{24} & x_{31} \cdots \\
x_{10} & x_{14} & x_{19} & x_{25} & x_{32} & x_{40} \cdots \\
x_{15} & x_{20} & x_{26} & x_{33} & x_{41} & x_{50} \cdots \\
x_{21} & x_{27} & x_{34} & x_{42} & x_{51} & x_{61} \cdots \\
\vdots & \vdots & \vdots & \vdots & \vdots & \vdots
\end{array}
\quad
\begin{array}{c}
\text{to}
\end{array}
\quad
\begin{array}{cccccc}
x_1 & x_3 & x_6 & x_{10} & x_{15} & x_{21} \cdots \\
x_2 & x_4 & x_7 & x_{11} & x_{16} & x_{22} \cdots \\
x_5 & x_8 & x_{12} & x_{17} & x_{23} & x_{30} \cdots \\
x_9 & x_{13} & x_{18} & x_{24} & x_{31} & x_{39} \cdots ; \\
x_{14} & x_{19} & x_{25} & x_{32} & x_{40} & x_{49} \cdots \\
x_{20} & x_{26} & x_{33} & x_{41} & x_{50} & x_{60} \cdots \\
\vdots & \vdots & \vdots & \vdots & \vdots & \vdots
\end{array}
$$

in other words, they apply the permutation $\rho = (1)(2\,3)(4\,5\,6)(7\,8\,9\,10)\ldots$ to the cells. Exceptions occur only when ρ introduces an empty cell above a dot; for example, x_{10} might be empty when x_{11} isn't. But we can get the correct new diagram by moving the top row down, sorting it into its proper place after applying ρ in such cases. Such a move always reduces the number of occupied diagonals, so it cannot be part of a cycle. Thus every cycle consists entirely of permutations by ρ.

If any element of a diagonal is empty in a cyclic partition, all elements of the next diagonal must be empty. For if, say, x_5 is empty, repeated application of ρ will make x_5 adjacent to each of the cells x_7, x_8, x_9, x_{10} of the next diagonal. Therefore if $n = \binom{n_2}{2} + \binom{n_1}{1}$ with $n_2 > n_1 \geq 0$ the cyclic states are precisely those with $n_2 - 1$ completely filled diagonals and n_1 dots in the next. [This result is due to J. Brandt, *Proc. Amer. Math. Soc.* **85** (1982), 483–486. The origin of the problem is unknown; see Martin Gardner, *The Last Recreations* (1997), Chapter 2.]

71. When $n = 1 + \cdots + m > 1$, the starting partition $(m-1)(m-1)(m-2)\ldots 211$ has distance $m(m-1)$ from the cyclic state, and this is maximum. [K. Igusa, *Math. Magazine* **58** (1985), 259–271; G. Etienne, *J. Combin. Theory* **A58** (1991), 181–197.] In the general case, Griggs and Ho [*Advances in Appl. Math.* **21** (1998), 205–227] have conjectured that the maximum distance to a cycle is $\max(2n+2-n_1(n_2+1), n+n_2+1, n_1(n_2+1)) - 2n_2$ for all $n > 1$; their conjecture has been verified for $n \leq 100$. Moreover, the worst-case starting partition appears to be unique when $n_2 = 2n_1 + \{-1, 0, 2\}$.

72. (a) Swap the jth occurrence of k in the partition $n = j \cdot k + \alpha$ with the kth occurrence of j in $k \cdot j + \alpha$, for every partition α of $n - jk$. For example, when $n = 6$ the swaps are

$$6, \ 51, \ 42, \ 411, \ 33, \ 321, \ 3111, \ 222, \ 2211, \ 21111, \ 111111.$$
$$\text{a} \quad \text{bl} \quad \text{fg} \quad \text{clg} \quad \text{hi} \quad \text{jkl} \quad \text{dlkh} \quad \text{n2i} \quad \text{m2ln} \quad \text{elmjf} \quad \text{ledcba}$$

(b) $p(n-k) + p(n-2k) + p(n-3k) + \cdots$. [A. H. M. Hoare, *AMM* **93** (1986), 475–476.]

SECTION 7.2.1.5

1. Whenever m is set equal to r in step H6, change it back to $r - 1$.

2. **L1.** [Initialize.] Set $l_j \leftarrow j - 1$ and $a_j \leftarrow 0$ for $1 \leq j \leq n$. Also set $h_1 \leftarrow n$, $t \leftarrow 1$, and set l_0 to any convenient nonzero value.

  L2. [Visit.] Visit the t-block partition represented by $l_1 \ldots l_n$ and $h_1 \ldots h_t$. (The restricted growth string corresponding to this partition is $a_1 \ldots a_n$.)

  L3. [Find j.] Set $j \leftarrow n$; then, while $l_j = 0$, set $j \leftarrow j - 1$ and $t \leftarrow t - 1$.

  L4. [Move j to the next block.] Terminate if $j = 0$. Otherwise set $k \leftarrow a_j + 1$, $h_k \leftarrow l_j$, $a_j \leftarrow k$. If $k = t$, set $t \leftarrow t + 1$ and $l_j \leftarrow 0$; otherwise set $l_j \leftarrow h_{k+1}$. Finally set $h_{k+1} \leftarrow j$.

  L5. [Move $j + 1, \ldots, n$ to block 1.] While $j < n$, set $j \leftarrow j + 1$, $l_j \leftarrow h_1$, $a_j \leftarrow 0$, and $h_1 \leftarrow j$. Return to L2. ∎

3. Let $\tau(k, n)$ be the number of strings $a_1 \ldots a_n$ that satisfy the condition $0 \leq a_j \leq 1 + \max(k-1, a_1, \ldots, a_{j-1})$ for $1 \leq j \leq n$; thus $\tau(k, 0) = 1$, $\tau(0, n) = \varpi_n$, and $\tau(k, n) = k\tau(k, n-1) + \tau(k+1, n-1)$. [S. G. Williamson has called $\tau(k, n)$ a "tail coefficient"; see *SICOMP* **5** (1976), 602–617.] The number of strings that are generated by Algorithm H before a given restricted growth string $a_1 \ldots a_n$ is $\sum_{j=1}^{n} a_j \tau(b_j, n - j)$, where $b_j = 1 + \max(a_1, \ldots, a_{j-1})$. Working backwards with the help of a precomputed table of the tail coefficients, we find that this formula yields 999999 when $a_1 \ldots a_{12} = 010220345041$.

4. The most common representatives of each type, subscripted by the number of corresponding occurrences in the GraphBase, are $\mathtt{zzzzz}_0$, $\mathtt{ooooh}_0$, $\mathtt{xxxix}_0$, $\mathtt{xxxii}_0$, $\mathtt{ooops}_0$, $\mathtt{llull}_0$, $\mathtt{llala}_0$, $\mathtt{eeler}_0$, $\mathtt{iitti}_0$, $\mathtt{xxiii}_0$, $\mathtt{ccxxv}_0$, $\mathtt{eerie}_1$, $\mathtt{llama}_1$, $\mathtt{xxvii}_0$, $\mathtt{oozed}_5$, $\mathtt{uhuuu}_0$, $\mathtt{mamma}_1$, $\mathtt{puppy}_{28}$, $\mathtt{anana}_0$, $\mathtt{hehee}_0$, $\mathtt{vivid}_{15}$, $\mathtt{rarer}_3$, $\mathtt{etext}_1$, $\mathtt{amass}_2$, $\mathtt{again}_{137}$, $\mathtt{ahhaa}_0$, $\mathtt{esses}_1$, $\mathtt{teeth}_{25}$, $\mathtt{yaaay}_0$, $\mathtt{ahhhh}_2$, $\mathtt{pssst}_2$, $\mathtt{seems}_7$, $\mathtt{added}_6$, $\mathtt{lxxii}_0$, $\mathtt{books}_{184}$, $\mathtt{swiss}_3$, $\mathtt{sense}_{10}$, $\mathtt{ended}_3$, $\mathtt{check}_{160}$, $\mathtt{level}_{18}$, $\mathtt{tepee}_4$, $\mathtt{slyly}_5$, $\mathtt{never}_{154}$, $\mathtt{sells}_6$, $\mathtt{motto}_{21}$, $\mathtt{whooo}_2$, $\mathtt{trees}_{384}$, $\mathtt{going}_{307}$, $\mathtt{which}_{151}$, $\mathtt{there}_{174}$, $\mathtt{three}_{100}$, $\mathtt{their}_{3834}$. (See S. Golomb, *Math. Mag.* **53** (1980), 219–221. Words with only two distinct letters are, of course, rare. The 18 representatives listed here with subscript 0 can be found in larger dictionaries or in English-language pages of the Internet.)

5. (a) $112 = \rho(0225)$. The sequence is $r(0)$, $r(1)$, $r(4)$, $r(9)$, $r(16)$, $\ldots$, where $r(n)$ is obtained by expressing n in decimal notation (with one or more leading zeros), applying the ρ function of exercise 4, then deleting the leading zeros. Notice that $n/9 \le r(n) \le n$.

(b) $1012 = r(45^2)$. The sequence is the same as (a), but sorted into order and with duplicates removed. (Who knew that $88^2 = 7744$, $212^2 = 44944$, and $264^2 = 69696$?)

6. Use the topological sorting approach of Algorithm 7.2.1.2V, with an appropriate partial ordering: Include c_j chains of length j, with their least elements ordered. For example, if $n = 20$, $c_2 = 3$, and $c_3 = c_4 = 2$, we use that algorithm to find all permutations $a_1 \ldots a_{20}$ of $\{1, \ldots, 20\}$ such that $1 \prec 2$, $3 \prec 4$, $5 \prec 6$, $1 \prec 3 \prec 5$, $7 \prec 8 \prec 9$, $10 \prec 11 \prec 12$, $7 \prec 10$, $13 \prec 14 \prec 15 \prec 16$, $17 \prec 18 \prec 19 \prec 20$, $13 \prec 17$, forming the restricted growth strings $\rho(f(a_1) \ldots f(a_{20}))$, where ρ is defined in exercise 4 and $(f(1), \ldots, f(20)) = (1, 1, 2, 2, 3, 3, 4, 4, 4, 5, 5, 5, 6, 6, 6, 6, 7, 7, 7, 7)$. The total number of outputs is, of course, given by (48).

7. Exactly ϖ_n. They are the permutations we get by reversing the left-right order of the blocks in (2) and dropping the '|' symbols: 1234, 4123, 3124, 3412, $\ldots$, 4321. [See A. Claesson, *European J. Combinatorics* **22** (2001), 961–971. S. Kitaev, in "Partially ordered generalized patterns," *Discrete Math.*, to appear, has discovered a far-reaching generalization: Let π be a permutation of $\{0, \ldots, r\}$, let g_n be the number of permutations $a_1 \ldots a_n$ of $\{1, \ldots, n\}$ such that $a_{k-0\pi} > a_{k-1\pi} > \cdots > a_{k-r\pi} > a_j$ implies $j > k$, and let f_n be the number of permutations $a_1 \ldots a_n$ for which the pattern $a_{k-0\pi} > a_{k-1\pi} > \cdots > a_{k-r\pi}$ is avoided altogether for $r < k \le n$. Then $\sum_{n \ge 0} g_n z^n / n! = \exp(\sum_{n \ge 1} f_{n-1} z^n / n!)$.]

8. For each partition of $\{1, \ldots, n\}$ into m blocks, arrange the blocks in decreasing order of their smallest elements, and permute the non-smallest block elements in all possible ways. If $n = 9$ and $m = 3$, for example, the partition 126|38|4579 would yield 457938126 and eleven other cases obtained by permuting $\{5, 7, 9\}$ and $\{2, 6\}$ among themselves. (Essentially the same method generates all permutations that have exactly k cycles; see the "unusual correspondence" of Section 1.3.3.)

9. Among the permutations of the multiset $\{k_0 \cdot 0, k_1 \cdot 1, \ldots, k_{n-1} \cdot (n-1)\}$, exactly

$$\binom{k_0 + k_1 + \cdots + k_{n-1}}{k_0, k_1, \ldots, k_{n-1}} \frac{k_0}{(k_0 + k_1 + \cdots + k_{n-1})} \frac{k_1}{(k_1 + \cdots + k_{n-1})} \cdots \frac{k_{n-1}}{k_{n-1}}$$

have restricted growth, since $k_j / (k_j + \cdots + k_{n-1})$ is the probability that j precedes $\{j + 1, \ldots, n - 1\}$.

The average number of 0s, if $n > 0$, is $1 + (n - 1)\varpi_{n-1} / \varpi_n = \Theta(\log n)$, because the total number of 0s among all ϖ_n cases is $\sum_{k=1}^{n} k \binom{n-1}{k-1} \varpi_{n-k} = \varpi_n + (n - 1)\varpi_{n-1}$.

10. Given a partition of $\{1, \ldots, n\}$, construct an oriented tree on $\{0, 1, \ldots, n\}$ by letting $j - 1$ be the parent of all members of a block whose least member is j. Then relabel

the leaves, preserving order, and erase the other labels. For example, the 15 partitions
in (2) correspond respectively to

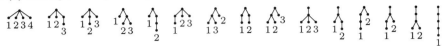

To reverse the process, take a semilabeled tree and assign new numbers to its nodes
by considering the nodes first encountered on the path from the root to the smallest
leaf, then on the path from the root to the second-smallest leaf, etc. The number of
leaves is $n + 1$ minus the number of blocks. [This construction is closely related to
exercise 2.3.4.4–18 and to many enumerations in that section. See P. L. Erdős and
L. A. Székely, *Advances in Applied Math.* **10** (1989), 488–496.]

11. We get pure alphametics from 900 of the 64855 set partitions into at most 10
blocks for which $\rho(a_1 \ldots a_{13}) = \rho(a_5 \ldots a_8 a_1 \ldots a_4 a_9 \ldots a_{13})$, and from 563,527 of the
13,788,536 for which $\rho(a_1 \ldots a_{13}) < \rho(a_5 \ldots a_8 a_1 \ldots a_4 a_9 \ldots a_{13})$. The first examples
are aaaa + aaaa = baaac, aaaa + aaaa = bbbbc, and aaaa + aaab = baaac; the
last are abcd + efgd = dceab (goat + newt = tango) and abcd + efgd = dceaf
(clad + nerd = dance). [The idea of hooking a partition generator to an alphametic
solver is due to Alan Sutcliffe.]

12. (a) Form $\rho((a_1 a_1') \ldots (a_n a_n'))$, where ρ is defined in exercise 4, since we have $x \equiv y$
(modulo $\Pi \vee \Pi'$) if and only if $x \equiv y$ (modulo Π) and $x \equiv y$ (modulo Π').

(b) Represent Π by links as in exercise 2; represent Π' as in Algorithm 2.3.3E;
and use that algorithm to make $j \equiv l_j$ whenever $l_j \neq 0$. (For efficiency, we can assume
that Π has at least as many blocks as Π'.)

(c) When one block of Π has been split into two parts; that is, when two blocks
of Π' have been merged together.

(d) $\binom{t}{2}$;   (e) $(2^{s_1 - 1} - 1) + \cdots + (2^{s_t - 1} - 1)$.

(f) True: Let $\Pi \vee \Pi'$ have blocks $B_1 | B_2 | \cdots | B_t$, where $\Pi = B_1 B_2 B_3 | \cdots | B_t$. Then
Π' is essentially a partition of $\{B_1, \ldots, B_t\}$ with $B_1 \not\equiv B_2$, and $\Pi \wedge \Pi'$ is obtained by
merging the block of Π' that contains B_1 with the block that contains B_2. [A finite
lattice that satisfies this condition is called *lower semimodular*; see G. Birkhoff, *Lattice
Theory* (1940), §I.8. The majorization lattice of exercise 7.2.1.4–54 does not have this
property when, for example, $\alpha = 4111$ and $\alpha' = 331$.]

(g) False: For example, let $\Pi = 0011$, $\Pi' = 0101$.

(h) The blocks of Π and Π' are unions of the blocks of $\Pi \vee \Pi'$, so we can assume
that $\Pi \vee \Pi' = \{1, \ldots, t\}$. As in part (b), merge j with l_j to get Π in r steps, when Π
has $t - r$ blocks. These merges applied to Π' will each reduce the number of blocks by
0 or 1. Hence $b(\Pi') - b(\Pi \wedge \Pi') \leq r = b(\Pi \vee \Pi') - b(\Pi)$.

[In *Algebra Universalis* **10** (1980), 74–95, P. Pudlák and J. Tůma proved that *every*
finite lattice is a sublattice of the partition lattice of $\{1, \ldots, n\}$, for suitably large n.]

13. [See *Advances in Math.* **26** (1977), 290–305.] If the j largest elements of a t-block
partition appear in singleton blocks, but the next element $n - j$ does not, let us say
that the partition has order $t - j$. Define the "Stirling string" Σ_{nt} to be the sequence
of orders of the t-block partitions Π_1, Π_2, $\ldots$; for example, $\Sigma_{43} = 122333$. Then
$\Sigma_{tt} = 0$, and we get $\Sigma_{(n+1)t}$ from Σ_{nt} by replacing each digit d in the latter by the
string $d^d (d+1)^{d+1} \ldots t^t$ of length $\binom{t+1}{2} - \binom{d}{2}$; for example,

$$\Sigma_{53} = 122333233322333333333333.$$

The basic idea is to consider the lexicographic generation process of Algorithm H. Suppose $\Pi = a_1 \ldots a_n$ is a t-block partition of order j; then it is the lexicographically smallest t-block partition whose restricted growth string begins with $a_1 \ldots a_{n-t+j}$. The partitions covered by Π are, in lexicographic order, Π_{12}, Π_{13}, Π_{23}, Π_{14}, Π_{24}, Π_{34}, $\ldots$, $\Pi_{(t-1)t}$, where Π_{rs} means "coalesce blocks r and s of Π" (that is, "change all occurrences of $s-1$ to $r-1$ and then apply ρ to get a restricted growth string"). If Π' is any of the last $\binom{t}{2} - \binom{j}{2}$ of these, from $\Pi_{1(j+1)}$ onwards, then Π is the smallest t-block partition following Π'. For example, if $\Pi = 001012034$, then $n = 9$, $t = 5$, $j = 3$, and the relevant partitions Π' are $\rho(001012004)$, $\rho(001012014)$, $\rho(001012024)$, $\rho(001012030)$, $\rho(001012031)$, $\rho(001012032)$, $\rho(001012033)$.

Therefore $f_{nt}(N) = f_{nt}(N-1) + \binom{j}{2} - \binom{j}{2}$, where j is the Nth digit of Σ_{nt}.

14. E1. [Initialize.] Set $a_j \leftarrow 0$ and $b_j \leftarrow d_j \leftarrow 1$ for $1 \le j \le n$.

E2. [Visit.] Visit the restricted growth string $a_1 \ldots a_n$.

E3. [Find j.] Set $j \leftarrow n$; then, while $a_j = d_j$, set $d_j \leftarrow 1 - d_j$ and $j \leftarrow j - 1$.

E4. [Done?] Terminate if $j = 1$. Otherwise go to E6 if $d_j = 0$.

E5. [Move down.] If $a_j = 0$, set $a_j \leftarrow b_j$, $m \leftarrow a_j + 1$, and go to E7. Otherwise if $a_j = b_j$, set $a_j \leftarrow b_j - 1$, $m \leftarrow b_j$, and go to E7. Otherwise set $a_j \leftarrow a_j - 1$ and return to E2.

E6. [Move up.] If $a_j = b_j - 1$, set $a_j \leftarrow b_j$, $m \leftarrow a_j + 1$, and go to E7. Otherwise if $a_j = b_j$, set $a_j \leftarrow 0$, $m \leftarrow b_j$, and go to E7. Otherwise set $a_j \leftarrow a_j + 1$ and return to E2.

E7. [Fix $b_{j+1} \ldots b_n$.] Set $b_k \leftarrow m$ for $k = j+1, \ldots, n$. Return to E2. ∎

[This algorithm can be extensively optimized because, as in Algorithm H, j is almost always equal to n.]

15. It corresponds to the first n digits of the infinite binary string $01011011011\ldots$, because ϖ_{n-1} is even if and only if $n \bmod 3 = 0$ (see exercise 23).

16. 00012, 01012, 01112, 00112, 00102, 01102, 01002, 01202, 01212, 01222, 01022, 01122, 00122, 00121, 01121, 01021, 01221, 01211, 01201, 01200, 01210, 01220, 01020, 01120, 00120.

17. The following solution uses two mutually recursive procedures, $f(\mu, \nu, \sigma)$ and $b(\mu, \nu, \sigma)$, for "forward" and "backward" generation of $A_{\mu\nu}$ when $\sigma = 0$ and of $A'_{\mu\nu}$ when $\sigma = 1$. To start the process, assuming that $1 < m < n$, first set $a_j \leftarrow 0$ for $1 \le j \le n - m$ and $a_{n-m+j} \leftarrow j - 1$ for $1 \le j \le m$, then call $f(m, n, 0)$.

Procedure $f(\mu, \nu, \sigma)$: If $\mu = 2$, visit $a_1 \ldots a_n$; otherwise call $f(\mu - 1, \nu - 1, (\mu+\sigma) \bmod 2)$. Then, if $\nu = \mu + 1$, do the following: Change a_μ from 0 to $\mu - 1$, and visit $a_1 \ldots a_n$; repeatedly set $a_\nu \leftarrow a_\nu - 1$ and visit $a_1 \ldots a_n$, until $a_\nu = 0$. But if $\nu > \mu + 1$, change $a_{\nu-1}$ (if $\mu+\sigma$ is odd) or a_μ (if $\mu+\sigma$ is even) from 0 to $\mu - 1$; then call $b(\mu, \nu-1, 0)$ if $a_\nu + \sigma$ is odd, $f(\mu, \nu-1, 0)$ if $a_\nu + \sigma$ is even; and while $a_\nu > 0$, set $a_\nu \leftarrow a_\nu - 1$ and call $b(\mu, \nu-1, 0)$ or $f(\mu, \nu-1, 0)$ again in the same way until $a_\nu = 0$.

Procedure $b(\mu, \nu, \sigma)$: If $\nu = \mu + 1$, first do the following: Repeatedly visit $a_1 \ldots a_n$ and set $a_\nu \leftarrow a_\nu + 1$, until $a_\nu = \mu - 1$; then visit $a_1 \ldots a_n$ and change a_μ from $\mu - 1$ to 0. But if $\nu > \mu + 1$, call $f(\mu, \nu-1, 0)$ if $a_\nu + \sigma$ is odd, $b(\mu, \nu-1, 0)$ if $a_\nu + \sigma$ is even; then while $a_\nu < \mu - 1$, set $a_\nu \leftarrow a_\nu + 1$ and call $f(\mu, \nu-1, 0)$ or $b(\mu, \nu-1, 0)$ again in the same way until $a_\nu = \mu - 1$; finally change $a_{\nu-1}$ (if $\mu+\sigma$ is odd) or a_μ (if $\mu+\sigma$ is even) from $\mu - 1$ to 0. And finally, in both cases, if $\mu = 2$ visit $a_1 \ldots a_n$, otherwise call $b(\mu - 1, \nu - 1, (\mu+\sigma) \bmod 2)$.

Most of the running time is actually spent handing the case $\mu = 2$; faster routines based on Gray binary code (and deviating from Ruskey's actual sequences) could be substituted for this case. A streamlined procedure could also be used when $\mu = \nu - 1$.

18. The sequence must begin (or end) with $01 \ldots (n-1)$. By exercise 32, no such Gray code can exist when $0 \neq \delta_n \neq (1)^{0+1+\cdots+(n-1)}$, namely when $n \bmod 12$ is 4, 6, 7, or 9.

The cases $n = 1, 2, 3$, are easily solved; and 1,927,683,326 solutions exist when $n = 5$. Thus there probably are zillions of solutions for all $n \geq 8$ except for the cases already excluded. Indeed, we can probably find such a Gray path through all ϖ_{nk} of the strings considered in answer 28(e) below, except when $n \equiv 2k + (2, 4, 5, 7)$ (modulo 12).

Note: The generalized Stirling number $\left\{ {n \atop m} \right\}_{-1}$ in exercise 30 exceeds 1 for $2 < m < n$, so there can be no such Gray code for the partitions of $\{1, \ldots, n\}$ into m blocks.

19. (a) Change (6) to the pattern $0, 2, \ldots, m, \ldots, 3, 1$ or its reverse, as in endo-order $(7.2.1.3-(45))$.

(b) We can generalize (8) and (9) to obtain sequences $A_{mn\alpha}$ and $A'_{mn\alpha}$ that begin with $0^{n-m}01 \ldots (m-1)$ and end with $01 \ldots (m-1)\alpha$ and $0^{n-m-1}01 \ldots (m-1)a$, respectively, where $0 \leq a \leq m-2$ and α is any string $a_1 \ldots a_{n-m}$ with $0 \leq a_j \leq m-2$. When $2 < m < n$ the new rules are

$$A_{m(n+1)(\alpha a)} = \begin{cases} A_{(m-1)n(b\beta)}x_1, A^R_{mn\beta}x_1, A_{mn\alpha}x_2, \ldots, A_{mn\alpha}x_m, & \text{if } m \text{ is even}; \\ A'_{(m-1)nb}x_1, A_{mn\alpha}x_1, A^R_{mn\alpha}x_2, \ldots, A_{mn\alpha}x_m, & \text{if } m \text{ is odd}; \end{cases}$$

$$A'_{m(n+1)a} = \begin{cases} A'_{(m-1)nb}x_1, A_{mn\beta}x_1, A^R_{mn\beta}x_2, \ldots, A^R_{mn\beta}x_m, & \text{if } m \text{ is even}; \\ A_{(m-1)n(b\beta)}x_1, A^R_{mn\beta}x_1, A_{mn\beta}x_2, \ldots, A^R_{mn\beta}x_m, & \text{if } m \text{ is odd}; \end{cases}$$

here $b = m - 3$, $\beta = b^{n-m}$, and $(x_1, \ldots, x_m)$ is a path from $x_1 = m - 1$ to $x_m = a$.

20. 012323212122; in general $(a_1 \ldots a_n)^T = \rho(a_n \ldots a_1)$, in the notation of exercise 4.

21. The numbers $\langle s_0, s_1, s_2, \ldots \rangle = \langle 1, 1, 2, 3, 7, 12, 31, 59, 164, 339, 999, \ldots \rangle$ satisfy the recurrences $s_{2n+1} = \sum_k \binom{n}{k} s_{2n-2k}$, $s_{2n+2} = \sum_k \binom{n}{k} (2^k + 1) s_{2n-2k}$, because of the way the middle elements relate to the others. Therefore $s_{2n} = n! \, [z^n] \exp((e^{2z} - 1)/2 + e^z - 1)$ and $s_{2n+1} = n! \, [z^n] \exp((e^{2z} - 1)/2 + e^z + z - 1)$. By considering set partitions on the first half we also have $s_{2n} = \sum_k \left\{ {n \atop k} \right\} x_k$ and $s_{2n+1} = \sum_k \left\{ {n+1 \atop k} \right\} x_{k-1}$, where $x_n = 2x_{n-1} + (n-1)x_{n-2} = n! \, [z^n] \exp(2z + z^2/2)$. [T. S. Motzkin considered the sequence $\langle s_{2n} \rangle$ in *Proc. Symp. Pure Math.* **19** (1971), 173.]

22. (a) $\sum_{k=0}^{\infty} k^n \Pr(X = k) = e^{-1} \sum_{k=0}^{\infty} k^n/k! = \varpi_n$ by (16). (b) $\sum_{k=0}^{\infty} k^n \Pr(X = k) = \sum_{k=0}^{\infty} k^n \sum_{j=0}^{m} \binom{j}{k} (-1)^{j-k}/j!$, and we can extend the inner sum to $j = \infty$ because $\sum_k \binom{j}{k} (-1)^k k^n = 0$ when $j > n$. Thus we get $\sum_{j=0}^{\infty} (k^n/k!) \sum_{l=0}^{\infty} (-1)^l/l! = \varpi_n$. [See J. O. Irwin, *J. Royal Stat. Soc.* **A118** (1955), 389–404; J. Pitman, *AMM* **104** (1997), 201–209.]

23. (a) The formula holds whenever $f(x) = x^n$, by (14), so it holds in general. (Thus we also have $\sum_{k=0}^{\infty} f(k)/k! = e f(\varpi)$, by (16).)

(b) Suppose we have proved the relation for k, and let $h(x) = (x-1)^k f(x)$, $g(x) = f(x+1)$. Then $f(\varpi + k + 1) = g(\varpi + k) = \varpi^k g(\varpi) = h(\varpi + 1) = \varpi h(\varpi) = \varpi^{k+1} f(\varpi)$. [See J. Touchard, *Ann. Soc. Sci. Bruxelles* **53** (1933), 21–31. This symbolic "umbral calculus," invented by John Blissard in *Quart. J. Pure and Applied Math.* **4** (1861), 279–305, is quite useful; but it must be handled carefully because $f(\varpi) = g(\varpi)$ does not imply that $f(\varpi)h(\varpi) = g(\varpi)h(\varpi)$.]

(c) The hint is a special case of exercise 4.6.2–16(c). Setting $f(x) = x^n$ and $k = p$ in (b) then yields $\varpi_n \equiv \varpi_{p+n} - \varpi_{1+n}$.

(d) Modulo p, the polynomial $x^N - 1$ is divisible by $g(x) = x^p - x - 1$, because $x^{p^k} \equiv x + k$ and $x^N \equiv x^{\bar{p}} \equiv x^{\underline{p}} \equiv x^p - x \equiv 1$ (modulo $g(x)$ and p). Thus if $h(x) = (x^N - 1)x^n/g(x)$ we have $h(\varpi) \equiv h(\varpi + p) \equiv \varpi^p h(\varpi) \equiv (\varpi^p - \varpi)h(\varpi)$; and $0 \equiv g(\varpi)h(\varpi) \equiv \varpi^{N+n} - \varpi^n$ (modulo p).

24. The hint follows by induction on e, because $x^{p^e} = \prod_{k=0}^{p-1}(x - kp^{e-1})^{p^{e-1}}$. We can also prove by induction on n that $x^n \equiv r_n(x)$ (modulo $g_1(x)$ and p) implies

$$x^{p^{e-1}n} \equiv r_n(x)^{p^{e-1}} \quad (\text{modulo } g_e(x), \, pg_{e-1}(x), \, \ldots, \, p^{e-1}g_1(x), \text{ and } p^e).$$

Hence $x^{p^{e-1}N} = 1 + h_0(x)g_e(x) + ph_1(x)g_{e-1}(x) + \cdots + p^{e-1}h_{e-1}(x)g_1(x) + p^e h_e(x)$ for certain polynomials $h_k(x)$ with integer coefficients. Modulo p^e we have $h_0(\varpi)\varpi^n \equiv h_0(\varpi + p^e)(\varpi + p^e)^n = \varpi^{p^e}h_0(\varpi)\varpi^n \equiv (g_e(\varpi) + 1)h_0(\varpi)\varpi^n$; hence

$$\varpi^{p^{e-1}N+n} = \varpi^n + h_0(\varpi)g_e(\varpi)\varpi^n + ph_1(\varpi)g_{e-1}(\varpi)\varpi^n + \cdots \equiv \varpi^n.$$

[A similar derivation applies when $p = 2$, but we let $g_{j+1}(x) = g_j(x)^2 + 2[j = 2]$, and we obtain $\varpi_n \equiv \varpi_{n+3\cdot 2^e}$ (modulo 2^e). These results are due to Marshall Hall; see *Bull. Amer. Math. Soc.* **40** (1934), 387; *Amer. J. Math.* **70** (1948), 387–388. For further information see W. F. Lunnon, P. A. B. Pleasants, and N. M. Stephens, *Acta Arith.* **35** (1979), 1–16.]

25. The first inequality follows by applying a much more general principle to the tree of restricted growth strings: In any tree for which $\deg(p) \geq \deg(\text{parent}(p))$ for all non-root nodes p, we have $w_k/w_{k-1} \leq w_{k+1}/w_k$ when w_k is the total number of nodes on level k. For if the $m = w_{k-1}$ nodes on level $k-1$ have respectively $a_1, \ldots, a_m$ children, they have at least $a_1^2 + \cdots + a_m^2$ grandchildren; hence $w_{k-1}w_{k+1} \geq m(a_1^2 + \cdots + a_m^2) \geq (a_1 + \cdots + a_m)^2 = w_k^2$.

For the second inequality, note that $\varpi_{n+1} - \varpi_n = \sum_{k=0}^{n}\left(\binom{n}{k} - \binom{n-1}{k-1}\right)\varpi_{n-k}$; thus

$$\frac{\varpi_{n+1}}{\varpi_n} - 1 = \sum_{k=0}^{n-1}\binom{n-1}{k}\frac{\varpi_{n-k}}{\varpi_n} \leq \sum_{k=0}^{n-1}\binom{n-1}{k}\frac{\varpi_{n-k-1}}{\varpi_{n-1}} = \frac{\varpi_n}{\varpi_{n-1}}$$

because, for example, $\varpi_{n-3}/\varpi_n = (\varpi_{n-3}/\varpi_{n-2})(\varpi_{n-2}/\varpi_{n-1})(\varpi_{n-1}/\varpi_n)$ is less than or equal to $(\varpi_{n-4}/\varpi_{n-3})(\varpi_{n-3}/\varpi_{n-2})(\varpi_{n-2}/\varpi_{n-1}) = \varpi_{n-4}/\varpi_{n-1}$.

26. There are $\binom{n-1}{n-t}$ rightward paths from ⓝ to ⓣ; we can represent them by 0s and 1s, where 0 means "go right," 1 means "go up," and the positions of the 1s tell us which $n-t$ of the elements are in the block with 1. The next step, if $t > 1$, is to another vertex at the far left; so we continue with a path that defines a partition on the remaining $t-1$ elements. For example, the partition $14|2|3$ corresponds to the path 0010 under these conventions, where the respective bits mean that $1 \not\equiv 2$, $1 \not\equiv 3$, $1 \equiv 4$, $2 \not\equiv 3$. [Many other interpretations are possible. The convention suggested here shows that ϖ_{nk} enumerates partitions with $1 \not\equiv 2$, $\ldots$, $1 \not\equiv k$, a combinatorial property discovered by H. W. Becker; see *AMM* **51** (1944), 47, and *Mathematics Magazine* **22** (1948), 23–26.]

27. (a) In general, $\lambda_0 = \lambda_1 = \lambda_{2n-1} = \lambda_{2n} = 0$. The following list shows also the restricted growth strings that correspond to each loop via the algorithm of part (b):

0,0,0,0,0,0,0,0,0 0123	0,0,1,0,0,0,0,0,0 0012	0,0,1,1,1,0,0,0,0 0102
0,0,0,0,0,0,1,0,0 0122	0,0,1,0,0,0,1,0,0 0011	0,0,1,1,1,0,1,0,0 0100
0,0,0,0,1,0,0,0,0 0112	0,0,1,0,1,0,0,0,0 0001	0,0,1,1,1,1,1,0,0 0120
0,0,0,0,1,0,1,0,0 0111	0,0,1,0,1,0,1,0,0 0000	0,0,1,1,11,1,1,0,0 0101
0,0,0,0,1,1,1,0,0 0121	0,0,1,0,1,1,1,0,0 0010	0,0,1,1,2,1,1,0,0 0110

(b) The name "tableau" suggests a connection to Section 5.1.4, and indeed the theory developed there leads to an interesting one-to-one correspondence. We can represent set partitions on a triangular chessboard by putting a rook in column l_j of row $n + 1 - j$ whenever $l_j \neq 0$ in the linked list representation of exercise 2 (see the answer to exercise 5.1.3–19). For example, the rook representation of 135|27|489|6 is shown here. Equivalently, the nonzero links can be specified in a two-line array, such as $\binom{1\,2\,3\,4\,8}{3\,7\,5\,8\,9}$; see 5.1.4–(11).

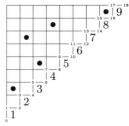

Consider the path of length $2n$ that begins at the lower left corner of this triangular diagram and follows the right boundary edges, ending at the upper right corner: The points of this path are $z_k = (\lfloor k/2 \rfloor, \lceil k/2 \rceil)$ for $0 \le k \le 2n$. Moreover, the rectangle above and to the left of z_k contains precisely the rooks that contribute coordinate pairs $\frac{i}{j}$ to the two-line array when $i \le \lfloor k/2 \rfloor$ and $j > \lceil k/2 \rceil$; in our example, there are just two such rooks when $9 \le k \le 12$, namely $\binom{2\,4}{7\,8}$. Theorem 5.1.4A tells us that such two-line arrays are equivalent to tableaux (P_k, Q_k), where the elements of P_k come from the lower line and the elements of Q_k come from the upper line, and where both P_k and Q_k have the same shape. It is advantageous to use decreasing order in the P tableaux but increasing order in the Q tableaux, so that in our example they are respectively

k	P_k	Q_k	k	P_k	Q_k	k	P_k	Q_k
2	$\boxed{3}$	$\boxed{1}$	7	$\boxed{7\,5}$	$\boxed{2\,3}$	12	$\boxed{8}\\\boxed{7}$	$\boxed{2}\\\boxed{4}$
3	$\boxed{3}$	$\boxed{1}$	8	$\boxed{8\,5}\\\boxed{7}$	$\boxed{2\,3}\\\boxed{4}$	13	$\boxed{8}$	$\boxed{4}$
4	$\boxed{7}\\\boxed{3}$	$\boxed{1}\\\boxed{2}$	9	$\boxed{8}\\\boxed{7}$	$\boxed{2}\\\boxed{4}$	14	$\boxed{8}$	$\boxed{4}$
5	$\boxed{7}$	$\boxed{2}$	10	$\boxed{8}\\\boxed{7}$	$\boxed{2}\\\boxed{4}$	15	$\cdot$	$\cdot$
6	$\boxed{7\,5}$	$\boxed{2\,3}$	11	$\boxed{8}\\\boxed{7}$	$\boxed{2}\\\boxed{4}$	16	$\boxed{9}$	$\boxed{8}$

while P_k and Q_k are empty for $k = 0$, 1, 17, and 18.

In this way every set partition leads to a vacillating tableau loop $\lambda_0, \lambda_1, \ldots, \lambda_{2n}$, if we let λ_k be the integer partition that specifies the common shape of P_k and Q_k. (The loop is 0, 0, 1, 1, 11, 1, 2, 2, 21, 11, 11, 11, 11, 1, 1, 0, 1, 0, 0 in our example.) Moreover, $t_{2k-1} = 0$ if and only if row $n + 1 - k$ contains no rook, if and only if k is smallest in its block.

Conversely, the elements of P_k and Q_k can be uniquely reconstructed from the sequence of shapes λ_k. Namely, $Q_k = Q_{k-1}$ if $t_k = 0$. Otherwise, if k is even, Q_k is Q_{k-1}

with the number $k/2$ placed in a new cell at the right of row t_k; if k is odd, Q_k is obtained from Q_{k-1} by using Algorithm 5.1.4D to delete the rightmost entry of row t_k. A similar procedure defines P_k from the values of P_{k+1} and t_{k+1}, so we can work back from P_{2n} to P_0. Thus the sequence of shapes λ_k is enough to tell us where to place the rooks.

Vacillating tableau loops were introduced in the paper "Crossings and nestings of matchings and partitions" by W. Y. C. Chen, E. Y. P. Deng, R. R. X. Du, R. P. Stanley, and C. H. Yan (preprint, 2005), who showed that the construction has significant (and surprising) consequences. For example, if the set partition Π corresponds to the vacillating tableau loop λ_0, λ_1, ..., λ_{2n}, let's say that its *dual* Π^D is the set partition that corresponds to the sequence of transposed shapes λ_0^T, λ_1^T, ..., λ_{2n}^T. Then, by exercise 5.1.4–7, Π contains a "k-crossing at l," namely a sequence of indices with $i_1 < \cdots < i_k \le l < j_1 < \cdots < j_k$ and $i_1 \equiv j_1, \ldots, i_k \equiv j_k$ (modulo Π), if and only if Π^D contains a "k-nesting at l," which is a sequence of indices with $i_1' < \cdots < i_k' \le l < j_k' < \cdots < j_1'$ and $i_1' \equiv j_1', \ldots, i_k' \equiv j_k'$ (modulo Π^D). Notice also that an involution is essentially a set partition in which all blocks have size 1 or 2; the dual of an involution is an involution having the same singleton sets. In particular, the dual of a perfect matching (when there are no singleton sets) is a perfect matching.

Furthermore, an analogous construction applies to rook placements in *any* Ferrers diagram, not only in the stairstep shapes that correspond to set partitions. Given a Ferrers diagram that has at most m parts, all of size $\le n$, we simply consider the path $z_0 = (0,0), z_1, \ldots, z_{m+n} = (n,m)$ that hugs the right edge of the diagram, and stipulate that $\lambda_k = \lambda_{k-1} + e_{t_k}$ when $z_k = z_{k-1} + (1,0)$, $\lambda_k = \lambda_{k-1} - e_{t_k}$ when $z_k = z_{k-1} + (0,1)$. The proof we gave for stairstep shapes shows also that every placement of rooks in the Ferrers diagram, with at most one rook in each row and at most one in each column, corresponds to a unique tableau loop of this kind.

[And much more is true, besides! See S. Fomin, *J. Combin. Theory* **A72** (1995), 277–292; M. van Leeuwen, *Electronic J. Combinatorics* **3**, 2 (1996), paper #R15.]

28. (a) Define a one-to-one correspondence between rook placements, by interchanging the positions of rooks in rows j and $j+1$ if and only if there's a rook in the "panhandle" of the longer row:

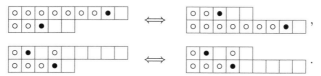

(b) This relation is obvious from the definition, by transposing all the rooks.
(c) Suppose $a_1 \ge a_2 \ge \cdots$ and $a_k > a_{k+1}$. Then we have

$$R(a_1, a_2, \ldots) = x R(a_1 - 1, \ldots, a_{k-1} - 1, a_{k+1}, \ldots) + y R(a_1, \ldots, a_{k-1}, a_k - 1, a_{k+1}, \ldots)$$

because the first term counts cases where a rook is in row k and column a_k. Also $R(0) = 1$ because of the empty placement. From these recurrences we find

$$R(1) = x + y; \quad R(2) = R(1,1) = x + xy + y^2; \quad R(3) = R(1,1,1) = x + xy + xy^2 + y^3;$$
$$R(2,1) = x^2 + 2xy + xy^2 + y^3;$$
$$R(3,1) = R(2,2) = R(2,1,1) = x^2 + x^2 y + xy + 2xy^2 + xy^3 + y^4;$$
$$R(3,1,1) = R(3,2) = R(2,2,1) = x^2 + 2x^2 y + x^2 y^2 + 2xy^2 + 2xy^3 + xy^4 + y^5;$$
$$R(3,2,1) = x^3 + 3x^2 y + 3x^2 y^2 + x^2 y^3 + 3xy^3 + 2xy^4 + xy^5 + y^6.$$

(d) For example, the formula $\varpi_{73}(x,y) = x\varpi_{63}(x,y) + y\varpi_{74}(x,y)$ is equivalent to $R(5,4,4,3,2,1) = xR(4,3,3,2,1) + yR(5,4,3,3,2,1)$, a special case of (c); and $\varpi_{nn}(x,y) = R(n-2,\dots,0)$ is obviously equal to $\varpi_{(n-1)1}(x,y) = R(n-2,\dots,1)$.

(e) In fact $y^{k-1}\varpi_{nk}(x,y)$ is the stated sum over all restricted growth strings $a_1 \dots a_n$ for which $a_2 > 0, \dots, a_k > 0$.

29. (a) If the rooks are respectively in columns $(c_1,\dots,c_n)$, the number of free cells is the number of inversions of the permutation $(n+1-c_1)\dots(n+1-c_n)$. [Rotate the right-hand example of Fig. 35 by $180°$ and compare the result to the illustration following Eq. 5.1.1–(5).]

(b) Each $r \times r$ configuration can be placed in, say, rows $i_1 < \dots < i_r$ and columns $j_1 < \dots < j_r$, yielding $(m-r)(n-r)$ free cells in the unchosen rows and columns; there are $(i_2-i_1+1) + 2(i_3-i_2-1) + \dots + (r-1)(i_r-i_{r-1}-1) + r(m-i_r)$ in the unchosen rows and chosen columns, and a similar number in the chosen rows and unchosen columns. Furthermore

$$\sum_{1 \le i_1 < \dots < i_r \le m} y^{(i_2-i_1+1)+2(i_3-i_2-1)+\dots+(r-1)(i_r-i_{r-1}-1)+r(m-i_r)}$$

may be regarded as the sum of $y^{a_1+a_2+\dots+a_{m-r}}$ over all partitions $r \ge a_1 \ge a_2 \ge \dots \ge a_{m-r} \ge 0$, so it is $\binom{m}{r}_y$ by Theorem C. The polynomial $r!_y$ generates free cells for the chosen rows and columns, by (a). Therefore the answer is $y^{(m-r)(n-r)} \binom{m}{r}_y \binom{n}{r}_y r!_y = y^{(m-r)(n-r)} m!_y n!_y / ((m-r)!_y (n-r)!_y r!_y)$.

(c) The left-hand side is the generating function $R_m(t+a_1,\dots,t+a_m)$ for the Ferrers diagram with t additional columns of height m. For there are $t+a_m$ ways to put a rook in row m, yielding $1 + y + \dots + y^{t+a_m-1} = (1 - y^{t+a_m})/(1-y)$ free cells with respect to those choices; then there are $t + a_{m-1} - 1$ available cells in row $m-1$, etc.

The right-hand side, likewise, equals $R_m(t+a_1,\dots,t+a_m)$. For if $m-k$ rooks are placed into columns $> t$, we must put k rooks into columns $\le t$ of the k unused rows; and we have seen that $t!_y/(t-k)!_y$ is the generating function for free cells when k rooks are placed on a $k \times t$ board.

[The formula proved here can be regarded as a polynomial identity in the variables y and y^t; therefore it is valid for arbitrary t, although our proof assumed that t is a nonnegative integer. This result was discovered in the case $y = 1$ by J. Goldman, J. Joichi, and D. White, *Proc. Amer. Math. Soc.* **52** (1975), 485–492. The general case was established by A. M. Garsia and J. B. Remmel, *J. Combinatorial Theory* **A41** (1986), 246–275, who used a similar argument to prove the additional formula

$$\sum_{t=0}^{\infty} z^t \prod_{j=1}^{m} \frac{1 - y^{a_j+m-j+t}}{1-y} = \sum_{k=0}^{n} k!_y \left(\frac{z}{1-yz}\right) \dots \left(\frac{z}{1-y^k z}\right) R_{m-k}(a_1,\dots,a_m).$$

(d) This statement, which follows immediately from (c), also implies that we have $R(a_1,\dots,a_m) = R(a_1',\dots,a_m')$ if and only if equality holds for all x and for any nonzero value of y. The Peirce polynomial $\varpi_{nk}(x,y)$ of exercise 28(d) is the rook polynomial for $\binom{n-1}{k-1}$ different Ferrers diagrams; for example, $\varpi_{63}(x,y)$ enumerates rook placements for the shapes 43321, 44221, 44311, 4432, 53221, 53311, 5332, 54211, 5422, and 5431.

30. (a) We have $\varpi_n(x,y) = \sum_m x^{n-m} A_{mn}$, where $A_{mn} = R_{n-m}(n-1,\dots,1)$ satisfies a simple law: If we don't place a rook in row 1 of the shape $(n-1,\dots,1)$, that row has $m-1$ free cells because of the $n-m$ rooks in other rows. But if we do put a rook there, we leave 0 or 1 or $\cdots$ or $m-1$ of its cells free. Hence $A_{mn} = y^{m-1}A_{(m-1)(n-1)} + (1 + y + \cdots + y^{m-1})A_{m(n-1)}$, and it follows by induction that $A_{mn} = y^{m(m-1)/2}\{{n \atop m}\}_y$.

(b) The formula $\varpi_{n+1}(x, y) = \sum_k \binom{n}{k} x^{n-k} y^k \varpi_k(x, y)$ yields

$$A_{m(n+1)} = \sum_k \binom{n}{k} y^k A_{(m-1)k}.$$

(c) From (a) and (b) we have

$$\frac{z^n}{(1 - z)(1 - (1+q)z)\ldots(1 - (1+q+\cdots+q^{n-1})z)} = \sum_k \left\{{k \atop n}\right\}_q z^k;$$

$$\sum_k \binom{n}{k}_q (-1)^k q^{\binom{k}{2}} e^{(1+q+\cdots+q^{n-k-1})z} = q^{\binom{n}{2}} n!_q \sum_k \left\{{k \atop n}\right\}_q \frac{z^k}{k!}.$$

[The second formula is proved by induction on n, because both sides satisfy the differential equation $G'_{n+1}(z) = (1 + q + \cdots + q^n)e^z G_n(qz)$; exercise 1.2.6–58 proves equality when $z = 0$.]

Historical note: Leonard Carlitz introduced q-Stirling numbers in *Transactions of the Amer. Math. Soc.* **33** (1933), 127–129. Then in *Duke Math. J.* **15** (1948), 987–1000, he derived (among other things) an appropriate generalization of Eq. 1.2.6–(45):

$$(1 + q + \cdots + q^{m-1})^n = \sum_k \left\{{n \atop k}\right\}_q q^{\binom{k}{2}} \frac{m!_q}{(m-k)!_q}.$$

31. $\exp(e^{w+z} + w - 1)$; therefore $\varpi_{nk} = (\varpi + 1)^{n-k} \varpi^{k-1} = \varpi^{n+1-k}(\varpi - 1)^{k-1}$ in the umbral notation of exercise 23. [L. Moser and M. Wyman, *Trans. Royal Soc. Canada* (3) **43** (1954), Section 3, 31–37.] In fact, the numbers $\varpi_{nk}(x, 1)$ of exercise 28(d) are generated by $\exp((e^{xw+xz} - 1)/x + xw)$.

32. We have $\delta_n = \varpi_n(1, -1)$, and a simple pattern is easily perceived in the generalized Peirce triangle of exercise 28(d) when $x = 1$ and $y = -1$: We have $|\varpi_{nk}(1, -1)| \leq 1$ and $\varpi_{n(k+1)}(1, -1) \equiv \varpi_{nk}(1, -1) + (-1)^n$ (modulo 3) for $1 \leq k < n$. [In *JACM* **20** (1973), 512–513, Gideon Ehrlich gave a combinatorial proof of an equivalent result.]

33. Representing set partitions by rook placements as in answer 27 leads to the answer ϖ_{nk}, by setting $x = y = 1$ in exercise 28(d). [The case $k = n$ was discovered by H. Prodinger, *Fibonacci Quarterly* **19** (1981), 463–465.]

34. (a) Guittone's *Sonetti* included 149 of scheme 01010101232323, 64 of scheme 01010101234234, two of scheme 01010101234342, seven with schemes used only once (like 01100110234432), and 29 poems that we would no longer consider to be sonnets because they do not have 14 lines.

(b) Petrarch's *Canzoniere* included 115 sonnets of scheme 01100110234234, 109 of scheme 01100110232323, 66 of scheme 01100110234324, 7 of scheme 01100110232232, and 20 others of schemes like 01010101232323 used at most three times each.

(c) In Spenser's *Amoretti*, 88 of 89 sonnets used the scheme 01011212232344; the exception (number 8) was "Shakespearean."

(d) Shakespeare's 154 sonnets all used the rather easy scheme 01012323454566, except that two of them (99 and 126) didn't have 14 lines.

(e) Browning's 44 *Sonnets From the Portuguese* obeyed the Petrarchan scheme 01100110232323.

Sometimes the lines would rhyme (by chance?) even when they didn't need to; for example, Browning's final sonnet actually had the scheme 01100110121212.

Incidentally, the lengthy cantos in Dante's *Divine Comedy* used an interlocking scheme of rhymes in which $1 \equiv 3$ and $3n - 1 \equiv 3n + 1 \equiv 3n + 3$ for $n = 1, 2, \ldots$.

35. Every incomplete n-line rhyme scheme Π corresponds to a singleton-free partition of $\{1, \ldots, n{+}1\}$ in which $(n{+}1)$ is grouped with all of Π's singletons. [H. W. Becker gave an algebraic proof in *AMM* **48** (1941), 702. Notice that $\varpi'_n = \sum_k \binom{n}{k}(-1)^{n-k}\varpi_k$, by the principle of inclusion and exclusion, and $\varpi_n = \sum_k \binom{n}{k}\varpi'_k$; we can in fact write $\varpi' = \varpi - 1$ in the umbral notation of exercise 23. J. O. Shallit has suggested extending Peirce's triangle by setting $\varpi_{n(n+1)} = \varpi'_n$; see exercises 38(e) and 33. In fact, ϖ_{nk} is the number of partitions of $\{1, \ldots, n\}$ with the property that $1, \ldots, k-1$ are not singletons; see H. W. Becker, *Bull. Amer. Math. Soc.* **58** (1954), 63.]

36. $\exp(e^z - 1 - z)$. (In general, if ϑ_n is the number of partitions of $\{1, \ldots, n\}$ into subsets of allowable sizes $s_1 < s_2 < \cdots$, the exponential generating function $\sum_n \vartheta_n z^n/n!$ is $\exp(z^{s_1}/s_1! + z^{s_2}/s_2! + \cdots)$, because $(z^{s_1}/s_1! + z^{s_2}/s_2! + \cdots)^k$ is the exponential generating function for partitions into exactly k parts.)

37. There are $\sum_k \binom{n}{k}\varpi'_k \varpi'_{n-k}$ possibilities of length n, hence 784,071,966 when $n = 14$. (But Pushkin's scheme is hard to beat.)

38. (a) Imagine starting with $x_1 x_2 \ldots x_n = 01 \ldots (n{-}1)$, then successively removing some element b_j and placing it at the left, for $j = 1, 2, \ldots, n$. Then x_k will be the kth most recently moved element, for $1 \leq k \leq |\{b_1, \ldots, b_n\}|$; see exercise 5.2.3–36. Consequently the array $x_1 \ldots x_n$ will return to its original state if and only if $b_n \ldots b_1$ is a restricted growth string. [Robbins and Bolker, *Æquat. Math.* **22** (1981), 281–282.]

In other words, let $a_1 \ldots a_n$ be a restricted growth string. Set $b_{-j} \leftarrow j$ and $b_{j+1} \leftarrow a_{n-j}$ for $0 \leq j < n$. Then for $1 \leq j \leq n$, define k_j by the rule that b_j is the k_jth distinct element of the sequence $b_{j-1}, b_{j-2}, \ldots$. For example, the string $a_1 \ldots a_{16} = 0123032303456745$ corresponds in this way to the σ-cycle 6688448628232384.

(b) Such paths correspond to restricted growth strings with $\max(a_1, \ldots, a_n) \leq m$, so the answer is $\left\{{n \atop 0}\right\} + \left\{{n \atop 1}\right\} + \cdots + \left\{{n \atop m}\right\}$.

(c) We may assume that $i = 1$, because the sequence $k_2 \ldots k_n k_1$ is a σ-cycle whenever $k_1 k_2 \ldots k_n$ is. Thus the answer is the number of restricted growth strings with $a_n = j - 1$, namely $\left\{{n-1 \atop j-1}\right\} + \left\{{n-1 \atop j}\right\} + \left\{{n-1 \atop j+1}\right\} + \cdots$.

(d) If the answer is f_n we must have $\sum_k \binom{n}{k} f_k = \varpi_n$, since σ_1 is the identity permutation. Therefore $f_n = \varpi'_n$, the number of set partitions without singletons (exercise 35).

(e) Again ϖ'_n, by (a) and (d). [Consequently $\varpi'_p \bmod p = 1$ when p is prime.]

39. Set $u = t^{p+1}$ to obtain $\frac{1}{p+1} \int_0^\infty e^{-u} u^{(q-p)/(p+1)} \, du = \frac{1}{p+1} \Gamma\left(\frac{q+1}{p+1}\right)$.

40. We have $g(z) = cz - n \ln z$, so the saddle point occurs at n/c. The rectangular path now has corners at $\pm n/c \pm mi/c$; and $\exp g(n/c + it) = (e^n c^n/n^n) \exp(-t^2 c^2/(2n) + it^3 c^3/(3n^2) + \cdots)$. The final result is $e^n (c/n)^{n-1}/\sqrt{2\pi n}$ times $1 + n/12 + O(n^{-2})$.

(Of course we could have obtained this result more quickly by letting $w = cz$ in the integral. But the answer given here applies the saddle point method mechanically, without attempting to be clever.)

41. Again the net result is just to multiply (21) by c^{n-1}; but in this case the *left* edge of the rectangular path is significant instead of the right edge. (Incidentally, when $c = -1$ we cannot derive an analog of (22) using Hankel's contour when x is real and positive, because the integral on that path diverges. But with the usual definition of z^x, a suitable path of integration does yield the formula $-(\cos \pi x)/\Gamma(x)$ when $n = x > 0$.)

42. We have $\oint e^{z^2} dz/z^n = 0$ when n is even. Otherwise both left and right edges of the rectangle with corners $\pm\sqrt{n/2} \pm in$ contribute approximately

$$\frac{e^{n/2}}{2\pi(n/2)^{n/2}} \int_{-\infty}^{\infty} \exp\left(-2t^2 - \frac{(-it)^3}{3}\frac{2^{3/2}}{n^{1/2}} + \frac{(it)^4}{n} - \cdots\right) dt,$$

when n is large. We can restrict $|t| \le n^\epsilon$ to show that this integral is $I_0 + (I_4 - \frac{4}{9}I_6)/n$ with relative error $O(n^{9\epsilon-3/2})$, where $I_k = \int_{-\infty}^{\infty} e^{-2t^2}t^k \, dt$. As before, the relative error is actually $O(n^{-2})$; we deduce the answer

$$\frac{1}{((n-1)/2)!} = \frac{e^{n/2}}{\sqrt{2\pi}(n/2)^{n/2}}\left(1 + \frac{1}{12n} + O\left(\frac{1}{n^2}\right)\right), \qquad n \text{ odd.}$$

(The analog of (22) is $(\sin \frac{\pi x}{2})^2/\Gamma((x-1)/2)$ when $n = x > 0$.)

43. Let $f(z) = e^{e^z}/z^n$. When $z = -n+it$ we have $|f(z)| < en^{-n}$; when $z = t+2\pi in + i\pi/2$ we have $|f(z)| = |z|^{-n} < (2\pi n)^{-n}$. So the integral is negligible except on a path $z = \xi + it$; and on that path $|f|$ decreases as $|t|$ increases from 0 to π. Already when $t = n^{\epsilon-1/2}$ we have $|f(z)|/f(\xi) = O(\exp(-n^{2\epsilon}/(\log n)^2))$. And when $|t| > \pi$ we have $|f(z)|/f(\xi) < 1/|1 + i\pi/\xi|^n = \exp(-\frac{n}{2}\ln(1 + \pi^2/\xi^2))$.

44. Set $u = na_2t^2$ in (25) to obtain $\Re\int_0^\infty e^{-u} \exp(n^{-1/2}c_3(-u)^{3/2} + n^{-1}c_4(-u)^2 + n^{-3/2}c_5(-u)^{5/2} + \cdots) \, du/\sqrt{na_2u}$ where $c_k = (2/(\xi+1))^{k/2}(\xi^{k-1} + (-1)^k(k-1)!)/k! = a_k/a_2^{k/2}$. This expression leads to

$$b_l = \sum_{\substack{k_1+2k_2+3k_3+\cdots=2l \\ k_1+k_2+k_3+\cdots=m \\ k_1,k_2,k_3,\ldots\ge 0}} \left(-\frac{1}{2}\right)^{l+m} \frac{c_3^{k_1}}{k_1!} \frac{c_4^{k_2}}{k_2!} \frac{c_5^{k_3}}{k_3!} \cdots,$$

a sum over partitions of $2l$. For example, $b_1 = \frac{3}{4}c_4 - \frac{15}{16}c_3^2$.

45. To get $\varpi_n/n!$ we replace $g(z)$ by $e^z - (n+1)\ln z$ in the derivation of (26). This change multiplies the integrand in the previous answer by $1/(1 + it/\xi)$, which is $1/(1 - n^{-1/2}a(-u)^{1/2})$ where $a = -\sqrt{2/(\xi+1)}$. Thus we get

$$b_l' = \sum_{\substack{k+k_1+2k_2+3k_3+\cdots=2l \\ k_1+k_2+k_3+\cdots=m \\ k,k_1,k_2,k_3,\ldots\ge 0}} \left(-\frac{1}{2}\right)^{l+m} a^k \frac{c_3^{k_1}}{k_1!} \frac{c_4^{k_2}}{k_2!} \frac{c_5^{k_3}}{k_3!} \cdots,$$

a sum of $p(2l) + p(2l-1) + \cdots + p(0)$ terms; $b_1' = \frac{3}{4}c_4 - \frac{15}{16}c_3^2 + \frac{3}{4}ac_3 - \frac{1}{2}a^2$. [The coefficient b_1' was obtained in a different way by L. Moser and M. Wyman, *Trans. Royal Soc. Canada* (3) **49**, Section 3 (1955), 49–54, who were the first to deduce an asymptotic series for ϖ_n. Their approximation is slightly less accurate than the result of (26) with n changed to $n + 1$, because it doesn't pass exactly through the saddle point. Formula (26) is due to I. J. Good, *Iranian J. Science and Tech.* **4** (1975), 77–83.]

46. Eqs. (13) and (31) show that $\varpi_{nk} = (1 - \xi/n)^k\varpi_n(1 + O(n^{-1}))$ for fixed k as $n \to \infty$. And this approximation also holds when $k = n$, but with relative error $O((\log n)^2/n)$.

47. Steps (H1, ..., H6) are performed respectively $(1, \varpi_n, \varpi_n - \varpi_{n-1}, \varpi_{n-1}, \varpi_{n-1}, \varpi_{n-1} - 1)$ times. The loop in H4 sets $j \leftarrow j - 1$ a total of $\varpi_{n-2} + \varpi_{n-3} + \cdots + \varpi_1$ times; the loop in H6 sets $b_j \leftarrow m$ a total of $(\varpi_{n-2} - 1) + \cdots + (\varpi_1 - 1)$ times. The ratio ϖ_{n-1}/ϖ_n is approximately $(\ln n)/n$, and $(\varpi_{n-2} + \cdots + \varpi_1)/\varpi_n \approx (\ln n)^2/n^2$.

48. We can easily verify the interchange of summation and integration in

$$\frac{e\varpi_x}{\Gamma(x+1)} = \frac{1}{2\pi i} \oint \frac{e^{e^z}}{z^{x+1}} \, dz = \frac{1}{2\pi i} \oint \sum_{k=0}^{\infty} \frac{e^{kx}}{k! \, z^{x+1}} \, dz$$

$$= \sum_{k=0}^{\infty} \frac{1}{k!} \frac{1}{2\pi i} \oint \frac{e^{kz}}{z^{x+1}} \, dz = \sum_{k=0}^{\infty} \frac{1}{k!} \frac{k^x}{\Gamma(x+1)}.$$

49. If $\xi = \ln n - \ln \ln n + x$, we have $\beta = 1 - e^{-x} - \alpha x$. Therefore by Lagrange's inversion formula (exercise 4.7–8),

$$x = \sum_{k=1}^{\infty} \frac{\beta^k}{k} [t^{k-1}] \left(\frac{f(t)}{1 - \alpha f(t)} \right)^k = \sum_{k=1}^{\infty} \sum_{j=0}^{\infty} \frac{\beta^k}{k} \alpha^j \binom{k+j-1}{j} [t^{k-1}] f(t)^{j+k},$$

where $f(t) = t/(1 - e^{-t})$. So the result follows from the handy identity

$$\left(\frac{z}{1 - e^{-z}} \right)^m = \sum_{n=0}^{\infty} \begin{bmatrix} m \\ m-n \end{bmatrix} \frac{z^n}{(m-1)(m-2)\ldots(m-n)}.$$

(This identity should be interpreted carefully when $n \geq m$; the coefficient of z^n is a polynomial in m of degree n, as explained in *CMath* equation (7.59).)

The formula in this exercise is due to L. Comtet, *Comptes Rendus Acad. Sci.* (A) **270** (Paris, 1970), 1085–1088, who identified the coefficients previously computed by N. G. de Bruijn, *Asymptotic Methods in Analysis* (1958), 25–28. Convergence for $n \geq e$ was shown by Jeffrey, Corless, Hare, and Knuth, *Comptes Rendus Acad. Sci.* (I) **320** (1995), 1449–1452, who also derived a formula that converges somewhat faster.

(The equation $\xi e^\xi = n$ has complex roots as well. We can obtain them all by using $\ln n + 2\pi i m$ in place of $\ln n$ in the formula of this exercise; the sum converges rapidly when $m \neq 0$. See Corless, Gonnet, Hare, Jeffrey, and Knuth, *Advances in Computational Math.* **5** (1996), 347–350.)

50. Let $\xi = \xi(n)$. Then $\xi'(n) = \xi/((\xi + 1)n)$, and the Taylor series

$$\xi(n + k) = \xi + k\xi'(n) + \frac{k^2}{2}\xi''(n) + \cdots$$

can be shown to converge for $|k| < n + 1/e$.

Indeed, much more is true, because the function $\xi(n) = -T(-n)$ is obtained from the tree function $T(z)$ by analytic continuation to the negative real axis. (The tree function has a quadratic singularity at $z = e^{-1}$; after going around this singularity we encounter a logarithmic singularity at $z = 0$, as part of an interesting multi-level Riemann surface on which the quadratic singularity appears only at level 0.) The derivatives of the tree function satisfy $z^k T^{(k)}(z) = R(z)^k p_k(R(z))$, where $R(z) = T(z)/(1 - T(z))$ and $p_k(x)$ is the polynomial of degree $k - 1$ defined by $p_{k+1}(x) = (1 + x)^2 p_k'(x) + k(2 + x)p_k(x)$. For example,

$$p_1(x) = 1, \quad p_2(x) = 2 + x, \quad p_3(x) = 9 + 10x + 3x^2, \quad p_4(x) = 64 + 113x + 70x^2 + 15x^3.$$

(The coefficients of $p_k(x)$, incidentally, enumerate certain phylogenetic trees called Greg trees: $[x^j]\,p_k(x)$ is the number of oriented trees with j unlabeled nodes and k labeled nodes, where leaves must be labeled and unlabeled nodes must have at least two children. See J. Felsenstein, *Systematic Zoology* **27** (1978), 27–33; L. R. Foulds and R. W. Robinson, *Lecture Notes in Math.* **829** (1980), 110–126; C. Flight, *Manuscripta* **34** (1990), 122–128.) If $q_k(x) = p_k(-x)$, we can prove by induction that $(-1)^m q_k^{(m)}(x) \geq 0$ for $0 \leq x \leq 1$. Therefore $q_k(x)$ decreases monotonically from k^{k-1} to $(k-1)!$ as x goes from 0 to 1, for all $k, m \geq 1$. It follows that

$$\xi(n+k) = \xi + \frac{kx}{n} - \left(\frac{kx}{n}\right)^2 \frac{q_2(x)}{2!} + \left(\frac{kx}{n}\right)^3 \frac{q_3(x)}{3!} - \cdots, \qquad x = \frac{\xi}{\xi+1},$$

where the partial sums alternately overshoot and undershoot the correct value if $k > 0$.

51. There are two saddle points, $\sigma = \sqrt{n+5/4} - 1/2$ and $\sigma' = -1 - \sigma$. Integration on a rectangular path with corners at $\sigma \pm im$ and $\sigma' \pm im$ shows that only σ is relevant as $n \to \infty$ (although σ' contributes a relative error of roughly $e^{-\sqrt{n}}$, which can be significant when n is small). Arguing almost as in (25), but with $g(z) = z + z^2/2 - (n+1)\ln z$, we find that t_n is well approximated by

$$\frac{n!}{2\pi}\int_{-n^\epsilon}^{n^\epsilon} e^{g(\sigma) - a_2 t^2 + a_3 i t^3 + \cdots + a_l(-it)^l + O(n^{(l+1)\epsilon - (l-1)/2})}\,dt, \qquad a_k = \frac{\sigma+1}{k\sigma^{k-1}} + \frac{[k=2]}{2}.$$

The integral expands as in exercise 44 to

$$\frac{n!\,e^{(n+\sigma)/2}}{2\sigma^{n+1}\sqrt{\pi a_2}}\left(1 + b_1 + b_2 + \cdots + b_m + O(n^{-m-1})\right).$$

This time $c_k = (\sigma+1)\sigma^{1-k}(1 + 1/(2\sigma))^{-k/2}/k$ for $k \geq 3$, hence $(2\sigma+1)^{3k}\sigma^k b_k$ is a polynomial in σ of degree $2k$; for example,

$$b_1 = \frac{3}{4}c_4 - \frac{15}{16}c_3^2 = \frac{8\sigma^2 + 7\sigma - 1}{12\sigma(2\sigma+1)^3}.$$

In particular, Stirling's approximation and the b_1 term yield

$$t_n = \frac{1}{\sqrt{2}}n^{n/2}e^{-n/2+\sqrt{n}-1/4}\left(1 + \frac{7}{24}n^{-1/2} - \frac{119}{1152}n^{-1} - \frac{7933}{414720}n^{-3/2} + O(n^{-2})\right)$$

after we plug in the formula for σ — a result substantially more accurate than equation 5.1.4–(53), and obtained with considerably less labor.

52. Let $G(z) = \sum_k \Pr(X = k)z^k$, so that the jth cumulant κ_j is $j!\,[t^j]\ln G(e^t)$. In case (a) we have $G(z) = e^{e^{\xi z} - e^\xi}$; hence

$$\ln G(e^t) = e^{\xi e^t} - e^\xi = e^\xi(e^{\xi(e^t-1)} - 1) = e^\xi \sum_{k=1}^{\infty}(e^t - 1)^k \frac{\xi^k}{k!}, \qquad \kappa_j = e^\xi \sum_k \left\{\begin{matrix} k \\ j \end{matrix}\right\}\xi^k\,[j \neq 0].$$

Case (b) is sort of a dual situation: Here $\kappa = j = \varpi_j\,[j \neq 0]$ because

$$G(z) = e^{e^{-1}-1}\sum_{j,k}\left\{\begin{matrix} k \\ j \end{matrix}\right\}e^{-j}\frac{z^k}{k!} = e^{e^{-1}-1}\sum_j \frac{(e^{z-1} - e^{-1})^j}{j!} = e^{e^{z-1}-1}.$$

[If $\xi e^\xi = 1$ in case (a) we have $\kappa_j = e\varpi\,[j \neq 0]$. But if $\xi e^\xi = n$ in that case, the mean is $\kappa_1 = n$ and the variance σ^2 is $(\xi+1)n$. Thus, the formula in exercise 45 states that the mean value n occurs with approximate probability $1/\sqrt{2\pi\sigma}$ and relative error $O(1/n)$. This observation leads to another way to prove that formula.]

53. We can write $\ln G(e^t) = \mu t + \sigma^2 t^2/2 + \kappa_3 t^3/3! + \cdots$ as in Eq. 1.2.10–(23), and there is a positive constant δ such that $\sum_{j=3}^{\infty} |\kappa_j| |t|^j/j! < \sigma^2 t^2/6$ when $|t| \leq \delta$. Hence, if $0 < \epsilon < 1/2$, we can prove that

$$[z^{\mu n + r}]\, G(z)^n = \frac{1}{2\pi} \int_{-\pi}^{\pi} \frac{G(e^{it})^n\, dt}{e^{it(\mu n + r)}}$$

$$= \frac{1}{2\pi} \int_{-n^{\epsilon-1/2}}^{n^{\epsilon-1/2}} \exp\left(-irt - \frac{\sigma^2 t^2 n}{2} + O(n^{3\epsilon - 1/2})\right) dt + O(e^{-cn^{2\epsilon}})$$

as $n \to \infty$, for some constant $c > 0$: The integrand for $n^{\epsilon-1/2} \leq |t| \leq \delta$ is bounded in absolute value by $\exp(-\sigma^2 n^{2\epsilon}/3)$; and when $\delta \leq |t| \leq \pi$ its magnitude is at most α^n, where $\alpha = \max |G(e^{it})|$ is less than 1 because the individual terms $p_k e^{kit}$ don't all lie on a straight line by our assumption. Thus

$$[z^{\mu n + r}]\, G(z)^n = \frac{1}{2\pi} \int_{-\infty}^{\infty} \exp\left(-irt - \frac{\sigma^2 t^2 n}{2} + O(n^{3\epsilon - 1/2})\right) dt + O(e^{-cn^{2\epsilon}})$$

$$= \frac{1}{2\pi} \int_{-\infty}^{\infty} \exp\left(-\frac{\sigma^2 n}{2}\left(t + \frac{ir}{\sigma^2 n}\right)^2 - \frac{r^2}{2\sigma^2 n} + O(n^{3\epsilon - 1/2})\right) dt + O(e^{-cn^{2\epsilon}})$$

$$= \frac{e^{-r^2/(2\sigma^2 n)}}{\sigma\sqrt{2\pi n}} + O(n^{3\epsilon - 1}).$$

By taking account of κ_3, κ_4, ... in a similar way we can refine the estimate to $O(n^{-m})$ for arbitrarily large m; thus the result is valid also for $\epsilon = 0$. [In fact, such refinements lead to the "Edgeworth expansion," according to which $[z^{\mu n + r}]\, G(z)^n$ is asymptotic to

$$\frac{e^{-r^2/(2\sigma^2 n)}}{\sigma\sqrt{2\pi n}} \sum_{\substack{k_1 + 2k_2 + 3k_3 + \cdots = m \\ k_1 + k_2 + k_3 + \cdots = l \\ k_1, k_2, k_3, \ldots \geq 0 \\ 0 \leq s \leq l + m/2}} \frac{(-1)^s (2l + m)_{2s}}{\sigma^{4l + 2m - 2s} 2^s s!} \frac{r^{2l + m - 2s}}{n^{l + m - s}} \frac{1}{k_1!\, k_2! \ldots} \left(\frac{\kappa_3}{3!}\right)^{k_1} \left(\frac{\kappa_4}{4!}\right)^{k_2} \cdots \; ;$$

the absolute error is $O(n^{-p/2})$, where the constant hidden in the O depends only on p and G but not on r or n, if we restrict the sum to cases with $m < p - 1$. For example, when $p = 3$ we get

$$[z^{\mu n + r}]\, G(z)^n = \frac{e^{-r^2/(2\sigma^2 n)}}{\sigma\sqrt{2\pi n}}\left(1 - \frac{\kappa_3}{2\sigma^4}\left(\frac{r}{n}\right) + \frac{\kappa_3}{6\sigma^6}\left(\frac{r^3}{n^2}\right)\right) + O\left(\frac{1}{n^{3/2}}\right),$$

and there are seven more terms when $p = 4$. See P. L. Chebyshev, *Zapiski Imp. Akad. Nauk* **55** (1887), No. 6, 1–16; *Acta Math.* **14** (1890), 305–315; F. Y. Edgeworth, *Trans. Cambridge Phil. Soc.* **20** (1905), 36–65, 113–141; H. Cramér, *Skandinavisk Aktuarietidsskrift* **11** (1928), 13–74, 141–180.]

54. Formula (40) is equivalent to $\alpha = s \coth s + s$, $\beta = s \coth s - s$.

55. Let $c = \alpha e^{-\alpha}$. The Newtonian iteration $\beta_0 = c$, $\beta_{k+1} = (1 - \beta_k)ce^{\beta_k}/(1 - ce^{-\beta_k})$ rises rapidly to the correct value, unless α is extremely close to 1. For example, β_7 differs from $\ln 2$ by less than 10^{-75} when $\alpha = \ln 4$.

56. (a) By induction on n, $g^{(n+1)}(z) = (-1)^n \left(\dfrac{\sum_{k=0}^{n} \binom{n}{k} e^{(n-k)z}}{\alpha(e^z - 1)^{n+1}} - \dfrac{n!}{z^{n+1}}\right)$.

(b) $\sum_{k=0}^{n} \binom{n}{k} e^{k\sigma}/n! = \int_{0}^{1} \cdots \int_{0}^{1} \exp(\lfloor u_1 + \cdots + u_n \rfloor \sigma)\, du_1 \ldots du_n$
$$< \int_{0}^{1} \cdots \int_{0}^{1} \exp((u_1 + \cdots + u_n)\sigma)\, du_1 \ldots du_n = (e^{\sigma}-1)^n/\sigma^n.$$

The lower bound is similar, since $\lfloor u_1 + \cdots + u_n \rfloor > u_1 + \cdots + u_n - 1$.

(c) Thus $n!\,(1-\beta/\alpha) < (-\sigma)^n g^{(n+1)}(\sigma) < 0$, and we need only verify that $1-\beta/\alpha < 2(1-\beta)$, namely that $2\alpha\beta < \alpha+\beta$. But $\alpha\beta < 1$ and $\alpha+\beta > 2$, by exercise 54.

57. (a) $n + 1 - m = (n+1)(1 - 1/\alpha) < (n+1)(1 - \beta/\alpha) = (n+1)\sigma/\alpha \leq 2N$ as in answer 56(c). (b) The quantity $\alpha + \alpha\beta$ increases as α increases, because its derivative with respect to α is $1 + \beta + \beta(1-\alpha)/(1-\beta) = (1 - \alpha\beta)/(1-\beta) + \beta > 0$. Therefore $1 - \beta < 2(1 - 1/\alpha)$.

58. (a) The derivative of $|e^{\sigma+it} - 1|^2/|\sigma + it|^2 = (e^{\sigma+it} - 1)(e^{\sigma-it} - 1)/(\sigma^2 + t^2)$ with respect to t is $(\sigma^2 + t^2)\sin t - t(2\sin\frac{t}{2})^2 - (2\sinh\frac{\sigma}{2})^2 t$ times a positive function. This derivative is always negative for $0 < t \leq 2\pi$, because it is less than $t^2 \sin t - t(2\sin\frac{t}{2})^2 = 8u\sin u \cos u(u - \tan u)$ where $t = 2u$.

Let $s = 2\sinh\frac{\sigma}{2}$. When $\sigma \geq \pi$ and $2\pi \leq t \leq 4\pi$, the derivative is still negative, because we have $t \leq 4\pi \leq s^2 - \sigma^2/(2\pi) \leq s^2 - \sigma^2/t$. Similarly, when $\sigma \geq 2\pi$ the derivative remains negative for $4\pi \leq t \leq 168\pi$; the proof gets easier and easier.

(b) Let $t = u\sigma/\sqrt{N}$. Then (41) and (42) prove that

$$\int_{-\tau}^{\tau} e^{(n+1)g(\sigma+it)}\, dt =$$

$$\frac{(e^{\sigma}-1)^m}{\sigma^n \sqrt{N}} \int_{-N^\epsilon}^{N^\epsilon} \exp\left(-\frac{u^2}{2} + \frac{(-iu)^3 a_3}{N^{1/2}} + \cdots + \frac{(-iu)^l a_l}{N^{l/2-1}} + O(N^{(l+1)\epsilon-(l-1)/2})\right) du,$$

where $(1-\beta)a_k$ is a polynomial of degree $k-1$ in α and β, with $0 \leq a_k \leq 2/k$. (For example, $6a_3 = (2 - \beta(\alpha+\beta))/(1-\beta)$ and $24a_4 = (6 - \beta(\alpha^2 + 4\alpha\beta + \beta^2))/(1-\beta)$.) The monotonicity of the integrand shows that the integral over the rest of the range is negligible. Now trade tails, extend the integral over $-\infty < u < \infty$, and use the formula of answer 44 with $c_k = 2^{k/2}a_k$ to define $b_1, b_2, \ldots$.

(c) We will prove that $|e^z - 1|^m \sigma^{n+1}/((e^\sigma - 1)^m |z|^{n+1})$ is exponentially small on those three paths. If $\sigma \leq 1$, this quantity is less than $1/(2\pi)^{n+1}$ (because, for example, $e^\sigma - 1 > \sigma$). If $\sigma > 1$, we have $\sigma < 2|z|$ and $|e^z - 1| \leq e^\sigma - 1$.

59. In this extreme case, $\alpha = 1 + n^{-1}$ and $\beta = 1 - n^{-1} + \frac{2}{3}n^{-2} + O(n^{-3})$; hence $N = 1 + \frac{1}{3}n^{-1} + O(n^{-2})$. The leading term $\beta^{-n}/\sqrt{2\pi N}$ is $e/\sqrt{2\pi}$ times $1 - \frac{1}{3}n^{-1} + O(n^{-2})$. (Notice that $e/\sqrt{2\pi} \approx 1.0844$.) The quantity a_k in answer 58(b) turns out to be $1/k + O(n^{-1})$. So the correction terms, to first order, are

$$\frac{b_j}{N^j} = [z^j] \exp\left(-\sum_{k=1}^{\infty} \frac{B_{2k} z^{2k-1}}{2k(2k-1)}\right) + O\left(\frac{1}{n}\right),$$

namely the terms in the (divergent) series corresponding to Stirling's approximation

$$\frac{1}{1!} \sim \frac{e}{\sqrt{2\pi}}\left(1 - \frac{1}{12} + \frac{1}{288} + \frac{139}{51840} - \frac{571}{2488320} - \cdots\right).$$

60. (a) The number of m-ary strings of length n in which all m digits appear is $m!\,\{{n \atop m}\}$, and the inclusion-exclusion principle expresses this quantity as $\binom{m}{0}m^n - \binom{m}{1}(m-1)^n + \cdots$. Now see exercise 7.2.1.4–37.

(b) We have $(m-1)^n/(m-1)! = (m^n/m!)m\exp(n\ln(1-1/m))$, and $\ln(1-1/m)$ is less than $-n^{\epsilon-1}$.

(c) In this case $\alpha > n^\epsilon$ and $\beta = \alpha e^{-\alpha}e^{\beta} < \alpha e^{1-\alpha}$. Therefore $1 < (1-\beta/\alpha)^{m-n} < \exp(nO(e^{-\alpha}))$; and $1 > e^{-\beta m} = e^{-(n+1)\beta/\alpha} > \exp(-nO(e^{-\alpha}))$. So (45) becomes $(m^n/m!)(1 + O(n^{-1}) + O(ne^{-n^\epsilon}))$.

61. Now $\alpha = 1 + \frac{r}{n} + O(n^{2\epsilon-2})$ and $\beta = 1 - \frac{r}{n} + O(n^{2\epsilon-2})$. Thus $N = r + O(n^{2\epsilon-1})$, and the case $l = 0$ of Eq. (43) reduces to

$$n^r \left(\frac{n}{2}\right)^r \frac{e^r}{r^r \sqrt{2\pi r}}\left(1 + O(n^{2\epsilon-1}) + O\left(\frac{1}{r}\right)\right).$$

(This approximation meshes well with identities such as $\left\{{n \atop n-1}\right\} = \binom{n}{2}$ and $\left\{{n \atop n-2}\right\} = 2\binom{n}{4} + \binom{n+1}{4}$; indeed, we have

$$\left\{{n \atop n-r}\right\} = \frac{n^{2r}}{2^r r!}\left(1 + O\left(\frac{1}{n}\right)\right) \qquad \text{as } n \to \infty$$

when r is constant, according to formulas (6.42) and (6.43) of *CMath*.)

62. The assertion is true for $1 \leq n \leq 10000$ (with $m = \lfloor e^\xi - 1\rfloor$ in 5648 of those cases). E. R. Canfield and C. Pomerance, in a paper that nicely surveys previous work on related problems, have shown that the statement holds for all sufficiently large n, and that the maximum occurs in *both* cases only if $e^\xi \bmod 1$ is extremely close to $\frac{1}{2}$. [*Integers* **2** (2002), A1, 1–13.]

63. (a) The result holds when $p_1 = \cdots = p_n = p$, because $a_{k-1}/a_k = (k/(n+1-k)) \times ((n-\mu)/\mu) \leq (n-\mu)/(n+1-\mu) < 1$. It is also true by induction when $p_n = 0$ or 1. For the general case, consider the minimum of $a_k - a_{k-1}$ over all choices of $(p_1,\ldots,p_n)$ with $p_1 + \cdots + p_n = \mu$: If $0 < p_1 < p_2 < 1$, let $p_1' = p_1 - \delta$ and $p_2' = p_2 + \delta$, and notice that $a_k' - a_{k-1}' = a_k - a_{k-1} + \delta(p_1 - p_2 - \delta)\alpha$ for some α depending only on $p_3, \ldots, p_n$. At a minimum point we must have $\alpha = 0$; thus we can choose δ so that either $p_1' = 0$ or $p_2'=1$. The minimum can therefore be achieved when all p_j have one of three values $\{0, 1, p\}$. But we have proved that $a_k - a_{k-1} > 0$ in such cases.

(b) Changing each p_j to $1 - p_j$ changes μ to $n - \mu$ and a_k to a_{n-k}.

(c) No roots of $f(x)$ are positive. Hence $f(z)/f(1)$ has the form in (a) and (b).

(d) Let $C(f)$ be the number of sign changes in the sequence of coefficients of f; we want to show that $C((1-x)^2 f) = 2$. In fact, $C((1-x)^m f) = m$ for all $m \geq 0$. For $C((1-x)^m) = m$, and $C((a + bx)f) \leq C(f)$ when a and b are positive; hence $C((1-x)^m f) \leq m$. And if $f(x)$ is any nonzero polynomial whatsoever, $C((1-x)f) > C(f)$; hence $C((1-x)^m f) \geq m$.

(e) Since $\sum_k \left[{n \atop k}\right]x^k = x(x+1)\ldots(x+n-1)$, part (c) applies directly with $\mu = H_n$. And for the polynomials $f_n(x) = \sum_k \left\{{n \atop k}\right\}x^k$, we can use part (c) with $\mu = \varpi_{n+1}/\varpi_n - 1$, if $f_n(x)$ has n real roots. The latter statement follows by induction because $f_{n+1}(x) = x(f_n(x) + f_n'(x))$: If $a > 0$ and if $f(x)$ has n real roots, so does the function $g(x) = e^{ax}f(x)$. And $g(x) \to 0$ as $x \to -\infty$; hence $g'(x) = e^{ax}(af(x) + f'(x))$ also has n real roots (namely, one at the far left, and $n - 1$ between the roots of $g(x)$).

[See E. Laguerre, *J. de Math.* (3) **9** (1883), 99–146; W. Hoeffding, *Annals Math. Stat.* **27** (1956), 713–721; J. N. Darroch, *Annals Math. Stat.* **35** (1964), 1317–1321; J. Pitman, *J. Combinatorial Theory* **A77** (1997), 297–303.]

64. We need only use computer algebra to subtract $\ln \varpi_n$ from $\ln \varpi_{n-k}$.

65. It is ϖ_n^{-1} times the number of occurrences of k-blocks plus the number of occurrences of ordered pairs of k-blocks in the list of all set partitions, namely $(\binom{n}{k}\varpi_{n-k} + \binom{n}{k}\binom{n-k}{k}\varpi_{n-2k})/\varpi_n$, minus the square of (49). Asymptotically, $(\xi^k/k!)(1+O(n^{4\epsilon-1}))$.

66. (The maximum of (48) when $n = 100$ is achieved for the partitions $7^1 6^2 5^4 4^6 3^7 2^6 1^4$ and $7^1 6^2 5^4 4^6 3^8 2^5 1^3$.)

67. The expected value of M^k is ϖ_{n+k}/ϖ_n. By (50), the mean is therefore $\varpi_{n+1}/\varpi_n = n/\xi + \xi/(2(\xi+1)^2) + O(n^{-1})$, and the variance is

$$\frac{\varpi_{n+2}}{\varpi_n} - \frac{\varpi_{n+1}^2}{\varpi_n^2} = \left(\frac{n}{\xi}\right)^2 \left(1 + \frac{\xi(2\xi+1)}{(\xi+1)^2 n} - 1 - \frac{\xi^2}{(\xi+1)^2 n} + O\left(\frac{1}{n^2}\right)\right) = \frac{n}{\xi(\xi+1)} + O(1).$$

68. The maximum number of nonzero components in all parts of a partition is $n = n_1 + \cdots + n_m$; it occurs if and only if all component parts are 0 or 1. The maximum level is also equal to n.

69. At the beginning of step M3, if $k > b$ and $l = r - 1$, go to M5. In step M5, if $j = a$ and $(v_j - 1)(r - l) < u_j$, go to M6 instead of decreasing v_j.

70. (a) $\left|\begin{smallmatrix}n-1\\r-1\end{smallmatrix}\right| + \left|\begin{smallmatrix}n-2\\r-1\end{smallmatrix}\right| + \cdots + \left|\begin{smallmatrix}r-1\\r-1\end{smallmatrix}\right|$, since $\left|\begin{smallmatrix}n-k\\r-1\end{smallmatrix}\right|$ contain the block $\{0, \ldots, 0, 1\}$ with k 0s. The total, also known as $p(n-1, 1)$, is $p(n-1) + \cdots + p(1) + p(0)$.

(b) Exactly $N = \left\{\begin{smallmatrix}n-1\\r\end{smallmatrix}\right\} + \left\{\begin{smallmatrix}n-2\\r-2\end{smallmatrix}\right\}$ of the r-block partitions of $\{1, \ldots, n-1, n\}$ are the same if we interchange $n-1 \leftrightarrow n$. So the answer is $N + \frac{1}{2}(\left\{\begin{smallmatrix}n\\r\end{smallmatrix}\right\} - N) = \frac{1}{2}(\left\{\begin{smallmatrix}n\\r\end{smallmatrix}\right\} + N)$, which is also the number of restricted growth strings $a_1 \ldots a_n$ with $\max(a_1, \ldots, a_n) = r - 1$ and $a_{n-1} \leq a_n$. And the total is $\frac{1}{2}(\varpi_n + \varpi_{n-1} + \varpi_{n-2})$.

71. $\lfloor \frac{1}{2}(n_1+1) \ldots (n_m+1) - \frac{1}{2} \rfloor$, because there are $(n_1+1) \ldots (n_m+1) - 2$ *compositions* into two parts, and half of those compositions fail to be in lexicographic order unless all n_j are even. (See exercise 7.2.1.4–31. Formulas for up to 5 parts have been worked out by E. M. Wright, *Proc. London Math. Soc.* (3) **11** (1961), 499–510.)

72. Yes. The following algorithm computes $a_{jk} = p(j, k)$ for $0 \leq j, k \leq n$ in $\Theta(n^4)$ steps: Start with $a_{jk} \leftarrow 1$ for all j and k. Then for $l = 0, 1, \ldots, n$ and $m = 0, 1, \ldots, n$ (in any order), if $l + m > 1$ set $a_{jk} \leftarrow a_{jk} + a_{(j-l)(k-m)}$ for $j = l, \ldots, n$ and $k = m, \ldots, n$ (in increasing order).

(See Table A-1. A similar method computes $p(n_1, \ldots, n_m)$ in $O(n_1 \ldots n_m)^2$ steps. Cheema and Motzkin, in the cited paper, have derived the recurrence relation

$$n_1 p(n_1, \ldots, n_m) = \sum_{l=1}^{\infty} \sum_{k_1, \ldots, k_m \geq 0} k_1 p(n_1 - k_1 l, \ldots, n_m - k_m l),$$

but this interesting formula is helpful for computation only in certain cases.)

Table A-1
MULTIPARTITION NUMBERS

n	0	1	2	3	4	5	6		n	0	1	2	3	4	5
$p(0,n)$	1	1	2	3	5	7	11		$P(0,n)$	1	2	9	66	712	10457
$p(1,n)$	1	2	4	7	12	19	30		$P(1,n)$	1	4	26	249	3274	56135
$p(2,n)$	2	4	9	16	29	47	77		$P(2,n)$	2	11	92	1075	16601	325269
$p(3,n)$	3	7	16	31	57	97	162		$P(3,n)$	5	36	371	5133	91226	2014321
$p(4,n)$	5	12	29	57	109	189	323		$P(4,n)$	15	135	1663	26683	537813	13241402
$p(5,n)$	7	19	47	97	189	339	589		$P(5,n)$	52	566	8155	149410	3376696	91914202

73. Yes. Let $P(m,n) = p(1,\ldots,1,2,\ldots,2)$ when there are m 1s and n 2s; then $P(m,0) = \varpi_m$, and we can use the recurrence

$$2P(m,n+1) = P(m+2,n) + P(m+1,n) + \sum_k \binom{n}{k} P(m,k).$$

This recurrence can be proved by considering what happens when we replace a pair of x's in the multiset for $P(m,n+1)$ by two distinct elements x and x'. We get $2P(m,n+1)$ partitions, representing $P(m+2,n)$, except in the $P(m+1,n)$ cases where x and x' belong to the same block, or in $\binom{n}{k}P(m,n-k)$ cases where the blocks containing x and x' are identical and have k additional elements.

Notes: See Table A-1. Another recurrence, less useful for computation, is

$$P(m+1,n) = \sum_{j,k} \binom{n}{k}\binom{n-k+m}{j} P(j,k).$$

The sequence $P(0,n)$ was first investigated by E. K. Lloyd, *Proc. Cambridge Philos. Soc.* **103** (1988), 277–284, and by G. Labelle, *Discrete Math.* **217** (2000), 237–248, who computed it by completely different methods. Exercise 70(b) showed that $P(m,1) = (\varpi_m + \varpi_{m+1} + \varpi_{m+2})/2$; in general $P(m,n)$ can be written in the umbral notation $\varpi^m q_n(\varpi)$, where $q_n(x)$ is a polynomial of degree $2n$ defined by the generating function $\sum_{n=0}^{\infty} q_n(x)z^n/n! = \exp((e^z + (x+x^2)z - 1)/2)$. Thus, by exercise 31,

$$\sum_{n=0}^{\infty} P(m,n)\frac{z^n}{n!} = e^{(e^z-1)/2} \sum_{k=0}^{\infty} \frac{\varpi_{(2k+m+1)(k+m+1)}}{2^k} \frac{z^k}{k!}.$$

Labelle proved, as a special case of much more general results, that the number of partitions of $\{1,1,\ldots,n,n\}$ into exactly r blocks is

$$n!\,[x^r z^n]\, e^{-x+x^2(e^z-1)/2} \sum_{k=0}^{\infty} e^{zk(k+1)/2} \frac{x^k}{k!}.$$

75. The saddle point method yields $Ce^{An^{2/3}+Bn^{1/3}}/n^{55/36}$, where $A = 3\zeta(3)^{1/3}$, $B = \pi^2\zeta(3)^{-1/3}/2$, and $C = \zeta(3)^{19/36}(2\pi)^{-5/6}3^{-1/2}\exp(1/3 + B^2/4 + \zeta'(2)/(2\pi^2) - \gamma/12)$. [F. C. Auluck, *Proc. Cambridge Philos. Soc.* **49** (1953), 72–83; E. M. Wright, *American J. Math.* **80** (1958), 643–658.]

76. Using the fact that $p(n_1,n_2,n_3,\ldots) \geq p(n_1+n_2,n_3,\ldots)$, hence $P(m+2,n) \geq P(m,n+1)$, one can prove by induction that $P(m,n+1) \geq (m+n+1)P(m,n)$. Thus

$$2P(m,n) \leq P(m+2,n-1) + P(m+1,n-1) + eP(m,n-1).$$

Iterating this inequality shows that $2^n P(0,n) = (\varpi^2 + \varpi)^n + O(n(\varpi^2 + \varpi)^{n-1}) = (n\varpi_{2n-1} + \varpi_{2n})(1 + O((\log n)^3/n))$. (A more precise asymptotic formula can be obtained from the generating function in the answer to exercise 75.)

78. 3 3 3 3 2 1 0 0 0
    1 0 0 0 2 2 3 2 0   (because the encoded partitions
    2 2 1 0 0 2 1 0 2   must all be (000000000))
    2 1 0 2 2 0 0 1 3

79. There are 432 such cycles. But they yield only 304 different cycles of set partitions, since different cycles might describe the same sequence of partitions. For example, (000012022332321) and (000012022112123) are partitionwise equivalent.

80. [See F. Chung, P. Diaconis, and R. Graham, *Discrete Mathematics* **110** (1992), 52–55.] Construct a digraph with ϖ_{n-1} vertices and ϖ_n arcs; each restricted growth string $a_1 \ldots a_n$ defines an arc from vertex $a_1 \ldots a_{n-1}$ to vertex $\rho(a_2 \ldots a_n)$, where ρ is the function of exercise 4. (For example, arc 01001213 runs from 0100121 to 0110203.) Every universal cycle defines an Eulerian trail in this digraph; conversely, every Eulerian trail can be used to define one or more universal sequences of restricted growth on the elements $\{0, 1, \ldots, n-1\}$.

An Eulerian trail exists by the method of Section 2.3.4.2, if we let the last exit from every nonzero vertex $a_1 \ldots a_{n-1}$ be through arc $a_1 \ldots a_{n-1}a_{n-1}$. The sequence might not be cyclic, however. For example, no universal cycle exists when $n < 4$; and when $n = 4$ the universal sequence 000012030110100222 defines a cycle of set partitions that does not correspond to any universal cycle.

The existence of a cycle can be proved for $n \geq 6$ if we start with an Eulerian trail that begins $0^n xyx^{n-3}u(uv)^{\lfloor (n-2)/2 \rfloor}u^{[n \text{ odd}]}$ for some distinct elements $\{u, v, x, y\}$. This pattern is possible if we alter the last exit of $0^k 121^{n-3-k}$ from $0^{k-1}121^{n-2-k}$ to $0^{k-1}121^{n-3-k}2$ for $2 \leq k \leq n-4$, and let the last exits of 0121^{n-4} and $01^{n-3}2$ be respectively $010^{n-4}1$ and $0^{n-3}10$. Now if we choose numbers of the cycle *backwards*, thereby determining u and v, we can let x and y be the smallest elements distinct from $\{0, u, v\}$.

We can conclude in fact that the number of universal cycles having this extremely special type is huge — at least

$$\left(\prod_{k=2}^{n-1} (k!\,(n-k))^{\left\{ {n-1 \atop k} \right\}} \right) \Big/ \left((n-1)!\,(n-2)^3 3^{2n-5} 2^2 \right), \qquad \text{when } n \geq 6.$$

Yet none of them are known to be readily decodable. See below for the case $n = 5$.

81. Noting that $\varpi_5 = 52$, we use a universal cycle for $\{1, 2, 3, 4, 5\}$ in which the elements are 13 clubs, 13 diamonds, 13 hearts, 12 spades, and a joker. One such cycle, found by trial and error using Eulerian trails as in the previous answer, is

(♠♠♠♠♠♣♡♢J♣♡♢♢♡♠♠♣♣♢♡♢♣♢♠♡♢♢♠♡♠♡♢♠♣♣♢♠♢♢♠♢♠♠♡♡♢♡♡♠♡♢♡♠♡♢♢♠♠♢♢).

(In fact, there are essentially 114,056 such cycles if we branch to $a_k = a_{k-1}$ as a last resort and if we introduce the joker as soon as possible.) The trick still works with probability $\frac{47}{52}$ if we call the joker a spade.

82. There are 13644 solutions, although this number reduces to 1981 if we regard

[domino equivalences] $\quad \boxed{} \equiv \boxed{} \equiv \boxed{}, \quad \boxed{} \equiv \boxed{}, \quad \boxed{} \equiv \boxed{}.$

The smallest common sum is $5/2$, and the largest is $25/2$; the remarkable solution

[domino sum equation]

is one of only two essentially distinct ways to get the common sum $118/15$. [This problem was posed by B. A. Kordemsky in *Matematicheskaĭa Smekalka* (1954); it is number 78 in the English translation, *The Moscow Puzzles* (1972).]

INDEX AND GLOSSARY

When an index entry refers to a page containing a relevant exercise, see also the *answer* to that exercise for further information. An answer page is not indexed here unless it refers to a topic not included in the statement of the exercise.

0–1 matrices, 120.

2-nomial coefficients, 89.

κ_t (Kruskal function), 19–21, 31–34, 102.

λ_t (Kruskal function), 20–21, 32–33.

μ_t (Macaulay function), 20–21, 32–33, 102.

ν (sideways sum), 20, 29, 88.

π (circle ratio), as "random" example, 2, 13, 27–29, 35, 80–81, 122.

ϖ_n, 64, *see* Bell numbers.

ϖ_n' (singleton-free partitions), 82.

ϖ_{nk}, 64, *see* Peirce triangle.

$\rho(\sigma)$: restricted growth string function, 78.

σ-cycles, 83.

$\sigma(n)$: sum of divisors, 55.

τ (Takagi function), 20–21, 32–33.

∂ (shadow), 18.

ϱ (upper shadow), 18.

Abel, Niels Henrik, 114.

Abelian groups, 60.

Active bits, 12.

Adjacent transpositions, 15–17, 30.

Ahlswede, Rudolph, 108.

Almkvist, Gert Einar Torsten, 116.

Alphametics, 78.

Alternating combinatorial number system, 9, 27.

Analysis of algorithms, 4–5, 25, 27, 29, 49–51, 58, 84.

Andrews, George W. Eyre, 37, 116.

Antichains of subsets, *see* Clutters.

Arbogast, Louis François Antoine, 65.

Arithmetic mean, 60, 84.

Asymptotic methods, 42–48, 56–58, 65–72, 83–85.

Atkin, Arthur Oliver Lonsdale, 114.

Auluck, Faqir Chand (फ़कीर चन्द औलक), 142.

Balanced partitions, 53.

Balanced ternary notation, 92.

Balls, 36.

Baseball, 26.

Basis of vector space, 26, 31.

Basis theorem, 34.

Beckenbach, Edwin Ford, 5.

Becker, Harold W., 129, 134.

Bell, Eric Temple, 64.

numbers, 64–65, 80–84, 123.

numbers, asymptotic value, 68–69, 83–84.

Bell-shaped curve, 70, 74, 84.

Bell-shaped sequence, 85.

Bellman, Richard Ernest, 19.

Bernoulli, Jacques (= Jakob = James), 16.

numbers, 64, 114.

Bessel, Friedrich Wilhelm, function, 44.

Binary partitions, 60.

Binary relations, 62.

Binary tree representation of tree, 27.

Binary vector spaces, 26, 31.

Binomial coefficients, 1, 32.

generalized, 33.

Binomial number system, *see* Combinatorial number system.

Binomial trees, 6–7, 27.

Bipartitions, 75–77, 141–142.

Birkhoff, Garrett, 126.

Bitner, James Richard, 8.

Bitwise manipulation, 4, 95, 109.

Björner, Anders, 102.

Blissard, John, 128.

Blocks, 61.

Bolker, Ethan David, 134.

Bonferroni, Carlo Emilio, 116.

Boolean functions, 34.

Bošković, Ruđer Josip (Бошковић, Руђер Јосип = Boscovich, Ruggiero Giuseppe = Roger Joseph), 117.

Bounded compositions, 16, 30, 31.

Brandt, Jørgen, 124.

Browning, Elizabeth Barrett, 82.

Bruijn, Nicolaas Govert de, 72, 136.

Brylawski, Thomas Henry, 118.

Buck, Marshall Wilbert, 30.

Bulgarian solitaire, 61.

Cache-hit patterns, 62.

Cai, Ning (蔡宁), 108.

Calabi, Eugenio, 89.

Canfield, Earl Rodney, 140.

Canonical bases, 26, 31.

Carlitz, Leonard, 122, 133.

Caron, Jacques, 93.

Catalan, Eugène Charles, 87.

Cauchy, Augustin Louis, 49, 57.

Cayley, Arthur, 120.

Change-making, 54.

Chase, Phillip John, 11–13, 16, 28–29, 96.

Chebyshev (= Tschebyscheff), Pafnutii Lvovich (Чебышев, Пафнутий Львович), 138.

Cheema, Mohindar Singh (मोहिंदर सिंह चीमा), 77, 141.

Chen, William Yong-Chuan (陈永川), 131.

Chinese rings, 28.

Chords, 10, 30.
Chung Graham, Fan Rong King
    (鍾金芳蓉), 108, 143.
Claesson, Anders Karl, 125.
Clements, George Francis, iv, 24–25,
    34, 105, 106.
Cliques, 31.
Clutters, 34.
Coalescence, 78.
Coalitions, 62.
Coins, 54.
Colex order, 5, 38, 53, 119.
Colman, Walter John Alexander, 115.
Colthurst, Thomas Wallace, 122.
Column sums, 60.
Combination generation, 1–18, 25–31, 35.
    Gray codes for, 8–18.
    homogeneous, 10–11, 16–17, 28–29,
        92, 96, 99.
    near-perfect, 11–17, 29.
    perfect, 15–17, 30.
Combinations, 1–36.
    dual, 2–4, 26–27, 29.
    of a multiset, 2–3, 16–18, 25, 33.
    with repetitions, 2–3, 11, 16–19,
        25, 33, 36, 39.
Combinatorial number system, 6, 27,
    31–32, 58, 88, 98, 124.
    alternating, 9, 27.
    generalized, 33.
Commutative groups, 60.
Complement in a torus, 21.
Complete binary tree, 90.
Complete graph, 108.
Completing the square, 43, 138.
Compositions, 2–4, 11, 25, 36, 56, 89, 141.
    bounded, 16, 30, 31.
Compression of a set, 23, 33, 106.
Comtet, Louis, 64, 136.
Conjugate of a partition, 40, 54, 58,
    60, 111, 117, 118.
    of a joint partition, 112.
    of a set partition, 80.
Consecutive integers, 54.
Contingency tables, 18, 31, 60.
Contour integration, 65–70.
Core set in a torus, 22–23, 33.
Corless, Robert Malcolm, 136.
Corteel, Sylvie Marie-Claude, 112.
Covering in a lattice, 58, 79.
Cramér, Carl Harald, 138.
Cribbage, 35.
Cross-intersecting sets, 31.
Cross order, 20–25, 33, 108.
Crossings in a set partition, 131.
Cumulants of a distribution, 84, 138.
Cycle, universal, of combinations, 35.
Cycles of a permutation, 125.
Cyclic permutations, 83.

Czerny, Carl, 98.

Danh, Tran-Ngoc, 108.
Dante Alighieri, 134.
Darroch, John Newton, 140.
Davidson, George Henry, 109.
Daykin, David Edward, 101, 108.
de Bruijn, Nicolaas Govert, 72, 136.
De Morgan, Augustus, 1, 56.
Debye, Peter Joseph William (= Debije,
    Petrus Josephus Wilhelmus), 66.
Decimal notation, 125.
Dedekind, Julius Wilhelm Richard, 44.
    sums, 44.
Delta sequences, 97, 98.
Deng, Eva Yu-Ping (邓玉平), 131.
Derbès, Joseph, 123.
Derivative, 32.
Descents of a permutation, 76, 122.
Diaconis, Persi Warren, 108, 143.
Diamond lemma, 119.
Dilogarithm function, 56, 114, 117.
Dimension of a vector space, 26.
Discrete torus, 60.
Distinct parts, 54, 55, 57, 58, 77.
Divisors, sum of, 55.
Dobiński, G., 65.
Dominoes, 35, 86.
Doubly bounded partitions, 49, 57, 59.
Du, Rosena Ruo-Xia (杜若霞), 131.
Dual of a combination, 2–4, 26–27, 29.
Dual of a set partition, 131.
Dual set in a torus, 22–23.
Dual size vector, 34.
Duality, 33, 106.
Dudeney, Henry Ernest, 78.
Durfee, William Pitt, 39.
    rectangle, 111.
    square, 39–40, 48, 112.
Dvořák, Stanislav, 88.
Dyson, Freeman John, 114.

e, as "random" example, 134.
Eades, Peter Dennis, 16, 97.
Eckhoff, Jürgen, 102.
Edgeworth, Francis Ysidro, expansion, 138.
Ehrlich, Gideon (גדעון ארליך), 8, 53,
    63, 64, 93, 133.
Elementary symmetric functions, 120.
Elliptic functions, 44.
End-around swaps, 30.
Endo-order, 14, 29, 128.
Engel, Konrad Wolfgang, 107.
Enveloping series, 47, 57, 85, 137.
Enns, Theodore Christian, 97.
Equivalence relations, 62, 78.
Erdős, Pál (= Paul), 19, 46, 57.
Erdős, Péter L., 126.
Etienne, Gwihen, 124.

Euler, Leonhard (Ейлеръ, Леонардъ = Эйлер, Леонард), 41, 50, 54, 55, 122.
  summation formula, 42, 56.
  trails, 108, 109, 143.
Eulerian numbers, 84, 114.
Evolutionary trees, 137.
Exponential generating functions, 65, 82, 134, 142.
Exponential growth, 42.

Felsenstein, Joseph, 137.
Fenichel, Robert Ross, 25.
Fenner, Trevor Ian, 110, 111.
Ferrers, Norman Macleod, 39.
  diagrams, 39–40, 45, 48, 51, 72, 81, 118, 120, 123, 131.
  diagrams, generalized, 112.
Fibonacci, Leonardo, of Pisa [= Leonardo filio Bonacci Pisano], recurrence, 42.
First-element swaps, 16–17, 30.
Fisher, Ronald Aylmer, 116.
Five-letter English words, 78.
Fixed points of a permutation, 80.
Flight, Colin, 137.
Flye Sainte-Marie, Camille, 108.
Foulds, Leslie Richard, 137.
Fourier, Jean Baptiste Joseph, series, 43.
Fraenkel, Aviezri S (אביעזרי פרנקל), 90.
Frankl, Péter, 102, 103.
Franklin, Fabian, 54, 57.
Fristedt, Bert, 118.

Gale, David, 120.
Gamma function, 67–68, 114.
Gaps, 54.
Gardner, Martin, 124.
Garsia, Adriano Mario, 132.
Garvan, Francis Gerard, 114.
Generalized Bell numbers, 81, 84.
Generalized Stirling numbers, 82, 128.
Generating functions, 29, 41, 45, 54–55, 57, 61, 65, 82, 98, 134, 142.
Genlex order, 9–13, 16–17, 28–29, 95, 100.
  for Gray codes, 31.
Geometric mean, 60, 84.
Goldman, Alan Joseph, 132.
Golomb, Solomon Wolf, 2, 25, 125.
Gonnet Haas, Gaston Henry, 136.
Good, Irving John, 135.
Gordon, Basil, 77.
Graham, Ronald Lewis (葛立恒), 108, 143.
Gray, Frank, binary code, 8, 100, 109, 128.
  codes for binary partitions, 121.
  codes for combinations, 8–18, 27–30.
  codes for partitions, 51–53, 60, 122.
  codes for set partitions, 63–64, 79.
  codes, reflected, 122.
Greene, Curtis, 119.
Greg, Walter Wilson, trees, 137.

Grid paths, 2–3, 25.
Griggs, Jerrold Robinson, 124.
Groups, commutative, 60.
Guittone d'Arezzo, 82.
Gumbel, Emil Julius, distribution, see Fisher.
Gupta, Hansraj (हंसराज गुप्ता), 116.

Hack, 98.
Haigh, John, 74.
Hall, Marshall, Jr., 115, 129.
Hamilton, William Rowan, cycles, 97.
  paths, 16, 30, 97, 99.
Handy identity, 136.
Hankel, Hermann, 68, 134.
  contour, 84.
Hardy, Godfrey Harold, 44, 45, 56, 57, 113, 121.
Hare, David Edwin George, 136.
Heine, Heinrich Eduard, 55.
Henrici, Peter Karl Eugen, 43.
Hickey, Thomas Butler, 16, 97.
Hilbert, David, basis theorem, 34.
Hilton, Anthony John William, 31, 102.
Hindenburg, Carl Friedrich, 38, 65.
Ho, Chih-Chang Daniel (何志昌), 124.
Hoare, Arthur Howard Malortie, 124.
Hoeffding, Wassily, 140.
Homogeneous generation, 10–11, 28–30, 96.
  scheme K_{st}, 10, 16–17, 29, 92, 99.
Homogeneous polynomials, 34.
Hooks, 111–112.
Hume, Alexander, v.
Hurlbert, Glenn Howland, 109.
Hutchinson, George Allen, 62, 77.
Hyperbolic functions, 84.
Hypergraphs, 18.

Igusa, Kiyoshi (井草潔), 124.
Inclusion-exclusion principle, 46, 57, 134, 139.
Incomplete gamma function, 67.
ind α: the index of α, 77.
Index of a permutation, 77, 122.
Integer partitions, 37–61, 74–77, 80, 130.
Internet, ii, iii, 26, 125.
Intervals of the majorization lattice, 49, 57, 59.
Inversions of a permutation, 41, 81.
Involutions, 84, 131.
Irwin, Joseph Oscar, 128.
Ising, Ernst, configurations, 26, 31, 89.
Iteration versus recursion, 12–14, 29.

Jackson, Bradley Warren, 109.
Jacobi, Carl Gustav Jacob, 42, 56.
    symbol, 115.
Janson, Carl Svante, iv.
Jeffrey, David John, 136.
Jenkyns, Thomas Arnold, 11.
Joichi, James Tomei (城市東明), 112, 132.
Joint partitions, 55.
Jolivald, Philippe (= Paul de Hijo), 108.

Katona, Gyula (Optimális Halmaz), 19.
Keyboard, 10, 30.
Kirchhoff, Gustav Robert, law, 49.
Kitaev, Sergey Vladimirovich (Китаев,
    Сергей Владимирович), 125.
Kleber, Michael Steven, 122.
Kleitman, Daniel J (Isaiah Solomon), 119.
Klimko, Eugene Martin, 110.
Knapsack problem, 7.
Knopp, Marvin Isadore, 114.
Knuth, Donald Ervin (高德纳), i, ii,
    iv, 89, 136.
Kordemsky, Boris Anastas'evich
    (Кордемский, Борис Анастасьевич),
    143.
Korsh, James F., 89.
Kramp, Christian, 65.
Kruskal, Joseph Bernard, Jr., 19–20.
    function κ_t, 19–21, 31–34, 102.
    function λ_t, 20–21, 32–33.
    –Katona theorem, 19.

Labeled objects, 36, 78, 137.
Labelle, Gilbert, 142.
Lagrange (= de la Grange), Joseph Louis,
    Comte, inversion formula, 136.
Laguerre, Edmond Nicolas, 140.
Landau, Hyman Garshin, 59.
Laplace (= de la Place), Pierre Simon,
    Marquis de, 67.
Lattice paths, 2–3, 25, 41.
Lattices of partitions, 58–59, 78–79.
Law of large numbers, 84.
Leck, Uwe, 108.
Left-to-right minima, 78.
Lehmer, Derrick Henry, 5, 30, 56, 97, 115.
Lehner, Joseph, 46, 57.
Lexicographic generation, 4–7, 16–19,
    25–27, 29, 31, 37–38, 40, 53–54, 62,
    75–77, 79, 98, 118.
Li₂ (dilogarithm), 56, 114, 117.
Limericks, 82.
Lindström, Bernt Lennart Daniel,
    24–25, 34, 107.
Linked lists, 27, 53, 78, 90.
Linusson, Hans Svante, 106.
Lipschutz, Seymour Saul, 89.
Littlewood, John Edensor, 120, 121.

Liu, Chao-Ning (劉兆寧), 8.
Lloyd, Edward Keith, 142.
Logarithm, as a multivalued function,
    68, 136.
Loizou, Georghios (Λοΐζου, Γεώργιος),
    110, 111.
Loopless generation, 8, 25, 27, 28, 92,
    96, 97, 110.
Lorenz, Max Otto, 120.
Lovász, László, 32, 102.
Lovejoy, Jeremy Kenneth, 112.
Lucas, François Édouard Anatole, 108.
Lüneburg, Heinz, 90.
Lunnon, William Frederick, 129.

Macaulay, Francis Sowerby, 19, 34, 101.
    function μ_t, 20–21, 32–33, 102.
MacMahon, Percy Alexander, 60, 61, 75.
Magic trick, 86.
Majorization, 120.
    lattice, 58–60, 126.
Malfatti, Giovanni Francesco Giuseppe, 115.
Marshall, Albert Waldron, 121.
Matchings, perfect, 131.
Matrix multiplication, 94.
Matsumoto, Makoto (松本眞), 103.
Matsunaga, Yoshisuke (松永良弼), 65.
McCarthy, David, 11.
McKay, Brendan Damien, 108.
McKay, John Keith Stuart, 37.
Mean values, 60, 84.
Meißner, Otto, 123.
Mellin, Robert Hjalmar, transforms, 42, 56.
Mems, 49.
Middle levels conjecture, 98.
Milne, Stephen Carl, 79.
Min-plus matrix multiplication, 94.
Minimal partition, 58.
Misiurewicz, Michał, 123.
Mixed radix notation, 123.
MMIX computer, ii, iv, 30.
modulo Π, 62.
Moments of a distribution, 80, 141.
Monomial symmetric functions, 120.
Monomials, 34.
Monotone Boolean functions, 34.
Mor, Moshe (משה מור), 90.
Moser, Leo, 71, 133, 135.
Most recently used replacement, 134.
Motzkin, Theodor Samuel
    (תיאודור שמואל מוצקין), 77, 128, 141.
Mountain passes, 66.
Muirhead, Robert Franklin, 120.
Multicombinations: Combinations
    with repetitions, 2–3, 11, 16–19,
    25, 33, 36, 39.
Multipartition numbers, tables, 141.
Multipartitions: Partitions of a multiset,
    75–77, 85, 143.

Multisets, 2, 87.
   combinations of, 2–3, 16–18, 25, 33.
   permutations of, 4, 14–15, 29, 30, 41, 89.

n-tuples, 36.
Naudé, Philippe (= Philipp), der
   jüngere, 41.
Near-perfect combination generation,
   11–17, 29.
Near-perfect permutation generation, 15, 29.
Nestings in a set partition, 131.
Newton, Isaac, rootfinding method, 69, 138.
Nijenhuis, Albert, 8, 57.
Normal distribution, 74.
Nowhere differentiable function, 32.

Odlyzko, Andrew Michael, 45.
Oettinger, Ludwig, 123.
Olive, Gloria, 97.
Olkin, Ingram, 121.
Olver, Frank William John, 72.
Onegin, Eugene (Онѣгинъ, Евгеній), 83.
Order ideal, 33.
Order of a set partition, 126.
Ordered factorizations, 123.
Organ-pipe order, 14.
Oriented trees, 78, 137.
Overpartitions, see Joint partitions.

P-partitions, 60.
Pak, Igor Markovich (Пак, Игорь
   Маркович), 112.
Part-count form, 39, 53, 78.
Partial order, 60.
Partition lattice, 78–79.
Partition numbers, 41–47, 55–57.
   tables of, 42, 46, 141.
Partitions, 36–86, 89.
   balanced, 53.
   doubly bounded, 49, 57, 59.
   of a multiset, 74–77, 85, 143.
   of a set, 37, 61–86.
   of an integer, 37–61, 74–77, 80, 130.
   ordered, see Compositions.
   random, 46–48, 57, 72–74.
   sums over, 39, 65, 135, 138.
   with distinct parts, 54, 55, 57, 58, 77.
   without singletons, 45, 82, 117, 131, 134.
Pascal, Ernesto, 6.
Paths on a grid, 2–3, 25, 41.
Patterns in permutations, 125.
Payne, William Harris, 9, 28.
Peirce, Charles Santiago Sanders, 64.
   triangle, iv, 64, 80–82, 84, 132, 134, 142.
Pentagonal numbers, 41, 55.
Perfect combination generation, 15–17, 30.
Perfect partitions, 61.
Permutations, 36, 78.
   of a multiset, 4, 14–15, 29, 30, 89, 123.

Petrarca, Francesco (= Petrarch), 82.
Phylogenetic trees, 137.
Pi (π), as "random" example, 2, 13,
   27–29, 35, 80–81, 122.
Piano, 10, 30.
Pigeons, 36–37.
Pitman, James William, 85, 128, 140.
Pittel, Boris Gershon (Питтель, Борис
   Гершонович), 74.
Plain changes, 10.
Playing cards, 35, 86.
Pleasants, Peter Arthur Barry, 129.
Poetry, 82–83.
Poinsot, Louis, 35, 108.
Poisson, Siméon Denis, 114.
   distribution, 73, 80.
   summation formula, 43, 56.
Pólya, György (= George), 111, 121.
Polyhedron, 18, 33.
Polynomial ideal, 34.
Pomerance, Carl, 140.
Postorder traversal, 27.
Powers of 2, 60.
Preorder traversal, 7, 27, 94.
Probability distribution functions,
   46, 74, 80, 84.
Prodinger, Helmut, 133.
Pudlák, Pavel, 126.
Pure alphametics, 78.
Pushkin, Alexander Sergeevich (Пушкинъ,
   Александръ Сергѣевичъ), 83.

q-multinomial coefficients, 30.
q-nomial coefficients, 15, 30, 89, 98, 132.
q-nomial theorem, 112, 116.
q-Stirling numbers, 82, 128.

Rademacher, Hans, 44, 45, 56, 57.
   functions, 32.
Radix sorting, 76–77.
Ramanujan Iyengar, Srinivasa (ஸ்ரீனிவாஸ
   ராமானுஜன் ஐயங்கார்), 44, 45,
   56, 57, 113, 114.
Random partitions, 46–48.
   generating, 57.
Random set partitions, 72–74.
   generating, 74.
Ranking a combination, 6, 9, 19, 29,
   90, 91, 98.
Read, Ronald Cedric, 16, 97.
Reagan, Ronald Wilson, 83.
Real roots, 85.
Recurrences, 26, 42, 50, 55, 91–93, 141.
Recursion, 10–12.
   versus iteration, 12–14, 29.
Recursive coroutines, 16.
Recursive procedures, 127.
Refinement, 78.
Reflected Gray code, 28, 122.
Regular solids, 33.

Reingold, Edward Martin (ריינגולד,
יצחק משה בן חיים), 8.
Reiss, Michel, 108.
Remmel, Jeffrey Brian, 132.
Replacement selection sorting, 90.
Residue theorem, 65, 68.
Restricted growth strings, 62–64, 78,
129, 130, 134, 141.
Reversion of power series, 90.
Revolving door property, 8, 29–30, 51.
scheme Γ_{st}, 8–10, 16–17, 27–29.
Rhyme schemes, 62, 82–83.
Riemann, Georg Friedrich Bernhard,
surface, 136.
Rim representation, 40–41, 48, 54, 58.
Robbins, David Peter, 134.
Robinson, Robert William, 108, 137.
Rook polynomials, 80–81.
Rooks, nonattacking, 80–81, 130–131.
Roots of a polynomial, 85.
Roots of unity, 30, 44, 115.
Round-robin tournaments, 59.
Row sums, 60.
Row-echelon form, 88.
Rucksack filling, 7, 27.
Ruskey, Frank, iv, 30, 63, 79.
Ruzsa, Imre Zoltán, 103.
Ryser, Herbert John, 120.

Sachkov, Vladimir Nikolaevich (Сачков,
Владимир Николаевич), 74.
Saddle point method, 44, 65–72, 83–85, 142.
Savage, Carla Diane, 51, 98.
Schur, Issai, 121.
Schützenberger, Marcel Paul, 19, 102, 107.
Score vectors, 59.
Second-smallest parts, 58.
Self-conjugate partitions, 54, 80, 121.
Semilabeled trees, 78.
Semimodular lattices, 126.
Sequences, totally useless, 78.
Set partitions, 37, 61–86.
conjugate of, 80.
dual of, 131.
Gray codes for, 63–64, 79.
order of, 126.
random, 72–74.
shadow of, 79.
universal sequences for, 86.
Seth, Vikram (विक्रम ‍सेठ), ii, 83.
Shadows, 18–25, 31–34.
of binary strings, 35.
of set partitions, 79.
of subcubes, 34.
Shakespeare (= Shakspere), William, 82.
Shallit, Jeffrey Outlaw, 134.
Shape of a random partition, 48, 57.
Shape of a random set partition, 72–73.
Shields, Ian Beaumont, 98.

Sibling links, 27.
Sideways sum, 20, 29, 88.
Sieve method, 123.
Simões Pereira, José Manuel dos Santos, 89.
Simplexes, 18.
Simplicial complexes, 33–34, 107.
Simplicial multicomplexes, 34.
Size vectors, 33, 34.
Smallest parts, 57, 58.
Sonnets, 82.
Spenser, Edmund, 82.
Sperner, Emanuel, theory, 107.
Spread set in a torus, 22–25, 33.
Stable sorting, 76–77, 122.
Stachowiak, Grzegorz, 97.
Stack frames, 75.
Stam, Aart Johannes, 74, 85.
Standard set in a torus, 22–24, 33.
Stanford GraphBase, ii, iii, 78.
Stanley, Richard Peter, 14, 36, 39,
102, 122, 131.
Stanton, Dennis Warren, 112.
Star transpositions, 16–17, 30.
Stephens, Nelson Malcolm, 129.
Stirling, James,
approximation, 67, 69, 71, 139.
cycle numbers, 140.
subset numbers, asymptotic value, 70–72.
subset numbers, generalized 82, 128.
Stirling strings, 126.
Subcubes, 31, 34.
Sums over all partitions, 39, 65, 135, 138.
Sutcliffe, Alan, 126.
Sutherland, Norman Stuart, iii.
Swapping with the first element, 16–17, 30.
Swinnerton-Dyer, Henry Peter Francis, 114.
Sylvester, James Joseph, 54, 113.
Symmetric functions, 39, 120.
Symmetrical mean values, 60.
Székely, László Aladár, 126.

Tableau shapes, 40, 80, see Ferrers diagrams.
Tail coefficients, 124.
Takagi, Teiji (高木貞治), 20, 103.
function, 20–21, 32–33.
Tang, Donald Tao-Nan (唐道南), 8.
Tarry, Gaston, 108.
Taylor, Brook, series, 71, 136.
Temperley, Harold Neville Vazeille, 48.
Ternary strings, 28, 108.
Terquem, Olry, 35.
Tippett, Leonard Henry Caleb, 116.
Tokushige, Norihide (徳重典英), 103.
Topological sorting, 61, 97, 125.
Török, Éva, 96.
Torus, n-dimensional, 20–25, 33.
Touchard, Jacques, 128.
Tournament, 59.
Trace, 40, 48, 54, 112.
Trading tails, 67, 139.

Transitive relations, 62.
Tree function, 70, 136.
Tree of losers, 90.
Tree of partitions, 54.
    of restricted growth strings, 129.
Tree traversal, 54.
Triangles, 20.
Triangulation, 88.
Trick, magic, 86.
Trie traversal, 9–10.
Tripartitions, 75.
Triple product identity, 42, 56.
Trost, Ernst, 123.
Tůma, Jiří, 126.
Twelvefold Way, 36, 53.
Two-line arrays, 130–131.

Umbral notation, 128, 133, 134, 142.
Union-find algorithm, 126.
Unit vectors, 22.
Universal cycles of combinations, 35.
Universal sequences for set partitions, 86.
Unlabeled objects, 36, 78, 137.
Unranking a combination, 27, 29.
Unranking a partition, 58.
Unranking a set partition, 78.
Unusual correspondence, 125.
Up-down partitions, 60, 122.
Upper shadow, 18.
Urns, 36.
Useless sequences, 78.

Vacillating tableau loops, 80.
van Zanten, Arend Jan, 91.
Vector partitions, 75–77, 85.
Vector spaces, 26, 31.
Vershik, Anatoly Moiseevich (Вершик, Анатолий Моисеевич), 48, 117.

Walsh, Timothy Robert Stephen, 9, 99.
Wang, Da-Lun (王大倫), 20, 22.
Wang, Ping Yang (王平, née 楊平), 20, 22.
Wegner, Gerd, 102.
Whipple, Francis John Welsh, 22.
White, Dennis Edward, 132.
Whitworth, William Allen, 65.
Wiedemann, Douglas Henry, 30.
Wilf, Herbert Saul, 8, 57, 89.
Williams, Aaron Michael, 97.
Williamson, Stanley Gill, 124.
Wong, Roderick Sue-Chuen (王世全), 72.
Wright, Edward Maitland, 141, 142.
Wyman, Max, 71, 133, 135.

Yakubovich, Yuri Vladimirovich (Якубович, Юрий Владимирович), 48, 74.
Yan, Catherine Huafei (颜华菲), 131.
Yee, Ae Ja (이애자), 113.

z-nomial coefficients, 15, 30, 89, 98, 132.
z-nomial theorem, 112, 116.
Zanten, Arend Jan van, 91.
Zeilberger, Doron (דורון ציילברגר), 55, 113.
Zeta function, 42, 114, 142.